CADKEY® Light™

▼ Computer aided design and drafting for engineers and technologists

Jon M. Duff, Ph.D.

Purdue University

Prentice Hall, Englewood Cliffs, New Jersey 07632

Library of Congress Cataloging-in-Publication Data

Duff, Jon M.
CADKEY Light: computer aided design and drafting for engineers and
technologists / Jon M. Duff.
     p.   cm.
Includes bibliographical references and index.
ISBN 0-13-117383-9 (College ed.).—ISBN 0-13-117748-6
(Professional ed.)
1. CADKey   I. Title
T385.D85 1991
620'.0042'028533—dc20   90-20197
                             CIP

Editorial/production supervision: Joe Scordato
Cover design: Bruce Kenselaar
Interior design: The West Highland Press
Manufacturing buyers: Linda Behrens/Patrice Fraccio
Acquisitions Editor: Doug Humphrey

CADKEY, CADKEY Light, CADKEY RENDER, CADKEY SOLIDS
PLOTFAST, and the CADKEY Advanced Design Language (CADL) are
registered trademarks or CADKEY, Inc.; Aldus PageMaker is a
registered trademark of Aldus Corporation; AutoCAD and DXF are
trademarks of Autodesk, Inc.; IBM and PC-DOS are registered
trademarks of International Business Machines Corporation; MS-DOS is
a trademark of Microsoft Corporation; INSTALL is a copyright of
Knowledge Corporation; Renderman is a registered trademark of
PIXAR Inc.

© 1991 by Prentice-Hall, Inc.
A Simon & Schuster Company
Englewood Cliffs, New Jersey 07632

Printed in the United States of America.
10 9 8 7 6 5 4 3 2

ISBN 0-13-117383-9 COLLEGE EDITION

ISBN 0-13-117748-6 PROFESSIONAL EDITION

Prentice-Hall International (UK) Limited, London
Prentice-Hall of Australia Pty. Limited, Sydney
Prentice-Hall Canada Inc., Toronto
Prentice-Hall Hispanoamericana, S.A., Mexico
Prentice-Hall of India Private Limited, New Delhi
Prentice-Hall of Japan, Inc., Tokyo
Simon & Schuster Asia Pte. Ltd., Singapore
Editora Prentice-Hall do Brasil, Ltda., Rio de Janeiro

Contents

PART ONE
Introduction to CADKEY
Light

C H A P T E R   F O U R

▼   **YOUR CADKEY** LIGHT **TUTOR**   **35**

C H A P T E R   F I V E

▼   **NAVIGATING IN CADKEY LIGHT**   **43**

PART TWO
CADKEY Light
Operations

CHAPTER SIX

▼ SCREEN CONTROLS 61

CHAPTER SEVEN

▼ EDITING FUNCTIONS 72

CHAPTER EIGHT

▼ CHARACTERISTICS OF GEOMETRIC ENTITIES 80

C H A P T E R   N I N E

▼ ATTRIBUTES OF GEOMETRIC ENTITIES   94

C H A P T E R   T E N

▼ LEVELS AND CONSTRUCTION DEPTH   103

C H A P T E R   E L E V E N

▼ 3D CADD—EXTRUSION   117

CHAPTER TWELVE

▼ 3D CADD-SWEEPING 127

CHAPTER THIRTEEN

▼ LIBRARY PATTERNS 142

CHAPTER FOURTEEN

▼ PART AND PATTERN FILES 156

Contents

P A R T   T H R E E
CADKEY Light Menus

C H A P T E R   E I G H T E E N

▼ POSITION MENU   213

C H A P T E R   N I N E T E E N

▼ MASKING MENU   223

C H A P T E R   T W E N T Y

▼ CREATE MENU   232

C H A P T E R   T W E N T Y - O N E

▼ EDIT MENU

273

C H A P T E R   T W E N T Y - T W O

▼ DETAIL MENU   284

Contents

C H A P T E R   T W E N T Y - S E V E N

P R E F A C E ▼

CADKEY Light

It is inconceivable that a technical worker in industry today—or a student preparing for a future technical career—might be uninformed concerning computer-aided design and drafting (CADD). CADD influences all of engineering and manufacturing. Everyone agrees on that. But CADD also plays an important role in personnel when CADD data are used to project manpower requirements for proposed production, in inventory control and contract proposals, and in marketing and distribution. 'CADKEY Light is your entry into this important activity of modern industry.

▼   WHO SHOULD USE THIS BOOK?

This book is intended to be a structured first experience in CADD for engineers and technologists. Many other technical majors may also find the need to understand CADD—scientists, medical researchers, economists, and industrial managers all will function in industries where CADD is an important activity. At Purdue University, where this material was developed, no fewer than 12 different majors in five separate colleges might take the introductory CADD course each semester. You can see that even though CADD is the direct concern of engineers and technologists, it also has become an important part of the academic preparation of many disciplines.

It is expected that each student has had a basic technical graphics course, or is receiving such instruction concurrently with CADKEY Light. The basics of geometric constructions, views and their placement, conventional line treatment, sectioning, and dimensioning are *not* covered in this book. Consult *Introduction to Engineering Drawing* by Warren J. Luzadder and Jon M. Duff, published by Prentice Hall, if you find the need for additional engineering drawing instruction.

▼   WHAT IS CADKEY LIGHT?

CADKEY Light marks a turn in the history of CADD software. With it, both students and professionals can purchase productive, industry-standard CADD software at a fraction of the commercial cost. With CADKEY Light, the vast majority of geometric operations and functions are available just as in the full-fledged version of CADKEY. Plus, the drawings created in CADKEY Light are compatible with this commercial version of CADKEY and may, through translation into DXF or IGES file formats, be compatible with hundreds of other CADD software tools.

CADKEY Light is particularly well suited as a personal CADD productivity tool. CADKEY and CADKEY Light are both powerful yet intuitive three-dimensional products that require a minimum amount of operating system (in this case MS-DOS) knowledge and present the user with a friendly and predictable interface that encourages design exploration.

CADKEY Light is a robust subset of CADKEY commercial CADD software with several advanced features removed to make the tool more accessible to students. For example, the CADKEY programming language CADL is not included in CADKEY Light, nor is CADKEY Solids. Likewise, advanced curves and surfaces are not supported. Still, CADKEY Light is a highly productive CADD tool—perfect for your personal computer at work or at home. And of course, the operations you learn with CADKEY Light are directly applicable to commercial CADKEY should you have that software available.

▼   THE SCOPE OF THIS BOOK

You will probably not be able to master or even explore all of CADKEY Light's many features in a single course. However, this text is the result of teaching an introductory CADD course with CADKEY Light in a way that students can accomplish the greatest results in the shortest possible time. This is especially important if you are a young engineer-in-training because CADD is a tool for you to accomplish other ends—engineering and design—and not an end in itself. For technologists, this course is a starting point for more in-depth CADD work in CADKEY Light, CADKEY, or other industrial CADD applications. After completing this first course each of you should be able to *apply* CADKEY Light to design and documentation tasks with little additional instruction.

This book could be used for either semester or quarter instruction and in one-, two-, or three-credit hour formats. It can also be used for individual self-paced instruction. You will notice that the required assignments in each chapter are very structured. This provides a *jumpstart* for each topic. These exercises become less specific as they progress, encouraging you to learn the commands. If you desire greater understanding and knowledge than would be afforded by a single activity, additional problems, without structured commands, are available at the end of many of the chapters.

An exercise disk is available from the publisher. This disk provides the part and pattern files necessary for many of the laboratory exercises. This disk is yours for the asking, as is an *Instructor's Guide* containing answers to the questions at the end of the chapters. Each student should also have a *data disk* on which to store complete part and pattern files.

▼ WHAT THIS BOOK CONTAINS

This book is divided into three parts. The first part is an introduction to CADKEY Light. This part helps develop an understanding of CADKEY Light, how it works, how you will create geometry in space, and how you can use CADKEY Light TUTOR as an aid in learning the software.

The second part is the meat of CADKEY Light. Here, you will solve geometric problems and learn many of CADKEY Light's commands. You will create parts and patterns, layers and text. You will learn editing and screen controls. This part culminates in applications of CADKEY Light. You will extrude and sweep models and turn those models into engineering drawings. As a final exercise, you will use CADKEY Light as a design tool to solve an engineering problem.

The final part lists all CADKEY Light commands and gives specific examples on how to use them. You may want to look through Part 3 before starting on Part 1 just to become familiar with the commands and some of the terms.

▼ ACKNOWLEDGMENTS

This book would not have been possible without the help and support of the people at CADKEY. President Peter Smith, Director Jimm Malloy, and Educational Representative Lilian Johnson have shown continuing interest in supporting engineering and technology education. Their help and encouragement is deeply appreciated. Because technical accuracy is important in a book such as this, the review of the chapters by Paul Mailhot at CADKEY was very helpful. My appreciation goes to Jonathan Katz, an aeronautical engineering student at Purdue who made numerous suggestions on the laboratory exercises.

Finally, hats off to the students who have used CADKEY Light. Their suggestions on sequencing and content have made a difference in its effectiveness and acceptance.

Jon M. Duff

PART ONE

Introduction to CADKEY Light

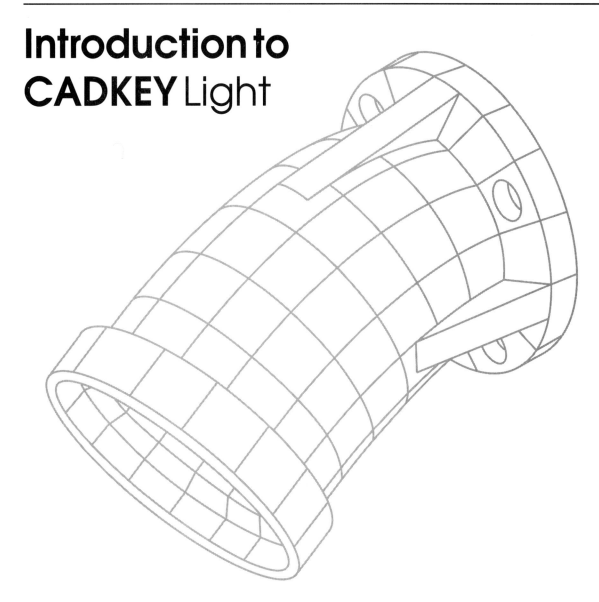

Introduction

A Design Approach
Chapter Organization
CADKEY Light and CADD
A Brief Discussion of CADD

There has been much change in engineering graphics, engineering design, and computer-aided design and drafting (CADD) in the past 10 years. CADD today is a common tool on the desk of nearly every engineer and technologist—a link to all engineering information including data on design, materials, manufacturing, testing, inventory, and marketing. This book may be your first introduction to CADD. If it is, you (or your teacher) have chosen wisely. You will experience an industry-standard CADD tool that has been heralded as the easiest to learn and one of the most powerful.

This book cannot include everything about CADKEY Light. It is a first course, a first experience to demonstrate the power and flexibility of CADKEY. It will lead you through the vast majority of CADKEY Light functions and operations in a sequence that has been tested and proven with thousands of engineering students.

This course *will not* prepare you to be a CADKEY operator. Why not? A productive CADKEY operator is the result of technical knowledge about materials and manufacturing, operations, and corporate procedures. Add to this in-depth experience in CADKEY and you have a super-productive member of the engineering team.

You are beginning the process of gaining this knowledge. With this course in CADKEY Light, you will be prepared to pick up CADKEY later and, combined with other skills and knowledge gained through courses and work experience, use CADKEY as the foundation for engineering design and drawing. Many of the short-cuts available in CADKEY Light are *not* presented in this course. CADKEY Light has provided several options for speeding up the operation of the program through function key combinations and through the *immediate mode* set of commands. If you are going to be a CADKEY operator you will want to learn these. However, as a first CADD experience, this author believes that it is more imperative to first understand *why* something works or is important than to learn the fastest way to execute a command.

▼   A DESIGN APPROACH

This course takes a design approach. It is based on the idea that engineers visualize in three-dimensional space. They solve problems, assemble mechanisms, and build buildings, highways, and spacecraft in 3-D. Then, after the parameters of the design are established and the volumes and relationships are set, standard engineering drawings can be produced that document the geometric relationships of the design in such a way that the design can be estimated, contracted, completed, and evaluated.

Each chapter in Part 2 contains step-by-step exercises that explains the important CADKEY Light topics under discussion. If you follow each exercise exactly, you will arrive at the desired solution. The exercises are brief and can be repeated for better understanding. Then, after you have completed the exercises, additional similar problems are presented without a step-by step solution. Repeat the step-by-step exercise if you are unsure of how to approach these additional problems.

Chapter 17, *CADKEY Light as a Design Tool*, will encourage you to use CADKEY Light to solve geometric problems. Only a few hints are given as to possible strategies to use. There will not be one right answer. What is important here is the *process* that you will go through to analyze the geometry and plan which CADKEY Light functions are appropriate. In fact, you should be spending almost as much time off the computer in planning, analyzing, and sketching as you do on the computer. You will find that your time in front of the monitor, which may be limited in a classroom situation, is more productive if you have done adequate preliminary analysis. Additional design problems for further study are included at the end of selected chapters.

With CADKEY Light comes CADKEY Light TUTOR. This set of interactive screens and exercises are blended into this first course if you need extra preparation before attempting the exercises. CADKEY Light TUTOR can be used as a first exercise or as a review once this course is completed. Its operation is explained in detail in Chapter 4. If you do not need tutoring, proceed directly to the chapter exercises.

▼   CHAPTER ORGANIZATION

Each chapter is laid out in the same manner and uses a system of "cards" to present supporting information. First, engineering design graphics knowledge that you need is outlined. Next, those general CADD concepts that CADKEY Light is demonstrating are presented. This is followed by those CADKEY Light TUTOR exercises that may be particularly helpful to complete before attacking the chapter exercises. With this information in mind, the chapter exercises should be completed. Beside the exercises are cards briefly explaining the location and function of the command being used. Finally, additional problems are presented to give you the opportunity to apply the CADKEY Light operations completed in the step-by-step exercise.

Drafting Topics

It is assumed that you either have taken an introductory course in drafting, engineering drawing, or technical graphics...or you are concurrently taking a course that combines traditional graphics instruction with CADKEY Light. To alert you to the engineering design graphics topics that are used in the current chapter, a card like that in Fig. 1-1 is used. With it you will find engineering design graphics topics important in the current discussion. If any of the topics are unfamiliar, you may want to consult *Fundamentals of Engineering Drawing* or *Introduction to Engineering Drawing*, both by Warren J. Luzadder and Jon M. Duff.

Fig. 1-1. Drafting topic card.

General CADD Topics.

CADKEY Light is an application of concepts and principles of CADD that transcend all CADD software. It is important to understand how CADKEY Light performs a certain operation. However, it is more important to understand the body of knowledge of which CADKEY Light makes use. Figure 1-2 shows the card used to list CADD topics. Use this card as a review to test your understanding of CADD concepts. If you are unsure of any, refer to one or more of the CADD references in the bibliography found in Appendix B.

Fig. 1-2. CADD topic card.

CADKEY Light Tutor Topics

Rather than complete the entire CADKEY Light Tutor, this course uses the tutor to introduce particular CADKEY Light operations as they are needed. If this is your first CADD experience, or if you are having difficulty in navigating in CADKEY Light, complete the tutor exercises before continuing on with each step-by-step exercise. The tutor card is shown in Fig. 1-3.

You may have access to the full CADKEY Light documentation. For this reason, some chapters conclude with a "Further CADKEY Light Reading" where those sections of the CADKEY Light documentation that may be of particular interest are listed.

Fig. 1-3. Tutor topic card.

CADKEY Light Commands

The location and function of the CADKEY Light commands being used in an exercise are shown on a card like that in Fig. 1-4. The first time a command is encountered, its card will be placed beside the place in the exercise where it is used. Glance to the card before you attempt a command of which you are unsure. Later, when a command is used again, it will not appear on a card. If you need a refresher on a command, refer to Part 3, CADKEY Light Menus.

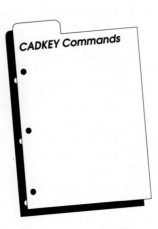

Fig. 1-4. CADKEY Light command card.

CADKEY in Industry

To give you an idea of how CADKEY is used in industry, cards like that shown in Fig. 1-5 are used in this course to present products that have been designed using CADKEY.

You may want to flip through this book to get an overview of any of the topics presented on these cards. This is an excellent way to review for examinations or to just test your own knowledge.

Fig. 1-5. CADKEY in industry card.

▼ CADKEY LIGHT **AND CADD**

The data base you create in CADKEY Light is perfectly compatible with CADKEY, CADKEY Light's big brother. So here, CADKEY and CADKEY Light will be discussed identically.

CADKEY's design world is automatically three-dimensional. Even when you intentionally make two-dimensional drawings in CADKEY, as you will in Chapter 10, you do so in three-dimensional space. CADKEY fits perfectly in the CADD design process where models are created first and drawings come second. In CADKEY Light you will create *wire frame* models. Wire frame descriptions are the lowest level of three-dimensional design but also the easiest to learn and understand.

CADKEY operates under MS-DOS, PS/2, and UNIX operating systems so it is accessible to the vast majority of industries. CADKEY may also be operated on a Macintosh II computer using either hardware or software that emulates the MS-DOS operating system.

CADKEY produces a data base in its own native format. It can translate that data into Hewlett Packard Graphic Language (HPGL), Drawing Exchange Format (DXF), and Initial Graphic Exchange Standard (IGES) for exchange with other CADD systems and machine tools.

The wire frame description you complete in CADKEY Light can be *postprocessed*. That is, the data base you create in CADKEY Light can be used in CADKEY Solids, a program that creates solid models from your wire frame. Additionally, the model can be used in CADKEY Render, a photorealistic program that uses RenderMan techniques to produce life like computer simulations.

▼ A BRIEF DISCUSSION OF CADD

Computer-aided design is referred to as CAD. It is the activity of formulating and defining the nature of a problem using computers. It is a modeling activity that does not rely on standard engineering drawings. The result of the CAD activity is a numerical description of the geometry, materials, and processes required to realize the design.

Computer-aided design and drafting is referred to as CADD. It encompasses the first activity and includes the generation of industry-standard documents, commonly called engineering drawings. In this course you will learn CADKEY Light by first defining three-dimensional geometry and then by using that geometry to produce standard engineering drawings. In doing so, you will be involved in the CADD process.

It is helpful to understand how CADD functions within engineering and technology before learning CADKEY Light. There is some debate whether or not CADD is a technique, fundamentally different from other approaches to engineering activities, or whether CADD is a tool, an application of existing engineering techniques. For the purposes of this course, CADD will be considered a tool. True, it presents several unique and interesting changes in how engineers approach design, manufacturing, assembly, and construction. But it still relies, for the most part, on engineering principles and techniques that are tool-independent.

CADD Equipment

You will be working on a graphics microcomputer equipped specifically to run CADKEY Light. There are, of course, many configurations of monitors, keyboards, input devices (mice, tablets), and computers themselves. If you will be installing CADKEY Light yourself, refer to Chapter 3, *Installing CADKEY Light*. If CADKEY Light has already been installed for you, you may want to begin with Chapter 5, *Navigating in CADKEY Light*.

Suffice to say, CADD programs such as CADKEY Light require more than minimal computing power. To use a CADD program effectively, your computer should have maximum memory installed, the fastest central processor and math coprocessor, the most capable graphics processor board, the fastest and largest capacity hard disk, the most accurate mouse or graphics tablet, the fastest and most flexible printer or plotter, and the largest and highest resolution monitor. Now of course you may not have access to or be able to afford all of these features. Each one you have to do without reduces the performance of the CADD software and lowers your productivity.

CADD Process

Engineering drawing has often been referred to as the "language of industry." Drawings (plots) provide a common basis for evaluating the feasibility of a design, for comparing it to previous designs, and integrating designs from dissimilar sources. Engineering drawings still fulfill a vital role in industry where engineering data must be shared among vendors without compatible CADD equipment or when communicating with management, suppliers, or the end user.

The Traditional Engineering Process. Before CADD (and in non-CADD environments today), engineering drawings were used to communicate between the designer and machine operators who interpreted the information on the drawings into setup instructions and manufacturing operations. This required both designer and operator to interpret the drawings the same way. There was much room for variation, and the process was often long and tedious. Consider the following as an outline of the engineering process before CADD:

Drafting Topics

▼ Drafting has no data base. The fundamental difference between drawings in CADD and in manual drafting is that CADD drawings are simply a representation of the data base and not the data base itself.

- Idea
- Sketch
- Engineering Drawings
- Prototype
- Testing
- Drawing Revisions
- Manufacturing or Construction

Notice how engineering drawings were made early in the process. This is because the data base—the description of the geometry of the design—was contained only in the designer's head, and until it was formalized in the manner of an engineering drawing, it could not be evaluated. Note also that a prototype had to be constructed for testing (both destructive and nondestructive).

What Makes CADD a Unique Tool? CADD encompasses a set of functions, several of which are unique to the point that they set CADD apart from other engineering design tools. CADD can be used simply as a very smart and powerful drafting tool. All of the manual techniques draftsmen have used for hundreds of years can be directly applied in CADD, using the computer's ability to easily and accurately create parallels, perpendiculars, angles, arcs, and text. It is no wonder that many CADD computers are used as powerful drafting machines. But this is a gross underutilization of CADD and not what makes the tool

▼ Changes in the labor force. Not all change brought about by CADD has been in the area of equipment. CADD provides the tools for each person to be involved to a greater degree with more of the engineering process.

unique. Let us look at how CADD computers function to see how they are unique.

First, CADD computers are *digital computers*. That is, they use digital electronics rather than analog electronics. Because of this, CADD computers are supremely flexible. Their logic does not rely on physical components being wired in such a way that the desired result is possible. The same computer that manages inventory, does the payroll, controls machine tools, or delivers training, can be used for CADD.

This flexibility has brought the most sweeping change to the technical labor force since the industrial revolution. Throughout history, industry has been based on a *division of labor*. There was a distinct difference between draftsmen and model makers; between tool makers and machinists; between printers and technical writers. With digital technology one individual, sitting at a computer, can design a part, test it through simulation, play "what if" games with production schedules, create machine tool paths and material-handling specifications, send the part description to the shop floor where a tool creates the part, and finally bring text, illustrations, and video images together for technical documentation.

The use of *conceptual space* also makes CADD, and in our case CADKEY Light, unique. A designer can model three-dimensional space without worrying about the materials and processes of modeling. A designer can combine geometry in an unlimited number of different schemes. A designer might take a week or more to conceptualize and test several designs using traditional manual design techniques, while a CADD designer can sort through hundreds of possible solutions in the same time. In fact, using *parametric design techniques*, the CADD computer can be programmed to ask for parameters surrounding the design and then automatically generate possible combinations, recording them as they are completed so that the designer might evaluate them later.

The CADD Engineering Process. Compare the traditional process on page 9 with that used in CADD:

- Idea

- Sketch

- Data Base Definition

- Testing of the Data Base

- Data Base Modification

- Manufacturing or Construction

- Engineering Drawings if Needed

The fundamental difference lies in the concept that in CADD, a numeric description of the geometry exists independent of the engineering drawing. This numeric description is referred to as the *data base*. In fact, one might consider the engineering drawing to be simply a reflection of the data base. In CADKEY Light, you will not be making drawings of lines and arcs on the monitor. Instead, you will be defining the geometric data base representative of your design in 3-D space.

Once this data base has been defined, it can be tested and evaluated just like a prototype may have been evaluated in the traditional engineering process. If corrections are necessary, they can be made and the model evaluated again without another prototype constructed. This demonstrates the power of the numeric data base. The CADD process produces engineering drawings only if they are needed. Then, the tested and corrected data base can be communicated directly to a computer numerically controlled (CNC) machine for manufacturing or assembly.

CADD Applications. Almost every type of product benefits from the CADD process. Anything that can be formed, finished, machined, assembled, constructed, or fabricated can be done faster, more consistently, with less waste, and with faster turnaround by using CADD.

CADD is not an either-or decision. That is, certain aspects of CADD can be integrated into traditional engineering with some benefit. For example, a company may not have computer numerically controlled machines themselves but still choose to do their design and engineering drawing on CADD. This provides greater control of design variability and quicker response for revisions. A company may adopt CADD because as a subcontractor to a larger company, they are *required* to supply engineering data in electronic format. Finally, another company may use CADD's ability to extract part and material data from electronic engineering drawings in order to supply the finance and inventory departments with up-to-date information on current and proposed products.

Many companies find themselves straddling two sides of the engineering fence. On one side are thousands of manual drawings created before CADD and on the other are electronic drawings created from CADD data bases. What is the company to do? There exist methods for translating manual paper drawings into CADD drawings. This process is a *raster to vector conversion* called scanning.

It is a tedious and imperfect process that results in an electronic two-dimensional data base. It does not produce a three-dimensional model, one that can be tested and sent directly to manufacturing. For these reasons, most companies convert manual drawings to electronic drawings on an as-needed basis.

You will notice throughout this course that many CADKEY applications are featured on *CADKEY in Industry* highlight cards, like the one on the previous page. When looking at these, keep in mind the CADD engineering process steps outlined on page 10 and try to imagine how those steps are implemented.

CADKEY and CAD-CAM

Many of you have heard of CAD-CAM, the acronym for *computer-aided design—computer-aided manufacturing*. You may be wondering how CADKEY fits into this process. CAD-CAM describes a process where computers are used to assist in the intregated process of design and manufacturing. CADKEY functions as a *front end* for the CAD-CAM process by easily and rapidly defining the geometry that will be used later in manufacturing. CADKEY's powerful editing features allow the geometry to be revised so that the CAD-CAM process is a loop—the manufacturing process provides feedback data for CADKEY so that adjustments can be made to the design.

CADKEY and Technical Publications

Today's technical publications rely on the engineering data base for much of its drawing and technical information. Because of this, many industries find CADKEY to be a perfect companion to their parts and operating manuals, their specification sheets, and their engineering drawings.

CADKEY 3-D geometry can be used as the basis for traditional technical illustrations done by hand. Or CADKEY models can be easily edited to produce finished technical illustrations that can be merged electronically with the publication.

▼ SUMMARY

This course is designed to be completed in sequence. The chapter exercises build progressively—fundamental exercises are presented in the early chapters while more advanced design problems are found in the later chapters. Upon completing this course, you should understand the CADD design process and how CADKEY Light in particular is used to create models. You should understand how those models are translated into standard engineering drawings. Finally, you should be in a good position to evaluate CADD tools for their effectiveness.

If you move on to CADKEY, all of the conceptual and operational topics learned here will be directly applicable. If presented with a different CADD program, your CADKEY Light knowledge will be easily transferred to the new software, making you productive in a very short time.

▼ QUESTIONS

1. Describe the difference between CAD and CADD.

2. Is CADD a tool or a technique? What is the difference?

3. Why is the data base so important in CADD ?

4. What is the relationship of the paper drawing to the data base?

5. What is considered the language of industry?

6. Describe the changes made in the engineering process by CADD.

7. What is parametric design? Suggest three products that would be appropriate for parametric design.

8. How does CADKEY Light function as the front end for CAD-CAM?

9. What has CADD done to the traditional divisions of labor in engineering?

10. What is meant when it is said that a data base has been postprocessed?

C H A P T E R ▼ T W O

Understanding **CADKEY** Light

This chapter should be read before installing, configuring, or operating CADKEY Light. Valuable material is presented that will provide for a deeper understanding of CADD in general and CADKEY Light in particular. The questions at the end of this chapter test your understanding of basic CADKEY Light program concepts.

▼ INTRODUCTION

Before beginning CADKEY Light operations, it is helpful to understand how the program is organized and how it functions. You can benefit from this chapter without CADKEY Light being installed on your computer.

Understanding CADKEY Light, and successfully using the program as a design tool, does not require in-depth knowledge of your computer. Likewise, it does not require a programmer's understanding of how the program itself works. It does, however, require an understanding of CADKEY Light's components. Most designers find that they can productively use a tool such as CADKEY Light only after the point where they can predict what the program expects. Then they can predict what the program will do with the instructions they give.

You probably want to know what CADKEY Light can accomplish. This program complements, by providing a powerful drawing utility, many applications available on MS-DOS computers. CADKEY Light is not a word processor; it is not a spread sheet; it is not a slide maker; it is not desktop publishing. CADKEY Light is computer-aided design and drafting.

▼ IN THIS CHAPTER

| Components
| Hard Disk Organization
| CADKEY Light Files
| The Most Important Keys
| Input Modes

CADKEY Light creates the most fundamental 3-D CADD description—the *wire frame*. This is a collection of vertices representing corners or points on the surface of your object, and lines or wires connecting these vertices (Fig. 2-1). It does not create a *surface model*, nor does it create a *solid model*.

The CADKEY Light wire frame can, however, be postprocessed by CADKEY 4 and its utilities to produce solid models that can be evaluated by techniques such as *finite element analysis* or turned into photo realistic renderings for simulation or animation. The wire frame description can also be translated into machine instructions for manufacturing or into intermediate formats for communication with other CADD computers. In short, CADKEY Light can be your entry to virtually any and all CADD processes.

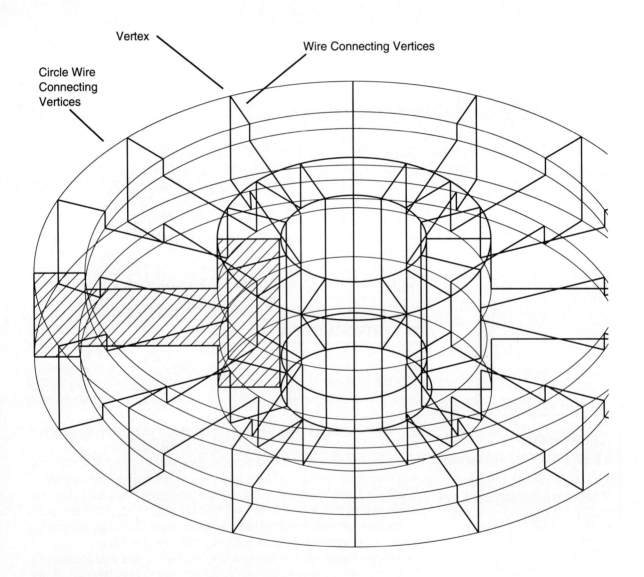

Fig. 2-1. A wire frame model with its compents identified.

CADKEY Light allows you to work directly in three dimensions, in up to four windows or *viewports*. These viewports are regions of the screen through which the data base (your design) is viewed and are entirely configurable. They can represent top, front, and side views or *any* set of views you desire.

CADKEY Light provides a full range of tools for creating and editing geometry. You will be able to create any regular or irregular geometric shape in two or three dimensions, in any position in space. You can then modify that geometry by editing or scaling.

Semi-automatic dimensioning is a feature of CADKEY Light. With this technique, CADKEY Light automatically keeps track of distances, lengths, and sizes. When you want to dimension a part, CADKEY Light automatically displays the correct numerical values. You only have to decide where to place the dimension.

You can place text in any position in space and edit that text afterward if necessary. You can choose or change text size, style, justification, and color. If you have text that you use repeatedly, you can create a text file that is used by CADKEY Light for notes.

Your creativity and productivity will not be restricted in any way by CADKEY Light. It is up to you to devise new and novel ways to use CADKEY Light as a design and documentation tool.

▼ COMPONENTS OF CADKEY LIGHT

CADKEY Light is a collection of small programs designed to allow you to easily define geometry in three dimensions. Rather than being one large program, CADKEY Light keeps program segments on your hard disk where they can quickly be retrieved when needed. Do not be concerned if CADKEY Light causes the access light on your hard disk to blink. It is simply retrieving information that it needs. Once installed, CADKEY Light requires little or no maintenance on your part.

The Operating System

CADKEY Light functions under the MS-DOS operating system. In order to do this CADKEY Light must conform to DOS in several important areas—file naming and file location in particular. If you are unfamiliar with DOS commands you will want to study *DOS Commands You Need to Know* in Chapter 3. CADKEY Light allows you to execute certain DOS commands (rename files, move files, delete files, etc.) from within the program, though you may not need to do this unless you are quite familiar with DOS and the CADKEY Light program itself.

CADKEY Light Configuration

A separate program named **CONFIG** allows you tailor CADKEY Light for your application. CADKEY Light looks to the information created by **CONFIG** each time you begin a work session and sets up the program accordingly.

You must configure CADKEY Light for your particular computer because there are variations in monitors, mice, tablets, and plotters. It is important for you to know exact model name, number, and specifications so you can communicate this to CADKEY Light. CADKEY, INC. has preconfigured CADKEY Light to satisfy the requirements of

CADKEY Commands

▼ CONFIG
A program that identifies your hardware configuration and creates the file **CONFIG.DAT** that CADKEY uses each time it is started.

most users so you won't have to make a great number of decisions about how the program runs. As a beginning user of CADKEY Light you should accept CADKEY Light's default configuration, changing only those parameters concerning your monitor, input device, graphics card, and printer/plotter.

After you have become familiar with CADKEY Light and the operation of the program, you may want to change certain aspects of how CADKEY Light displays drawings and information. To do this you will have to run the CONFIG program again and restart CADKEY Light to see your changes.

CADKEY Light Program

CADKEY Light is assembled from several individual program segments during installation and placed into directories and subdirectories that facilitate program operation. You will find CADKEY Light very friendly in that it asks questions when you have provided inappropriate information; it may correct you when you make mistakes. It may refuse to accept actions that it knows might get you in trouble.

CADKEY Light allows you to change certain commands without interrupting what you are doing. This is especially helpful when you are in the middle of a command and realize that you are on the wrong level, or at the wrong construction depth, or in the wrong view. These are called *immediate mode commands* and are noted in Part 3.

CADKEY Light TUTOR

This set of CADKEY files is a self-paced introduction to CADKEY Light and requires a separate installation. Once installed, TUTOR can be accessed from CADKEY Light after closing the current part. TUTOR introduces the features and operations of CADKEY Light in eight structured exercises. Each TUTOR exercise takes 15–25 minutes to complete. The sections are progressive; that is, the results of one section are used as the basis for the next section. For this reason, TUTOR exercises are most effective when completed in sequence.

This course makes use of TUTOR as supplementary exercises. You may want to sit down and complete TUTOR from beginning to end before you begin Chapter 5. Or, you may find TUTOR best when used as a beginning exercise for each chapter. In this case, use the TUTOR Topic Cards that appear at the beginning of the chapters to direct your activities. Finally, CADKEY Light TUTOR may serve your needs best as a review of the program's features and operations.

CADKEY Light Data Base

The 2-D drawings and 3-D models you create in CADKEY Light are both saved in a three-dimensional data base compatible with CADKEY 4. This data base is the numeric description of your design and is the information used to display your design on the screen, print on a printer, plot to a plotter, drive a machine tool or communicate with other CADD computers (Fig. 2-2). Since each use of the data base requires the geometric data to be in a different format, translators are used to change CADKEY Light files into a format understood by the various devices.

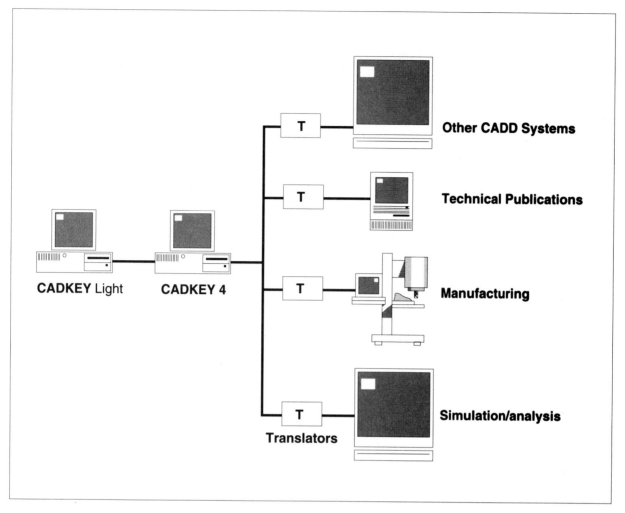

Fig. 2-2. CADKEY Light is your entry into the full range of CADD activities.

CADKEY Light Interface

CADKEY Light is a menu-driven computer program. You execute commands from a hierarchial menu that lists the commands by name, removing the need to memorize which commands are under which menus and how they are spelled.

All menu selections are numbered as shown in Fig. 2-3. A command can be executed by either selecting the item with your input device or by striking the corresponding function key. Designers experienced in CADKEY utilize these function key equivalents extensively, although beginners will generally choose to pick commands from the menu using their mouse or tablet pen.

The history line along the upper edge of the screen gives you a visual record of where you are in CADKEY Light's menu structure. Note in Fig. 2-3 that the exact command history is shown. When an item from the very last menu is selected, an asterisk (*) appears beside it. It does not appear in the history line. The CADKEY Light interface is covered in detail in Chapter 5.

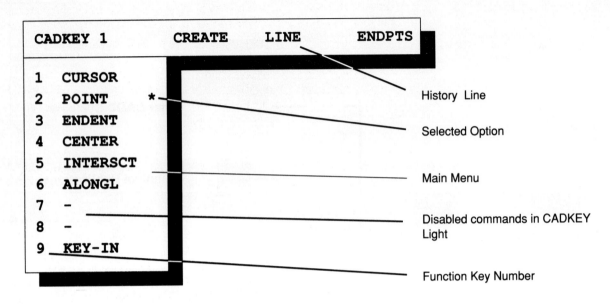

Fig. 2-3. CADKEY Light main menu with history line.

▼ HARD DISK ORGANIZATION

During installation, CADKEY Light creates directories and subdirectories and places into them the appropriate program and data files. You have no control over this. As a beginning CADKEY Light user you should accept this organization. More advanced CADKEY users can redesign this directory and subdirectory structure to fit their individual needs.

To operate CADKEY Light it is helpful to visualize this structure so that files are saved in the appropriate places on the hard disk or on your own disks.

Directories Created During INSTALL

\cadkey directory. Contains the CADKEY Light program and related files. This directory is one level removed from the hard disk or *root* level of your computer's hard disk. When you turn on your computer you are at the root (c:) level.

\prt subdirectory. The subdirectory where CADKEY Light part files are stored. You may want to store your part files in this subdirectory while you are working on them because your computer will save and retrieve them much faster from the hard disk than from a diskette. However, always *back up* your work on your own data disks before finishing your work session. This is especially true if others will be working on your computer.

\ptn subdirectory. The subdirectory where CADKEY Light library pattern files are kept. These patterns should also be used on the hard disk and backed up onto data disks.

\db subdirectory. The subdirectory where CADKEY Light stores portions of your work that exceed the memory of your computer. You should not store part or pattern files in this subdirectory.

\sf subdirectory. The subdirectory where CADKEY Light stores scratch files. These scratch files can be used to recover your work in the event your computer malfunctions or "crashes." You should not store part or pattern files in this subdirectory.

\not subdirectory. The subdirectory where you will store text files for notes that are used repeatedly. You should not store part or pattern files in this subdirectory.

\plt subdirectory. The subdirectory where you will store plot files that are written to disk rather than sent to a plotter.

The hard disk, represented by the description c:, may be thought of as a filing cabinet like that shown in Fig. 2.4. Your data disk in drive a: could be thought of as a separate but smaller filing cabinate that may have one or more drawers.

The drawers of this cabinet correspond to first-level directories. In this case, \cadkey is a drawer in the c: cabinet. Within this drawer are folders or subdirectories. Five folders are created in the \cadkey drawer automatically during the installation. Individual files can be considered documents in the folders.

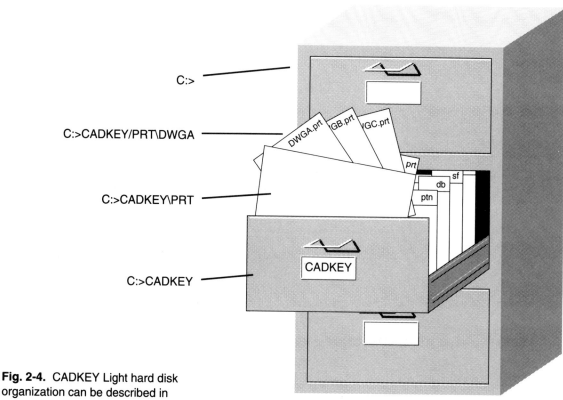

C:>

C:>CADKEY/PRT\DWGA

C:>CADKEY\PRT

C:>CADKEY

Fig. 2-4. CADKEY Light hard disk organization can be described in terms of cabinets, drawers, folders, and documents.

As a comparison consider the example of the structure of CADKEY Light. Refer to Fig. 2-4.

cabinet	drawer	folder	document

```
c:
    \cadkey
        \prt
            drawingA.prt
        \ptn
            patternA.ptn
        \db
            overflow.db
        \sf
            temp.sf
        \not
            text.not
```

Carefully use this organization. For example, store part files in the **\prt** folder in the **\cadkey** drawer. Notice that files carry extensions that match the title of the subdirectories in which they reside.

▼ CADKEY LIGHT FILES

CADKEY Light creates two types of geometric files: part files and pattern files. There are no differences in geometry or data base structure between the two types of files, only in how CADKEY Light identifies and uses them. It is important to distinguish the difference between the two and how they are used in CADD.

Part Files

To begin a work session CADKEY Light must either recall a part file or begin a new one. Part files can be considered as the base geometry or drawing to which other pieces can be added. For that reason, parts cannot be placed on other parts. Part files are stored in the **\prt** subdirectory or on your data disks.

When you execute the command sequence **FILES—PART—SAVE**, CADKEY Light automatically places the file extension .PRT on the file name you specify. Then, when you want that file again, CADKEY Light will display only those files that have the .PRT file extension. To combine two parts, save one as a pattern and place it (retrieve it) into the

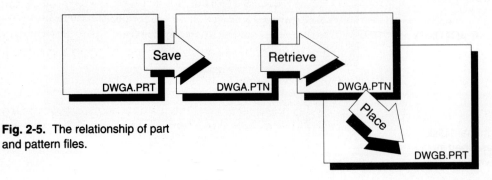

Fig. 2-5. The relationship of part
and pattern files.

part as shown diagramatically in Fig. 2-5. To add DWGA to DWGB, save DWGA as a pattern and retrieve it into DWGB.

Pattern Files

As shown in Fig. 2-5, a pattern file can be retrieved into a part file. This means that a pattern file cannot be displayed at the beginning of a work session without first loading an existing part file or beginning a new part file.

Pattern files allow, for example, the repeated use of electrical, mechanical, and hydraulic symbols. When you execute the command sequence **FILES—PATTERN—CREATE**, CADKEY Light automatically places the file extension .PTN on the file name you specify. Pattern files are stored in the **\ptn** subdirectory or on your data disk.

Disk Text Files

Notes that will be used repeatedly can be created in a word processor or text editor and placed into CADKEY Light. Once saved in ASCII or text-only format and placed in the **\not** subdirectory, these text files can be used again and again. Each line of text can be only 128 characters long, including spaces, and the total length of the note cannot exceed 1,024 characters. Characters outside this range are ignored.

▼ Keys make the difference. Use keyboard shortcuts for your most common commands and notice a marked increase in efficiency and performance.

▼ THE MOST IMPORTANT KEYS IN CADKEY LIGHT

Five keys are important to mention at the start because their use controls much of what you do in CADKEY Light. The menu equivalents of these keys are contained in the *Break Area*. See *The CADKEY Light Screen* in Chapter 5 for a complete description of these menu items. Due to the fact that keyboards are not designed with these keys in uniform position, their exact position cannot be shown in a figure.

The Escape Key

Located somewhere on your keyboard (usually at one or more of the corners) is the escape key, marked **ESC**. This key terminates the current command and returns you to the main CADKEY Light menu. Use this key to cancel commands that have been entered but not executed.

The F10 Function Key

You will notice that there are never 10 options in a CADKEY Light menu. This is to reserve the F10 function key as a back-up command. Each time you strike the F10 key, you are returned one step backward through the menu structure. Use this key when you want to change previously entered commands in the chain without leaving the command entirely.

The Backspace or Delete Key

When CADKEY Light requires that you enter values by the keyboard, the backspace or delete key removes typing as long as the **ENTER** key has not been struck.

The Alt or CTRL Keys

When either of these keys are held down, another key assigned to an immediate mode invokes that command.   For example, by holding down **ALT** key and then pressing the V key (called ALT-V) the active view can be changed in the middle of a command. The immediate mode allows commands to be executed within commands from different menus.

The Enter or Return Key

After entering keyboard information such as text or numbers, or when accepting CADKEY Light defaults, press the Enter (sometimes called **RETURN** or **CR** for carriage return) key once. When this is expected, the command will be presented <Enter>.

▼   INPUT MODES IN CADKEY LIGHT

Menu Selection

Use menu selection with your mouse or tablet pen for most commands as you are learning CADKEY Light. The shape of the cursor alerts you to where you are on the screen and what action CADKEY Light may take.

When you move the CADKEY cursor into a menu area, notice that it changes the selection to reverse video. When the cursor is moved into an inactive area of the screen, the cursor turns into a small circle.

When the cursor is in a drawing window it appears as a cross.   The size of the cross is specified in the CONFIG program. When selecting from pop-up windows for color, line type, or line width, the cursor becomes a pointer. See Fig. 2-6.

Function Keys

As you become more familiar with the program you will recognize that certain function key sequences can be memorized to increase your efficiency.   These sequences are found in Part 3.

Keyboard Entry

Some commands require that you respond with numerical values or text entry.   The keyboard is used for this.   Pay particular attention to the prompt line at the bottom of the screen where CADKEY Light's expectations are displayed.   For example, some commands require that you accept keyboard entry by striking the **ENTER** key, while other commands require that you accept through a menu selection.

Graphic Cursor— appears when cursor is in a viewport.

Circle—appears when cursor is in an area of the menu where no selection is possible.

Arrow—appears when a menu selection is expected.

CREATE   **Reverse Video—** shows that a menu option has been picked.

Fig. 2-6. CADKEY Light cursors.

▼   SUMMARY

Successful operation of CADKEY Light is a combination of understanding how the program functions and acquiring experience using the tool. Knowing how CADKEY Light is organized on your hard disk provides a fast mental picture of where your files are and how you can find them.

Knowing what kind of files CADKEY Light generates allows you to efficiently plan your design work so that repetitive tasks make use of the powerful functions of the software.

Although a graphics program should make limited use of keyboard entry, knowing a few critical key strokes will accelerate your use of CADKEY Light.

If CADKEY Light has already been installed on your computer, you can skip directly to Chapter 4 and begin familiarizing yourself with CADKEY Light TUTOR. If you need to install CADKEY Light, carefully follow the steps outlined in the next chapter.

▼ QUESTIONS

1. What is the most fundamental 3-D modeling method in CADD?

2. Describe viewports and their function.

3. What does the program **CONFIG** do?

4. What are directories used for? When would you create your own?

5. What must be done to CADKEY Light's data base to communicate with machines or dissimilar CADD systems?

6. What are the two types of geometric files created in CADKEY Light? Describe the differences and similarities of the two.

7. Describe the function of the **ESC** key.

8. What is the function of the **F10** key? When might it not work?

9. Under what circumstances would you use the backspace or delete key?

10. When are the **ALT** or **CTRL** keys used?

11. What would you do if you hit the <Enter> key by accident and had typed an incorrect number in the prompt line?

12. Try to think of a use for using disk text files. How would you create a disk text file?

Installing **CADKEY** Light

▼ IN THIS CHAPTER

Equipment Requirements
DOS Commands to Know
CADKEY Light Disks
Hardware Information
Installation Procedures
CONFIG Program
Start CADKEY Light

If CADKEY Light is the first software you have installed on an MS-DOS computer, you should be prepared to spend approximately 60 to 90 minutes to read this chapter and complete the installation operation.

▼ INTRODUCTION

If CADKEY Light has been installed on your computer, you may turn to Chapter 4 to begin familiarization with the program using TUTOR. If later you want to change any of the settings in the CONFIG program, refer to page 29 where CADKEY Light's configuration settings are discussed

If CADKEY Light is not on your computer, carefully read this chapter in total before you begin installation. Then go back and follow the installation procedures. This course assumes that your IBM or compatible computer has already been set up and ready for CADKEY Light installation. If not, follow the procedures that came with your computer for setup and installation of either PC-DOS or MS-DOS.

As an overview, to install CADKEY Light you will follow these steps:

- Assure that you have the appropriate equipment.

- Install CADKEY Light on your hard disk.

- Configure CADKEY Light for your hardware.

- Start CADKEY Light and verify operation.

▼   MINIMUM EQUIPMENT REQUIREMENTS

CADKEY Light will operate correctly on any IBM, Compaq, or fully compatible computer having the following minimum configuration:

- XT or AT model configuration

- DOS version 2.1 or higher

- One floppy disk drive 5.25" or 3.5"

- 640K RAM

- A hard disk with at least 3MB of free space

- A CADKEY Light–supported graphics card

- An input device supported by CADKEY Light

When you start your computer, the version of DOS and the amount of RAM installed in you computer will be displayed on the screen. CADKEY Light supports virtually all popular monitors, graphics cards, input devices, and printers. When you run the CONFIG program, you will be presented with lists of supported devices from which to choose. Before beginning the installation process you will want to find and write down the model names and numbers of these devices so that during CONFIG you can respond appropriately.

▼   DOS COMMANDS YOU NEED TO KNOW

Several DOS commands are used during the installation process. To study all of the aspects of these commands, refer to the manuals that came with your computer. This list is simply meant to be a starting point for more in-depth study of DOS. If you use CADKEY Light for an extended period of time, you will want to become more familiar with DOS commands.

After you have turned on your computer and it has loaded DOS and checked its memory, a command line awaits your keyboard input. For the purpose of these examples, consider that DOS is installed on your hard disk and that the hard disk is the **c:** drive. The internal floppy disk drive is named **a:**.

If a second drive is installed, it is called **b:**. Commands in DOS are not case-sensitive. That is, you can type upper or lower case with the same results. You must, however pay strict attention to the characters and spaces. The examples in this book are shown in lower case. Spaces are noted by the → character.

The command line displays the *path* from the current drive, into the current directory. This is consistent with the way CADKEY Light directs files in the program itself. For example, if the command line displayed were

```
>c:\cadkey\prt
```

you would know that you are currently in the **\prt** subdirectory inside the **\cadkey** directory on the **c:** (hard disk) drive.

Format Disks

---
format→**a:** <Enter>

After this command is entered, DOS prompts you to place the disk in drive a:. The status of the format is displayed and when complete, you have the opportunity to continue formatting as many disks as you want. New disks must be formatted before they are used.

Old disks may be reformatted to erase previous data and be used again. You will want to format several data disks to hold your models and drawings. Also, you will want to make back-up copies of the CADKEY Light program disks.

Copy the Entire Contents of One Disk to Another

---
copy→**a:*.***→ **b:** <Enter>

This command copies existing files from the first drive specified (in this case **a:**) to the second drive (in this case **b:**). The asterisks are called "wild card" characters and mean "all file names and all extensions." The copied files will have the same names as the original files. Files in lower level directories are not copied.

You should make copies of your CADKEY Light disks before installation. You may want to back up valuable CADKEY Light part and pattern files for security.

---
xcopy→**a:*.***→ **b:**→**/s**→**/e** <Enter>

This command copies all files and all directories including lower level directories if they exist. The switches **/s** and **/e** copy all files and all directories even if the directories are empty.

Make a New Directory

---
md *directory name* <Enter>

Use this command when you want to create a directory to contain special parts or patterns. The directory is created on the current drive and within the current directory. For example, you may want to make a directory to hold all of the models and drawings for a single project so that they can be located easily. CADKEY Light creates its required directories during installation so you don't have to make directories before installation.

If you write files to disk so that they can be printed from a computer without CADKEY Light, you may want to create a **\pnt** directory.

Change into a Directory

---
cd *directory name* <Enter>

You will want to change into the CADKEY directory each time you begin a work session. Or you may want to create a batch file as described

CADD Topics

▼ **The Operating System.** The disk operating system (DOS) controls how you access and save information on both your hard disk and diskettes.

on page 31 to automate this process. For example, if after installation you wanted to change from the **c:** drive into the **\prt** subdirectory on the same drive the command would be

---
cd\cadkey\prt<Enter>

Back Up Through the Directory Path

---
cd.. <Enter>

This allows you to back up one level in the directory structure. For example, if the command line shows

>c:\cadkey\ptn

and you added the command

>c:\cadkey\ptn→**cd..**

you would be returned to the CADKEY directory and the command line would read

>c:\cadkey

---
cd <Enter>

Returns you to the root (highest level) of the current drive. For example, the highest level of the hard disk is the **c:** level.

Change to a Different Drive

---
a: <Enter>

Use this command if you want the **a:** internal drive to be the current drive. You might need to do this if you wanted to view then copy CADKEY Light files from this disk to another.

View Files in the Current Directory

---
dir <Enter>

This presents a list of all files (CADKEY and non-CADKEY) in the current directory. CADKEY Light allows you to list either part or pattern files from within the program itself.

View the Files on Another Drive

---
dir→**a:** <Enter>

This allows you to list the files on the disk in the **a:** drive without making that disk the current drive.

Delete a File in the Current Directory

---

del→*file name.extension* <Enter>

To use this command you must type the file's name and extension exactly. You must be very careful with this command. DOS will immediately delete the file without a prompt.

▼ YOUR CADKEY LIGHT DISKS

If you are installing CADKEY Light, make back-up disks before you begin the installation. Refer to the DOS copy command on the previous page or your system documentation. Use the back-up copies for the actual installation.

CADKEY Light is available on six (6) 5.25" and three (3) 3.25" diskettes. These are numbered in order and are called for at the appropriate time by the installer program.

▼ HARDWARE INFORMATION

Disks are inserted shutter first and label up. Insert the disks straight in and not up or down at an angle. If your disk drive is equipped with a locking handle, carefully and smoothly raise and lower it. If your disk drive is equipped with an eject button, carefully and firmly press the button straight in.

Store your CADKEY Light master disks in a safe place. Store your back-up disks in another place. Always use the back-up disks to install CADKEY Light.

▼ INSTALLATION

Follow these steps to install CADKEY Light:

1. Turn on your computer and allow it to warm up. When the command line shows >c:, you are ready to install CADKEY Light.

2. Insert CADKEY Light program disk 1 into drive a:.

3. Change the current drive to the drive holding disk 1.

    a: <Enter>

4. Run the installation program by typing

    >a:**install**<Enter>

The installation procedure prompts you for appropriate responses. If at any time you want to abort the installation procedure, press the **ESC** key. Note: This may leave CADKEY Light partially installed on your hard disk.

5. When you are prompted to identify the drive on which the CADKEY Light program will be installed, press the <Enter> key to accept drive c: as the location for the program.

6. The default directory name for CADKEY Light is **\cadkey**. Press <Enter> to accept this default.

7. CADKEY Light is automatically installed on your hard disk and in the directory specified. Subdirectories **\prt** and **\ptn** are created automatically into which sample part and pattern files are copied.

8. When installation is completed, you are returned to the DOS prompt in the **\cadkey** directory.

▼   SYSTEM CONFIGURATION

CADKEY Light reads information from a file named CONFIG.DAT each time it is started. This file informs CADKEY Light of the specifications of your monitor, graphics card, input device, printer/plotter, and program parameters. To modify CONFIG.DAT for your computer, the program CONFIG, which was placed in the **\cadkey** directory during installation, is run. Type the following command:

$$>c:\backslash cadkey \rightarrow \textbf{config}$$

You are presented with the CONFIG main menu. Not all of the menu choices need to be made. In this configuration, you will accept many of CADKEY Light's defaults. After becoming familiar with CADKEY you may want to go back and rerun CONFIG to custom tailor the program to your needs. If at any time you select the wrong item and accept it with an <Enter>, reselect the item from the main config menu and redo your selection.

Note: In the event your monitor, input device, or printer/plotter is not on the supported list, do one of the following:

• Accept the default selection and see if CADKEY Light operates correctly.

• Check your documentation to see if your device is compatible with one of those listed.

Graphics Options

Graphics Device. CONFIG will present a list of graphics cards supported by CADKEY Light. Use PgUp/PgDn to view the full list of graphics devices. Enter the number of the graphics card or, if yours is not on the list, accept the default device.

Graphics Display Monitors. Choose the number of the monitor that matches the one with your system. If your monitor is not listed (remember to use PgUp/PgDn to view additional selections), choose a monitor with the same screen dimensions as yours.

The horizontal screen measurement is equal to the distance of 80 characters. The vertical measurement is equal to the distance of 25 lines. If the dimensions of your monitor are unique, choose:

22) Enter screen dimensions

Input Device

To select the correct driver for your input device select:

2) Set input device options

Type the number of the device from the displayed list. When prompted, choose the serial port (COM1 or COM2) to which your tablet or mouse is connected. If you are using a tablet without a unique application overlay, simply accept the default active area. If your tablet includes an overlay, follow the directions for identifying digitizing and function areas.

Printer/Plotter Options

CADD Topics

▼ A Graphics Card. This circuit board determines the number of colors you can display and the graphic resolution of your monitor.

If you have a plotter attached to your computer, CADKEY Light must be able to find and use the correct driver when you plot. Select your plotter from the list by typing its corresponding number.

If your plotter is not on the list, check to see if it is compatible with one of the listed plotters. Accept the defaults installed with CADKEY Light unless you know that your plotter differs in specification.

If you do not have a plotter, choose the **NONE** option. Printers are selected in the same manner. Select the model by number. From the main config menu choose either:

3) Set plotter options
4) Set printer options

Both printers and plotters must be attached to your computer at the serial or parallel port specified in the **CONFIG** program. As a **CONFIG** option, you may choose to write the printer or plotter file to disk. This would be advisable if you want to transport plot files on disk to another computer for plotting, one that does not have CADKEY Light installed. Unless a full path is specified in the **CONFIG** program, the plot file is written to the current directory.

Accepting Defaults

The **CONFIG** program may ask you several questions during each step of the configuration. For the purposes of this initial configuration accept all defaults other than those mentioned in this section. Because there may conceivably be hundreds of different configurations—and some of them not supported by CADKEY Light—you may have to run the **CONFIG** program more than once to arrive at the desired configuration.

Exit and Save Configuration

When you have finished with these configuration choices, you will want them saved in **CONFIG.DAT** so that CADKEY Light will use them the next time the program is run. At this point you can return to any of the menu choices and change your selection. When complete, choose:

8) Exit and save changes

Configuration changes are saved in the **CONFIG.DAT** file and you are returned to DOS at the the **c:\cadkey** prompt.

▼   START CADKEY LIGHT

CADKEY Light can be started in a number of ways. In this section we will present two methods and run the program to determine if the installation and configuration was successful.

Load Device Driver—Type Commands

To begin CADKEY Light, you must provide a means to tell DOS which graphics device to place in memory so that the program can be displayed correctly on the screen. Depending on the graphic board you have, you will probably want to load one of the following files:

herc.exe	(monochrome monitor)
ibmcga.exe	(low res color monitor)
ibmvga.exe	(high res color monitor)

Figure 3-1 shows the DOS start-up sequence with your commands in **boldface.**

```
>C:cd\cadkey           (makes cadkey the active directory)
>C:\cadkey ibmvga       (loads the ibmvga graphics device driver)

>CADKEY GDT 3.51                              .
>Copyright CADKEY INC 1988                    .
>IBM EGA/VGA Adapter 1.1                       .
>    grdev=IBMVGA                             .
>    grmode=0 EGA (10h) XXXXXXXXX .
>    grmode=1 VGA (12h) XXXXXXXXX .
>(Use -r flag to remove)                      .
>                                             .
>Loading driver                              .
>C:\cadkey cadkey       (executes the CADKEY program)
```

Fig. 3-1. The start up sequence if you manually change directory and load the graphics device driver.

Load Device Driver—Use Batch File

To keep from typing this every time you start CADKEY Light, place a batch file (cadkey.bat) at the **c:** directory (root) level. If you are unfamiliar with the IBM PC, you may want to secure help on this from someone experienced in using the DOS text editor. If you are in a class, your instructor will be able to copy this small file onto your hard disk. To start CADKEY Light with this batch file in place, type:

c:cadkey <Enter>

The statements in the batch file are executed and CADKEY Light is started. The batch file contains the statements shown in Fig. 3-2.

```
c:              (makes c: the current drive)
cd\cadkey       (makes \cadkey the current directory)
ibmvga          (loads the graphics driver)
cadkey          (runs the cadkey program)
```

Fig. 3-2. Statements in the CADKEY batch file.

Launch the Program

By either typing the driver commands, or by executing a batch file, start CADKEY Light. After the system initializes, you are presented with a screen as shown in Fig. 3-3.

Follow these steps to determine that CADKEY Light has been properly installed and configured.

1. Press the **ESC** key to begin your work session.

2. CADKEY Light opens an unnamed work session and displays the default windows and menus in default orientation and colors (Fig. 3-4).

3. Move the cursor around the screen to assure that the correct input driver has been loaded.

4. Cursor select from the menu at the upper left of the screen. Note that the menus change as they are selected.

5. Press the **ESC** key once.

5. Choose **EXIT** from the break menu in the middle of the left side. Do not save this file.

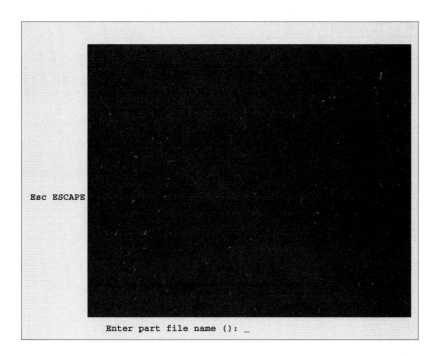

Esc ESCAPE

Enter part file name (): _

Fig. 3-3. The initial CADKEY Light screen.

If CADKEY Light does not display the screen as shown in Fig. 3-4, or if cursor action is not smooth, restart your computer (**CTRL–ALT–DEL**) and confirm that the model numbers of your monitor and input device are registered in the **CONFIG** program.

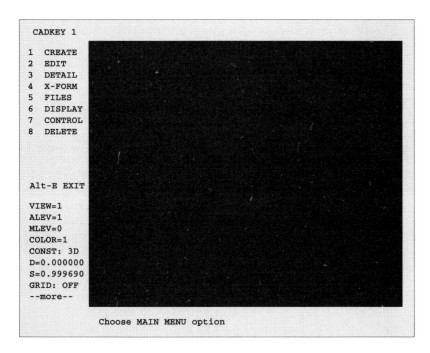

CADKEY 1

1   CREATE
2   EDIT
3   DETAIL
4   X-FORM
5   FILES
6   DISPLAY
7   CONTROL
8   DELETE

Alt-E EXIT

VIEW=1
ALEV=1
MLEV=0
COLOR=1
CONST: 3D
D=0.000000
S=0.999690
GRID: OFF
--more--

Choose MAIN MENU option

Fig. 3-4. The CADKEY Light program screen. You are ready to start modeling.

▼ SUMMARY

CADKEY Light must be installed and configured correctly for the program to function as designed. To operate confidently with DOS, a small number of commands must be learned. The **INSTALL** program automatically asks you for the appropriate disks at the correct time.

To quickly configure CADKEY Light for your computer, write down model numbers and names before running the **CONFIG** program. Then, accept all configuration defaults other than those that are hardware-specific for your computer. Later, as you become more confident with CADKEY Light, you may want to experiment with program settings to tune CADKEY Light to your needs.

▼ QUESTIONS

1. What is the difference between **INSTALL** and **CONFIG**?

2. What is the function of the **CONFIG.DAT** file?

3. What would be one possible situation when **CONFIG** would not have to be run and the information in the **CONFIG.DAT** file used as it was installed?

4. What is the difference between the DOS commands **COPY** and **XCOPY**? How would you know when to use one or the other?

5. What is the function of the **CADKEY.BAT** file?

6. What must **CADKEY.BAT** contain and where must it reside?

7. What happens when you respond with **ESC** to the initial CADKEY Light screen?

8. Where does CADKEY Light think you want to save part files? Pattern files?

9. How can you begin an empty, unnamed part file?

10. What is DOS? What is CADKEY Light's relationship to DOS?

11. How could you determine the active drive at DOS level? Within the CADKEY Light program?

Your **CADKEY** Light **TUTOR**

▼ IN THIS CHAPTER

Using TUTOR
An Overview
Installing TUTOR
Rerunning CONFIG
Start TUTOR

▼ INTRODUCTION

CADKEY Light TUTOR contains a set of structured interactive exercises that introduce many of the features of CADKEY Light. It is totally self-paced. That is, you can take as long as you need to read the instructions that CADKEY Light TUTOR presents on the screen. You can also repeat TUTOR as many times as you want to better understand any of the operations.

TUTOR is not a free-standing application. It requires that CADKEY Light be installed and properly configured. TUTOR adds an item to the **FILES** menu so that the geometry you create during the tutorial may appear in CADKEY Light for further refinement. You will start CADKEY Light first and then begin TUTOR.

▼ USING TUTOR WITH THIS BOOK

How you use TUTOR depends on how you are using this book. If you are part of an organized course and TUTOR is a scheduled activity, you will benefit from completing the tutorial exercises before beginning more technical problems. Or, you may want to complete the TUTOR exercises but in the order they are presented on the TUTOR cards that begin Chapters 6 through 16.

If you have CADD experience in CADKEY or another package, you may want to bypass TUTOR and immediately begin the chapter exercises. Later, complete TUTOR as a review to test your understanding of the software.

▼ AN OVERVIEW OF CADKEY LIGHT TUTOR

TUTOR Exercises

If you have read Chapter 3, you are somewhat familiar with how the CADKEY Light program functions. That information will not be repeated here. If you are unsure of anything in this chapter, you may want to reread previously presented information.

TUTOR is organized around the creation of a 3-D model, its editing, and presentation as a standard engineering drawing. The object used in TUTOR, called the *Finger Guide*, is shown in Fig. 4-1. Notice that it exhibits many of the geometric features common to manufactured parts. The eight exercises should be completed in order because the outcome of one exercise is used as the basis for the next.

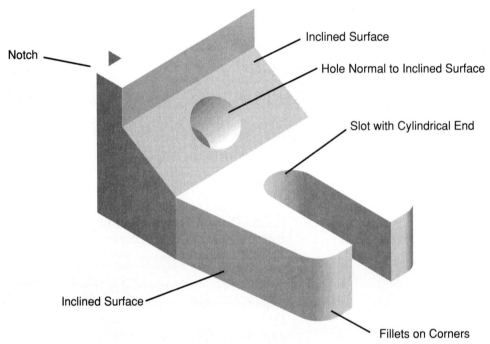

Notch

Inclined Surface

Hole Normal to Inclined Surface

Slot with Cylindrical End

Inclined Surface

Fillets on Corners

Fig. 4-1. The Finger Guide used in CADKEY Light TUTOR.

TUTOR Windows

The TUTOR screen contains many of the same information areas as does CADKEY Light itself. The main TUTOR screen is shown in Fig. 4-2 with its components identified.

In addition to this main screen, TUTOR uses three colored windows to present information at important times during the tutoring process.

Dialog windows present information to you that the TUTOR feels is important enough to interrupt your activity. They can appear at the bottom of the screen or be large enough to cover the entire viewport. Read the information in this gray background window and then press <Enter>.

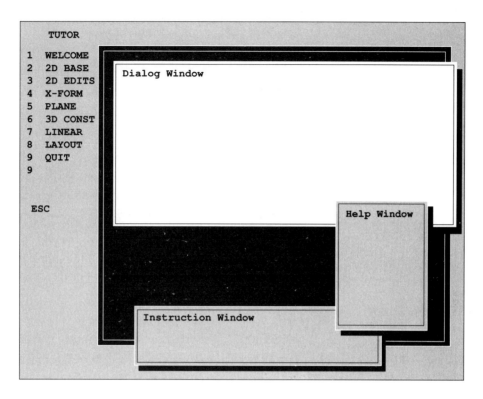

Fig. 4-2. The CADKEY TUTOR screen, Main Menu, and windows.

Instruction windows have a blue background and give directions as on how to complete the TUTOR exercises. They appear at the bottom of the screen and remain until you complete the operation described in the instruction window.

Help windows will appear if you enter information or make selections that the TUTOR feels are inappropriate or outright incorrect. The help window will tell you what you did wrong and suggest a correct action.

TUTOR Menu Choices

The TUTOR menu operates the same way as the menus in CADKEY Light. You may cursor pick the menu selections or you may use the function key number to the left of the menu item. Once you have chosen a TUTOR exercise, the main CADKEY Light menu appears in its place.

WELCOME. This exercise introduces many of the basic program functions. You choose options from the various menus, select geometry, and enter information through the prompt line.

2D BASE. You learn 2-D construction and editing techniques by constructing the base of the Finger Guide.

2D EDITS. The base constructed in the previous exercise is edited in this exercise. Geometric entities are trimmed and extended into position.

X-FORMS. The first two exercises were essentially 2-D. In this exercise you will begin to build the 3-D model from the 2-D base.

PLANE.   The powerful feature of building planes in 3-D is demonstrated in this exercise.

3D CONST. CADKEY Light's ability to define multiple views is featured in this exercise. Construction and editing in 3-D complete the wire frame model.

LINEAR.   In this exercise you learn the difference between part and pattern files by creating your own pattern geometry. You practice choosing and placing linear and nonlinear dimensions.

LAYOUT.   The final exercise leads you through the making of an engineering drawing based on your 3-D model of the Finger Guide. Level selection, pattern retrieval, and part filing complete your work in CADKEY Light TUTOR.

QUIT. At any time you can quit CADKEY Light TUTOR and return to the CADKEY Light program. The geometry you create in TUTOR can be saved as part files and opened in CADKEY Light for further practice.

TUTOR Illustrations

It is important for TUTOR to be run on a color computer. Each exercise makes use of color to alert you to what may be the desired action. At the beginning of each step an illustration is presented to show you what the Finger Guide will look like at the end of the step. These illustrations make use of color to explain your actions.

- **Dashed yellow lines** represent entities you will create while in TUTOR.

- **White entities** show that they have been selected.

- **Dashed red lines** show entities or parts of entities that will be deleted.

- **Green lines** represent entities after they have been created.

The Repeat Menu

By pressing the **ESC** key, TUTOR displays the Repeat Menu as shown in Fig. 4-3. The three choices allow you to choose your own pacing of the TUTOR exercises. The **ESC** key also provides a way to quit TUTOR without returning to the main TUTOR menu. When you have completed a step, TUTOR presents a review screen and displays the repeat menu.

CONTINUE.   Returns you to the step you were on when you hit the **ESC** key. During a review session, this command exits the review and begins the next step in the tutorial.

```
1   CONTINUE
2   REPEAT
3   QUIT
```

Fig. 4-3. The TUTOR Repeat Menu.

REPEAT.   Allows you to repeat a step as often as you wish. When you repeat, you are returned to the first screen of the current step.

QUIT. Allows you to leave the tutorial and return to CADKEY Light. If you choose to **SAVE** the part, it will automatically appear in CADKEY Light. If you choose to **DELETE** the construction, all work since the last save is lost.

▼ **Back up program disks.** Before you install TUTOR, make a copy of the disk. Use this copy during installation.

▼   INSTALLING CADKEY LIGHT **TUTOR**

CADKEY Light TUTOR must be installed separately, after CADKEY Light itself has been installed. Once installed, TUTOR is available from the **FILES** menu.

As an overview, to install CADKEY Light TUTOR you will follow these steps:

- Assure that you have the proper equipment.

- Install TUTOR on your hard disk.

- Configure CADKEY Light for TUTOR.

- Start CADKEY Light and begin TUTOR.

To help you with the installation, several conventions have been followed when describing TUTOR installation. First, any text that you are required to type is shown in **boldface** at the command line. The information at the command line, either displayed by the computer or that you have previously typed, is shown in normal type.
For example consider the following prompt line:

```
>c:\cadkey
```

You know that this is information currently displayed at the prompt line. The computer is waiting for input from the keyboard. Now consider the following addition:

>c:\cadkey→**config** <Enter>

This line shows that you have been instructed to press the space bar once and type the word **config**. The <Enter> specification represents a return. This is sometimes called a *carriage return*.

Equipment

If you have installed CADKEY Light successfully, you have the correct hardware configuration for TUTOR. If you haven't installed CADKEY Light, refer to page 28. Install CADKEY Light before installing TUTOR. In the event that your CADD system has a monochrome monitor, TUTOR will still operate correctly. However, the benefit of the TUTOR experience will be lessened without the color cues mentioned in the previous section.

Installation

Follow these steps to install TUTOR:

1.   Turn on your computer and allow it to warm up. When the command line shows >c:, you are ready to install TUTOR.

2.   Insert the TUTOR disk into drive a:.

3.   Change the current drive to the drive holding TUTOR.

>c:**a:** <Enter>

4.   Run the installation program by typing

>a:**install** <Enter>

You will be prompted to identify the directory into which TUTOR will be installed. Accept the \cadkey directory as the target directory to hold TUTOR.

▼   RERUNNING CONFIGURATION

If you have already configured CADKEY Light, you have identified correct graphic and input devices, monitor, and printer/plotter. Two configuration settings need to be checked so that TUTOR instructions and dialog window text will make sense. Accept all other selections and values without change.

1.   Assure that you are in the \cadkey directory.

>c:\cadkey

2. Run the configuration program.

    >c:\cadkey→**config**

3. Select from the configuration menu.

    5) Set Program Options

4. Select the Unit Mode for CADKEY.

    1) Inches

5. Select Entity Highlighting Style.

    2) Flashing Markers

6. After completing these two selections choose

    8) Exit and save changes

You are returned to the >c:cadkey DOS subdirectory.

▼   START TUTOR

When you start TUTOR, CADKEY Light checks to see if a part is currently active in the work space. If one is on the screen, you are given the opportunity to save it before beginning TUTOR. Before you actually participate in the exercises, you should assure that the installation and configuration were successful by running TUTOR once from the CADKEY Light Main Menu.

1. Begin CADKEY Light as outlined on page 32 by either manually changing to the \cadkey directory and loading the appropriate device drivers or by executing the **CADKEY.BAT** batch file.

2. When presented with the initial screen, respond by pressing the **ESC** key.

3. CADKEY Light opens an unnamed work session. From the main menu select

    FILES-TUTOR

The main TUTOR screen signals that you are ready to begin your TUTOR session. You can reenter TUTOR at any of the eight menu sections.

4. Choose **QUIT** from the TUTOR Main Menu. You are returned to the main CADKEY Light program screen. If you wish, you can **LOAD** the part file created in the TUTOR program for further refinement in CADKEY Light.

▼ SUMMARY

TUTOR is a perfect way to receive your first instruction in CADKEY Light. You will design a 3-D wire frame model using many of CADKEY Light's drawing and editing functions. Then, TUTOR shows you how this model can be used as the basis for an engineering drawing.

When TUTOR is installed, the CADKEY Light **FILES** menu is changed so that TUTOR appears as an option. Once installed, you can go back and review TUTOR exercises at any time. The part geometry that you create in TUTOR is fully compatible with CADKEY Light.

You may choose to complete TUTOR in its entirety or complete the sections as they apply to the exercises in this book. In the chapters that follow, TUTOR exercises that reinforce the topics under discussion appear on topic cards with reference to the appropriate exercises.

▼ QUESTIONS

1. Is TUTOR a free-standing program that can be run without installing CADKEY Light?

2. Can models created in TUTOR be opened from CADKEY Light? What does this tell you about TUTOR's data base?

3. Describe the difference between dialog, instruction, and help windows.

4. What is the function of the **ESC** key during the operation of TUTOR?

5. Discuss the purpose of the different line styles and colors in the operation of TUTOR.

6. Why does the **config** program have to be run again when installing TUTOR?

7. If you didn't install TUTOR on your computer yourself, how could you tell from within the CADKEY Light program if it had in fact been installed ?

8. What would happen if you tried to **LOAD** a TUTOR part file from within CADKEY Light?

Navigating in CADKEY Light

After reading the previous chapters, you are ready to begin learning how CADKEY Light actually models geometry. If you have completed TUTOR, this chapter will further explain the ins and outs of operating the software.

This chapter is about navigating around in CADKEY Light. So much of CADD involves knowledge of where you are in the command structure, how to find and retrieve, whether or not to save, responding correctly when prompted, and knowing what a program is waiting for when nothing happens. All of these activities support the real function of CADKEY Light—creating 3-D model geometry. You will probably find that after you are comfortable doing all of the "housekeeping" chores involved in operating CADKEY Light, you will be able to attend to the task of model making.

▼ INTRODUCTION

You have CADKEY Light installed and configured on your computer. You have formatted several data disks. You are now ready to get some "driving time." In Chapter 3 you opened CADKEY Light to confirm that your graphic and input drivers were correctly installed. You exited without saving.

Now you will practice the operations that will help make CADKEY Light a familiar tool. To do this follow this procedure:

• Understand the CADKEY Light interface, screen, and menus.

• Understand CADKEY Light operating commands.

• Practice these operations by completing the navigation exercises at the end of this chapter.

It is important to practice each operation directly after reading its description.

▼ THE CADKEY LIGHT SCREEN

The heart of CADKEY Light is the way that it communicates with you. It is important to know where information is found in each region of the screen. Your screen is comprised of seven distinct functional areas. Figure 5-1 shows the location of these regions.

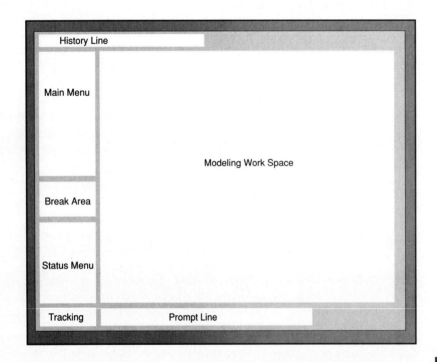

Fig. 5-1. CADKEY Light screen with menu areas identified.

The Modeling Work Space

This region of the screen presents from 1 to 4 *viewports*. A viewport is a region of the screen through which model geometry is viewed. A typical viewport organization is shown in Fig. 5-2. However, any view of the model geometry can be taken and stored for display. Only four views can be displayed at one time, and only one viewport can be the active viewport. You create geometry in the active viewport, and it is simultaneously displayed in all others.

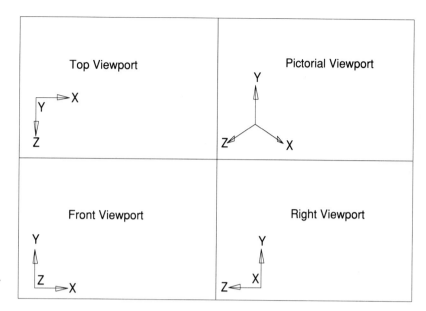

Fig. 5-2. Typical organization of four
CADKEY Light viewports.

The Main Menu Area

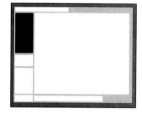

CADKEY Light's menus appear along the left edge of your screen,
outside the modeling workspace. You can select menu items in any of
three ways.

Menu Pick. Move your cursor to the menu area. Note that the cross
hairs change to a circle when in an inactive (dead) region of the border.
When the cursor is moved onto a menu item, the function's name is
immediately shown in reverse video. Click once with your input device
to select the highlighted menu item.

Function Key Equivalent. Every menu item has a number beside it. To
select the menu item using function keys (F Keys), the cursor does not
have to be moved. Only the corresponding function key needs to be
depressed once.

Immediate Mode. By combining the CTL or ALT keys and a keystroke,
some, but not all, of CADKEY Light commands and settings can be
changed without leaving the current command. See Part 3 for immediate
mode commands listed with their corresponding menu selections.

The History Line

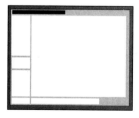

Because there can be only one menu displayed at a time, the history of
your current command sequence is displayed at the top of the screen.
For example, were the history line to display the sequence shown in Fig.
5-3, you would know that CADKEY Light is waiting for you to identify
by free cursor position the beginning and end of a line.

```
CREATE    LINE    ENDPTS    ENDENT
```

Fig 5-3. History Line displays the command sequence for easy reference.

The Break Area

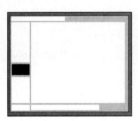

Directly below the main menu area is a region where three commands can be displayed. These can be selected by either cursor or keyboard entry.

Back Up (F10). At any time you can back up through the command sequence one step each time the F10 key is depressed. Use this break function to change previous selections without completely escaping from the entire command sequence and returning to the main menu. This selection is not available at the root level of the main menu.

Escape (ESC). To return to the main CADKEY Light menu—the root level— press the ESC key once. This cancels all commands in the active sequence. Incomplete model geometry (as in a line with only one end point specified) is not completed and is lost. The **ESC** command has no affect at the root level.

Exit (ALT-E). When at the root level of the menu, this break function prompts you to save the current part geometry before returning to DOS. You may choose it with a cursor selection or by holding down the **ALT** key while depressing the **E** key once.

The Status Menu

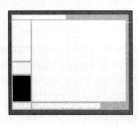

Settings and parameters that control the operation of CADKEY Light can be changed in this menu without leaving the selected command. For example, in the middle of a command you may decide to change the active view because the construction is more appropriately done elsewhere. The top view may be the active view when instead you want the construction to be made in the front view. This change is done through the status menu. All status menu items can't be shown at once. The **--more--** selection causes the status menu to scroll, displaying additional selections.

The Cursor Tracking Window

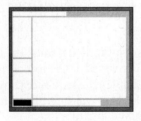

You have the option to display or not display the position of the cursor in either world or view space. If cursor tracking is off, numbers appear in this region only when spatial position is entered while executing a command. When cursor tracking is turned on, the position of the cursor is constantly displayed when it is the work space. If *world coordinates* have been chosen from the status menu, the cursor's position relative to the world origin (X, Y, Z) is shown. If *view coordinates* has been chosen, the cursor's position relative to the view origin (XP, YP) is displayed.

This area also shows which page (1–3) of the status menu is currently displayed.

```
ENTER SCALE FACTOR (1) = >_
```

Fig 5-4. Prompt line with default value displayed.

The Prompt Line

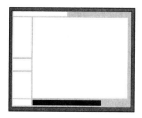

When CADKEY Light needs to communicate with you it displays text in the form of a prompt line at the bottom of the screen, below the work space. Sometimes this may be instructions, a warning, or an error message. To make sure that you read these messages, CADKEY Light waits for a specific response (like an <Enter> or a menu choice) before it continues. Figure 5-4 shows a prompt line and a default value presented. To accept the default, press <Enter>. To change the current value or selection, type a substitute and then press <Enter>. Use the back space or delete key to change keyboard entry. This value remains active until changed by another keyboard entry.

▼ START A NEW WORK SESSION

CADKEY Light allows you to begin a new untitled work session when you start the program from DOS. The program begins with all configuration defaults in place.

Procedure

1. Begin the CADKEY Light program.

2. When presented with the initial screen, you have two options:

   • Begin a new work session.

   • Load an existing part file.

3. Press **ESC** to begin a new work session.

Tutor Topics

▼ TUTOR Assignment. Begin CADKEY Light and choose TUTOR from the **FILES** menu. Complete the **WELCOME** exercises.

▼ OPEN AN EXISTING PART FILE

You can open an existing part file either from the initial screen or from the CADKEY Light program itself. Type only the file name and *not* the extension. For example, a correct file name would be:

PARTA

An incorrect file name would be:

FILEA.prt

Use this procedure to continue work on partially completed model geometry, to edit models or drawings, or to simply visually check the file. Or this technique can be used to build custom configurations for part geometry. An empty part file can be used as a configuration template from which to start new work sessions.

Procedure Upon Start Up

1. Begin the CADKEY Light program.

2. When presented with the initial screen you have two options:

    • Type the name of the file and CADKEY Light will automatically look inside the \prt subdirectory for that file.

    • Type the drive name and then the file A:FILENAME and CADKEY Light will look for the file on the named drive.

3. Press <Enter> when the file name is complete. CADKEY Light retrieves the part file and displays it in the work space. Program settings reflect their status when the part file was saved.

Procedure During Program Operation

First, determine the name and location of the desired part file. You then have two options for identifying the file:

    • Do it by remembering the file's name and location.

    • Let CADKEY Light display the part files on the target drive.

1. Choose **FILES-PART-LOAD** from the menu. You will be prompted to save the part geometry currently in the work space. Use this option if you know the location and name of the desired file. If you simply type the file name, CADKEY Light looks for the part file in the **\prt** subdirectory. If you type a drive specification as part of the file name (as in A:FILENAME), CADKEY Light looks to that drive for the file.

2. Press <Enter>. CADKEY Light retrieves the part file and displays it in the work space. A misspelling here will cause an error message. Press <Enter> and carefully retype the file name. Also, assure that the file is on the target disk. Program settings reflect their status when the part file was saved.

To Review a List of Part Files

1. Choose **FILES-PART-LST/LOAD** from the menu. CADKEY Light prompts you for the drive from which you want a list of part files. Type the drive specification such as **a:**.

```
prt/                                    page:   1

PARTA   .       .       .       .

PARTB   .       .       .       .

.       .       .       .       .

.       .       .       .       .

.       .       .       .       .

.       .       .       .       .

.       .       .       .       .

.       .       .       .       .
```

Fig. 5-5. The part selection window from the **LST/LOAD** command.

2. Press <Enter>. A window appears with a list of the part files (Fig. 5.5). Only part files are displayed by using this command. Files of other types, such as pattern (.PTN) files are not displayed even though they may reside in that subdirectory.

3. Move your cursor to the desired file. The file's name changes to reverse video. Click once to select that file. You are prompted to save the current part. CADKEY Light retrieves the part file and displays it in the work space. Program settings reflect their status when the part file was saved.

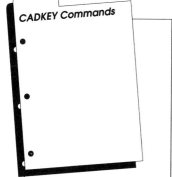

CADKEY Commands

▼ Open a new untitled part.
Create a blank part file to start a fresh part from inside CADKEY Light.

▼ CLOSE AND OPEN ANOTHER PART

When you are finished with a part and want to begin another, or if you need to check something on a different model or drawing, you will want to close the current part and load another. Do not exit CADKEY Light and reenter the program from DOS. Perform this operation from within the CADKEY Light program itself.

Procedure

1. Choose **FILES-PART-LOAD** from the menu. CADKEY Light prompts you to save the current part. This is true even though you may have just saved the part in anticipation of closing it to load another. This final prompt allows you to save the part on a back-up disk immediately before loading the second part.

2. Follow the procedure for opening an existing part file as outlined in the previous section.

It is interesting to note that in CADKEY Light the only way to begin a fresh or empty work session is to **ESC** from the initial screen after start-up from DOS. To get around this, and to open a fresh work session from inside CADKEY Light, you may want to save a *blank part file* and load it as an alternative to exiting the program altogether.

▼   SAVE A PART IN THE \PRT SUBDIRECTORY

When you configured CADKEY Light, you accepted a default path for saving part files as **c:\cadkey\prt**. This means that CADKEY Light will save parts automatically on your hard disk, inside the **\cadkey** directory, inside the **\prt** subdirectory unless explicitly told to do otherwise.

Part geometry stored on your hard disk will load, save, and generally operate much faster than the same part stored on a diskette. For this reason, you will probably want to use the **\prt** subdirectory as the working location for your parts and the a: diskette as the back-up location.

Procedure

1.   Choose **FILES-PART-SAVE** from the menu.

2.   If this is a new part that has never been saved, type the file name and press <Enter>.

3.   If this is a file that has been loaded from your hard disk, CADKEY Light remembers the path to that file. Press <Enter> to overwrite the file on top of its previous version.

4.   If the file has been loaded from the diskette drive, you will have to redirect the path CADKEY Light uses to find the correct storage location. Type:

       c:\cadkey\prt→filename <Enter>

▼   SAVE A PART ON THE A: DRIVE

Use the a: drive to save part geometry on removable diskettes. Remember, if others are using your computer, they may delete files in the \prt subdirectory. Always save your files on diskette before ending your work session. To save your part geometry on the a: drive:

1.   Choose **FILES-PART-SAVE** from the menu.

2.   Direct the file to the a: drive by typing:

       a:filename<Enter>

CADKEY Light remembers that this is the path to this file. The next time you save the file, it will automatically be directed to this location.

▼ RETRIEVE A PATTERN FILE

A pattern file is a geometric figure that has been saved for the purpose of being used repeatedly in part files. It is one of the truly unique aspects of CADD. A pattern file cannot exist without being included in a part file. A pattern file cannot be plotted, printed, or displayed directly. It must be output after being retrieved and placed in a part file.

Pattern files should be saved in either the **\ptn** subdirectory on your hard disk or on your data disk in drive a:. You may, of course, create specialized subdirectories to contain related patterns. CADKEY Light automatically assigns the **.ptn** file extension to your pattern's file name. *Do not include the extension as part of the file name.*

Pattern geometry is placed into the work space in relation to the active view, normal (perpendicular) to the screen z axis. You may want to think of this in terms that the pattern file is placed *parallel* to the screen in the active view. For example, Fig. 5-6 shows three figures: **circle.ptn**, **square.ptn**, and **triangle.ptn**.. The circle, to be seen as a circle in the front view, must be placed in that view. The square, to be seen as a square in the top view, must be placed in the top view. Similarly, if the triangle is to be seen in true shape and size in the side view, it must be placed in the side view.

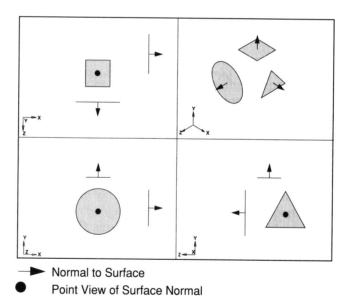

Fig. 5-6. Orientation of pattern normal with the screen z axis of the active view.

➤ Normal to Surface
● Point View of Surface Normal

Characteristics of Patterns

Pattern Base. Each pattern is created relative to a pattern base or origin. This base controls where the pattern will be placed relative to the insertion point. In Fig. 5-7 a pattern is identified by its base at point A. Note that when placed in a part, the base is aligned with the cursor insertion point. The same pattern has been saved with a different base point in Fig. 5-8. The same insertion point results in entirely different results.

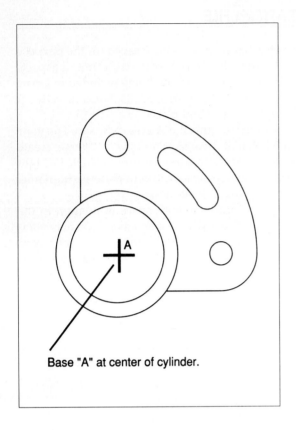

Base "A" at center of cylinder.

Fig. 5-7. Pattern base at insertion point.

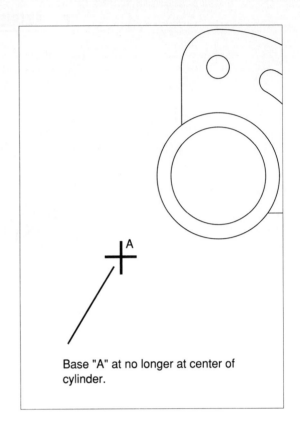

Base "A" at no longer at center of cylinder.

Fig. 5-8. Same insertion point, different pattern base.

CADKEY Light cannot show you the location of the pattern base before clicking on the insertion point. If you don't know (or can't remember) where the pattern base is located, make sure you group the pattern so that it can be easily deleted if placed incorrectly.

Pattern Scale. Patterns are scaled at the time of placement. Because of this, it is important to create a pattern at a convenient size so that later it can be easily scaled. The pattern in Fig. 5-9 was created with a horizontal dimension of 10.00". Sometimes this is called a *unitary* (as in 1.0, 10.0, or 100.0) dimension because this dimension can be treated as a unit. At time of placement, the pattern could be scaled at .56, resulting in a pattern 5.60" across. This technique is especially important when designing parts which are based on the same design—and are proportional in sizes—but which vary along some important dimension.

Pattern Rotation. Pattern geometry can be rotated about the screen z axis (ZV). Rotation is specified counter-clockwise in positive degrees, or clockwise in negative degrees (Fig. 5-10).

Pattern Grouping. Pattern geometry can be placed as a single named group or as ungrouped geometry. Grouping a pattern allows the group to be moved, scaled, modified, or deleted as a single entity. The entities (lines, circles, arcs, text, etc.) in an ungrouped pattern can be individually identified and modified.

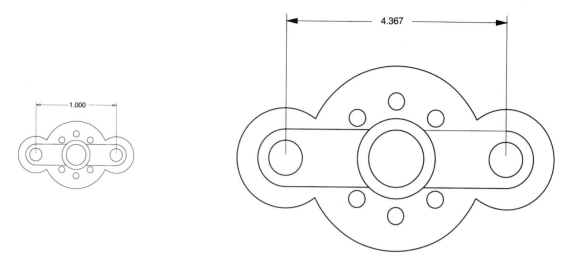

Fig. 5-9. The result of scaling a figure of unitary dimensions. In this case, a scale factor of 4.367 was used to arrive at the final dimension.

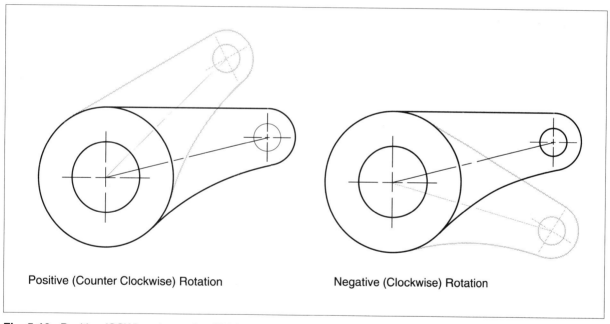

Positive (Counter Clockwise) Rotation   Negative (Clockwise) Rotation

Fig. 5-10. Positive (CCW) and negative (CW) rotation of a pattern during retrieving and placing.

Pattern Level. You are given the option to place the pattern on the current level or to specify a different level. Many industries have strict guidelines controlling on which levels or layers certain information is placed. This feature allows you to continue placing dissimilar pattern geometry without explicitly changing the current level.

Procedure to Retrieve a Pattern

1. Begin with a part file active in the work space.

2. Make the appropriate view active by clicking once in that view.

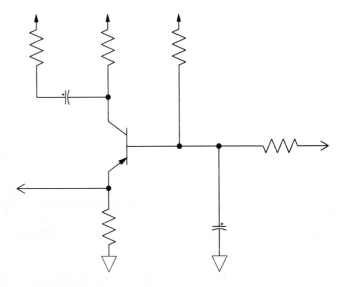

▼ Pattern Libraries. When pattern files are grouped together by similar topics, they form libraries.

3. If you know the name and location of the desired pattern file, choose **FILES-PATTERN-RETRIEV** from the main menu.

4. If you don't know the name or location of the pattern file, choose **FILES-PATTERN-LST/RTRV** from the main menu.

5. In either case, type the path to the desired pattern file. The default path is >c:cadkey\ptn. Type **a:** to change to the diskette drive.

6. Either type the pattern name (with **RETRIEV**) or cursor select the pattern from the displayed list (with **LST\RTRV**).

7. Respond to the questions concerning scale, rotation, and grouping.

8. Cursor select the insertion point by clicking once.

Fig. 5-11. Electrical drawing making use of repetitive symbology. Several of the figures have been rotated before placing.

CADKEY Light keeps the cursor loaded with the selected pattern after each placement. This allows you to continue placing the pattern without retrieving it each time. Use the **F10** key to back up and change any of the pattern characteristics while keeping the cursor loaded with the pattern. Figures 5-11 and 5-12 show the use of pattern symbology

▼ EXIT CADKEY LIGHT

When you exit CADKEY Light, you are returned to your computer's operating system (DOS) with control at the \cadkey subdirectory. The prompt line should look like the following:

```
c:cadkey>
```

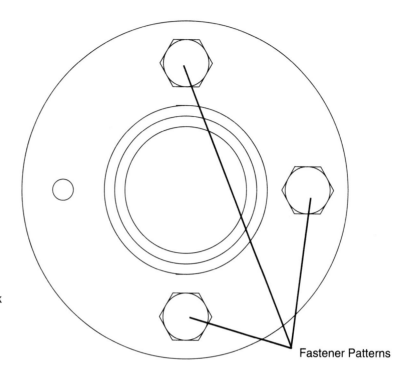

Fig. 5-12. Patterns provide for quick and accurate fastener placement.

Fastener Patterns

You can exit CADKEY Light at the Main Menu by invoking the command with **ALT-E**. This causes the program to ask whether or not you want to save the current part file. CADKEY Light will ask you this even though you have just saved the part and have not done anything else since the save. This gives you the opportunity to *back up* the file on another disk before actually exiting CADKEY Light. You can also change to the root (c : >) level of the hard disk by typing the following:

cd.. (cd followed by two periods) and <Enter>

▼ SUMMARY

CADKEY Light presents a consistent way to navigate through the CADD program. You should now understand where to look for specific information in the CADKEY Light screen as well as how to find and load part files. The difference between part and pattern files is fundamental to the operation of CADKEY Light. You should appreciate the importance of pattern base location as well as the scale at which patterns are originally created. With these things in mind, you are ready to begin creating models in Part 2 of this book.

▼ QUESTIONS

1. What is the purpose of the history line?

2. How may you back up through the history line?

3. The modeling work space contains regions through which the geometry is viewed. What are these regions called?

4. What are the two methods of selecting items from the main menu?

5. What are the two methods of selecting items from the status menu?

6. What three items are shown in the break area? Are all three always shown?

7. How do you know if CADKEY Light is expecting a keyboard entry?

8. What is the difference between world and view coordinates?

9. Explain how you would decide in which viewport to place a pattern. What would be the result of placing the pattern in different viewports?

10. Why don't you have to include the appropriate file extension with the file name when you load or save a file?

11. What is the difference between **LOAD** and **LST/LOAD**?

12. What is the difference between **RETRIEV** and **LST/RTRV**?

13. What function does **ALT-E** perform? When can you envoke this command?

▼ NAVIGATION EXERCISES

For the purposes of the exercises that follow, it is assumed that CADKEY Light has been installed as suggested in the software documentation and that you have a mouse as an input device. If the software is installed differently, or if you have a graphics tablet as an input device, familiarize yourself with that information before beginning the exercises.

To complete these exercises, you must follow the directions exactly. It is helpful to read all the steps of a particular operation before beginning the procedure.

On the following pages are step-by-step navigation exercises. Follow them carefully. As you are performing the CADKEY Light operations, ask yourself these questions:

• Do I know what this operation is intended to accomplish?

• Can I predict ahead of time what CADKEY Light expects of me in terms of the information I supply?

• Do I know where I am in the CADKEY Light command structure?

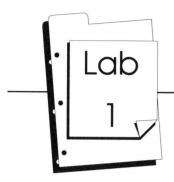

CADKEY Light Navigation Exercises

Start Up Computer

1. Turn monitor switch to on position.
2. Turn power switch on base unit to on position.
3. Computer is ready when c:\> prompt is displayed. Insert your exercise disk into drive a:.

Note: If you aren't using the exercise disk available with this book, you will need to format a disk, create, and save a part file before you can load a part from the a: drive.

Open CADKEY Light

1. At the c:\> prompt, type **cadkey**.
2. When prompted for a part file name, press **ESC** key (usually at upper left of keyboard).
3. CADKEY Light opens a new, unnamed part file.

Close CADKEY Light

1. Cursor select **EXIT** from the middle break menu.
2. Cursor select **NO** from the main menu. The program is terminated.
3. Control is returned to the computer at c:\cadkey>.

Note: If your computer has a *DOS shell* installed (as with DOS 5.0) you will want CADKEY Light listed there as a program. References to C:\> should then be disregarded when using the shell.

Open a Part File from the Initial Screen

1. Type **cadkey** at the c:\cadkey> prompt.
2. Type **a:link** and then <Enter>.
3. CADKEY opens the part file link.prt from your exercise disk.

The ESC Key

The **ESC** key returns you to the main (root) menu level, canceling all incomplete commands.

1. Choose **CREATE-LINE-ENDPTS.**
2. Choose **ESC.**
3. You are returned to the root level of the menu.

> **Note:** CADKEY Light will use the default part file path as established in the **config.dat** file. If you made the a: drive the default, it will look there. Otherwise, the default path is c:\cadkey\prt. If you are confused, enter the full path and file name.

Close a Part File and Open Another

You may either cursor select main menu items or use the function keys corresponding to the menu item.

1. Choose **FILES-PART-LST/LD**from the Main Menu.
2. Accept the c:\cadkey\PRTpath with <Enter>.
3. Cursor choose any part from the list displayed.
4. Answer **NO** to saving the current part.
5. **ESC** to the main menu.

Save a Part File on the a: Drive

1. Choose **FILES-PART-SAVE**.
2. Type a:<*your initials*>. As an example, **a:JMD**.
3. CADKEY saves the part on the diskette in drive a:.
4. Drive a: becomes the path for saving this part while active.
5. **ESC** to the main menu.

The F10 Key

The F10 function key backs up through the menu structure.

1. Choose **CREATE-LINE-ENDPTS**
2. Either press the **F10** key or choose **F10 BACK-UP** from the middle break menu.
3. The active command backs up one step. Note this in the history line at the top of the screen.
4. Press **F10** again. You are returned to the Main Menu.

Exit CADKEY Light

1. Choose **EXIT** from the break menu.
2. Respond **NO** to saving the part.
3. Control is returned to DOS at the c:\cadkey> level.
4. Type **cd..**(cd followed by two periods) and <Enter>.
5. Control is returned to c:\> the root level of your hard disk, the place you started.

End Lab 1

CADKEY Light
Operations

Screen Controls

▼ INTRODUCTION

In this chapter you will gain experience in setting up your CADKEY Light environment. Most CADD systems allow the user to define views and assign views to regions of the screen called *viewports*. CADKEY Light provides several methods for defining views that are fast and intuitive. The Display Menu is covered in detail in Chapter 25.

The first part of this chapter presents the conceptual material around which the Lab Assignment will later be completed. This is the organization of material that will be followed throughout the rest of the book: first a general discussion and then a tutorial lab assignment.

When your system starts up, a single viewport will be displayed. This is the case even if you have saved a part with four viewports active. The part will still appear in a single viewport. If you want your original views back, you will have to reassign them. In this chapter, you will be presented with a standard view representation arrangement. You will first create a part file that has this view arrangement and save it to be used as the template for subsequent labs.

▼ AUTOMATIC VIEWPORTS

CADKEY Light provides two options for viewport arrangement—one or four viewports. Any view can be displayed in any viewport. However, most designers find that if the views have a set spatial relationship, greater meaning can be derived from looking at the views together. We call this *view alignment*. For the purposes of this book, we will rearrange the default viewports into a system where depth is a horizontal dimension in and out of the screen in the front view. You will save this organization as a part file named **BLANK** and use it to begin all of our CADKEY Light exercises.

Study Fig. 6-1 carefully. It represents the CADKEY Light default views. Compare this to Fig. 6-2. Notice that the view names have stayed the same. However, the position of the view relative to the world axis system has been changed to place world axis depth, Z, in a horizontal position where positive Z runs out of the screen in the front view. This is a preferable orientation of views and the one we will use in this book. In the following two figures the position of the world axis system relative to the viewports has been represented with CADKEY Light's axis marker.

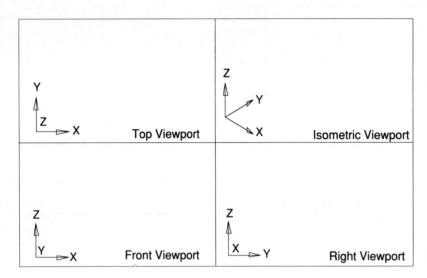

Fig. 6-1. Default CADKEY Light view assignments.

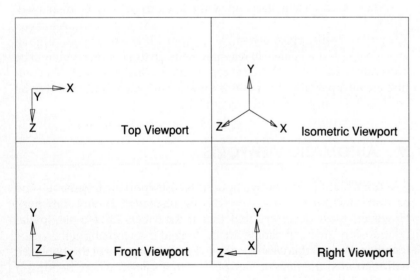

Fig. 6-2. Redefined views with world Z seen as a point in the front viewport.

▼ WORLD AXIS MARKERS

An icon that represents the orientation of the world axes can be displayed in each view. Its position is not related to the origin of the work space but always appears in the lower left corner of the viewport. In Fig. 6-3 three planes have been created and a small marker placed at 0, 0, 0 to mark the origin. All three of the planes intersect at 0, 0, 0—the origin of the work space. You will create these three planes as visual reminders of

- the location of the origin of the work space.

- the position of depth=0 construction reference planes in each view.

Because the three planes are unitary, the views will be sized and aligned correctly when zoomed to fill the viewport. The planes, when assigned to a reserved level, can be easily blanked or redisplayed.

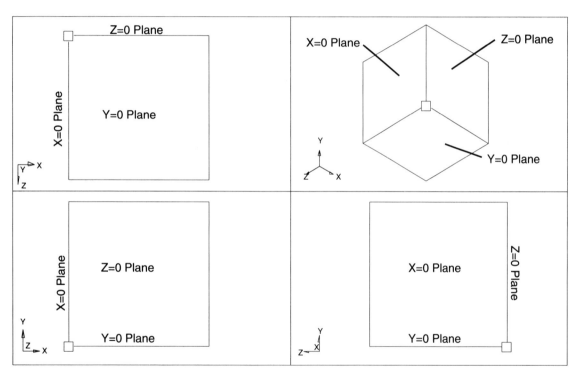

Fig. 6-3. Viewports with depth=0 construction reference planes installed.

Note in Fig. 6-3, the relation of the construction planes to the world axes seen normally in each view. In the front view, the construction plane is called the *x-y plane*. In the top view the plane is called the *x-z plane*. In the right view the construction plane is called the *z-y plane*. The construction plane in the isometric view is not normal to any of the three axes.

▼　DEFINE YOUR VIEWS

CADKEY Light contains eight preset views. View 1 is the view that you will use as your front view because it contains the point view of positive Z. To get your top, right, and isometric views in correct arrangement, you will need to rotate the viewport. Although you will move your view around a stationary world axis system, you will tell CADKEY Light how to do this by specifying the effect of the rotation on the world axes. For example, Fig. 6-4 shows the rotation of direction of view in order to produce a top view. CADKEY Light produces this view by rotating the top of the world axis system *out* (Fig. 6-5). The top of the world axis system can be rotated in or out; the right of the axis system can be rotated in or out; the entire axis system can be rotated clockwise (Fig. 6-6) or counter clockwise parallel to the current viewport.

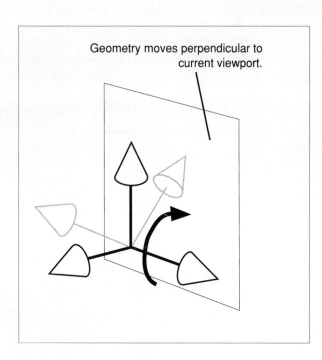

Fig. 6-4. Create a new view by rotating the top of the world axis system into the viewport.

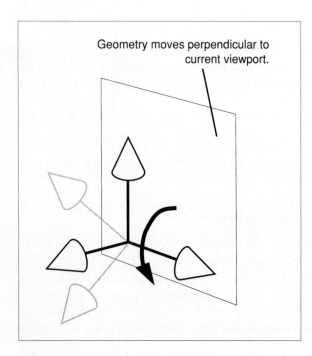

Fig. 6-5. Create a new view by rotating the top of the world axis system out of the viewport.

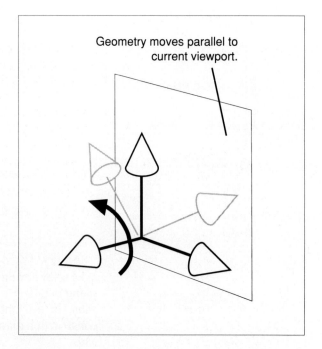

Fig. 6-6. Create a new view by rotating the world axis system counter clockwise.

CADKEY Light View Name	View #	Your View	Point View Axis
Top	**1**	**Front**	**+Z**
Front	2		-Y
Right	3		+X
Left	4		-X
Bottom	5		-Z
Back	6		+Y
Isometric	7		None
Axonometric	8		None
	9	**Top**	**+Y**
	10	**Right**	**+X**
	11	**Isometric**	**None**

Fig. 6-7. CADKEY Light standard views and the three views you create.

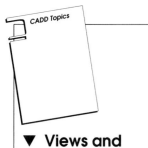

▼ Views and Viewports.

A *view* is the direction of sight taken from a certain vantage. A *viewport* is the region of the screen, perpendicular to the view, into which the geometry of the world is mapped.

▼   SAVE YOUR NEW VIEWS

After you have the views in their desired positions, you must save them as part of the file. Because CADKEY Light has the eight preset views, you will want to assign the next view number to the top view, the next to the right side view, and the next to your isometric view. Figure 6-7 shows the organization of views after you have saved yours. After you have set up the views in **BLANK**, you will have 11 preset views, one of which (View 1) is Light's top view. This View 1 will be your front view. View 9 is your top view; View 10 your right side view; View 11 your isometric view.

When you save **BLANK**, these view positions and their respective numbers are saved along with the file. When you load **BLANK** again, View 1 will be shown in a single viewport. To redisplay your views with the construction reference planes, select the four-view icon from **DISPLAY—VIEWPORTS—AUTOSET**, and assign view numbers 9, 10, and 11 to the top, right, and isometric viewports.

If you don't explicitly save the views, they will not be saved with the part file and will be unavailable the next time you load the part. It is important to realize that when you choose **DISPLAY—VIEW—SAVE** and click in a viewport, CADKEY Light assigns the next available number to that view (if it hasn't already been saved). The current number of saved views are displayed on the prompt line.

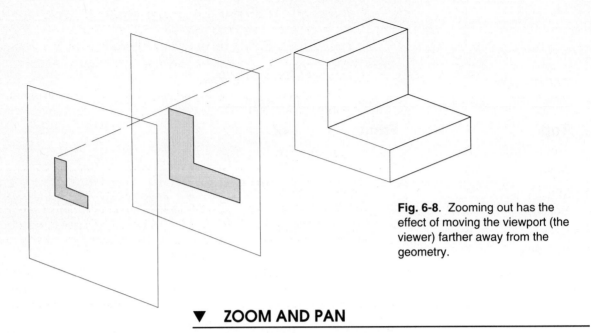

Fig. 6-8. Zooming out has the effect of moving the viewport (the viewer) farther away from the geometry.

▼ ZOOM AND PAN

Zooming and panning allow the viewport to be moved around so that more, or less, of the geometry can be displayed. Zooming and panning do not change the actual size or scale of the geometry in the work space (Fig. 6-8).

Zooming is generally done in one viewport at a time unless a **ZOOM–AUTO** (**ALT-A**) is executed for all viewports. The display of the part in unzoomed or unpanned viewports remains the same. Zooming is often necessary to identify entities or place patterns. However, zooming is not a method that necessarily speeds up the drawing process. It can actually take longer to complete a model by zooming in and out. A preferable technique is to use level or entity masks to refine the selection of entities.

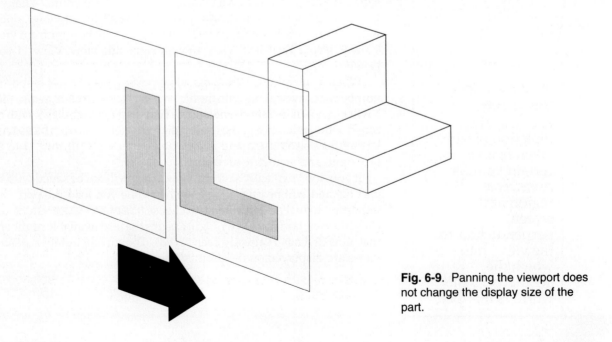

Fig. 6-9. Panning the viewport does not change the display size of the part.

Panning moves the viewport from side to side without moving it in or out (Fig. 6-9). Therefore, the geometry stays the same visual size as the result of a pan. Because entities generally have to be in a viewport to be selected, panning is the method to use when *small* lateral movements are needed.

In either case, the redisplay of geometry in the viewport can be halted by pressing the **ESC** key.

▼ SUMMARY

The preset views in CADKEY Light can be rearranged to provide an environment where world Z axis depth is perpendicular to the front viewport. New top, right, and isometric views numbered 9, 10, and 11 can be created and saved in a part file named **BLANK.** This file is used as a template for subsequent exercises.

Construction depth is an important concept in CADKEY Light. The position of current construction depth in relation to depth=zero is facilitated by creating construction reference planes each passing through 0, 0, 0, the origin of the work space.

CADKEY Light's world axis markers provide a reference of the current view coordinates (XV, YV, ZV) with world coordinates (X, Y, Z).

Viewport orientation to the world axes can be changed by creating new viewing positions, by zooming, and by panning. New viewing positions can be specified and saved as part of **BLANK**. CADKEY Light defaults to View 1, your front view. To see the top, right, and isometric views, a four-viewport screen display must be chosen and views 9, 10, and 11 assigned to the appropriate viewports. Zooming, although it may appear to change the size of part geometry, changes only the *display* of the geometry in the viewport. The part itself stays the same size. Panning moves the viewport left and right or up and down. The display of the part remains the same size as it is brought into or out of the viewport.

▼ QUESTIONS

1. What is the purpose of the template file **BLANK** ?

2. What is the default viewport set and assignment in CADKEY Light?

3. What is the relationship of the world axis icon and the origin of the work space in each view?

4. What is the relationship of XV, YV, and ZV axes to construction depth?

5. Assume that you are in the front viewport. Does the top of the axis system go in or out 90° to achieve the top view shown in Fig. 6-2?

6. Describe both zoom and pan in terms of the XV, YV, and ZV coordinates.

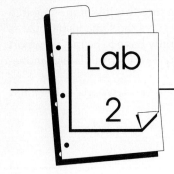

CADKEY Light Screen Control

Start Up Computer

Start CADKEY Light

ESC to a New Part Drawing

Insert your exercise disk into drive a:. Have a formatted data disk ready on which to save your exercise.

Turn on Display of Axis Markers

1. Choose **DISPLAY—AXES—DISP VW**
2. Choose **ON**.
3. **ESC** to the Main Menu.
4. CADKEY LIGHT displays the world axis marker in the lower left corner of the default viewport.

Create Multiple Viewports

1. Choose **DISPLAY—VWPORTS—AUTOSET**
2. Click once on the icon representing four views.
3. Click once on the lower left viewport to indicate the primary viewport.
4. **ESC** to the Main Menu.
5. CADKEY Light Displays four viewports with an axis marker displayed in each.

Front View—View 1

1. Choose **DISPLAY—VIEW**.
2 Click once in the lower left viewport.
3. Keyboard enter the number *1*, <Enter>.

Top View—New View

1. You are in the **DISPLAY—VIEW** menu.
2. Click once in the top viewport.
3. Choose **NEW—KEY-IN—TOP OUT**.
4. Keyboard enter the number *90*, <Enter>.
5. Choose **DONE**.

Right Side—New View

1. You are in the **DISPLAY—VIEW** menu.
2. Click once in the right viewport.
3. Choose **NEW—KEY-IN—CCW.**
4. Keyboard enter the number *90*, <Enter>.
5. Choose **DONE.**

Isometric—New View

1. You are in the **DISPLAY—VIEW** menu.
2. Click once on the pictorial viewport.
3. Keyboard enter the number *1*, <Enter>. The pictorial viewport is now the same as the front viewport.
4. Click again in the pictorial viewport.
5. Choose **NEW—KEY-IN—RGT OUT.**
6. Keyboard enter the number *45*, <Enter>.
7. Choose **TOP OUT.**
8. Keyboard enter the number *35.266*, <Enter>.
9. Choose **DONE.**
10. The viewport now shows an isometric orientation.
11. **ESC** to the Main Menu.

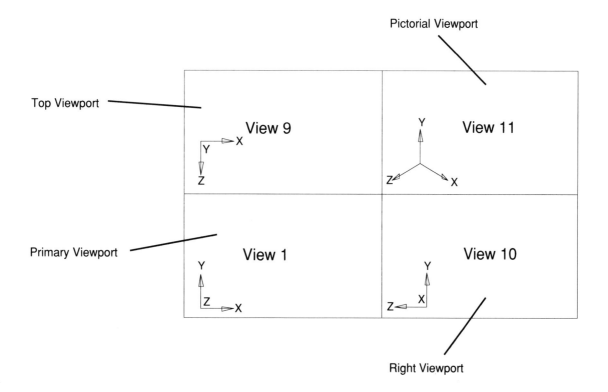

Save New Views

1. Choose **DISPLAY—VIEW**.
2. Click once in the top viewport.
3. Choose **SAVE**.
4. CADKEY Light assigns view 9 to the top view.
5. Click once on the right side view.
6. Choose **SAVE**.
7. CADKEY Light assigns view 10 to the right side view.
8. Click once in the isometric view.
9. Choose **SAVE**.
10. CADKEY Light assigns view 11 to the isometric view.
11. **ESC** to the Main Menu.

Save BLANK

1. Eject the exercise disk and insert your personal data disk if you have one. If not, use the exercise disk for your data.
2. Choose **FILES—PART—SAVE**.
3. Type **a:blank** to save the template on your data disk, <Enter>.
4. **ESC** to the Main Menu.

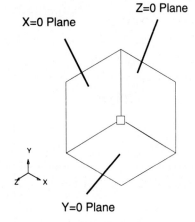

X=0 Plane

Z=0 Plane

Y=0 Plane

Place Reference Planes

1. Eject your data disk and reinsert the exercise disk.
2. Choose **FILES—PATTERN—RETRIEV**.
3. Keyboard enter **a:constrpl**.
4. Answer all prompts by accepting the defaults except **KEY IN** the number *99* for the desired level.
5. Select **COORD:WLD** and **CONSTR:3D** from the Status Menu.
6. Choose **KEY-IN** from the Position Menu. Place cursor in the front viewport.
7. Keyboard enter *0* (zero) for X, Y, and Z coordinates of the pattern base.
8. Construction planes and axes are placed on **BLANK** on level 99.

Turn on Level 99

1. Choose **DISPLAY—LEVELS—ADD** and keyboard enter **99** <Enter>.
2. Press **ALT—A** <Enter> to auto zoom viewports.

Exit CADKEY Light

1. Choose **EXIT** from the Break Menu.
2. Respond **YES.**

Start Light and Open BLANK

1. Type **cadkey** at the c: \cadkey> prompt.
2. At the initial screen, type **a:blank** <Enter>.
3. CADKEY opens the part file from your data disk in a single viewport with view 1.

Recall Saved Views

1. Choose **DISPLAY—VWPORTS—AUTOSET**
2. Click once on the icon representing four views
3. Click once on the lower left viewport to indicate the primary viewport.
4. **ESC** to the Main Menu.
5. Choose **DISPLAY—VIEW.**
6. Click once in the top viewport.
7. Keyboard enter the number 9, <Enter>.
8. Click once on the right side view.
9. Keyboard enter the number 10, <Enter>.
10. Click once in the isometric view.
11. Keyboard enter the number 11, <Enter>.
12. **ESC** to Main Menu.

Close CADKEY Light

1. Cursor select **EXIT** (**ALT—E**) from the middle Break Menu.
2. Choose **NO** from the Main Menu. You don't want to overwrite BLANK.
3. Control is returned to the computer at c: \cadkey>.

End Lab 2

Editing Functions

Complete the 2D
BASE and 2D
EDITS section of
TUTOR after
you have read
this chapter but
before working
on Lab 3.

▼ INTRODUCTION

Editing is the way to change the shape, size, or association of entities after they have been created. Sometimes it is faster to create the correct shape and later edit the entity to the correct size than it is to create the entity the correct size in the first place. Edits cannot be undone, so it is advisable to save your part file first before embarking on a major edit. Experienced designers learn to "rough out" their designs first, not being overly concerned with exact sizes and intersections. They know that they can use the power of CADKEY Light to tighten up their designs by editing.

In this chapter you will be introduced to the editing functions described in detail in Chapter 21. You will practice editing on a sample part file first, learning many of CADKEY Light's editing features. You won't have to create any geometry first...that will come in the next chapter.

In the **CONFIG** program you have the opportunity to specify how you wish entities to be marked when selected. Entity markers (small triangles placed on each entity near the location where you click your cursor) can be drawn or flashed. When drawn, they stay on the screen until it is redrawn. At no time do entity markers become a geometric or detail part of the data base. Entities can also be flashed white to show that they have been selected for editing. This has the advantage of not cluttering the display with marker triangles but has the disadvantage that it may be difficult to determine which of several close entities has been flashed, or after a few minutes, which one was selected at all.

Entities can be selected for editing in any viewport. You can switch from one viewport to another while selecting to get the best view of the target. If the wrong entity is selected, choose **F10** backup to reselect.

▼ WHAT CAN BE EDITED

Editing in CADKEY Light involves either lengthening or shortening a line or arc (**TRM/EXT**), punching a hole or gap in a line or arc (**DIVIDE**), breaking entities into sections that automatically assume different line attributes (**BREAK**), bringing a deleted entity or layer back into the data base (**RECALL**), or grouping geometric entities (**GROUP**). Many editing operations require the selection of geometric entities. You may want to selectively use the **DISPLAY—ZOOM—WINDOW** command to more easily identify entities for editing.

▼ TRIM AND EXTEND

For an entity to be trimmed or extended, it must be displayed in the viewport. The entity that is used to control the final position of the edited object is called the *trimming entity*. Entities that belong to groups can also be edited. Trim and extend has only one rule:

Always identify an entity on the portion that is to remain after the editing has been done.

To change the length of a line or arc use the **TRM/EXT** option. If a line is trimmed or extended, its angle is not changed. If an arc is trimmed its radius and center are not moved, only its arc length is altered. It is important to use the **TRM/EXT** function rather than trying to visually align constructions Because CADKEY Light can calculate intersections to a much greater level of accuracy than you can. This assures the validity of the geometric data base.

In Fig. 7-1 a preliminary construction has been done. Note that it would be virtually impossible to predict the beginning and ending angles of the arcs as they cross the circle. You would use CADKEY Light's powerful **TRM/EXT** options to complete the edit. This is shown in Fig. 7-2 on the next page. Several options exist for trimming entities. See Chapter 21 for a description of these options.

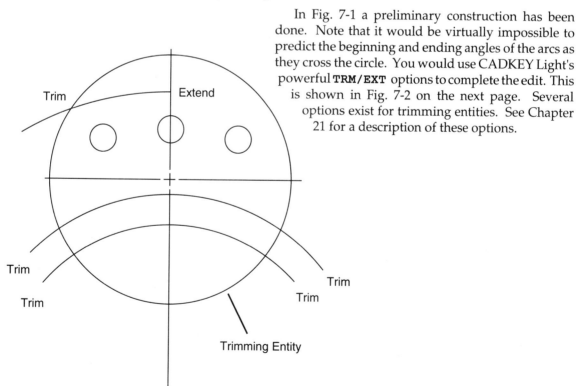

Fig. 7-1. Construction before trim and extend.

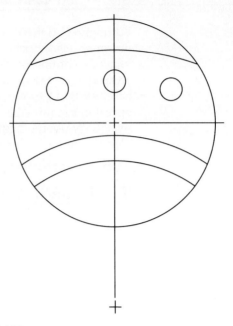

Fig. 7-2. Construction after trim
and extend.

▼ BREAK

When an entity is broken, it is split into two or more pieces. The position of the pieces in space is not altered. What makes this function powerful is that newly created divisions assume whatever attributes are active at the time of the break. This means that entities can be created whole, broken into parts, and those new parts' attributes changed in one step. This is much more efficient than creating individual entities and changing their attributes.

Consider the construction in Fig. 7-3. The lines extending from the ends of the arc need to change into dashed lines as they pass the solid horizontal line. This could be done by constructing separate lines, changing the current line style attribute each time. Or the lines could be constructed separately and the dashed segments changed as a group. But by setting the current line type to dashed first, and then breaking the lines, the lines can be divided and changed into dashed lines in the same step. Figure 7-4 shows the result of the breaking operation. Because the current line attribute was set to dashed, all broken portions assume this attribute.

Several options exist for breaking entities. See Chapter 21 for a description of these options.

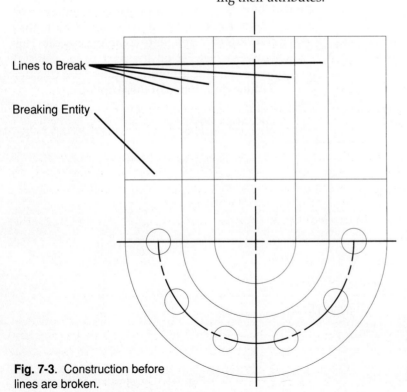

Lines to Break

Breaking Entity

Fig. 7-3. Construction before
lines are broken.

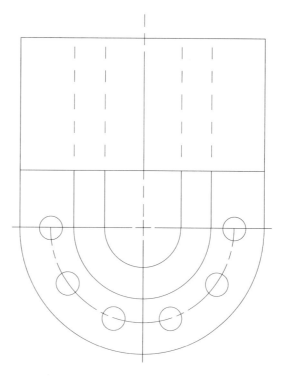

Fig. 7-4. Construction after lines have been broken. Note that the broken portions assume current line attribute—dashed.

▼ RECALL LAST DELETE

This option is kind of an *unedit*, but only for deleted entities, both geometric and detail. This means that lines that have been trimmed cannot be *untrimmed*. Lines that have been broken cannot be *unbroken*. **RECALL** only applies to those entities deleted since the part file was loaded. If the part is removed from the work space by loading another part file, all chance to recall deleted entities is lost. A deleted entity can be recalled once for each delete action.

The **LAST** deleted entity can be brought back into the data base. When an entire **LEVEL** has been deleted, it too can be recalled. Finally, **ALL** entities can be recalled that were deleted since the part file was loaded.

This option is used to restore a part file to its condition before a series of extensive deletes was accomplished. Of course, it may be more advantageous to first save the file, under another file name if necessary, and then reload the file. On the other hand, it may be faster to recall a single deleted entity rather than saving, deleting, and then reloading the file.

▼ GROUPING

The association of geometric and detail entities into a group is a powerful feature of CADD systems. CADKEY Light allows you to make groups and name them for easy identification. Although called an edit in CADKEY Light, grouping does not change attributes or sizes in the data base. It only associates entities for further editing.

You should create groups when entities will be deleted, moved, or scaled as a single unit or when attributes such as line style, line weight, color, or level assignment will be changed for associated geometry. Groups should have short descriptive names—short for ease of keyboarding and descriptive so that the names will have meaning.

When a group is selected, CADKEY Light will ask you if you want to act on the entire group or on the entity that was selected within the group. This provides a means to edit individual entities within a group without degrouping, changing, and regrouping.

▼ SUMMARY

Editing of entities requires that they be displayed in a viewport. Lines and arcs can be trimmed or extended. This may be a more efficient technique than attempting to create lines or arcs of the proper length at the beginning. When trimmed, a portion of a line or arc is removed by a trimming entity. When extended, the line or arc is made longer until it intersects the trimming entity.

When a line or arc is broken by a breaking entity, the original is split into segments. The original part retains the attributes in effect when the entity was created. The new portion assumes the current attribute assignments. If the attributes were not changed, both parts of the broken entity will look the same.

When something deleted is recalled, it is brought back into the data base and displayed on the screen. A single entity, a deleted level, or all deletions since loading the part file can be recalled once for each deletion.

Grouping objects together and assigning a group name provides a powerful method of editing. Choose short, easy-to-remember names.

▼ QUESTIONS

1. Why is it important to perform a save before a major editing operation?

2. On what portion of an entity must you click to identify it for editing?

3. What is the difference between **TRM/EXT** and **BREAK**?

4. Why is it important to know current attributes before beginning a **BREAK** operation?

5. On what changes will **RECALL** work? What strategies are available to correct mistakes made with other commands?

6. When would it be appropriate to create a group? How many objects can be included within a group?

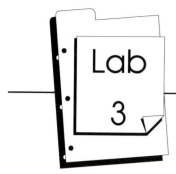

CADKEY Light
Editing

Start CADKEY Light

Load LAB3 From Your Exercise Disk

Display Problem A in the Viewport

Use **ALT—W** to zoom window around problem A.

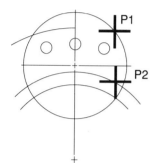

Trim Overhanging Arcs

1. Choose **EDIT—TRM/EXT—MODAL**.
2. Select the trimming entity (P1).
3. Select the entity to trim on the portion that will remain after the trim (P2).
4. Continue selecting until all arcs are trimmed.
5. **ESC** to the Main Menu.

Extend Arc to Intersection

1. Choose **EDIT—TRM/EXT—FIRST**.
2. Select the arc to extend (P1).
3. Select the trimming entity (P2).
4. **ESC** to the Main Menu.

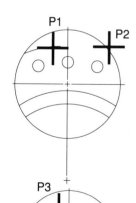

Group Arcs

1. Choose **EDIT—GROUP—MAKE**.
2. Keyboard the name **arcs** as the group name.
3. Choose **SINGLE**.
4. Select each of the three arcs P1, P2, P3, <Enter>.
5. **ESC** to the Main Menu.

Change Arc's Line Style

1. Choose **CONTROL—ATTRIB—L-TYPE—CHANGE** and pick the dashed line type.
2. Choose **GROUP—BY NAME**.
3. Keyboard enter the group name **arcs**, <Enter>.
4. **ESC** to the Main Menu.

Save File as LAB3A

Display Problem B in Viewport

Use **ALT–W** to zoom window around problem B.

Delete and Recall Single Entity

1. Choose **DELETE–SELECT–SINGLE**
2. Select one of the lines, <Enter>.
3. **ESC** to the Main Menu.
4. Choose **EDIT–RECALL–LAST.**
5. **ESC** to the Main Menu.

Set Current Line Type to Dashed

1. Choose **CONTROL–ATTRIB–L-TYPE–CURRENT**
2. Choose the dashed line type.
3. **ESC** to the Main Menu.

Break Lines

1. Choose **EDIT–BREAK–MODAL**

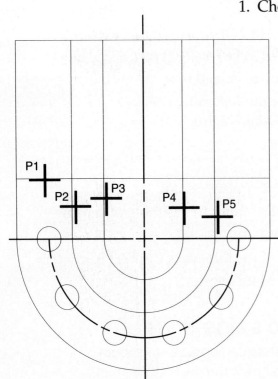

2 Select the breaking entity (P1).
3. Select the first line on the portion that will keep the original line type at tribute (P2).
4. Continue selecting lines (P3-P5) until all are broken and the type attribute is changed.
5. **ESC** to the Main Menu.

Save File as LAB3A

End Lab 3

▼   ADDITIONAL EXERCISES FOR PRACTICE

Shown below are additional editing exercises to give you practice with trim, extend, break, and group. These files are found on your CADKEY Light Exercise Disk. A small triangle mark lines to be edited by trim and extend. An **X** marks line segments that should be removed using the divide option.

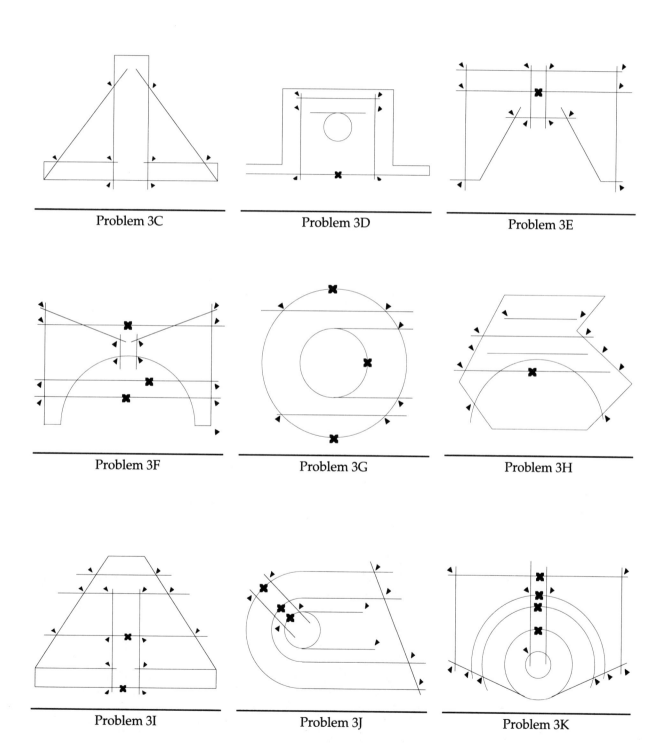

Problem 3C   Problem 3D   Problem 3E

Problem 3F   Problem 3G   Problem 3H

Problem 3I   Problem 3J   Problem 3K

Characteristics of Geometric Entities

▼ IN THIS CHAPTER

Position Masks
Modeling Components
Drafting Components
Construction Strategies
Lab 4

▼ INTRODUCTION

This chapter will introduce the basic geometric building blocks used in CADKEY Light. You are, by no means, limited to the *primitives* found in the Create Menu. As you will discover, custom geometry can be created and saved as geometric patterns, able to be placed at any scale and at any orientation in space.

But to understand CADKEY Light's capabilities, it is wise to first start with those geometric *entities* recognized by the system. All of the functions available in the Create Menu are discussed in Chapter 20. The explanations in this chapter are meant to prepare you to understand when and where the entities can and should be used. Exact operations are covered in Chapter 20. You may want to peruse these operations in *before* continuing with the reading of this chapter simply to have in mind the breadth of constructions possible in CADKEY Light.

The examples used in this chapter may not make use of the *immediate command* shortcuts available in CADKEY Light. These can be learned after the basics of geometric constructions have been practiced. The lab exercise in this chapter takes you step-by-step through the construction of a typical geometric problem using many of the commands available in the Create Menu. Complete this exercise before continuing on with the additional exercises.

This is the first chapter that makes heavy use of conventional engineering drawing conventions and practices. You should have most of these in hand as you learn to apply CADKEY Light to engineering design and documentation problems. But to refresh your memory, look for a Drafting Topic Card presented beside the text with important terms, definitions, or procedures.

▼ POSITION MASKS

Position masks are fundamental in constructing geometry. When a position mask is active, your freedom to position the cursor in space is controlled. You snap to the nearest feature that matches the chosen position option. For example, if **POINT** is chosen, CADKEY Light will search only for point entities within its search area. The search area is defined by the size of the cursor as set in the **CONFIG** program. The choice of position mask depends on the type of construction that you are doing.

Position masks are available from the Position Menu. This menu is displayed automatically when CADKEY Light expects spatial cursor input. When a position mask is active, an asterisk (*) appears beside the choice. This mask remains chosen as long as the function that called the Position Menu is active.

CADKEY Light prompts you for action in the prompt line at the bottom of the screen. Because geometric constructions often require multiple input points, the position mask can be changed for entry. Until you gain experience with these masks, it may be common to have the wrong mask active during a construction. Always glance to the Position Menu to check the active mask before entering a data point.

To assure that CADKEY Light selects the position you desire, display the part geometry in an unambiguous position. Note in Fig. 8-1(a) that two line entities visually coincide. Were the **ENDENT** mask active, you might not be able to predict which line's end would be selected. In Fig. 8-1(b), the view has been rotated slightly, allowing an unambiguous view of both lines.

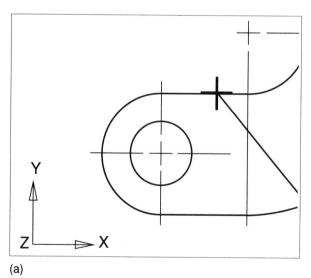

(a)

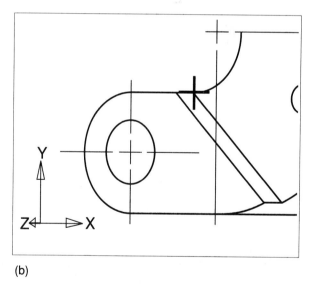

(b)

Fig. 8-1. Rotate view to present an unambiguous view of the geometry.

CURSOR   Allows the free positioning of the cursor in space. If grid snap is on, the cursor snaps to grid snap interval. CADKEY Light defaults to **CURSOR** positioning.

POINT   Positions the cursor at the nearest point entity.

ENDENT   Positions the cursor at the end of a line, end of an arc, or 0º position on a circle.

CENTER   Positions the cursor at the midpoint of a line or center of an arc or circle.

INTRSC   Positions the cursor at the intersection of two entities.

ALONGL   Positions the cursor at a point along a line at a specified distance from one of the ends.

POLAR   Positions the cursor at a polar position specified by center, radius, and angle.

DELTA   Positions the cursor at an offset distance from a known point.

KEY-IN   Positions the cursor at an absolute point in either world or view space.

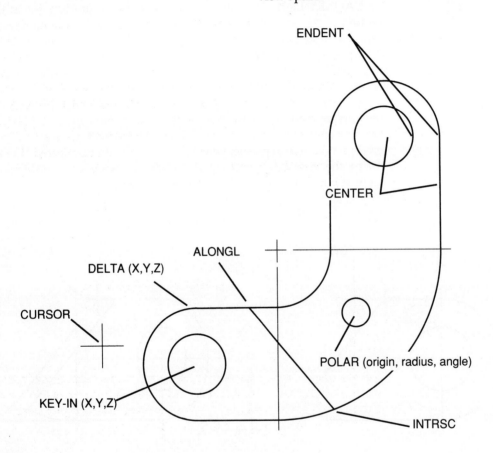

Fig. 8-2. Examples of location masks.

▼ MODELING COMPONENTS

It is important to recognize the function of entities as they are used to describe geometry on engineering models. With this knowledge, you will be able to choose the appropriate geometric entity to describe real-world geometry. Detail drafting entities—dimensions, notes, and labels—are not part of a model.

Modeling Components

Lines

On models, lines represent the intersection of surfaces or elements on surfaces (Fig. 8-3). Lines have end points, centers, points along, and form intersections with other entities.

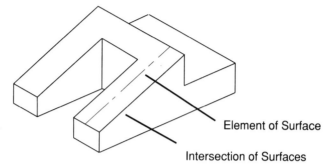

Fig. 8-3. Lines in a model.

Element of Surface

Intersection of Surfaces

Arcs

Arcs on models also represent the intersection of surfaces or elements on surfaces (Fig. 8-4). Arcs have end points, centers, and form intersections with other entities.

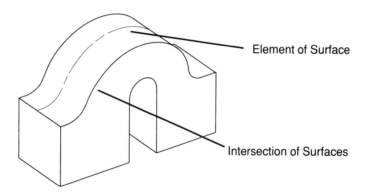

Element of Surface

Intersection of Surfaces

Fig. 8-4. Arcs in a model.

Circles

Circles are generally used to define the intersection of cylindrical surfaces and planes. For example, in Fig. 8-5 the two circles define the entrance and exit of a hole. Circles have centers, end points at zero degrees, and form intersections with other entities.

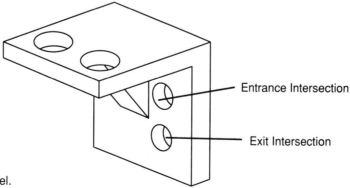

Entrance Intersection

Exit Intersection

Fig. 8-5. Circles in a model.

Points

Point entities are used to mark positions in space and do not correspond to any geometric feature on a model. They may, for example, be used to describe spatial position on surfaces that do not adhere to linear, circular, or spherical construction. In Fig. 8-6(a) a number of points have been located by their X, Y, Z coordinates. A *surface patch* like that shown in Fig. 8-6(b) can be generated by masking lines to the points. Points can be masked only with the **POINT** mask itself.

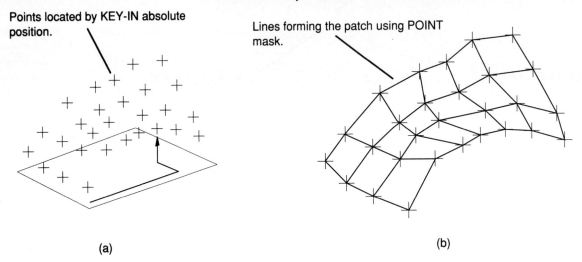

Points located by KEY-IN absolute position.

Lines forming the patch using POINT mask.

(a)

(b)

Fig. 8-6. Points in a model used to define a surface patch.

Polylines

Polylines consist of connected line segments and as such describe either the intersection of surfaces or elements of surfaces. For example, the lines passing through the points can be individual line segments or polylines. Polylines have end points, centers, and form intersections with other entities.

Fillets

This entity automates the construction of arcs that are tangent to lines or other arcs. As a geometric feature, a fillet describes the edge or limit of a cylindrical or toroidal surface (Fig. 8-7). An option under fillet is **CHAMFER**. This represents the edge of an angled plane surface between two intersecting plane surfaces. Fillets have end points, centers, and form intersections with other entities.

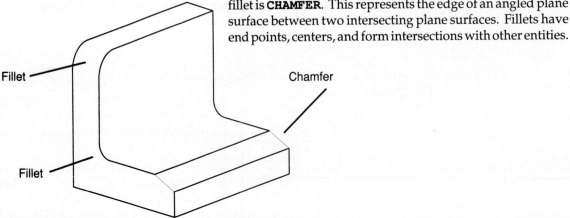

Fillet

Fillet

Chamfer

Fig. 8-7. Fillets in a model.

Polygons

A polygon generally represents the end view of a prismatic solid. This entity can be a regular polygon, a rectangular polygon, or an irregular polygon (Fig. 8-8). Polygons have center of sides, ends of sides, and form intersections with other entities.

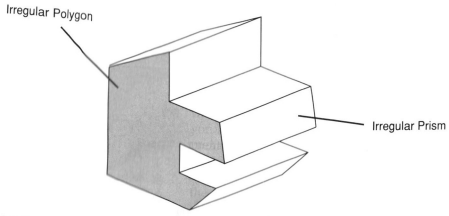

Irregular Polygon

Irregular Prism

Fig. 8-8. Polygon in a model.

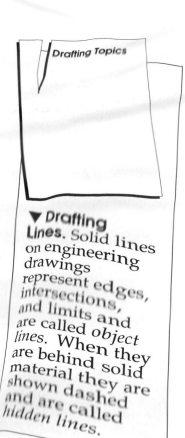

Drafting Topics

▼ **Drafting Lines.** Solid lines on engineering drawings represent edges, intersections, and limits and are called object lines. When they are behind solid material they are shown dashed and are called hidden lines.

▼ DRAFTING COMPONENTS

To use the power of CADKEY Light, engineering drawings are generally extracted from 3D models. True, a designer may choose to work on 2D portions, assembling a model along Z axis depth. But it is the integrity of the model that is of first concern because the model data base must be valid for subsequent postprocessing.

CADKEY Light is at its center *modeling* software. You are able to disregard either view or world depth and perform constructions in 2D space. You can use CADKEY Light to make traditional 2D engineering drawings. But engineering drawings require that the third dimension be visualized or assembled by simultaneously reading related 2D views. CADKEY Light, because it builds a true 3D data base, is able to present geometry in *any* view, once a 3D model is built.

All of the geometric entities used in modeling have their corresponding uses in drafting.

▼ CONSTRUCTION STRATEGIES

Three construction strategies are described in this section that rely heavily on the geometric constructions available in the Create Menu. All make use of 2D profiles that are somehow manipulated in 3D space. They are presented early in this book so that when described in detail later, they will be familiar. It is important to carefully analyze the geometric characteristics of a design so that the most efficient construction method may be applied to its description. The step-by-step exercise in Lab 4 provides practice in creating the 2D profile that will later form the basis of a 3D model.

Depth Construction

Profiles are constructed in 2D at specific depth settings. Intersections and elements of surfaces can then be added manually using position masks for accuracy (Fig. 8-9). This construction technique is appropriate for objects that change in profile as they recede along the depth axis.

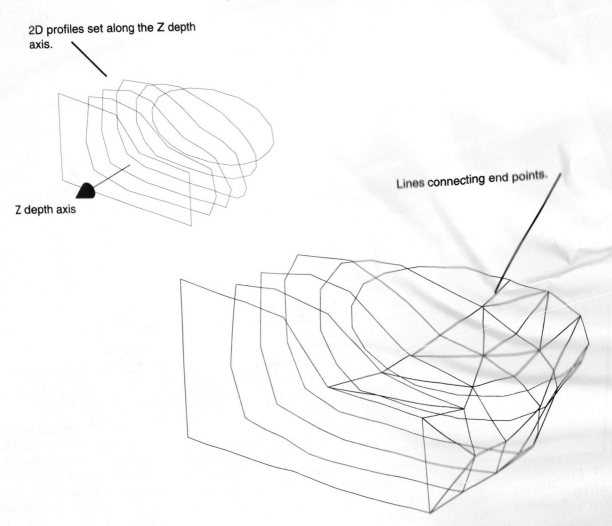

2D profiles set along the Z depth axis.

Z depth axis

Lines connecting end points.

Fig. 8-9. Depth construction of a model.

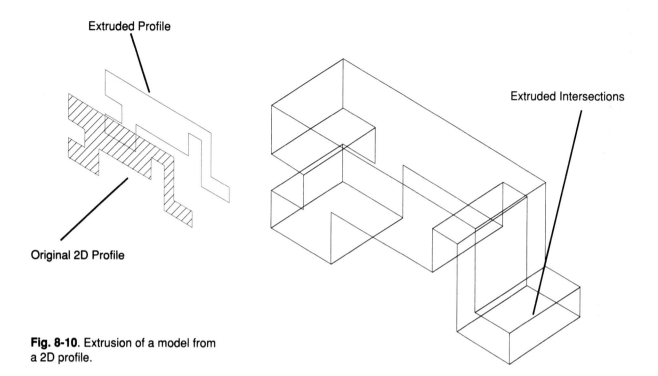

Extruded Profile

Extruded Intersections

Original 2D Profile

Fig. 8-10. Extrusion of a model from a 2D profile.

Sweeping

A 2D profile can be revolved about an axis and copied a specified number of times (Fig 8-11). The vertices of the profile are automatically connected and all redundant entities are removed. This technique is appropriate for turned or symmetrical parts.

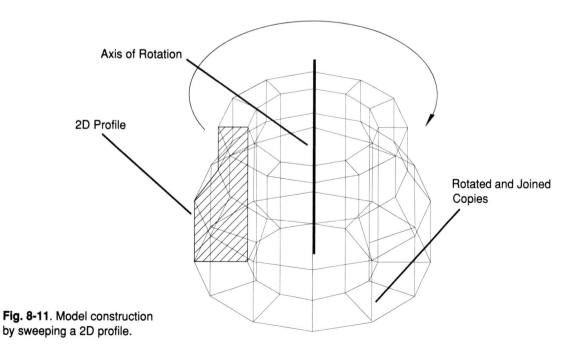

Axis of Rotation

2D Profile

Rotated and Joined Copies

Fig. 8-11. Model construction by sweeping a 2D profile.

▼ SUMMARY

To efficiently use the construction options available in CADKEY Light, the design must be analyzed to determine the most applicable construction strategy. Because lines, arcs, and circles do not exist in 3D models—rather they represent the intersection of surfaces—knowing which entity to use to represent a geometric feature is important for the validity of the model.

Three construction strategies might be considered when planning the modeling of an object. Depth construction is a powerful extension of 2D construction techniques. Extrusion automates model building when a consistent profile is present. Finally, sweeping provides a method of modeling parts that are symmetrical about an axis.

▼ QUESTIONS

1. How can you determine which position mask is active?

2. How can you keep CADKEY Light from being confused as to which entity you wish to select?

3. Describe the function of each of the position masks.

4. What is meant by an *unambiguous view*? How does this relate to selecting entities?

5. Describe the difference between a surface intersection and a surface element. Can they be the same?

6. Why is it important to extract engineering drawings from 3D model data rather than make the 3D models from 2D drawings?

7. What sort of objects are appropriate for depth, extrusion, and sweeping techniques?

8. Can the same profile be used for sweeping and extrusion?

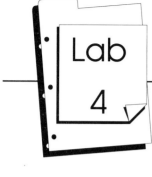

CADKEY Light
Constructions

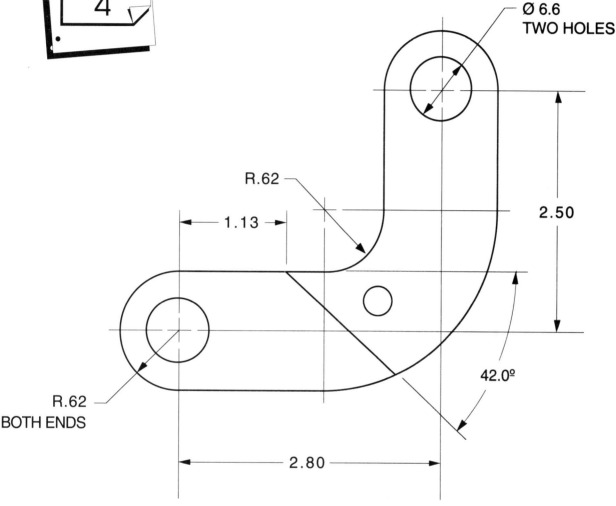

Ø 6.6
TWO HOLES

R.62

1.13

2.50

R.62
BOTH ENDS

42.0°

2.80

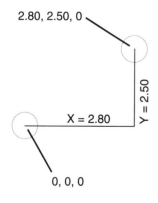

2.80, 2.50, 0

Y = 2.50

X = 2.80

0, 0, 0

Load BLANK From Your Data Disk

1. `GRID:OFF; SNAP:OFF.`
2. Choose **DISPLAY—VIEW** and keyboard enter **1** <Enter>.

Locate Holes

1. Choose **CREATE—CIRCLE—CTR+D**
2. Keyboard enter .66 as the diameter, <Enter>.
3. Choose **KEY-IN** from the Position Menu.
4. Keyboard enter 0, 0, 0 view coordinates, <Enter>.
5. Keyboard enter 2.80, 2.50. 0, <Enter>.
6. Press **ALT-A**.
7. **ESC** to the Main Menu.

Rounded Ends

1. Choose **CREATE—ARC—CTR+RAD.**
2. Keyboard enter .62 as radius, <Enter>.
3. Keyboard enter 90 and 270 as start and end angles.
4. Choose **CENTER** from the Position Menu.
5. Select the lower left hole (P1).
6. Press **F10** backup, <Enter>. Accept 0.62 radius.
7. Keyboard enter 0 and 180 as start and end angles.
8. Select the upper right hole (P2).
9. Press **ALT-A**
10. **ESC** to the Main Menu.

Save LAB4 on Your Data Disk

Rough Out the Sides

1. Choose **CREATE—LINE—ENDPTS—ENDENT**
2. Select the end of the arc, P1.
3. Choose **DELTA—ENDENT,** reselect P1.
4. Keyboard enter 4, 0, 0, <Enter>.
5. Choose **BACKUP—ENDENT.** Select P2.
6. Choose **DELTA—ENDENT,** reselect P2.
7. Keyboard enter 0 -3.5, 0, <Enter>.
8. Choose **BACKUP—ENDENT.** Select P3.
9. Choose **DELTA—ENDENT,** reselect P3.
10. Keyboard enter 0, -2.5, 0, <Enter>.
11. Choose **BACKUP—ENDENT.** Select P4.
12. Choose **DELTA—ENDENT,** reselect P4.
13. Keyboard enter 2.5, 0, 0, <Enter>.
14. **ESC** to the Main Menu.

Note: Select line on portion that is to remain after fillet trim.

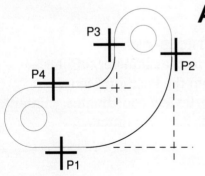

Add Fillets

1. Choose **CREATE—FILLET—ARC—TRIM**
2. Keyboard enter .62 as the fillet radius, <Enter>.
3. Select the first fillet entity (P3).
4. Select the second fillet entity (P4).
5. Keyboard enter 1.86 as the fillet radius, <Enter>.
6. Select the first fillet entity (P1).
7. Select the second fillet entity (P2).
8. **ESC** to the Main Menu.

Polygons

A polygon generally represents the end view of a prismatic solid. This entity can be a regular polygon, a rectangular polygon, or an irregular polygon (Fig. 8-8). Polygons have center of sides, ends of sides, and form intersections with other entities.

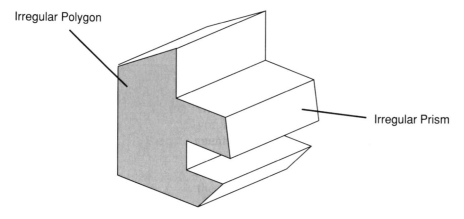

Irregular Polygon

Irregular Prism

Fig. 8-8. Polygon in a model.

Drafting Topics

▼ Drafting Lines. Solid lines on engineering drawings represent edges, intersections, and limits and are called *object lines*. When they are behind solid material they are shown dashed and are called *hidden lines*.

▼ DRAFTING COMPONENTS

To use the power of CADKEY Light, engineering drawings are generally extracted from 3D models. True, a designer may choose to work on 2D portions, assembling a model along Z axis depth. But it is the integrity of the model that is of first concern because the model data base must be valid for subsequent postprocessing.

CADKEY Light is at its center *modeling* software. You are able to disregard either view or world depth and perform constructions in 2D space. You can use CADKEY Light to make traditional 2D engineering drawings. But engineering drawings require that the third dimension be visualized or assembled by simultaneously reading related 2D views. CADKEY Light, because it builds a true 3D data base, is able to present geometry in *any* view, once a 3D model is built.

All of the geometric entities used in modeling have their corresponding uses in drafting.

▼ CONSTRUCTION STRATEGIES

Three construction strategies are described in this section that rely heavily on the geometric constructions available in the Create Menu. All make use of 2D profiles that are somehow manipulated in 3D space. They are presented early in this book so that when described in detail later, they will be familiar. It is important to carefully analyze the geometric characteristics of a design so that the most efficient construction method may be applied to its description. The step-by-step exercise in Lab 4 provides practice in creating the 2D profile that will later form the basis of a 3D model.

Depth Construction

Profiles are constructed in 2D at specific depth settings. Intersections and elements of surfaces can then be added manually using position masks for accuracy (Fig. 8-9). This construction technique is appropriate for objects that change in profile as they recede along the depth axis.

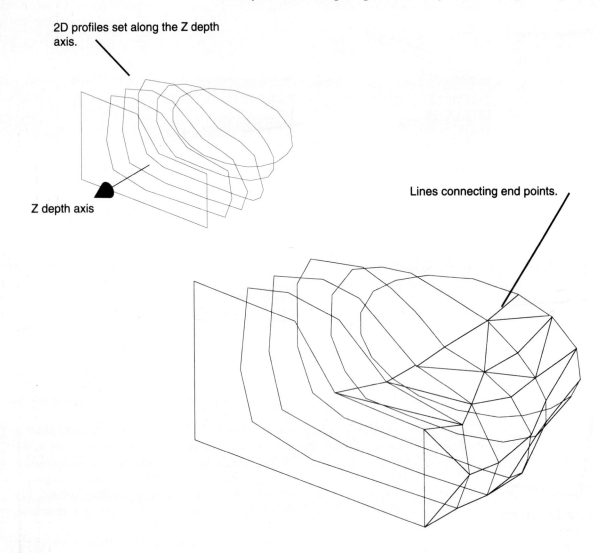

Fig. 8-9. Depth construction of a model.

Extrusion

A 2D profile can be translated relative to X, Y, and Z axes (either view or world) with the vertices of the 2D profiles joined automatically (Fig. 8-10). Each copied profile can be translated along any or all three ot the axes, allowing complex shapes to be extruded. If in joining the two profiles two entities connect the same two points, CADKEY solves this redundancy by removing one of the entities. This construction technique is appropriate for objects that do not change in profile over their length.

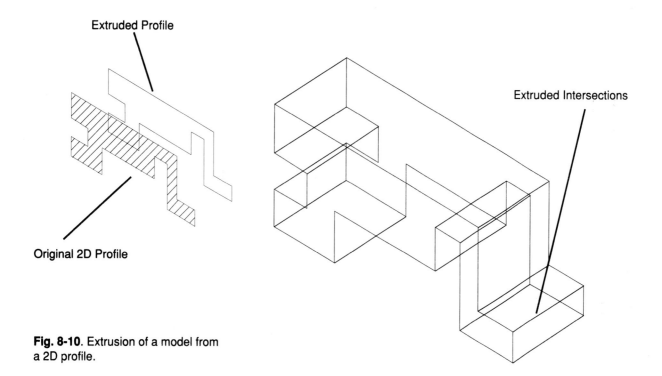

Extruded Profile

Extruded Intersections

Original 2D Profile

Fig. 8-10. Extrusion of a model from a 2D profile.

Sweeping

A 2D profile can be revolved about an axis and copied a specified number of times (Fig 8-11). The vertices of the profile are automatically connected and all redundant entities are removed. This technique is appropriate for turned or symmetrical parts.

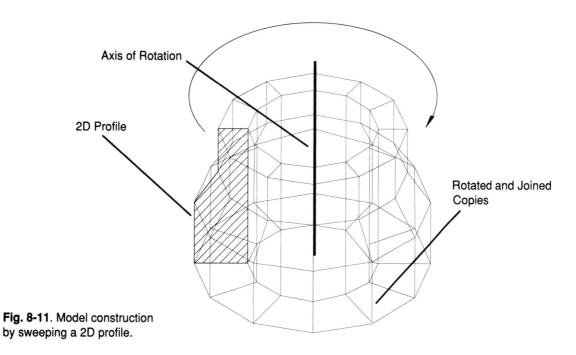

Axis of Rotation

2D Profile

Rotated and Joined Copies

Fig. 8-11. Model construction by sweeping a 2D profile.

▼ SUMMARY

To efficiently use the construction options available in CADKEY Light, the design must be analyzed to determine the most applicable construction strategy. Because lines, arcs, and circles do not exist in 3D models—rather they represent the intersection of surfaces—knowing which entity to use to represent a geometric feature is important for the validity of the model.

Three construction strategies might be considered when planning the modeling of an object. Depth construction is a powerful extension of 2D construction techniques. Extrusion automates model building when a consistent profile is present. Finally, sweeping provides a method of modeling parts that are symmetrical about an axis.

▼ QUESTIONS

1. How can you determine which position mask is active?

2. How can you keep CADKEY Light from being confused as to which entity you wish to select?

3. Describe the function of each of the position masks.

4. What is meant by an *unambiguous view*? How does this relate to selecting entities?

5. Describe the difference between a surface intersection and a surface element. Can they be the same?

6. Why is it important to extract engineering drawings from 3D model data rather than make the 3D models from 2D drawings?

7. What sort of objects are appropriate for depth, extrusion, and sweeping techniques?

8. Can the same profile be used for sweeping and extrusion?

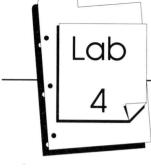

CADKEY Light
Constructions

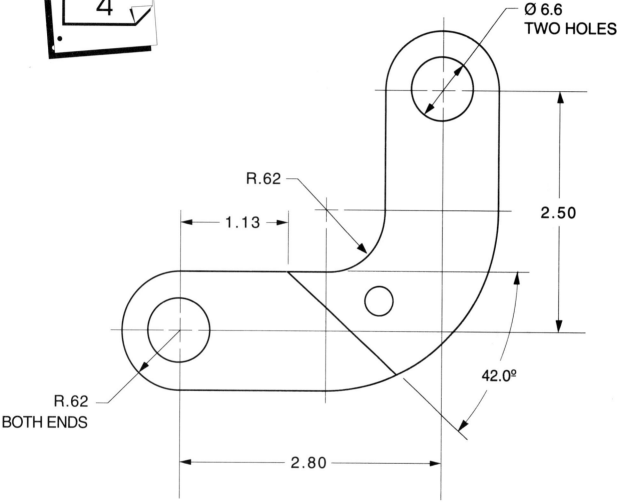

Ø 6.6
TWO HOLES

R.62

1.13

2.50

R.62
BOTH ENDS

42.0°

2.80

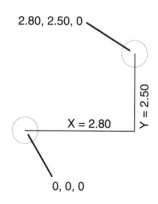

2.80, 2.50, 0

X = 2.80

Y = 2.50

0, 0, 0

Load BLANK From Your Data Disk

1. GRID:OFF; SNAP:OFF.
2. Choose DISPLAY—VIEW and keyboard enter 1 <Enter>.

Locate Holes

1. Choose CREATE—CIRCLE—CTR+D
2. Keyboard enter .66 as the diameter, <Enter>.
3. Choose KEY-IN from the Position Menu.
4. Keyboard enter 0, 0, 0 view coordinates, <Enter>.
5. Keyboard enter 2.80, 2.50. 0, <Enter>.
6. Press ALT-A.
7. ESC to the Main Menu.

Rounded Ends

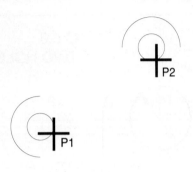

1. Choose **CREATE—ARC—CTR+RAD.**
2. Keyboard enter .62 as radius, <Enter>.
3. Keyboard enter 90 and 270 as start and end angles.
4. Choose **CENTER** from the Position Menu.
5. Select the lower left hole (P1).
6. Press **F10** backup, <Enter>. Accept 0.62 radius.
7. Keyboard enter 0 and 180 as start and end angles.
8. Select the upper right hole (P2).
9. Press **ALT-A**
10. **ESC** to the Main Menu.

Save LAB4 on Your Data Disk

Rough Out the Sides

1. Choose **CREATE—LINE—ENDPTS—ENDENT**
2. Select the end of the arc, P1.
3. Choose **DELTA—ENDENT,** reselect P1.
4. Keyboard enter 4, 0, 0, <Enter>.
5. Choose **BACKUP—ENDENT.** Select P2.
6. Choose **DELTA—ENDENT,** reselect P2.
7. Keyboard enter 0 -3.5, 0, <Enter>.
8. Choose **BACKUP—ENDENT.** Select P3.
9. Choose **DELTA—ENDENT,** reselect P3.
10. Keyboard enter 0, -2.5, 0, <Enter>.
11. Choose **BACKUP—ENDENT.** Select P4.
12. Choose **DELTA—ENDENT,** reselect P4.
13. Keyboard enter 2.5, 0, 0, <Enter>.
14. **ESC** to the Main Menu.

Note: Select line on portion that is to remain after fillet trim.

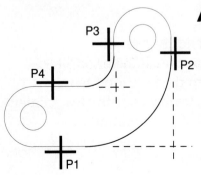

Add Fillets

1. Choose **CREATE—FILLET—ARC—TRIM**
2. Keyboard enter .62 as the fillet radius, <Enter>.
3. Select the first fillet entity (P3).
4. Select the second fillet entity (P4).
5. Keyboard enter 1.86 as the fillet radius, <Enter>.
6. Select the first fillet entity (P1).
7. Select the second fillet entity (P2).
8. **ESC** to the Main Menu.

Save LAB4 on Your Data Disk

Line at Angle

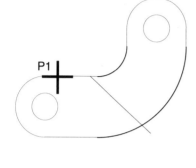

1. Choose **CREATE–LINE–ENDPNTS–ALONGL**
2. Cursor select the reference end of the line, P1.
3. Keyboard enter 1.13, the distance along the line, <Enter>.
4. Choose **POLAR–ALONGL**.
5. Reselect the reference end of the line, P1.
6. Keyboard enter 1.13, <Enter>.
7. Keyboard enter -42 as the inclination, <Enter>.
8. Keyboard enter 2.5 as an untrimmed length, <Enter>.
9. **ESC** to the Main Menu.

Trim Line to Intersection

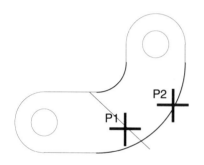

1. Choose **EDIT–TRM/EXT–FIRST.**
2. Select the line to trim (P1).
3. Select the trimming entity (P2).
4. **ESC** to the Main Menu.

Hole at Polar Coordinates

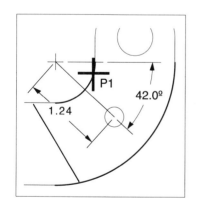

1. Choose **CREATE–CIRCLE–CTR+DIA**
2. Keyboard enter .30 as the diameter, <Enter>.
3. Choose **POLAR** as the position option for the hole.
4. Choose **CENTER** to mask the polar origin.
5. Select the upper fillet, P1.
6. Keyboard enter -42 as the polar angle, <Enter>.
7. Keyboard enter 1.24 as the polar radius, <Enter>.
8. **ESC** to the Main Menu.

Save Lab4 on Your Data Disk

End Lab 4

▼   ADDITIONAL EXERCISES FOR PRACTICE

The following problems are intended to provide practice in geometric constructions. Most of the problems are fully dimensioned—all of the size and location information is there. Some problems only specify the size of holes and the shape of the geometry. It is up to you to design the part around the holes by using dimensions of your choosing. Make use of parallelism, symmetry, and similar sizes. Refer to Chapter 20 for a complete description of the options found in the Create Menu.

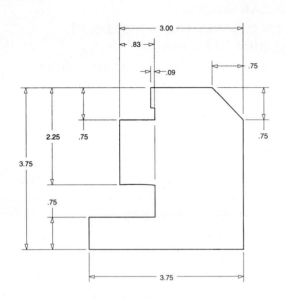

Problem 4A

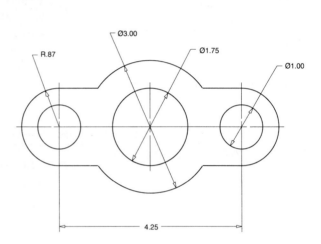

Problem 4B

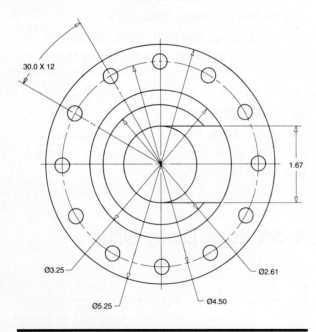

Problem 4C

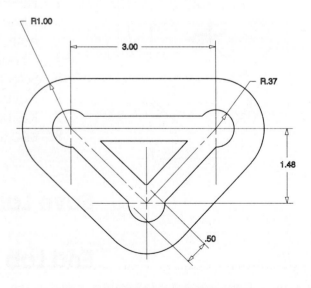

Problem 4 D

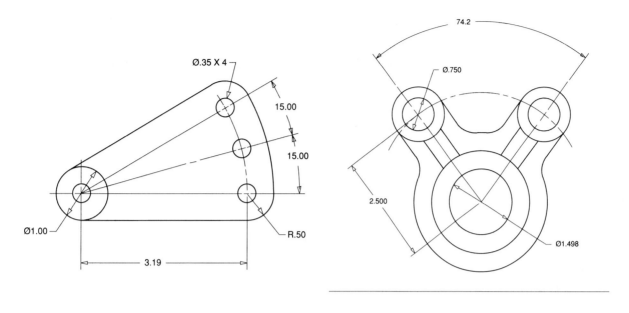

Problem 4E

Problem 4F

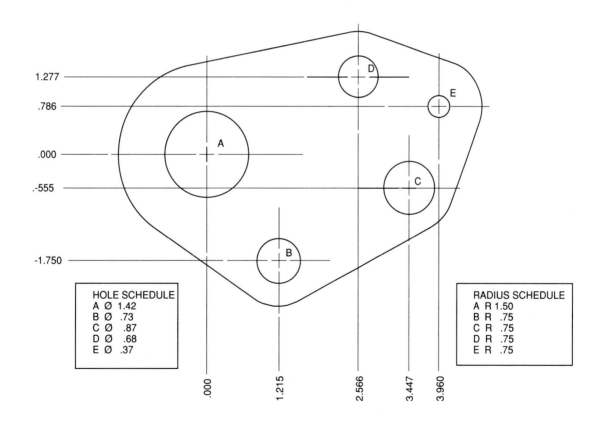

HOLE SCHEDULE
A Ø 1.42
B Ø .73
C Ø .87
D Ø .68
E Ø .37

RADIUS SCHEDULE
A R 1.50
B R .75
C R .75
D R .75
E R .75

Problem 4G

Attributes of Geometric Entities

▼ INTRODUCTION

Under the instructions of the **CONFIG.DAT** file at start-up, CADKEY Light sets the defaults of a number of attributes associated with entities. To begin a work session with other than these default settings, create custom templates (part files that are blank) with the settings you desire. For example, if you make terrain models, you may want a certain line color, type, and width to be the default. If you are designing microelectronics you may want different default attributes.

Attributes deal with how geometric entities, and some detail drafting entities, appear. Attributes *do not* in any way alter or influence the geometric description of the entity. In fact, many *postprocessing* activities disregard these attributes altogether and act only on the numerical portion of the data base.

Attributes are used for two reasons. First, certain attributes are accepted as *conventional* in the preparation of engineering drawings, Dashed lines, center lines, object lines of various weights—all have special meaning on documents and must be chosen wisely to communicate the desired information. The second use of attributes is by CADD designers to better communicate the design to themselves. For example, in the course of a design, lines of movement may be shown in red, axis lines in blue, temporary construction in green, and final geometry in white. These attribute assignments may not have meaning to anyone but the designer.

Attributes can be set in two ways. Attributes can be **CHANGED** so that all entities identified are changed while the new attribute is selected. When you return to the Main Menu, attribute settings are returned to their condition before the change. The **CURRENT** attribute setting can also be changed. This results in a permanent change in the default settings for this work session—until CADKEY Light is quit and restarted. All entities created after this point assume the **CURRENT** settings. As a review, entities that exist in the data base can have their attributes altered through **CHANGE**. New entities take their attributes from **CURRENT** settings.

Attributes can be checked using the **CONTROL–VERIFY** command. Attribute assignments will be displayed as numbers in the prompt line using a form of shorthand notation. See page 364 for a listing of these attributes.

▼ COLOR

The attribute of color is helpful when visualizing the components of a design. When you installed and configured CADKEY Light, you identified the color capabilities of your computer and its monitor. CADKEY Light uses this information to display the color palette of available choices.

Monochrome monitors, if they are of digital design, display only two colors (i.e., black and white, black and green, black and amber, etc.). Analog monitors may display levels of gray. Monochrome monitors are sensitive to color choices. Because contrast in a monochrome monitor is dependent on *value* differences, it is important that high value (bright) colors be chosen. Medium values may not be discernible at all on monochrome monitors. When using a monochrome monitor, these values should be set in the **CONFIG** program.

A logical and consistent methodology should be adopted for entity color. Unless you are told otherwise, consider the color assignments in the following table for part geometry. These components on a part are identified in Fig. 9-1.

Completed Geometry	Off White
Construction Geometry	Red
Temporary Geometry	Green
Axes of Symmetry	Blue
Locus of Action	Yellow

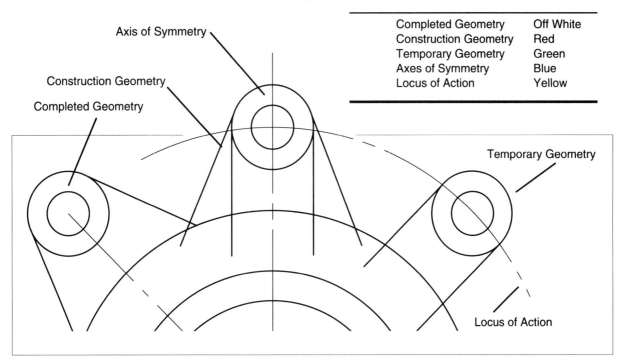

Fig. 9-1. Components that are candidates for color attribute assignment.

To efficiently use color, plan ahead. It is not efficient to change colors individually on single entities. Use the checklist in Fig. 9-2 to plan your color attribute assignments.

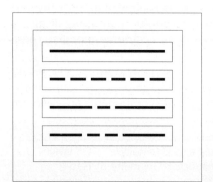

Immediate Commands	
ALT—X	color
ALT—T	line type
ALT—Y	line width
ALT—Z	pen number

Fig. 9-2. Attribute efficiency checklist.

✔ Use the *immediate mode* command to rapidly set current attribute.

✔ Set current attribute *before* beginning a series of similar operations.

✔ Group associated geometry and change attributes by group.

✔ Create patterns that can be grouped and assigned attributes.

✔ Assign geometry to layers that can be selectively displayed and changed.

✔ Change only that which enhances communication.

▼ LINE TYPE

CADKEY Light provides four line type choices (Fig. 9-3): solid, dashed, center, and phantom. These line types, when used to represent different geometric features, allow you to distinguish both functional and visual aspects of the model. Lines, when they are used in modeling or drafting, represent intersection boundaries, surface elements, or non-model entities such as axes or center lines. Line type does not in any way influence the validity of a model. That is, a model created in dashed lines is just as valid as a model created in solid lines.

Each of the four line types can be displayed in the range of colors that are available. Use the checklist in Fig. 9-2 to efficiently modify line type attributes. In Fig. 9-4, *before* and *after* are shown where a number of lines have been changed from solid (the default) to dashed with the **ALT-T** immediate mode command for line type.

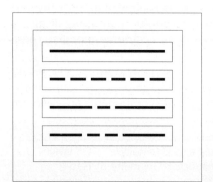

Fig. 9-3. Line types available in CADKEY Light.

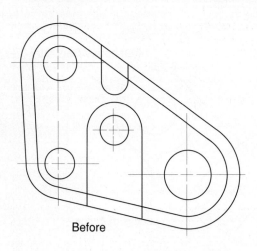

Before

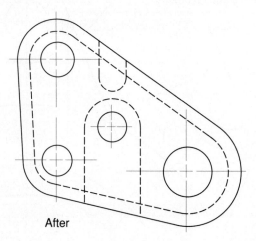

After

Fig. 9-4. Lines identified one after the other are changed to dashed.

Fig. 9-5. Line widths available in CADKEY Light.

▼ LINE WIDTH

CADKEY Light assumes that a single-stroke line (one screen pixel wide) is a line .3 millimeters in width. Wider lines can be selected in 3, 5, 7, 9, 11, 13, or 15 screen pixels in width corresponding to .9, 1.5, 2.1, 2.7, 3.3, 3.6, or 4.5 millimeters when plotted (Fig. 9-5). Wider lines are created on a plotter by over plotting. If it is important that a line be an exact specific width—as can be the case when preparing artwork for electronic circuits— use filled shapes rather than wide lines.

A word of caution, however. Line width, like line type, has nothing to do with the geometric validity of a model. Wide lines, thin lines, dashed lines, phantom lines, center lines—all are used to better communicate the design to *you*. Your choice of line type can, however, dramatically affect the time it takes to display the model during zooms, pans, and redraws. (Remember that **ESC** will halt the redisplay of the model after any operation that requires a redraw.) The wider the line, the longer the display time.

▼ PEN NUMBER

The attribute of pen number is applicable only when planning for plotter output. Pen number, like any attribute, has no affect on the geometric data base. But unlike color, line type, and line weight, pen number has nothing to do with how the model is displayed on your monitor.

The most efficient technique in using pen number is to divorce the process of assigning pen numbers for plotting from the modeling process itself. Because you may not know ahead of time which pen will be in what position in your plotter, it may be more efficient to set up the plotter and assign pen numbers *en masse*. The checklist in Fig. 9-2 can be used to plan a strategy for assigning pen numbers.

▼ OUTLINE AND FILL

Polygons and polylines can be drawn in the default outline mode, or filled with a color from the fill palette. Once filled, the outline becomes the fill color. This attribute is appropriate for several purposes.

Charts and Graphs

Presentation slides can be made more effective when contrasting color fills are used.

Rendering a Model

When placed in pictorial position, a 3D model can be "rendered" by selectively filling bound surfaces to give the illusion of a solid model. However, this is not a true surface model and questions of visibility are not resolved by the CADKEY Light program. The filled areas will be displayed in the order in which they reside in the data base.

A filled area may be helpful in visualizing a model. However, filled areas require extended redisplay times and may not be advisable *during the course of design*, when slow redraws may hinder creativity and productivity. Filling surfaces has no affect on the validity of the model itself.

▼ SUMMARY

Entity attributes attach nongeometric information to a model. These attributes aid in the visualization of a design and its conventional representation through engineering drawings and can be assigned to both geometric and detail drafting entities.

Color attributes can be used to facilitate visualization and construction. Line type can represent geometric conventions on engineering drawings or features of the model itself. Line weight adds another variable to the list of entity attributes. These three attributes— color, type, and width—can be assigned independently of one another. That is, you can have a red center line that is five pixels (1.5 mm) wide. Bound planar forms can be displayed either outline of filled. Pen numbers assign the task of plotting a line to a pen in a certain position in a pen plotter.

When attributes are *changed*, only selected entities are modified. When a *current* attribute setting is changed, all subsequent entities assume this new attribute.

It is important to plan and implement efficient methods for assigning attributes to entities. By grouping, layering, using immediate commands, and making similar constructions together, reduced instructions can be given to CADKEY Light to accomplish these changes.

▼ QUESTIONS

1. Describe the difference between a changed attribute and the current attribute.

2. Describe the relationship between entity attribute and entity geometry in the part data base.

3. What determines the range of colors available on your computer with CADKEY Light?

4. What operational techniques are available to ensure efficiency in attribute assignments?

5. Describe methods available to speed up redraws once wide lines or filled areas have been designated.

6. Discuss the difference between modeling and nonmodeling line types. Why are nonmodeling line types used in a model? In engineering drawings?

7. Describe the relationship between pen number and line width, line color, and line type.

CADKEY Light
Attributes

Lab

5

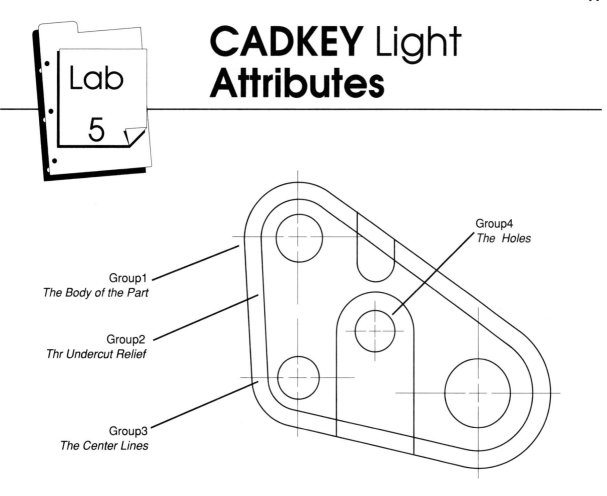

Group4
The Holes

Group1
The Body of the Part

Group2
Thr Undercut Relief

Group3
The Center Lines

Load LAB5 From Your Exercise Disk

Change Color

1. Choose **CONTROL—ATTRIB—COLOR—CHANGE**
2. Select the light blue color with a cursor click.
3. Choose **GROUP—BY NAME.**
4. Keyboard enter **Group3**, the group name of the centerlines, <Enter>.
5. Select the red color.
6. Choose **GROUP—BY NAME.**
7. Keyboard enter **Group1,** the body of the part, <Enter>.
8. Select the white color.
9. Choose **ALL DSP—ALL.** The entire part is displayed in white.
10. **ESC** to the Main Menu.

Change Line Type

1. Choose **CONTROL–ATTRIB–L-TYPE–CHANGE**
2. Select the dashed line type.
3. Choose **GROUP–BY NAME.**
4. Keyboard enter **Group2**, the group name of the undercut, <Enter>.
5. Select dashed line type.
6. Choose **SINGLE** and select P1-P6, the non-grouped hidden features. Press <Enter> when done.

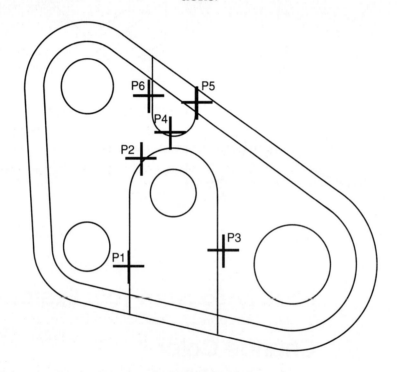

Save LAB5 on Your Data Disk

Eject the exercise disk and insert your personal data disk.

Change Line Width

1. Choose **CONTROL–ATTRIB–L-WIDTH–CHANGE**
2. Select the next to thinnest line (.9 mm).
3. Choose **GROUP–BY NAME.**
4. Keyboard enter **Group4**, the group name of the holes, <Enter>.
5. Esc to the Main Menu.

Set Current Line Color, Type, Width

1. Press **ALT-X** and select the green color.
2. Press **ALT—T** and select the solid line.
3. Press **ALT—Y** and select the thinnest line.
4. Choose **CREATE—LINE—RECTANG—CORNERS** and draw a rectangle around the figure.
5. **ESC** to the Main Menu.

Assign Pen Number

Note that assigning pen numbers to entities is useful only when plotting the drawing with a plotter that has multiple pens. The procedure here is to demonstrate the method of assigning these numbers. There will be no visible change in the drawing.

1. Choose **CONTROL—ATTRIB—PEN #—CHANGE**
2. Keyboard enter the number **2** as the pen number.
3. Choose **GROUP—BY NAME**.
4. Keyboard enter **GROUP2**, the hidden relief.
5. **ESC** to the Main Menu.

Change From Outline to Fill

1. Choose **CONTROL—ATTRIB—OUT/FIL.**
2. Choose **FILLED.**
3. Choose **GROUP—BY NAME**.
4. Cursor select the desired fill pattern.
5. Keyboard enter **GROUP4**, the holes <Enter>.

CADKEY Light alerts you that no entity has been found, The **FILL** option works only with polygons and polylines. There are none in your data base. Press <Enter>.

6. **ESC** to the Main Menu.

Exit CADKEY Light and Save LAB5

End Lab 5

▼   **ADDITIONAL EXERCISE FOR PRACTICE**

Load Lab5 From Your Data Disk

1. Delete the rectangle.
2. Turn all entities to yellow.
3. Return all line widths to single line.
4. Set **CURRENT** color to white.
5. Complete the constructions on the part you used in Lab 5 so that it matches the part below.

Hints: Use **DELTA** location for .667 holes. Use full circles and **CENTER** location for rounded ends —trim after tangents and parallels have been drawn.

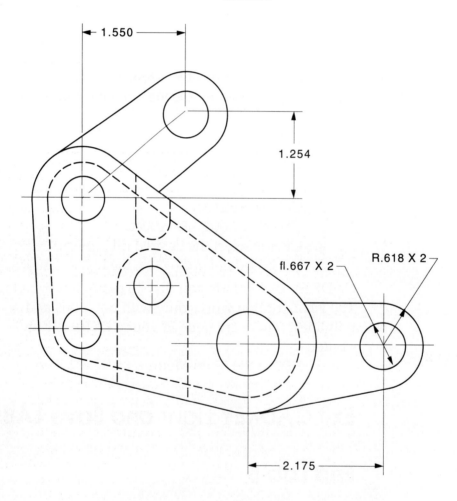

Problem 5A

Levels and Construction Depth

▼ IN THIS CHAPTER

Using Construction Depth
Using Levels
Lab 6

Tutor Topics

Complete the **X-FORM** exercise in CADKEY TUTOR. Pay particular attention to world and view construction axes.

▼ INTRODUCTION

These two features of CADKEY Light are fundamental to the effective use of CADD. Because they accomplish many of the same ends—although they are absolutely unrelated and independent—they are explained together, the better to show their similarities and differences.

Levels represent the *logical* association geometric and drafting entities. Levels exist only in the association of entities within the data base and *do not* represent actual physical or spatial levels. Levels provide a way for you to associate parts of the design logically, no matter where they exist in space.

Construction depth, on the other hand, *does* represent spatial position relative to the view depth axis (ZV), zero construction depth. Each viewport has an absolute Depth=0 position where ZV=0. For practical purposes, this construction depth is usually associated with a particular world axis direction. When working at a given construction depth, it is considered that you are working on a *construction plane* set at that construction depth. To visualize the relationship of view and world coordinate directions, it is helpful to display world axis markers in the viewports so that construction depth, in and out of the screen, can be associated with its corresponding position along a world axis. When an auxiliary viewing position is taken, construction depth remains normal (perpendicular) to the auxiliary viewport, although it is no longer aligned with a world axis.

Geometry at the same construction depth may be assigned to different levels (Fig. 10-1). In the example, the holes and the raised face of the boss exist at the same construction depth. However, the holes are assigned to a different level. This allows the holes to be selectively displayed, deleted, moved, etc.—all independently of the boss geometry.

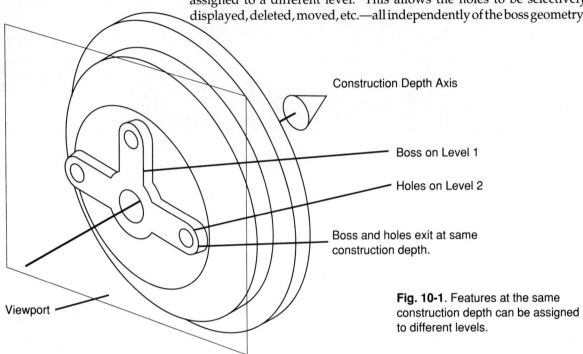

Construction Depth Axis

Boss on Level 1

Holes on Level 2

Boss and holes exit at same construction depth.

Viewport

Fig. 10-1. Features at the same construction depth can be assigned to different levels.

▼   USING CONSTRUCTION DEPTH

To use construction depth requires that the 2D/3D construction switch in the Status Menu be set to 3D. Thus set, three-dimensional input is possible in a viewport in which only two dimensions are apparent.

Construction depth is *not* view dependent. That is, setting depth equal to, say, -5.00 will set construction depth along the view Z axis to this value in *every* viewport. Three options are available to set current construction depth. You should work back and forth between the three, depending on the information available about the design.

A Quick Check of Depth

To determine current depth, observe the line in the Status Menu that displays depth. This is the current view depth of entities created in any and all viewports. To quickly check the depth of any geometric feature, follow these steps:

```
VIEW=1
ALEV=1
MLEV=0
COLOR=1
CONST: 3D
D=0.00000
S=0.999690
GRID: OFF
-- more --
```

1. Choose **CONTROL–VERIFY–COORD** or use the F-key shortcut **F7–F1–F2**.

2. Select the entity in the viewport in which you want to check depth.

3. Press <Enter> until XV, YV, ZV coordinates of the entity are displayed on the prompt line. The ZV value is the construction depth in the viewport used for selection.

4. **ESC** to the Main Menu.

The depth reported in the prompt line is viewport dependent. That is, to check depth in any viewport other than one where ZV depth corresponds to the desired dimensional direction results in depth that has little meaning.

Set Construction Depth-Value Option

Use an absolute value if you have planned ahead and positioned the part in view space such that the Depth=0 construction reference plane has meaning. In Fig. 10-2, an object has been positioned so that its reference datum coincides with Depth=0. The cylinder intersections can then be created by changing depth relative to the datum plane.

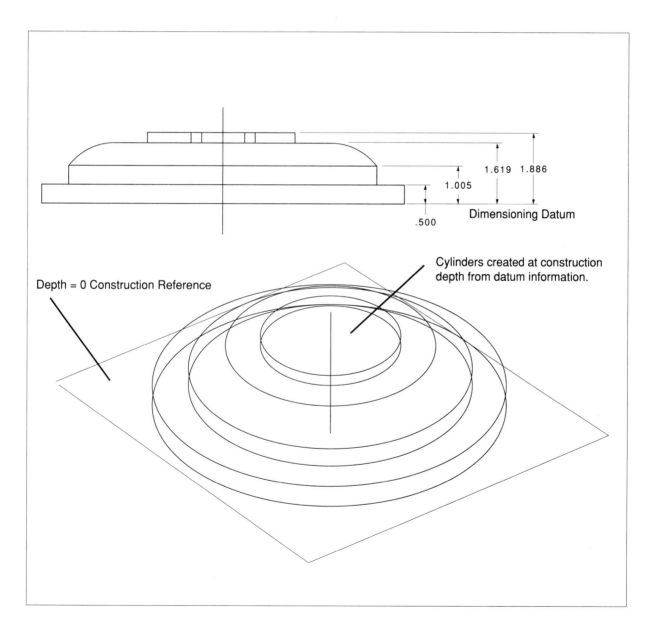

Fig. 10-2. Object placed so that datum dimensions correspond to construction depth.

Set Construction Depth-Position Option

The view depth of a position in space can be used to set the current construction depth. For example, the same part shown in Fig. 10-2 can be used to set construction depth at the vertical center using the **CENTER** position option in a view where the cylinder ends appear as edges (Fig. 10-3). Because View 1 and View 2 are perpendicular, one would rightly expect the construction planes of the two views to be perpendicular also.

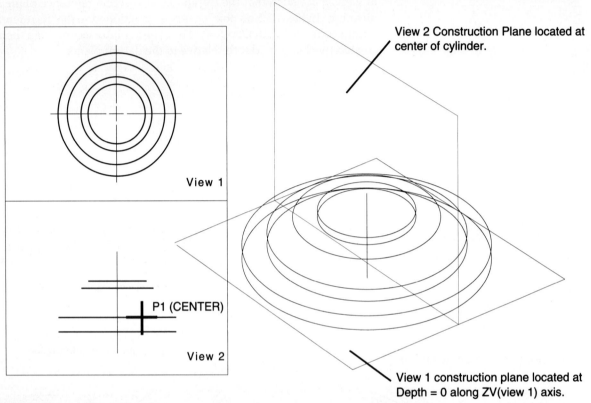

View 2 Construction Plane located at center of cylinder.

View 1 construction plane located at Depth = 0 along ZV(view 1) axis.

Fig. 10-3. Use position options to place construction depth at entity feature.

Set Construction Depth-Offset Option

This option is appropriate when the position of one feature is known relative to another feature but its absolute position relative to Depth=0 is not available (Fig. 10-4).

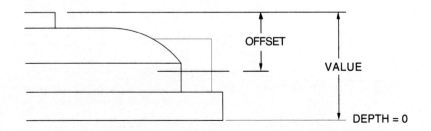

Fig. 10-4. Set current construction depth as an offset value from a known location.

Move Geometry to a New Construction Depth

Since construction depth is relative to each viewport's ZV axis, moving geometry relative to ZV should be done carefully. For example, consider the object in Fig. 10-5(a). Assume that the object must be made taller. The axis appears as a point in the top view. Change in ZV depth in the top view will result in the top of the object being moved parallel to ZV which is parallel to the cylinder's axis. But assume that the move is accomplished in the front view, parallel to ZV, in that view as shown in Fig. 10-5(b). The result is that the end of the cylinder is moved along the front ZV axis and an oblique cylinder top has been formed—not the desired result.

The watchword is to move geometry to new construction depth *only* in a view where ZV depth coincides with the axis of translation.

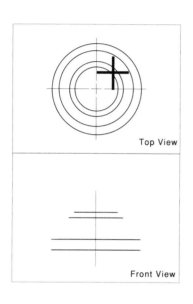

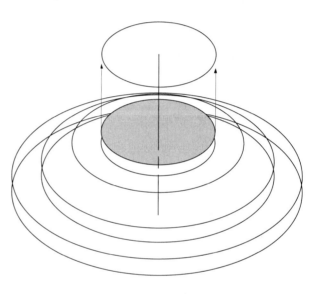

Fig. 10-5(a). Top of cylinder is moved upward along top view ZV axis.

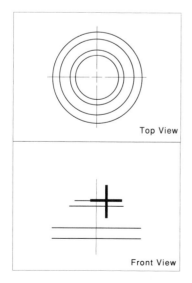

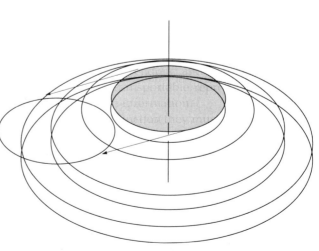

Fig. 10-5(b). Top of cylinder moved forward along front view ZV axis.

▼   USING LEVELS

The efficient use of levels is an indicator of the skill of a CADD designer. This is not a technique that comes easily to many and is not a requirement of operating CADKEY Light or of making models. Levels become, however, more important as the complexity of the model increases. When a model becomes complex, it becomes difficult to identify components, use location masks, and generally see what you are doing. Displaying all of a model may become time-consuming during pans, zooms, and redraws. Limiting the display to geometry of current interest speeds up the entire design process.

Levels become paramount when models are turned into engineering drawings. The different components of an assembly—parts, dimensions, notes, title block, and details—should have separate level assignment so that they can be combined or selectively displayed. It is entirely possible, and desirable, to produce the entire set of engineering drawings for a project—as many as 20 separate sheets—from a single part file by the effective use of layers.

CADKEY Light provides the opportunity to use 256 separate levels to logically separate components of your models. Practically, 10-20 levels are sufficient to accomplish most CADD tasks.

At start up, your system makes level 1 active. If a level is made active it is automatically displayed. Only one level can be active (able to receive constructions or detail entities) at a time. Additional levels can be displayed in any combination. Although a level is automatically displayed when it is made the active current level, it *can* be explicitly turned off. This means that it is possible to work on an active level and not see the results of your constructions.

Use the function key shortcut **F6—F6** to quickly enter the Level Menu.

Check Current Level Status

A glance to the Status Menu reveals the current active level. This setting tells you on which level constructions or details will be assigned. What is *not* immediately known are the levels, though not active, that are currently displayed. To check currently displayed levels choose **DISPLAY—LEVELS—LIST**. To check the level assignment of a particular entity follow these steps:

```
VIEW=1
ALEV=1
MLEV=0
COLOR=1
CONST: 3D
D=0.00000
S=0.999690
GRID: OFF
-- more --
```

1. Choose **CONTROL—VERIFY—COORD** or use the F-key shortcut **F7—F1—F2**.

2. Select the entity in any viewport.

3. Press <Enter> until the level is displayed on the prompt line.

4. **ESC** to the Main Menu.

Activate New Level

Press **CTL—L** to quickly keyboard enter the new active level. This level is added automatically to the display list. The display status (display on or off) of the previously active level is not changed by its deactivation. All entities created after this point are assigned to the new level and will be visible.

Move Geometry to a New Level

When an entity is moved to a new level it remains visible *only* if that level is currently displayed. If the level had not been previously added, you must add the level in order to see the moved entities. For example, consider that all entities on the object in Fig. 10-6 have been created on the default level, level 1. If the holes are moved to level 2 they will disappear (Fig. 10-7) until level 2 is added to the display list. Choose **DISPLAY—LEVELS—MOVE** to change level assignment. Then, without returning to the Main Menu, choose **F10—LIST** to add the level to the display list.

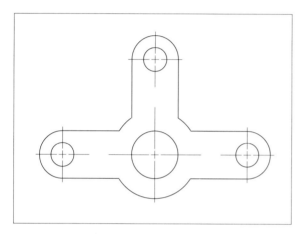

Fig. 10-6. All entities on same level.

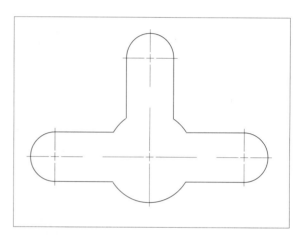

Fig. 10-7. Holes moved to level 2, which is not on the display list.

Selectively Display Levels

Levels are turned on interactively on a numerical list of levels (Fig 10-8). Choose the option from the menu that corresponds to the action you want to accomplish. Levels 1-256 can be turned on or off with a cursor click; a range of levels selected by click dragging from the start to the end. When finished turning levels on or off, press <Enter>. The result of turning levels on or off will be seen immediately when the screen is redrawn. The exception to level display is level 256 on which all entities will be hidden although they can be selected.

```
                    DISPLAYED LEVELS LIST TURN LEVEL(S) ON

             Cursor-indicate the level number to change.  To box select, move
             the cursor to another level number before releasing the button.

      1    2    3    4    5    6    7    8    9   10   11   12   13   14   15   16
     17   18   19   20   21   22   23   24   25   26   27   28   29   30   31   32
     33   34   35   36   37   38   39   40   41   42   43   44
     49   50   51   52   53   54   55   56   57   58   59
     65   66   67   68   69   70   71   72   73   74
     81   82   83   84   85   86   87   88   89
     97   98   99  100  101  102  103  104
```

Fig. 10-8. Level display window with levels turned on shown in reverse video.

▼   SUMMARY

Construction depth and levels both allow entities to be associated with other features for easy construction and editing. The difference lies in that construction depth describes a *spatial* association along an axis perpendicular to a given viewport, while layer describes a *logical* association in the data base.

Construction depth moves the position of the cursor in and out of a view. However, using a position mask overrides the depth setting and places the cursor at the depth of the mask.

Levels provide a powerful method of associating entities so that they can be acted on together. A single level is designated as being active and only levels that have been turned on will display their contents. Any number of levels (up to 256) can be displayed at the same time. Geometry can be created on one level and moved to another.

▼   QUESTIONS

1.   How can you determine where Depth = 0 is located in a view?

2.   What is the relationship of location options (CENTER, ENDENT, etc.) and construction depth?

3.   What is the relationship between the ZV axis and a construction plane in that view?

4.   How can construction depth be set to different values in different viewports?

5.   Describe how you can be sure that entities on the active layer are displayed?

6.   Describe the spatial relationship of construction planes in the top, front, right, and isometric views.

7.   Describe the difference between moving geometry to a new construction depth and to a new level.

8.   Discuss the advantages and disadvantages of these two approaches: creating geometry on the correct level vs. moving geometry to the correct level.

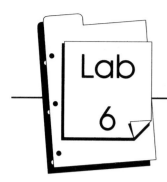

Lab 6

CADKEY Light
Levels and Depth

In this lab you will begin to model the part described orthographically in the views to the left. Note that many of the dimensions required to completely describe the geometry have been omitted to better illustrate those dimensions that are of importance in building the basic model description.

You will make use of construction depth to rough out the part's basic shape and assign certain geometry to layers to better complete the construction. Consider that the part is sitting at Depth = 0 where ZV is coincidental with the world Y axis. This places the model in the same view orientation as that shown in the detail views to the left.

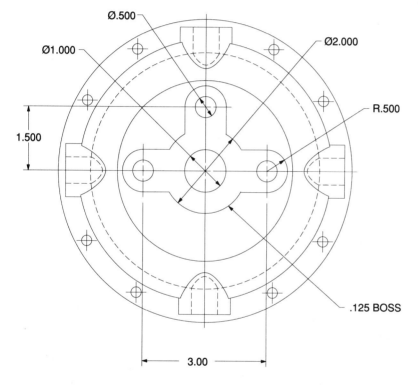

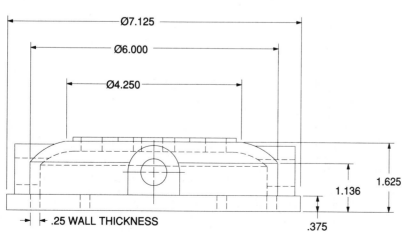

Load BLANK From Your Data Disk

Auto Set Viewports 1,9,10,11

Snap ON

Set Color Attribute

1. Press **ALT–X**. The color menu appears.
2. Cursor pick the color red.
3. Note in the Status Menu that **COLOR=2**.

Set Level

1. Press **CTRL–L**, the immediate command for levels.
2. Keyboard enter **10,** <Enter>.
3. You are now on level 10 with levels 1 and 10 turned on.

Construct the Flange

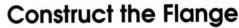

1. From the Status Menu **CONST:3D, COORD:VW, D=0.000000**.
2. Choose **CREATE–CIRCLE–CRT+DIA**
3. Keyboard enter **7.125**.
4. Allow the cursor to snap to a point near the middle of the top viewport. Click once.
5. Press **ALT–A**, the immediate mode command for auto scale, <Enter>.
6. Click once on the depth line in the Status Menu.
7. Choose **VALUE**.
8. Keyboard enter **.375**, <Enter>.
9. Allow the cursor to snap to the center of the first circle in the top viewport. Click once.

Construct the Body

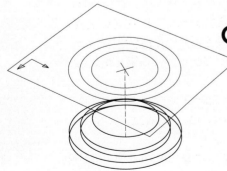

1. Press **F10**, backup.
2. Keyboard enter **6.00**, <Enter>.
3. Cursor snap to the center point. Click once.
4. Change depth value to **1.136**, <Enter>.
5. Cursor snap to the center point. Click once.
6. Press **F10**, backup.
7. Keyboard enter **4.250**, <Enter>.
8. Change depth value to **1.625**.

9. Cursor snap to the center. Click once.
10. **ESC** to the Main Menu.

Save LAB6 on Your Data Disk

Set Level

1. Press **CTRL—L**.
2. Keyboard enter **20**, <Enter>.

Set Attributes

1. Press **ALT—X**.
2. Cursor pick the color green.

Create Reference Point

1. Choose **CREATE—POINT—POSITN**
2. Cursor snap to the circles' center in the top view port. Click once.
3. **ESC** to the Main Menu.

Edit Display List

1. Choose **DISPLAY—LEVEL—LIST—TURN OFF**
2. Click once on Level 10, <Enter>.
3. **ESC** to the Main Menu.
4. You now see the green point at D = 1.625 around which the Boss will be constructed.

Bottom of Boss—Holes

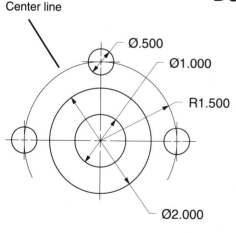

Center line

Ø.500
Ø1.000
R1.500
Ø2.000

1. Choose **CREATE—CIRCLE—CTR+DIA**
2. Accept the default diameter of (1), <Enter>.
3. Choose **POINT** and select the point entity in the top viewport.
4. **F10**, backup. Keyboard enter 2 as the new diameter, <Enter>. Select the point entity.
5. F10, backup. Keyboard enter .5 as the new diameter, <Enter>. Select the point entity.
6. Choose **POLAR—CENTER** and click once on either green circle.
7. Keyboard enter **0,** <Enter>.
8. Choose **CENTER.** Keyboard enter **1.50,** <Enter>.
9. Repeat steps 7 and 8 for circles at 90 and 180 degrees, rechoosing **CENTER** each time.
10. **ESC** to the Main Menu.

Bottom of Boss—Ends

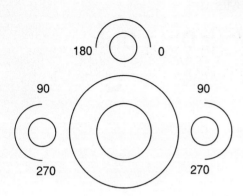

1. **SNAP:OFF**.
2. Choose **CREATE–ARC–CTR+DIA**
3. Accept the default diameter of (1), <Enter>.
4. Use the diagram to the left to enter start and end angle for the right end (CCW = positive).
5. Choose **CENTER** location mask.
6. Click once on the right-most hole.
7. **F10**, backup.
8. Repeat for remaining ends, changing start and end angles.
9. **ESC** to the Main Menu.

Bottom of Boss—Edges

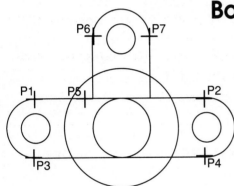

1. Choose **CREATE–LINE–ENDPTS–ENDENT**
2. Create edges across ends, P1-P2; P3-P4.
3. **ESC** to Main Menu.
4. Choose **CREATE–LINE-TAN/PRP–PRP PT**
5. Select line P5.
6. Choose **ENDENT**. Selectend of arc P6.
7. Reselect line P5.
8. Select end of arc P7.
9. **ESC** to the Main Menu.

Save LAB6 on Your Data Disk

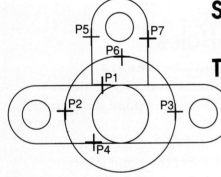

Trim Lines (use **ALT-W** as needed)

1. Choose **EDIT–TRM/EXT–DIVIDE**
2. Select entity to trim P1, trimming entities P2, P3
3. Select entity to trim P4, trimming entities P2, P3
4. **F10**, backup.
5. Choose **FIRST**.
6. Select entity to trim P5, trimming entity P6.
7. Select entity to trim P7, trimming entity P6.

Construct Arc

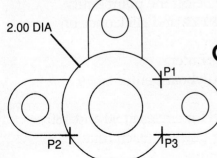

1. Press **ESC**.
2. Delete the 2.00 diameter circle.
3. Choose **CREATE–ARC–THREE-P–ENDENT**
4. Construct arc P1-P2-P3.

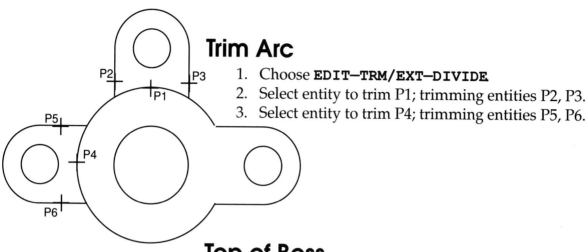

Trim Arc

1. Choose **EDIT—TRM/EXT—DIVIDE**
2. Select entity to trim P1; trimming entities P2, P3.
3. Select entity to trim P4; trimming entities P5, P6.

Top of Boss

1. Choose **X-FORM—TRANS-R—COPY—ALL DISP**
2. Click once in the top viewport (P1). Choose **ALL**.
3. Accept the default number of copies (1), <Enter>.
4. Click once in the top viewport to signal the view port of transformation (P2).
5. Keyboard enter dXV=**0** dYV=**0** dZV=**.125.**

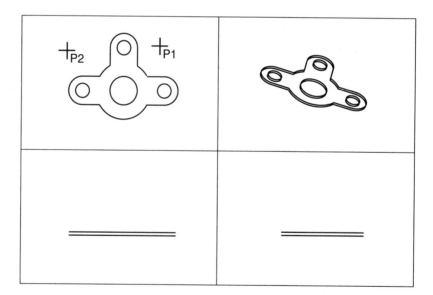

Redisplay Model

1. Choose **DISPLAY—LEVELS—LIST.**
2. Click once on Level 10, <Enter>.
3. **ESC** to the Main Menu.
4. Press **ALT—A,** <Enter>.

End Lab 6

▼ ADDITIONAL EXERCISES

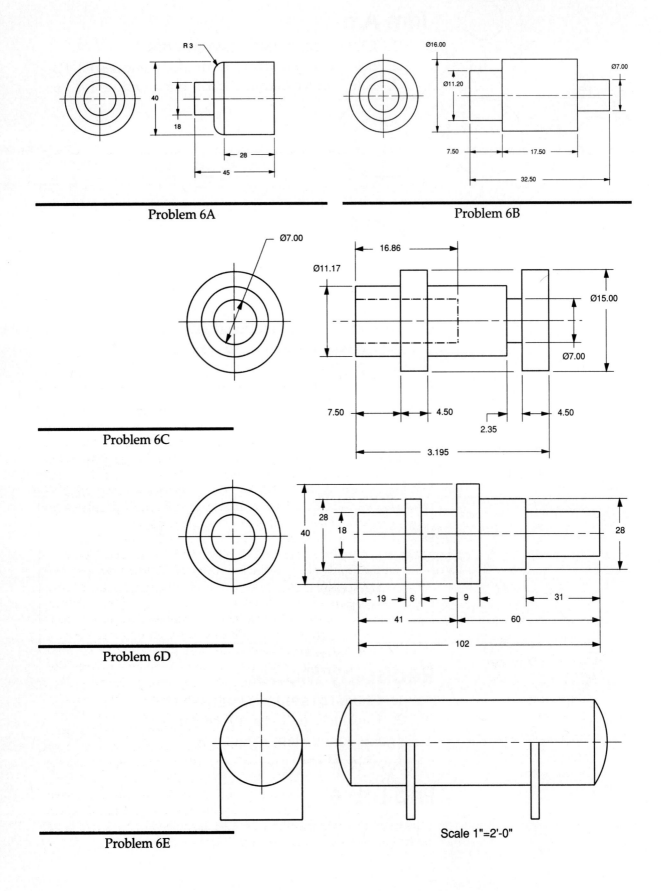

Problem 6A

Problem 6B

Problem 6C

Problem 6D

Problem 6E

Scale 1"=2'-0"

3D CADD—Extrusion

Tutor Topics

Complete the **PLANE** and **3D CONST** exercises in TUTOR. Use the pictorial viewport to observe the space relationships while you work.

▼ INTRODUCTION

In the previous chapter construction depth, as a technique for building 3D models, was presented. You have by now completed Laboratory Exercise 6 and possibly several of the additional exercises at the end of Chapter 10. The ability to quickly and easily manipulate construction depth is an important technique in building 3D geometry. This chapter will further explore 3D CADD space and present several additional methods for building models. In the next chapter you will apply these techniques to another modeling process…sweeping.

CADKEY Light, as you have been told, is a 3D design tool. That doesn't mean that you can't use CADKEY Light to make 2D diagrams—charts, graphs, or drawings—you can. In fact, CADKEY Light provides a way to suppress 3D constructions so that all constructions are done on a two-dimensional plane. In the course of completing a 3D model it may be helpful to disregard depth while certain profiles or sections are built.

The geometry you create in CADKEY Light exists in world space and is seen through viewports in view space. Both of these spaces have their own coordinate systems, which may or may not be aligned. When they *are* aligned, the relationship is easy to determine if the world axis markers are displayed. Understanding the relationship between view space and world space is important because a geometric condition that *appears* to exist in a viewport in view space may not exist in world space. It is generally the world space condition that is of greater importance. For example, Fig. 11-1(a) displays what appears to be a tangent condition between a circle and a line. Because this is observed in view space it may be said that the *projection* of the circle and the line satisfies the tangent condition. However, the geometry in world space is entirely different. The line, although tangent to a cylinder as defined by the circle, is not tangent to the circle itself. See Fig. 11-1(b).

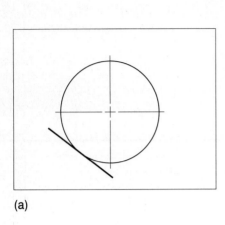

(a)   (b)

Fig. 11-1. The difference between view and world geometric relationships

▼ 2D AND 3D CONSTRUCTIONS

In this chapter you will be introduced to the CADD concept of *extrusion*, called **COPY—JOIN** in CADKEY Light. In order to use this technique in model building, a design must be carefully analyzed in order to identify the profile that will become the basis for the extrusion. Parts that have consistent cross-sections as shown in Fig. 11-2 or similar cross-sections as shown in Fig. 11-3 are prime candidates for extruding a 2D profile into 3D.

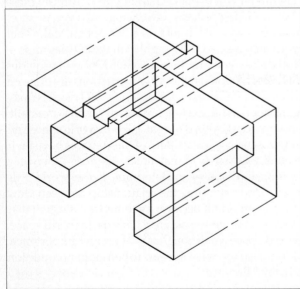

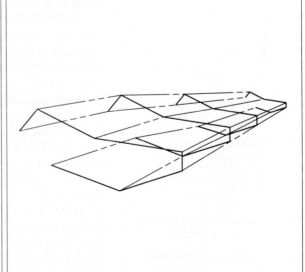

Fig. 11-2. Extrusion with a consistent cross-section.

Fig. 11-3 Extrusion with a similar but diminishing cross-section.

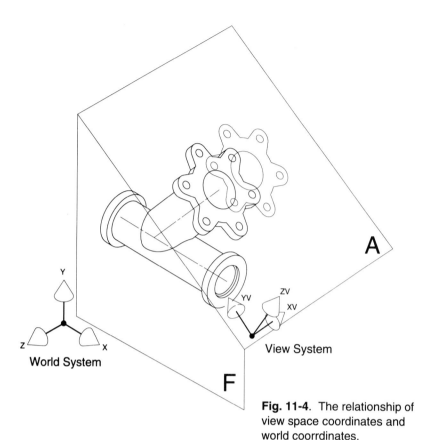

Y

Z ——— x

World System

YV   ZV
      XV

View System

A

F

Fig. 11-4. The relationship of view space coordinates and world coorrdinates.

View Space

Many new CADD designers want to know when it is appropriate to work in view coordinates and when it is better to work in world coordinates. The answer to this question depends on the nature of the part being designed. If view coordinates are not aligned with needed directions of measure (Fig. 11-4), then use the coordinates of that viewport.

The important dimensions of the angled flange are XV(A), YVA, and ZV(A). World Z depth does coincide with XV(A), however the other two flange dimensions do not correspond with world axis directions at all. In this case, view space in in View A is used to construct the flange on the inclined pipe.

World Space

When view space and world space are aligned, that is when X, Y, and Z world and view axes are coincidental, it doesn't matter which construction reference is used. But more often than not, the two axis systems are not aligned and view space is used.

▼ 3D IN VIEW SPACE

To make 3D constructions in view space, assure that the 2D/3D switch in the Status Menu is set to **3D** and that the coordinate switch is set to **VW**. Under these construction constraints, depth (ZV) will always be in and out of the screen. Use the chart in Fig. 11-5 to see the relationship between view depth and world depth.

View	View Depth
Front View	World Z
Top View	World Y
Right	World X
Isometric	Not aligned

Fig. 11-5. Chart of axis relationships.

To illustrate this, assume that a profile had been defined and that an extruded shape is desired. The profile is shown in Fig. 11-6 in the front viewport. Were the extrustion to be specified in the front view, the result would be as that shown in the other viewports. The correct extrusion *could* have been made if the profile had been extruded along YV in the top view or along XV in the side view. Study Fig. 11-6 to better understand the correct possibilities. When a view axis coincides with the axis of extrusion it may be used to direct the extrusion. The desired results *cannot* be attained in the isometric viewport because XV, YV, or ZV in the isometric viewport does not map to the extrusion axis.

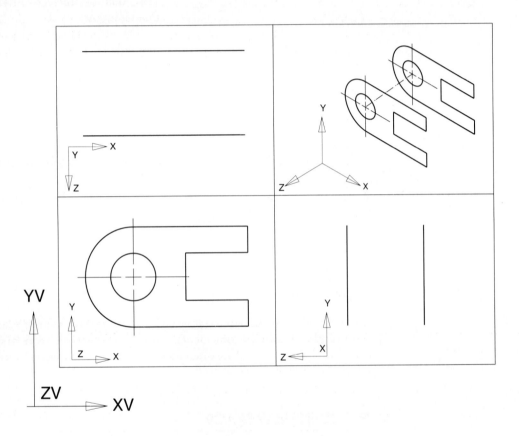

Fig.11-6. Extrusion along YV in the front, YV in the top, or XV in the side views.

▼   3D IN WORLD SPACE

The same extrusion in Fig. 11-6 can be accomplished in world space. Make sure that the coordinates switch in the Status Menu is set to **WLD**. Because the axis of extrusion coincides with the world Z axis, it doesn't matter in which view the geometry is selected for extension. The profile is extruded in world space and correctly displayed in each viewport. World space is view independent. To conclude this discussion, it is paramount in being able to predict the result of a 3D geometric construction that the current orientation of view and world space be fully understood.

▼   WORKING DIRECTLY IN 3D

CADKEY Light allows you to work directly in 3D space. For this reason the isometric view, where all three world axes are shown together, can be used to interactively model in world space. Any other viewport could also be used, but the geometry may coincide spatially, making identification difficult. See Fig. 8-1 on page 81.

For example, consider the two profiles in Fig. 11-7. They have been copied but not joined. Working in the isometric view, the two profiles can be joined with line entities using location masks. When a location mask such as **ENDENT** or **CENTER** is used, the current depth setting in the view is overridden. If the default **CURSOR** location is used, the two profiles will not be connected. Even though the profiles may *appear* connected, as shown in the isometric viewport in Fig. 11-8, the connections lie at construction depth in that view. This can easily be seen in the other three views.

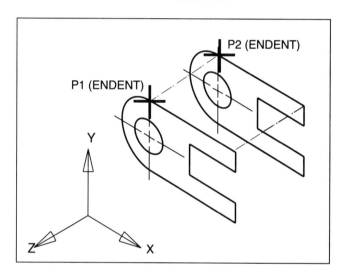

Fig. 11-7. Modeling in 3D using location masks.

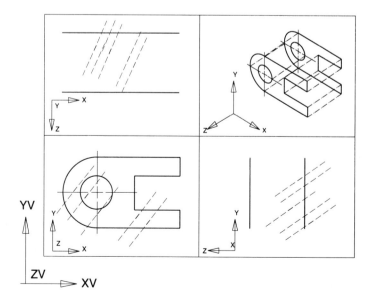

Fig. 11-8. Result of modeling with CURSOR location on current construction plane.

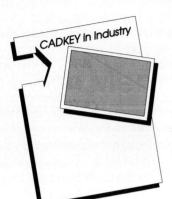

▼ SUMMARY

Extrusion, called **COPY–JOIN** in CADKEY Light, is a fundamental 3D construction technique. Some parts are appropriate for extrusion. These are parts that are consistent or similar (same shape but different size). The shape that is extruded is called the *profile*.

Extrusion is an important CADD construction technique because it parallels the manufacturing process that shares the same name. Many standard architectural and industrial shapes are extruded. These extrusions can be cut, joined, and modified with other shapes to arrive at complex designs. A good CADD designer recognizes classes of design problems that can be solved using extrusions because in almost all cases, an extrusion will be less expensive than were the company to manufacture the shape themselves.

When profiles are copied and joined, CADKEY Light solves redundancy in the data base. This means that when profiles are connected, two vertices are not connected twice. Use the **JOIN** option when you want to accept CADKEY Light's method of extrusion. Use **COPY** and make your own connections when you want connections other than those made by the system.

When the axis of extrusion coincides with one of the world or view axes, this axis can be used to direct the extrusion. Inclined or oblique extrusion axes must be aligned with ZV in a view where the axis appears as a point.

The construction switch found in the Status Menu provides a quick way to toggle between world and view coordinates. CADKEY Light looks to the position of this switch before requesting information in the prompt line. Make sure this switch is set the way you want it *before* beginning the extrusion.

You can construct directly in 3D using any of the options in the Locate Menu other than **CURSOR**. When **CURSOR** is used, all constructions are performed at current construction depth in the working view.

▼ QUESTIONS

1. What is the difference between **COPY** and **JOIN** when extruding a profile?

2. How might you check whether a geometric condition is true?

3. Describe the general class of parts that are appropriate for extrusion.

4. How can you quickly determine whether you are in world or view space?

5. When may a view axis be used as the axis of extrusion? When may a world axis be used?

6. Discuss the ramifications of using the isometric viewport to select geometry for extrusion.

7. Assume that the construction switch is set to **WLD**. What happens when you use the **CURSOR** location mask to connect extrusion profiles?

8. Describe a method for visually checking the results of direct 3D construction.

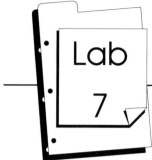

CADKEY Light
Extrusion

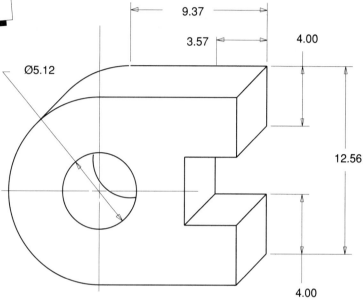

Load BLANK From Your Data Disk

Display Views 1, 9, 10, 11
Work in the front viewport.

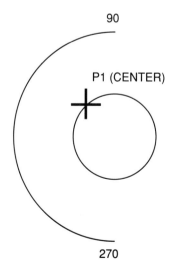

Create Rounded Ends
1. **COORD:WLD; D=0.000000; GRD:OFF; SNAP:OFF;** Color=RED; Level=1.
2. Choose **CREATE—CIRCLE—CTR+DIA**
3. Keyboard enter **5.12**, <Enter>.
4. Choose **KEY-IN** and keyboard enter X=**0**, Y=**0**, Z=**0** as the circle's center.
5. **ESC** to the Main Menu.
6. Choose **CREATE—ARC—CTR+DIA**
7. Keyboard enter **12.56**, <Enter>.
8. Keyboard enter **90** and **270** as start and end angles.
9. Choose **CENTER** and select circle, P1.
10. **ESC** to Main Menu. Press **ALT—A**, <Enter>.

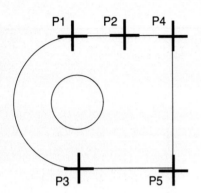

Create Notch End

1. Choose **CREATE—LINE—ENDPTS—ENDENT** and select P1.
2. Choose **DELTA—ENDENT** and reselect P1.
3. Keyboard enter dX=**9.37** dY=**0** dZ=**0**.
4. Press **F10—F10**.
5. Choose **PARALEL—THRU PT**.
6. Click once on the 9.37 line, P2.
7. Choose **ENDENT**, select P3.
8. Press **F10—F10—F10**. Choose **ENDPTS—ENDENT**.
9. Connect corners P4, P5.
10. **ESC** to Main Menu.

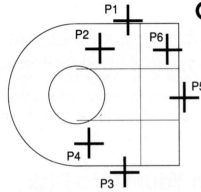

Create Notch

1. Choose **CREATE—LINE—PARALEL—AT DIST**
2. Keyboard enter **4.00**, <Enter>.
3. Select line P1, side P2.
4. Select line P3, side P4.
5. Press **F10**. Keyboard enter **3.57**, <Enter>.
6. Select line P5, side P6.
7. **ESC** to the Main Menu.

Trim Notch

1. Choose **EDIT—TRM/EXT—MODAL**
2. Select trimming entity P1, entities P2 and P3.
3. Press **F10, F10**. Choose **FIRST**.
4. Select entity P4, trimming entity P5.
5. Select entity P4, trimming entity P6.

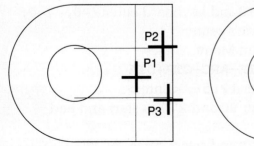
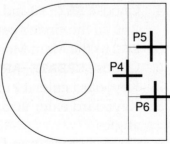
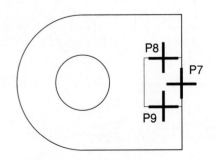

6. Press **F10**. Choose **DIVIDE**.
7. Select entity P7, trimming entities P8 and P9.
8. Press **ALT—A,** <Enter>.

Save LAB7 on Your Data Disk

Extrude Profile

1. **LEVEL=2**
2. Choose **X-FORM—TRANS-R—JOIN—ALL DISP—ALL**.
3. Cursor select the front viewport with one click.
4. Choose **ALL**. Accept default (1) copy, <Enter>.
5. Keyboard dX=**0** dY=**0** dZ=**7.37**.
6. Press **ALT—A,** <Enter>.
7. Choose **DISPLAY—LEVELS—REMOVE** and keyboard enter **2** <Enter>. CADKEY Light re moves the extrusion from the display list.
8. Press **F10** backup. Choose **LEVELS—ADD** and keyboard enter **2** <enter>. You now see both the original profile and the extrusion.

Exit CADKEY Light and Save LAB7

End Lab 7

Experiment

Before attempting one of the additional exercises, reload **LAB7** and delete level 2 (the extrusion). Save this as **EXPER7**. Perform the extrusion again with different depth values, multiple copies, and X and Y offsets for each copy.

▼   **ADDITIONAL EXERCISES**

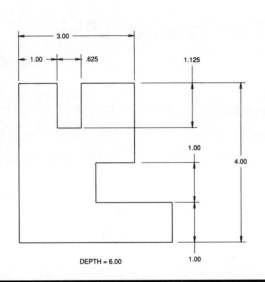

DEPTH = 6.00

Problem 7A

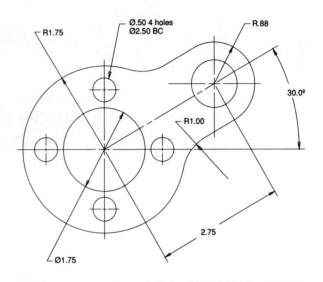

Problem 7B

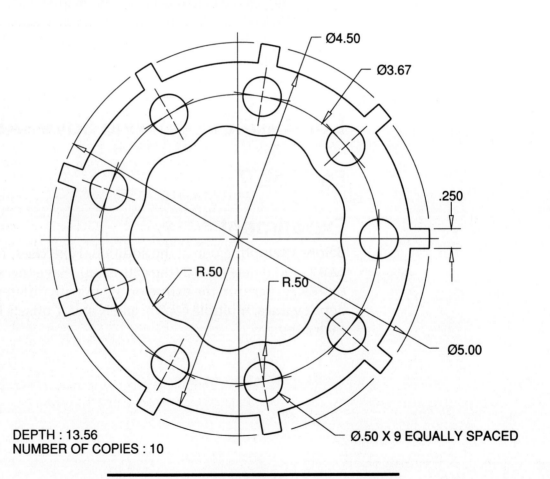

DEPTH : 13.56
NUMBER OF COPIES : 10

Problem 7C

3D CADD—Sweeping

▼ IN THIS CHAPTER

Angles and Copies
Break Down the Geometry
Choose Appropriate Strategy
To Join or Not to Join
Combine Copy and Join
Lab 8

▼ INTRODUCTION

Sweeping, called **2-D ROT** in CADKEY Light, provides a method for generating *surfaces of revolution.* Such surfaces are shapes described by a profile and generated by revolving or sweeping that profile about some axis. You may sweep a profile and connect the subsequent positions or simply deposit a profile without any connections. Two connected profiles are said to have been *joined*. Positive rotation is counterclockwise; negative rotation is counter-clockwise.

Examples of swept surfaces are cylinders and cones, spheres, and tori. But it is the ability to sweep much more complicated shapes that makes this a powerful construction tool. Any shape that you can draw in CADKEY Light can be used to sweep a model.

Certain information is necessary to perform a sweep. A profile must be defined that describes a consistent cross-section of the part being designed. The profile need not be a closed shape. The axis of rotation defines the center of the part around which the profile is rotated. This is usually described as a center line (Fig. 12-1). CADKEY Light rotates selected geometry parallel to the viewport in which the axis is identified as a point. Three-dimensional geometry can be rotated in this manner even though the rotation itself is 2D and about ZV in the designated viewport.

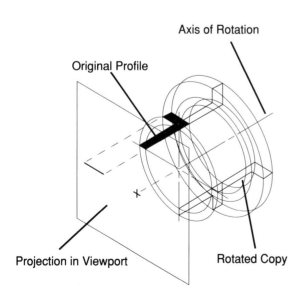

Fig. 12-1. Profile being rotated about an axis parallel to a viewport.

▼ ANGLES AND COPIES

CADKEY Light performs sweeping operations through **X-FORM—2D ROT**. This command requires you to specify the angle and number of copies. It is important to understand these two variables before sweeping your first model. Examples using angle and copies are found throughout this chapter.

Angle Between Copies

CADKEY Light expects you to determine the angle between each rotated and copied profile. To do this, determine the total degrees of the sweep and divide this by the number of copies desired. The result is angle between each copy (Fig. 12-2).

$$\frac{\text{Total Sweep Degrees}}{\text{Number of Copies}} = \text{Angle Between Copies}$$

Total sweep = 180º
Number of copies = 2
Angle = 90

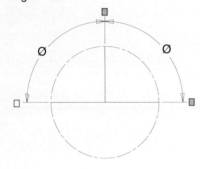

Fig. 12-2. Determine the sweep angle and number of copies to arrive at the angle between copies.

Number of Copies

Hint: You can enter the equation directly on the prompt line for number of copies.

CADKEY Light uses this integer to deposit a copy of the original profile at the angle specified. If **JOIN** is used to create connections between the profiles, connections are made from *the previous profile to the current profile*. This means that to create a completely swept and connected model, a final profile must be deposited on top of the original. CADKEY Light will check all joined connections and remove redundancy. However, the system *will not* remove the extra profile. Your options are to leave the sweep one copy short and manually connect the profiles, or delete the redundant profile. If the sweep is 360° and is done without joining, the total number of copies should be reduced by one (Fig. 12-3).

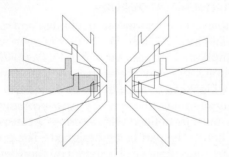

(a) Eleven copies at 30º unjoined to make 12 total profiles.

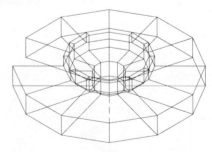

(b) Eleven copies at 30º joined to make 12 total profiles.

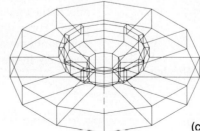

Fig. 12-3(a-c). Full sweep with JOIN deposits additional profile on top of the original.

(c) Twelve copies at 30º joined to make 13 total profiles.

▼ BREAK DOWN THE GEOMETRY

Some parts are appropriate for definition by sweeping. If the part is cylindrical, spherical, toroidal, ellipsoidal, hyperbolic, or parabolic, it probably can be modeled most efficiently by sweeping. Or, if the part is symmetrical about a central axis, it may have *any* cross-sectional shape.

When planning a sweep, it is important to include as much geometry in the sweep as possible. Individual profiles and connections can be edited later to further refine the model. However, don't misinterpret a sectional view and include features such as holes or ribs (Fig. 12-4) that will have to be removed later.

Complete all fillets and rounds on the profile. Use location masks to assure a valid, contiguous profile.

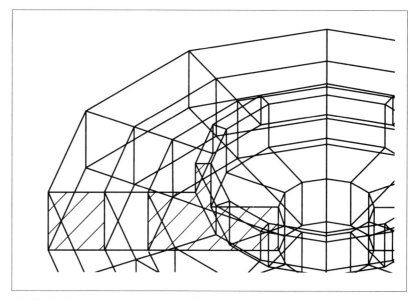

(a) Profile in orthographic.

(b) Holes included in the profile and swept.

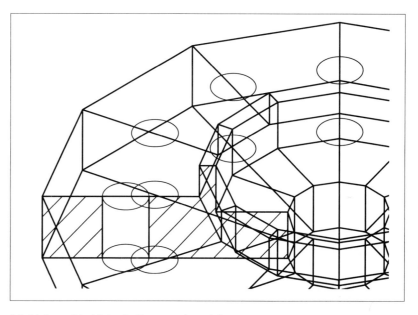

Fig. 12-4(a-c). Profile including holes.

(c) Holes added later to the swept model.

▼ CHOOSE APPROPRIATE STRATEGY

To successfully sweep a model it is helpful to have two adjacent (90º apart) views of the profile and the axis (Fig. 12-5). Note that in the front view the profile appears in edge and the axis of rotation a point view. In the top view, the normal view of the profile and axis or rotation are displayed. It is convenient if the sweep axis is at a grid snap point, although a location mask can be used to identify this position. Use the most appropriate selection option to select the geometry.

You can select the geometry in one view and the axis of rotation in another. *The rotation will be performed parallel to the viewport in which you have identified the axis of rotation.* Note the result of identifying the axis of rotation in the top and front viewports for the same profile (Fig 12-6). In both cases the profile was rotated about ZV. However, in the top view ZV does *not* coincide with the axis of rotation, producing something entirely different from the desired swept model.

Several classes of manufacturing processes are represented by sweeping. **Turning** operations done on a lathe, **casting** of symmetrical objects especially by centrifugal methods, and **spinning** of sheet material can all be modeled by sweeping. The following is a partial list of manufactured parts that can be modeled by sweeping.

Axles	Fasteners
Shafts	Lenses
Bearings	Glassware and ceramics
Bushings	Pipes and connectors
Gears	Pistons
Wheels	Valves
Tires	Pressure vessels
Pulleys	Storage tanks
Cylindrical covers	Tool profiles
Architectural structures	

It is tempting to specify a large number of profiles when sweeping...the greater the number of profiles the more the model *appears* solid. However the determining factor is not how the model appears, but rather how the model is to be used.

If the model is to be *postprocessed*, it is important to know how much information the postprocessor needs to understand the shape of the model. It may be necessary to only define an axis and a profile. If the model is to be used to check clearances, a rotated profile at a critical position may yield the desired information. If engineering drawings will be produced from the model, profiles at the limits of the object (right-left; front-rear) will help develop the final drawings.

Operationally it is advantageous to use a minimum number of profiles in sweeping a model because the greater the number of profiles, the larger the data base and the more difficult it becomes to discern detail.

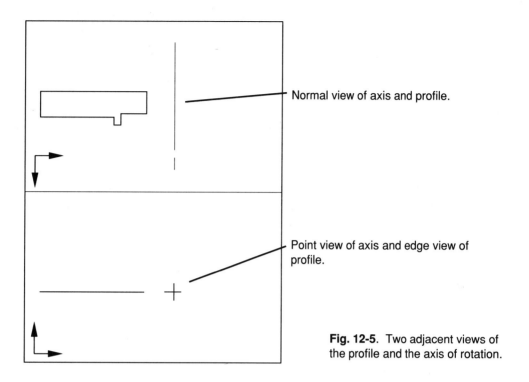

Normal view of axis and profile.

Point view of axis and edge view of profile.

Fig. 12-5. Two adjacent views of the profile and the axis of rotation.

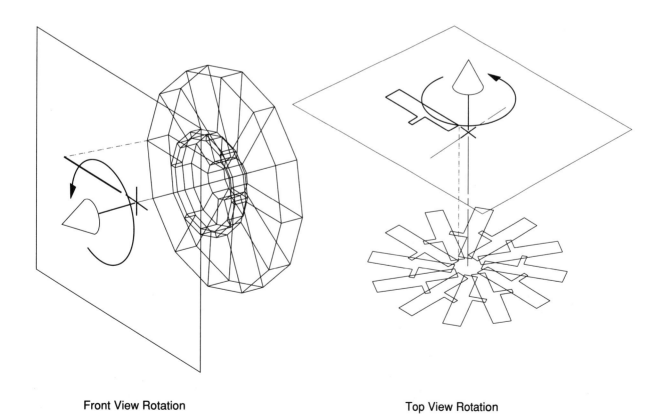

Front View Rotation

Top View Rotation

Fig. 12-6. Result of different axes of rotation.

CADKEY Light allows any number of copies to be made about the axis. It is important to know how CADKEY Light understands *angles* and *copies* to use this command. When you specify an angle, you tell the system how many degrees you want *between* each copy. For example in Fig. 12-7, two sweeps of the same profile have been done.

In the first example, the profile has been swept 90° with two copies. In the second example, the profile has been swept with two copies but with an angle of 360°. Where are the two additional profiles? They are directly on top of the original because *each* copy was rotated 360° before it was copied.

When making full 360° sweeps it is helpful to know the degree of rotation for a given number of profiles. These are shown to the left. The question always comes up "How many copies should I sweep?" Remember that you are creating a *wireframe* description of a part that will be *postprocessed* into a more sophisticated geometric data base. You could possibly get by with only three profiles at 90°. This might be sufficient information for another computer to understand that the shape is really cylindrical. But for *your* visualization, 12 to 24 copies is usually enough to portray the geometry accurately. The down side of increasing the number of copies is the possibility of decreased system performance as the number of elements in the data base increases.

Full Rotations	
4 copies	90 degrees
6 copies	60 degrees
8 copies	45 degrees
10 copies	36 degrees
12 copies	30 degrees
14 copies	25.714 degrees
16 copies	22.5 degrees
18 copies	20 degrees

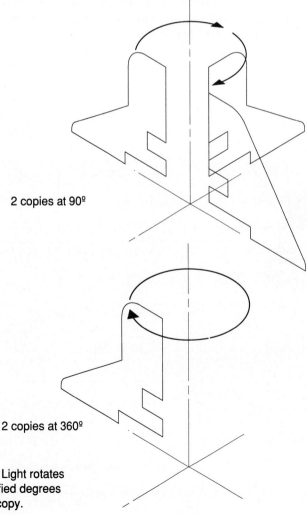

2 copies at 90°

2 copies at 360°

Fig. 12-7. CADKEY Light rotates the profile the specified degrees before depositing a copy.

▼   TO JOIN OR NOT TO JOIN

The decision of whether or not to join the revolved profiles is an important one. If the copies are not joined during rotation, it may be virtually impossible to later make the connections. In general, join the profiles when making a sweep. Don't join them when depositing individual features like tabs or mounting flanges like those shown in Fig. 12-8.

CADKEY Light joins each profile with a line or a polygon. This is shown in a table on page 317. Geometrically complex profiles take longer to join because each connection is checked for redundancy. This means that CADKEY Light assures that after the sweep, the profiles are connected by the minimum number of entities required to make the model.

▼   COMBINE COPY AND JOIN

It may be necessary to combine **2D ROT–COPY**, **2D ROT–JOIN**, and direct 3D construction on the same part. Examine the part shown in wire frame in Fig. 12-9. The semi-cylindrical ends are swept from common profiles. The mounting flanges, since they represent individual instances and not a continuous feature, are not swept. Rather, they are copied without being joined.

To finish the model, use direct construction in 3D. Corners of beginning and ending profiles are connected with lines using location masks.

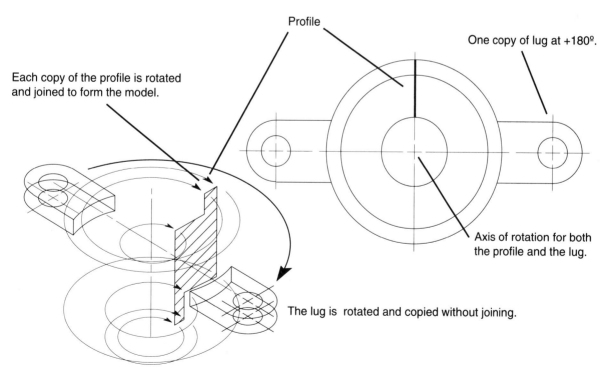

Profile

One copy of lug at +180º.

Each copy of the profile is rotated and joined to form the model.

Axis of rotation for both the profile and the lug.

The lug is rotated and copied without joining.

Fig. 12-8. An example of a part with swept (JOINED) and copied features.

In Fig. 12-9, the near portion of the part is swept +180º and joined. The original lug is copied four times at 45º without joining. To build the rear of the model, follow these steps:

1. Translate and copy the original profile to the left rear.

2. Sweep and join this profile -180º.

3. Translate and copy the lug to the rear.

4. Rotate and copy but do not join the lug four times at -45º.

5. Connect vertices of the profiles to form the left and right sides of the object.

In Lab 8 you will build the front portion of the housing model shown in Fig. 12-9. As an additional exercise, you can complete the entire model as described in the steps above. Additional swept shapes are shown in Fig. 12-10.

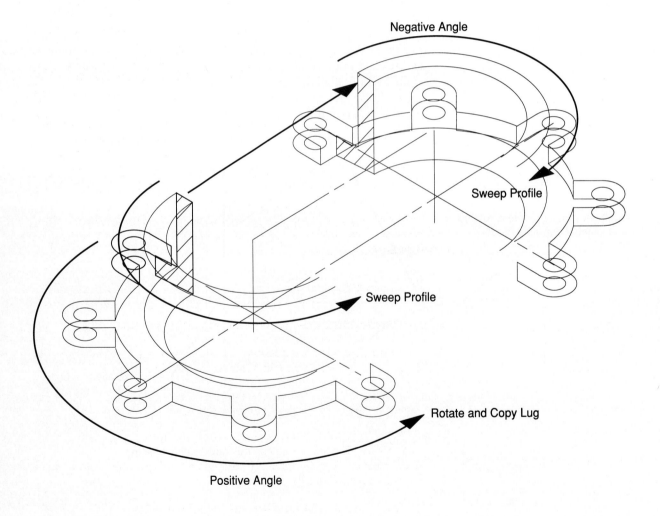

Fig. 12-9. Combining COPY, JOIN, and direct 3D construction.

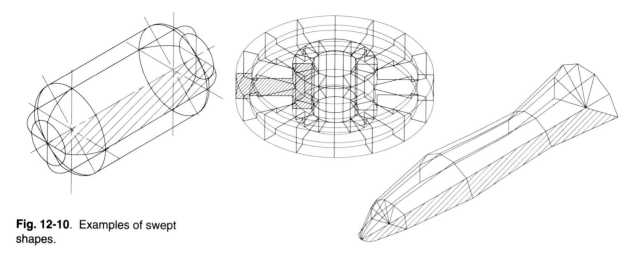

Fig. 12-10. Examples of swept shapes.

▼ SUMMARY

Sweeping is a powerful method to model parts with a consistent cross-section when that cross-section rotates around some axis. The shape that is rotated is called the *profile* and can be any 2D or 3D shape. Sweeping may represent turned, spun, or cast parts.

Swept models can have their profiles joined by lines and polygons to further refine the shape. CADKEY Light optimizes the model by removing redundant connections, assuring the most efficient description of the part.

To sweep a 3D part, the profile can be selected in any view. The axis of rotation, however, must be specified in a viewport where the axis of rotation coincides with ZV.

When specifying the number of copies, keyboard enter the total number of profiles *excluding* the original. The angle specified during the sweep represents the *angle between each of the copies*.

Sweeping is called **X-FORM—2-D ROT—JOIN**. This produces joined profiles. If you don't want the profiles joined, or if you are rotating and copying feet, tabs, lugs, or ribs, use **2-D ROT—COPY**.

▼ QUESTIONS

1. Describe the difference between extruding and sweeping.

2. What geometry is necessary to sweep a model? How must the geometry be displayed in CADKEY Light viewports?

3. Consider that you want to sweep 16 equal divisions. How many copies are specified? Through how many degrees?

4. Why is it important to sweep a minimum number of profiles?

5. Is the number of copies different if you want to join the profiles? Why or why not?

6. Describe the difference between **COPY** and **JOIN**.

7. What is the relationship of sweeping to various manufacturing processes?

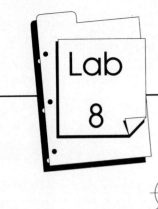

CADKEY Light Sweeping

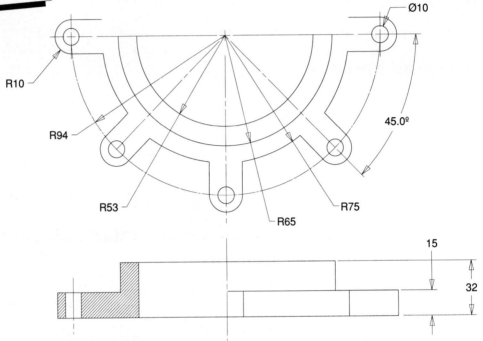

NOTE: DIMENSIONS ARE IN MILLIMETERS

Start CADKEY Light

Set Units

1. Type **CD CADKEY** and press <Enter> at the **C:** prompt.
2. Type **CONFIG**, press <Enter>.
3. Type **5**, <Enter>.
4. Press <Enter> until "Units Modes for CADKEY" is displayed.
5. Type **2** to change units to millimeters, <Enter>.
6. Continue to press <Enter> until you are returned to the Main Menu.
7. Type **8** to accept changes, <Enter>.
8. Type **CD**, <Enter>.

Load BLANK From Your Data Disk

Assign View 1 to a Single Viewport

1. `COORD:WLD; ALEV=2; COLOR=RED`

Create Profile

Use **ALT–H** to zoom half and **ALT–W** as necessary to zoom window during this part of the construction

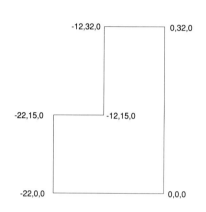

-12,32,0   0,32,0

-22,15,0   -12,15,0

-22,0,0   0,0,0

1. Choose **CREATE–POLYLIN–STRING–KEY-IN** and begin walking around the profile.
2. Starting point   X=**0**   Y=**0**   Z=**0**.
3. Ending point   X=**0**   Y=**32**   Z=**0**.
4. Ending point   X=**-12**   Y=**32**   Z=**0**.
5. Ending point   X=**-12**   Y=**15**   Z=**0**.
6. Ending point   X=**-22**   Y=**15**   Z=**0**.
7. Ending point   X=**-22**   Y=**0**   Z=**0**, <Enter>.
8. Respond **YES** to close current polyline entity.
9. Press **ALT–A**, <enter>. **ESC** to Main Menu.

Save LAB8 on your Data Disk

Create Axis

1. `COLOR=BLUE; ALEV=1; L-TYPE=CENTER`
2. Choose **CREATE–LINE–ENTPTS–KEY-IN**
3. Starting point   X=**53** Y=**0**   Z=**0**.
4. Ening point X=**53** Y=**32** Z=**0**.
5. **ALT–A**, **ESC** to Main Menu.

Display Views 1,9,10,11

Sweep Profile

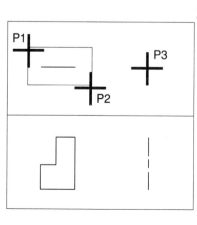

P1

P2

P3

1. `ALEV=2; L-TYPE=SOLID; COLOR=WHITE`
2. Choose **X-FORM–2D ROT–JOIN–WINDOW**.
3. Click once (P1) to define one corner and again (P2) of the selection window.
4. Keyboard enter **12** for the number of copies, <Enter>.
5. Choose **ENDENT** and cursor select the axis in the top view (P3).
6. Keyboard enter **15** for the angle between profiles, <Enter>.
7. **ESC** to Main Menu.
8. **ALT–A**, <Enter>.

Create Lug Profile

Hole

1. Choose **CREATE—CIRCLE—CTR+DIA**
2. Keyboard enter **10**, <Enter>.
3. Choose **KEY-IN** to locate center.
4. Keyboard enter   X=**-41**Y=**0**   Z=**0**.
5. **ALT—A**, and click once in the top viewport.

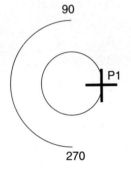

Rounded End

1. Choose **CREATE—ARC—CTR+DIA**
2. Keyboard enter **20**, <Enter>.
3. Start angle =**90**, <Enter>.
4. End angle=**270**, <Enter>.
5. Choose **CENTER** and select P1.

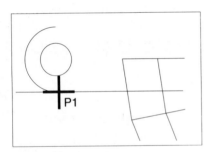

Sides

1. Press **ALT—W** and window zoom up on the lug in the top view.
2. Choose **CREATE—LINE—HRZ/VERT—HORIZTL—ENDENT** and select P1.
3. **ESC** to Main Menu.

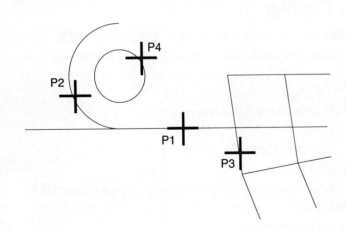

4. Choose **EDIT—TRM/EXT—FIRST.**
5. Select line P1, arc P2.
6. Reselect line P1, line P3.
7. **ESC** to Main Menu.
8. Choose **X-FORM—MIRROR—COPY—SINGLE** and reselect P1, <Enter>.
9. Choose **CENTER** and select circle P4.
10. Choose **DELTA—CENTER** and select P4. Keyboard enter: dX=**1**   dY=**0**   dZ=**0**
11. **ESC** to Main Menu.

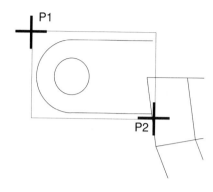

Extrude Lug

1. Choose **X-FORM—TRANS-R—COPY—SINGLE** and select the four entities of the lug, <Enter>.
2. Press <Enter> to accept the default (1) copy.
3. Keyboard enter   dX=**0**   dY=**15**   dZ=**0**.
4. **ESC** to Main Menu.

Rotate and Copy Lug

1. Press **ALT—A** and click once in the top viewport.
2. Choose **X-FORM—2D ROT—COPY—WINDOW** and carefully select the lug with corners P1 and P2.
3. Keyboard **4** as the number of copies, <Enter>.
4. Choose **ENDENT** and select the axis of rotation in the top view.
5. Keyboard enter **45** as the rotation angle, <Enter>.
6. **ESC** to Main Menu.

Reset Units to Inches

End Lab 8

Experiment

Finish this part so that it has identical ends separated by 100 mm. Use **ALT—W** and **ALT—P** to zoom and pan to complete intersections that have to be added or edited.

Hints:

1. Copy original profile and axis -100 mm along the Z axis.

2. Sweep this profile -15º with 12 copies.

3. Copy original lug -100 mm along the Z axis.

4. Rotate and copy this lug -45º with 4 copies.

5. Use direct 3D construction to complete sides.

6. Use **F10** backup to cancel an incorrect selection and reselect.

▼   ADDITIONAL EXERCISES

Use the following profiles to sweep model geometry. You may wish to copy without joining and later add circular connections or use **JOIN** function to automatically connect the profiles. Consult your instructor for suggested angles and number of copies.

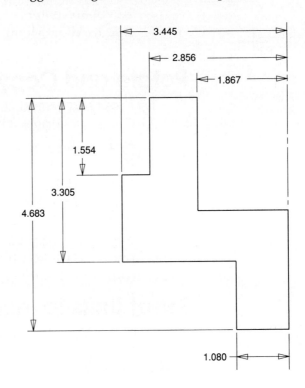

Problem 8A

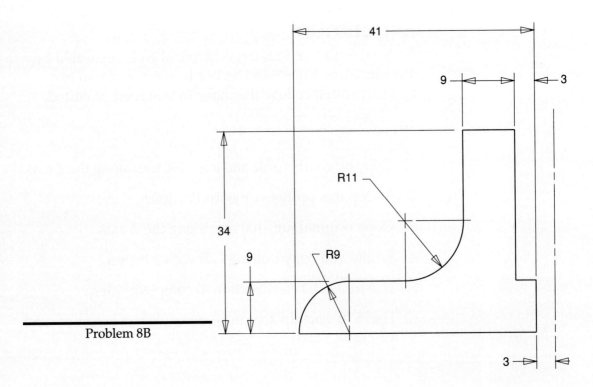

Problem 8B

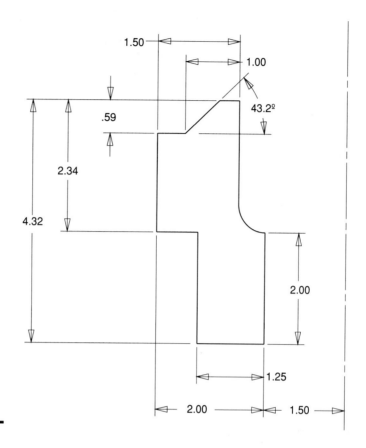

Problem 8C

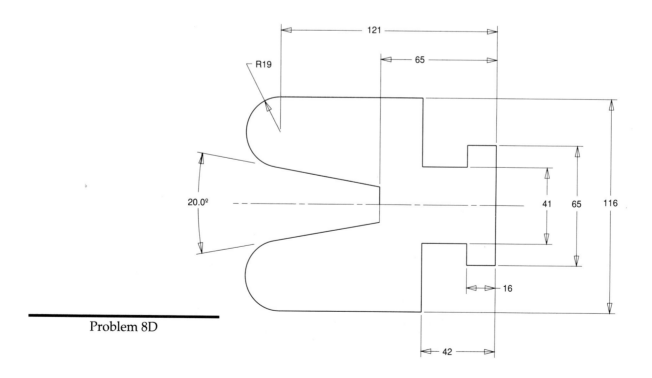

Problem 8D

Library Patterns

▼ **INTRODUCTION**

CADKEY Light provides a method for bringing together two separately created geometric files. The file that is retrieved from disk is called a *pattern*, while the file currently in memory is called a *part*.* Part files *cannot* be directly retrieved into other part files. To accomplish this, one part file must be saved as a pattern. A copy of the pattern is placed in the part file while the original is left untouched for future use.

The exact same geometry can exist as both part and pattern files. The only difference lies in the extension CADKEY Light automatically assigns to the file name when the file is saved. Parts have .PRT extensions. Patterns have .PTN extensions. The only geometric difference is that an origin, or *base* position, is associated with the pattern. The pattern is then placed by matching its base position with a user-specified location in the part.

Any and all entities—both 2D and 3D, both geometric and drafting—can be used to create a pattern. Patterns can also contain other patterns. The line type, color, layer, and other entity attributes in effect when the pattern was created remain in effect when the pattern is retrieved into a part.

When patterns are saved together with similar patterns on diskette or in a subdirectory on a hard disk, they become *pattern libraries*. Pattern libraries represent one of the most powerful characteristics of CADD. With patterns, repetitive design components can be retrieved, scaled, rotated, and placed in any part file, in any orientation in space. Experienced CADD designers always look for instances where repetitive geometry can be created using patterns.

* Do not confuse *pattern* with *hatch* or *fill*, two terms often used in CADD. Hatch is a group of lines filling a 2D area used in sectioning. Fill is a pattern of screen dots filling a 2D area used to make a model appear solid.

▼   HOW A PATTERN FUNCTIONS

At the time of creation, CADKEY Light needs to know three things about the pattern: the geometry to be included, the location of the pattern's base, and the position of ZV (the device Z axis) relative to the geometry.

Included Geometry

Any option from the Select Menu can be used to include geometric or drafting entities in a pattern. These entities can be selected in *any* viewport.

Pattern Base

The *base* is the reference point for placing the pattern in a part. When retrieved, unless you have personally created the pattern and remember where its base is located, the pattern may not be placed in the anticipated position. Consider Fig. 13-1. The base of a pattern (in this case a transistor) is identified. Unfortunately, it is not at a position that would facilitate the placing of the transistor on a line in an electronic diagram. The result would be that shown in Fig. 13-2. The transistor does not arrive at the expected location—the end of the line. If there is a First Rule of Patterns it might be:

"Locate the base of a pattern where it would logically exist based on the *function* of the pattern in a design. If there is no such point, locate the base at the pattern's geometric center."

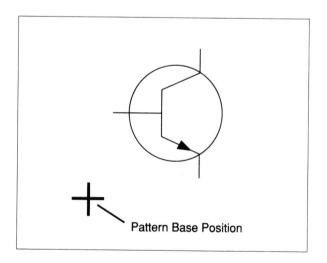
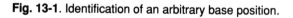

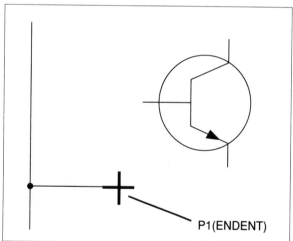

Fig. 13-1. Identification of an arbitrary base position.

Fig. 13-2. Placing pattern saved with an arbitrary base position.

If the **CURSOR** position mask is active, the base will be located at construction depth. Other position masks (such as **CENTER**, **ENDENT**, etc.) will locate the base at the depth of the masked feature. In Fig. 13-3(a), a pattern base is identified. Study in (b) the effect of different location masks on the position of the base.

The choice of viewport in which the base is identified is *very* important, as is discussed in the next section.

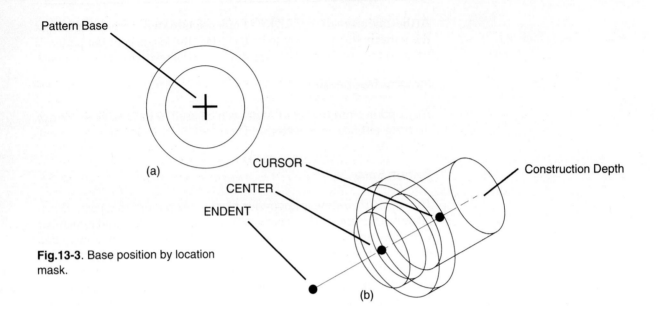

Fig.13-3. Base position by location mask.

▼ POSITION OF THE ZV AXIS

The pattern is saved with ZV sticking straight out toward the viewer and running through the base position. This is important because when retrieved, CADKEY Light matches base point to placing point and ZV(pattern) to ZV(part). This structure allows you to place a pattern normal to any surface.

A pattern is saved in a position that corresponds to how it will be placed in a part. Study Fig. 13-4 where a pin will be inserted into holes until the surface of the shoulder rests on the surface through which the hole is drilled. This means that the pattern should adhere to two rules.

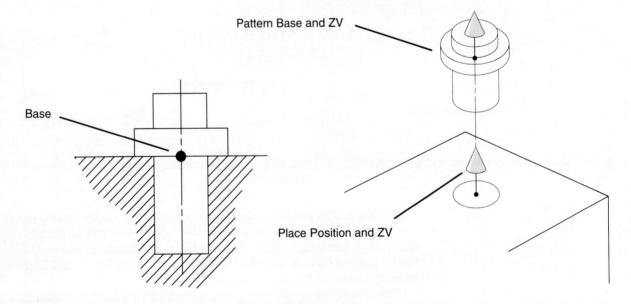

Fig.13-4. Pin rests with shoulder on surface through which hole is drilled.

1. Be created in a view looking down the axis of the pin.

2. Have its base located at the center of the circle defining the shoulder's surface.

The pin pattern, when saved, has a ZV orientation and base position like that shown in Fig. 13-5.

How then can this pin be inserted into holes drilled through horizontal, vertical, profile, and inclined planes? Figure 13-6 shows a part that satisfies this problem. In (a), the pin is retrieved and placed in the front viewport where hole "A" is seen normally. In (b), the pin is again retrieved and placed in the top

Fig.13-5. Pin pattern base and ZV axis orientation.

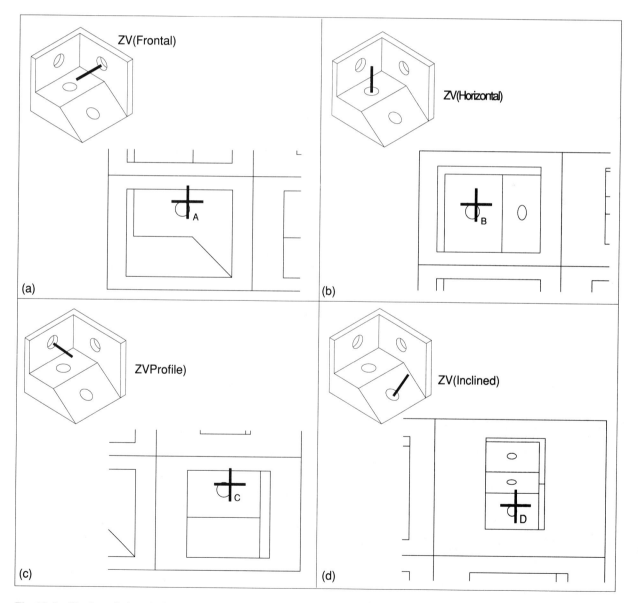

(a)

(b)

(c)

(d)

Fig.13-6. Placing pin into holes drilled through frontal, horizontal, profile, and inclined surfaces.

viewport where hole "B" is normal. Then in (c) and (d) the pin is placed in the side and inclined viewports, normal to profile and inclined holes. Notice that ZV(pattern) is always matched with ZV(viewport).

▼ CREATE PATTERN

Any geometry or drafting detail in the work space can be captured as a pattern. You may want to select a portion of your current design to save as a pattern if you think you might want to use it again. In this case you would have to distinguish between components included in the pattern and those not to be included. In general practice, however, patterns are created in blank unnamed part files. Follow these steps to create a pattern:

1. Create the pattern using CADKEY Light's geometric and detail drafting tools. It may be helpful to create the pattern in unitary dimensions. That is, some dimension on the pattern may be made to be 1, 10, 100, etc., so that the pattern can be scaled easily when placed into a part.

2. Display the pattern in a position that matches the position in which it will be placed into part files.

3. Choose **FILES—PATTERN—CREATE**.

4. Select the pattern using an option from the Select Menu. You can use any viewport for selection.

5. Identify the base position using an option from the Location Menu. The base point should be the logical point that will match some feature on the target part. The pattern can be moved around after placing, but it is more efficient to place it in the correct position in one step.

6. Assign a path and descriptive pattern name to the file. Study the examples below.

`a:pin`	saves pin.ptn on the diskette in drive a:
`c:/cadkey/ptn pin`	saves pin.ptn in the PTN subdirectory on your hard disk, drive c:
`c:/cadkey/ptn/fastnr pin`	saves pin.ptn in a subdirectory you created for fasteners inside the PTN subdirectory on your hard disk

CADKEY Commands

Tip:
Grid snap is effective only with the **CURSOR** location mask and at current construction depth. All other masks override snap and construction depth, placing the pattern at the depth of the feature.

▼ RETRIEVE PATTERN

You have two options when retrieving a pattern file. If you know the name and location of the file, choose **FILES—PATTERN—RETRIEV** and type the name of the file (without extension). If the pattern file is on the default drive, you can simply type the file name. If the file is on another drive, type the complete path to the file followed by a space and the file name. If you are unsure of the name or location of the pattern file, you will want to use **FILES—PATTERN—LST/RTV**.

Without specifying a path, CADKEY Light will use the path established in the **CONFIG.DAT** file when you ran the **CONFIG** program. To override this default, type the path you want to search. CADKEY Light displays a list of all files with .PRT extensions located at that path destination. Select the desired pattern with a cursor-click. Once retrieved, the pattern can be placed any number of times.

▼ PLACE PATTERN

When CADKEY Light has located the pattern file, several options are available. You must respond to these the first time the pattern is retrieved. These options can be changed for the same pattern by using **F10** to back up through the options.

Group

The entities can be grouped for easy manipulation. In general, you will want to group the pattern—especially if you are unsure of where the pattern base is located and might have to move it into final position.

Group Name

The default name of the group is the same as the name of the pattern. Press <Enter> to accept this. Type your own group name to override the default. Subsequent placing of the same pattern under the same group name causes *subgroups* to be created. By editing the group by name, all instances of its subgroups can be automatically edited. You can see that this is a powerful feature, but one that might result in disaster if such massive changes were not really desired.

Level

CADKEY Light allows you to assign the pattern to levels before actually placing the file. See Chapter 25 for a description of the options available with levels.

Scale

The pattern can be scaled up or down. Were the pattern unitary, its final size could be easily determined. That is, if the pattern were 10" on a side and the desired size is 3.37", a scale factor of .337 would produce the desired result. If the pattern is of indeterminate size, it can be placed first for informational purposes, deleted, and then replaced with an appropriate scale factor.

Rotation

The pattern can be rotated positively or negatively about ZV in the viewport in which it is being placed. When rotated, the base point position is rotated along with pattern entities...its position relative to the pattern remains the same (Fig. 13-7).

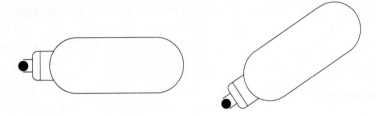

Fig. 13-7. Effect of rotation on pattern base position.

Location

The actual position of the base in the part file depends on the Location Menu option that you choose. In 2D, you may choose to place the pattern at ZV=0 construction depth. A practical way of doing this for schematics and diagrams is to deposit a point entity at the position you want the pattern base. In Fig. 13-8, five point entities have been created, each marking the location of a resistor. These points become placing points for each resistor's base. When the schematic is completed, the points can be deleted.

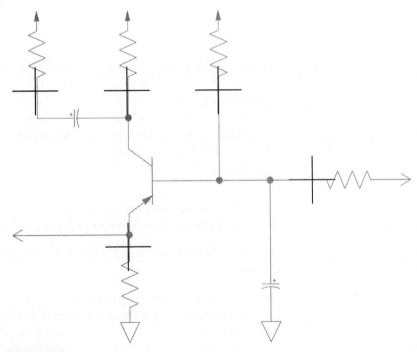

Fig. 13-8. Use point entities to mark location of pattern components in an electrical schematic.

▼ SUMMARY

A pattern is created and saved when a diagram or model is going to be used repeatedly. Any geometric or detail drafting entity can be included in a pattern as well as any and all entity parameters. Patterns can be grouped, assigned to levels, scaled, rotated, and placed using any option from the Locate Menu.

The *pattern base* is the reference point used to place the pattern. This base is matched with a placing point in the target part. Choose a logical position for the pattern base. The more you know about how the pattern is going to be used, the more intelligent will be your choice for the position of the base.

The ZV(pattern) will be aligned with ZV(part) in the viewport in which the placing point is indicated. When placing a part with which you are unfamiliar, group the pattern, choose **ENT-LEV** level assignment, full scale, and zero rotation. By choosing these options, you will be able to determine how the pattern was created. Discharge the pattern at a known position such as X=0, Y=0, Z=0. By doing this you will know the exact position of the pattern's base.

Patterns are saved in associated groups on diskette or hard disk subdirectories using descriptive file names. This way, libraries can be searched efficiently for the desired pattern.

Once placed, there is no link between the pattern and its original. That is, changes in the original pattern are not reflected in instances where it was placed. If grouped when placed, the pattern can be recognized as a named entity for accounting purposes, such as when building a Bill of Materials. If not grouped, pattern geometry simply is added to the individual geometry making up the part.

▼ QUESTIONS

1. Describe the difference between merging two part files and placing a pattern in a part. Can CADKEY Light do both of these?

2. Can geometry be selected in *any* viewport for inclusion in a pattern?

3. How may a pattern's base be identified *before* placing?

4. Describe the difference between *base point* and *placing point*.

5. What is the relationship between ZV(pattern) and ZV(part)?

6. Why is it advantageous to create a pattern with unitary dimensions.

7. What determines the storage location that will be searched for a desired pattern?

8. If you wanted to rotate a pattern about the X(world) axis when placing, in which viewport would the placing point have to be identified?

9. Which location mask would you use to snap the pattern base to a grid point?

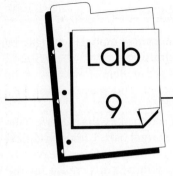

CADKEY Light
Library Patterns

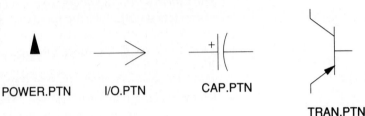

POWER.PTN   I/O.PTN   CAP.PTN

TRAN.PTN

RESIST.PTN   GROUND.PTN   CONNECT.PTN

Pattern Parameters

1. `GRD:ON; SNAP:ON; DEPTH = 0.00; VW = 1.`
2. Choose `DISPLAY—GRD/SNAP—GRID INC` and keyboard enter .1 as the value for X and Y grid increment.
3. `F10` backup.
4. Choose `SNAP INC` and keyboard enter **.05** for both X and Y values. `ESC` to Main Menu.
5. Choose `DISPLAY—ZOOM—WINDOW` and zoom to 20x20 grid area. `ESC` to Main Menu.

Create Resistor

Using the diagram to the right, create the resistor symbol. Eact dot represents a point on the .1 grid.

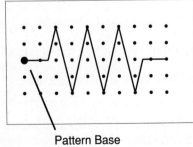

Pattern Base

1. Choose `FILES—PATTERN—CREATE—ALL DSP—ALL`.
2. Grid snap to the pattern base (the black dot); click once.
3. Name the file `a:RESIST` and press <Enter>.
4. `ESC` to the Main Menu.

Create Capacitor

1. Choose `DELETE—SELECT—ALL DSP—ALL` to remove the resistor from the work space.
2. Press `CTRL—R` to redraw the display. `ESC`.

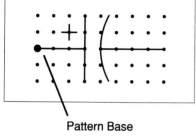

Pattern Base

Using the diagram to the left, create the capacitor symbol.

3. Grid snap to the pattern base; click once.
4. Choose **FILES—PATTERN—CREATE—ALL DSP—ALL.**
5. Name the file **a:CAP** and press <Enter>.
6. **ESC** to the Main Menu.

Create Transistor

1. Choose **DELETE—SELECT—ALL DISP—ALL** to remove the capacitor from the work space.
2. Press **CTRL—R** to redraw the display.

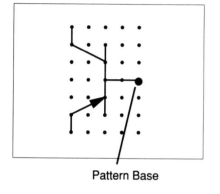

Pattern Base

Using the diagram to the left , create the transistor symbol. Choose **CREATE—POLYGON—STRING—FILLED** to draw the arrow.

3. Choose **FILES—PATTERN—CREATE—ALL DSP—ALL.**
4. Grid snap to the pattern base; click once.
5. Name the file **a:TRAN** and press <Enter>.
6. **ESC** to the Main Menu.

Create Power Out

1. Choose **DELETE—SELECT—ALL DISP—ALL** to remove the transistor from the work space.
2. Press **CTRL—R** to redraw the display.

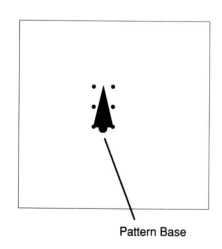

Pattern Base

Using the diagram to the left, create the power out symbol. Choose **CREATE—POLYGON—STRING—FILLED** to draw the arrow.

3. Choose **FILES—PATTERN—CREATE—ALL DISP—ALL**
4. Use the **CENTER** mask to identify the pattern base, click once.
5. Name the file **a:POWER** and press <Enter>.
6. **ESC** to the Main Menu.

Create Connector

1. Choose **DELETE—SELECT—ALL DSP—ALL** to remove the power out from the work space.
2. Press **CTRL—R** to redraw the display.

Using the diagram to the next page, create the connector symbol. Choose **CREATE—POLYGON—CTR+RAD.**

3. Keyboard enter **8** as the desired number of sides, <Enter>.

4. Press <Enter> to accept the default rotation of zero degrees.

5. Keyboard enter **.05** as the value of the radius.

6. Choose **CORNER;** choose **FILLED**.

7. Let cursor snap to a grid point, click once. **ESC** to the Main Menu.

8. Choose **FILES—PATTERN—CREATE—ALL DISP—ALL**.

9. Choose **CURSOR** from the Locate Menu. Snap to the center point of the polygon for the pattern base.

10. Name the file **a:CONNECT** and press <Enter>.

11. **ESC** to the Main Menu.

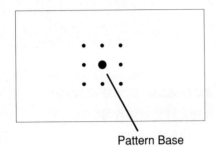

Pattern Base

Create Ground

1. Choose **DELETE—SELECT—ALL DISP—ALL** to remove the connector from the work space.

2. Press **CTRL—R** to redraw the display. Choose **CREATE—LINE—STRING**. Using the diagram to the left, create the ground symbol.

3. Choose **FILES—PATTERN—CREATE—ALL DISP—ALL**.

4. Use the **CENTER** mask to identify the pattern base; click once.

5. Name the file **a:GROUND** and press <Enter>.

6. **ESC** to the Main Menu.

Pattern Base

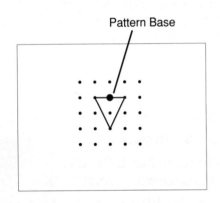

Create IO

1. Choose **DELETE—SELECT—ALL DSP—ALL** to remove the connector from the work space.

2. Press **CTRL—R** to redraw the display.

   Choose **CREATE—LINE—ENDPTS**. Using the diagram to the left, create the I/O symbol.

3. Choose **FILES—PATTERN—CREATE—ALL DSP—ALL**.

4. Use the **ENDENT** mask to identify the pattern base; click once.

5. Name the file **a:IO** and press <Enter>.

6. **ESC** to the Main Menu.

Pattern Base

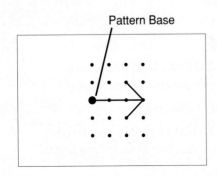

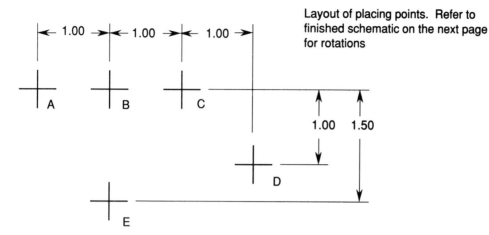

Layout of placing points. Refer to finished schematic on the next page for rotations

Create Placing Point Positions

1. Change grid and snap to .5.
2. **COORD:VW; CONSTR:2D.**
3. Using the information above, create five point entities. Choose **CREATE—POINT—POSITN—KEY-IN** and enter XV and YV data.

Place Resistors

1. Choose **FILES—PATTERN—RETRIEV**.
2. Keyboard enter **a:RESIST**, <Enter>.
3. Group the pattern, accept the default name, current level, zero rotation, and full scale.
4. Choose **POINT** from the Location Menu and click once on the position of the unrotated resistor (D).
5. Press **F10** backup. Change rotation to 90, <Enter>.
6. Place resistors A, B, and C.
7. Press **F10** backup. Change rotation to 270, <Enter>.
8. Place resistor E. These components become the controlling points for the rest of the schematic.
9. Save as **a:LAB9.**

Drafting Topics

▼ **Schematic Layout.** When designers lay out a schematic, they usually pick one or two components around which the other components will be balanced. Wires can then be roughed in, trimmed, and the other components placed.

Place Transistor

Determine the length of wire from point D so that the transistor will end up with its leads directly below point B. Save the schematic after retrieving and placing each pattern.

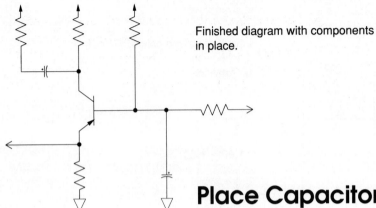

Finished diagram with components
in place.

Place Capacitors

Complete the wiring so that the capacitors can be placed.
Rotate the capacitors as necessary. Note, the position is
somewhat variable and relys on your sense of design and
balance. See schematic above left.

Place Power Out

Using the **ENDPTS** location mask, place the power out
pattern on the end of resistors A, B, and C.

Connect Components

Using the **ENDPTS** location mask, place the connector
pattern at the intersection of each wire.

Place I/O

Place the I/O pattern on the appropriate wires using
ENDPTS location mask. Rotate as necessary.

Place Ground

Using the **ENDPTS** location mask, place the two ground
symbols.

Delete Points

1. Choose **DELETE—SELECT—ALL DSP—ALL—BY
   TYPE—GEOM—POINT—DONE**
2. CADKEY Light deletes the points you used to
   place the patterns.

Save Schematic

End Lab 9

▼   ADDITIONAL EXERCISES

The two schematic sketches on this page make use of the patterns you created in Lab 9 and are similar to the type of sketches that are translated into CADD drawings. You may have to create additional patterns or unique symbols as necessary. Study each problem to determine which symbols should be placed first and around which the other symbols are balanced.

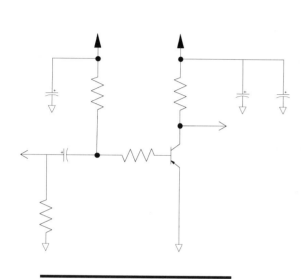

Problem 9A

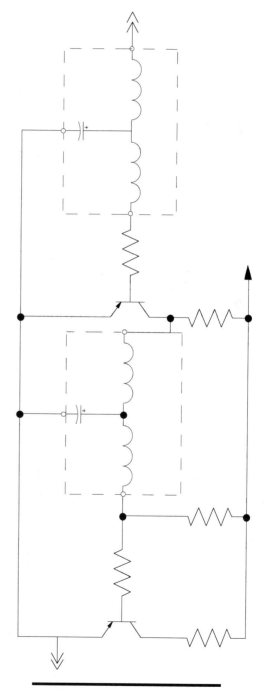

Problem 9B

Part and Pattern Files

▼ INTRODUCTION

In the previous chapter the manner in which CADKEY patterns function was explained. Particular attention was paid to the relationship of ZV(pattern) and ZV(part). Lab 9 provided experience in creating 2D electronic schematic patterns and using these to complete schematic diagrams. In this chapter the relationship of 3D parts and patterns will be further explained.

Experienced CADD designers analyze designs for subsets of geometry that can be created individually as patterns and later joined together. This accomplishes several things. First, extremely complicated part geometry can be attacked in smaller pieces. This means that redisplay and save times are faster and there is less "visual clutter" in the work space. Second, if several parts share common design features these can be used over and over, making the CADD design process even more efficient. This pattern strategy can be used for single objects and for assemblies.

Important in this analysis is seeing an underlying structure around which the individual patterns exist. This may simply be the center lines that define axes of symmetry of the object or may require a more careful analysis of how the object is subdivided.

Individual pattern pieces should be constructed at the same scale and saved in an orientation that makes their placement convenient. This was explained in detail in Figure 13-6. Remember that a part file must be active first for patterns to be retrieved and placed, even if it is an unnamed and unsaved blank part. Once the first pattern is placed, it is added to the geometry of the part.

You will notice that no additional exercises follow the laboratory exercise at the end of this or the next three chapters. Refer to any of the popular texts on engineering drawing for further assignments.

▼   BREAK DOWN GEOMETRY INTO PATTERNS

Take for example the assembly shown in Fig. 14-1 that will be used as
the basis for this chapter's lab exercise. It consists of three parts and four
fasteners. Rather than create the entire assembly as one part, the Pin,
Cap, and Body will be created as individual patterns. The base of each
pattern will be located so that common points of assembly will be
aligned. Finally, hex cap screws will be created and placed into the
mounting holes.

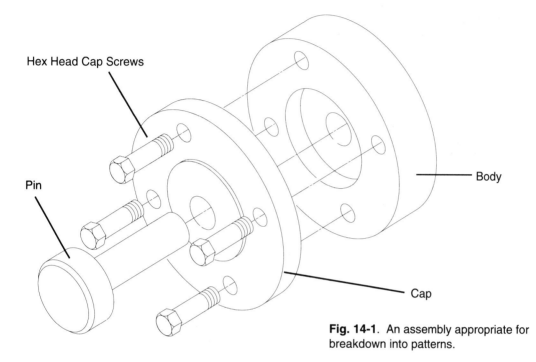

Fig. 14-1. An assembly appropriate for
breakdown into patterns.

▼   LOCATE BASE POSITIONS

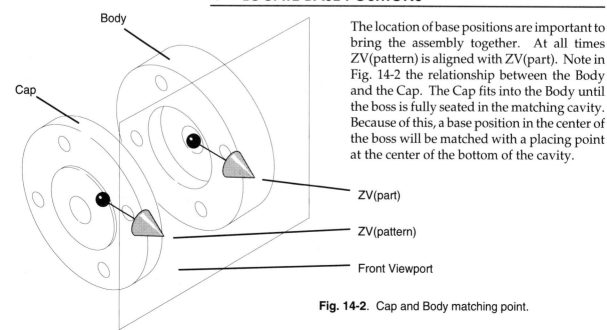

The location of base positions are important to
bring the assembly together. At all times
ZV(pattern) is aligned with ZV(part). Note in
Fig. 14-2 the relationship between the Body
and the Cap. The Cap fits into the Body until
the boss is fully seated in the matching cavity.
Because of this, a base position in the center of
the boss will be matched with a placing point
at the center of the bottom of the cavity.

Fig. 14-2. Cap and Body matching point.

The Pin, when inserted into the Cap and Body, rests with the underside of the head against the boss of the cap. Figure 14-3 shows the base at the center of the underside of the Pin's head and the placing point at the center of the Cap's boss.

Finally, mounting screws are inserted into holes with the underside of the fastener's head in the same plane as the entrance to the hole (Fig. 14-4).

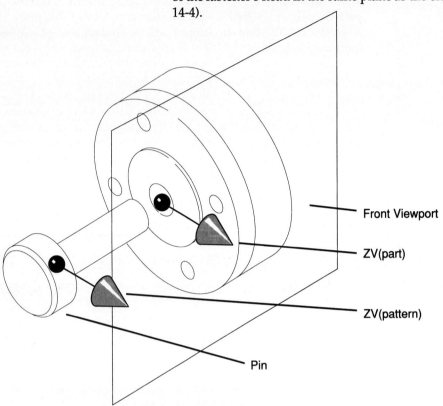

Fig. 14-3. Pin and Cap matching point.

Fig. 14-4. Hex Screw and Cap matching point.

▼ Mating Parts.
Model geometry may have to be edited to remove actual clerarances between mating parts when turning models into drawings.

▼ BUILD INDIVIDUAL PATTERNS

The individual patterns are constructed as usual. When it comes time for the pattern's base to be identified, a different approach from what has been described before is used. Pattern bases are identified in the profile rather than in the end view. Experience has shown that when several circular features are centered along the same axis, it becomes tedious to identify positions at various depth settings. By placing the patterns in the profile view, the **CENTER** location mask can be used with ease.

The exception to this is the fastener, which is saved as a pattern in a view showing the hex head from the end.

As a practical matter, the difference between modeling and drawing is never so evident as in this pattern—part construction. Conventionally, very small differences between mating parts are not shown on engineering drawings. In creating a model, sizes reflect actual measurements and tolerances. This may produce parts which *seem* not to align but which in fact show actual clearances.

▼ RETRIEVE AND PLACE GEOMETRY

The first pattern, the body, is placed into a blank part file. It may be helpful to place this first part at a known location in space so that coordinate distances are conveniently small. Use the **KEY-IN** position

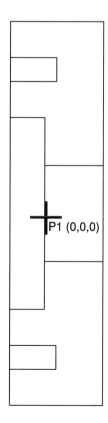

Fig. 14-5. Place Base pattern in front viewport at 0, 0, 0.

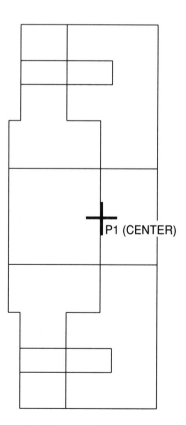

Fig. 14-6. Match CAP base point in front viewport with 0, 0, 0 or use CENTER location mask.

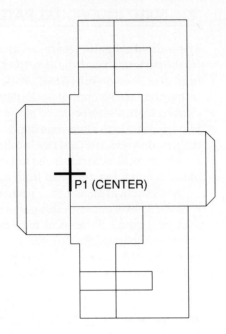

P1 (CENTER)

Fig. 14-7. Match Pin base point with placing point on Cap by using CENTER location mask.

mask to place the Body's base position at X=0, Y=0, Z=0 (Fig. 14-5). The Cap pattern's base is matched with the **CENTER** of the cavity depth (Fig. 14-6). Or, because the matching point is at 0, 0, 0, **KEY-IN** can be used again (P1). The Pin pattern's base is matched with the **CENTER** of the outside boss (Fig. 14-7).

Finally, the fasteners are placed in the mounting holes as shown in Fig. 14-8. To do this, switch to the left view* and place the screws into the holes using the **POINT** location mask (P1-P4). Point entities can be created at the center of holes against which the bases of the hex cap screws will be placed, making their alignment easier. You can later delete the points.

CADKEY in Industry

Pattern geometry accomplishes several goals in a production environment. First, no one wants to "redesign the wheel." If a part of a previous design can be used as the basis for subsequent projects, much time and effort can be saved. Also, this assures that similar or identical parts are the same size because they are from the same data base. This way you know right away if parts will fit.

Second, many designs are comprised of repetitive geometric features. These features can be saved as patterns and retrieved, scaled, rotated, and placed.

As a design strategy, it is often more efficient to break down a complex mechanism into smaller parts that can be modeled individually. The components can be assembled into the whole. This technique is effective even when the design is a single part but is most powerful when dealing with assemblies.

Left View. You have not saved a left view but can produce one by choosing `DISPLAY-VIEW-NEW-KEY-IN-RGT IN`. By rotating the axis system into the screen 90°, a left side view is produced. You can easily return to the front view with `DISPLAY-VIEW` and keyboard entering the number `1`.

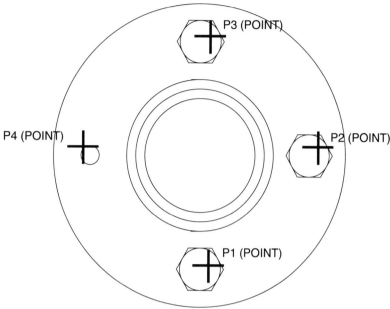

Fig. 14-8. Match Hex Screw base point with placing point on each hole. Note the change to the top viewport.

▼ SUMMARY

From this discussion of patterns something should be evident. Effective use of CADD requires planning, planning, planning. A CADD designer is much more efficient when design procedures are planned to make use of the uniquely powerful techniques inherent in CADD computers.

Paramount in this planning is the planning of the ZV(pattern) and ZV(part) orientation—in other words, in which *viewport* will the pattern's base position be identified. Once this decision has been made, the location of the pattern's *base* provides a handle with which to place the geometry. Finally, the *placing point* is the spot in the part file to which the pattern's base will be matched.

▼ QUESTIONS

1. How do you know when it is appropriate to use pattern geometry?

2. How do you know where to locate the pattern's base?

3. How do you know where to locate the placing point?

4. Can you make patterns out of portions of existing parts? What techniques would you use to accomplish this?

5. Assume that you load a part file that you have not personally constructed. Can you determine if pattern geometry is included in the part and, if so, which patterns were used?

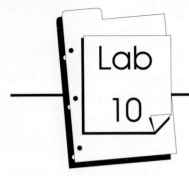

CADKEY Light
Parts and Patterns

This laboratory exercise makes use of the example presented in the first part of the chapter. If you have not studied pages 156-161, do so before starting this lab.

Three parts have been completed for you and are on your exercise disk. These are the Base, the Cap, and the Pin. You will create the Hex Cap Screw pattern and join all three together into an assembly. At the appropriate time, insert the exercise disk to retrieve these patterns. Finally, you will plot an isometric view of the assembly.

Start CADKEY Light with BLANK

1. `GRID:ON; SNAP:ON; COORD:WLD`.
2. Set views 1, 9, 10, 11 in 4 viewports.

Create Bolt Head

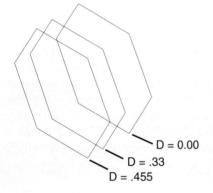

D = 0.00
D = .33
D = .455

1. `DEPTH=0.0000;` Work in the front viewport.
2. Choose **CREATE-POLYGON-CTR+RAD** with 6 sides, zero rotation, .5 radius as measured across flats, in **OUTLINE** form.
3. Let the cursor snap to a grid point and click once. **ESC** to Main Menu.
4. Choose **CREATE—POINT—POSITN** and snap to the same center point; click once. **ESC** to Main Menu.
5. Create another hexagon at the same point in the front view at **D=.33** and a third at **D=.45**.
6. Choose **CREATE-CIRCLE-CTR+RAD** with a radius of .5; cursor snap center of the hexagons in front view. **ESC** to the Main Menu.
7. Zoom in **(ALT-W)** on isometric view for the next steps.

Put Points at Intersections

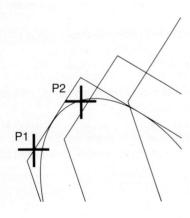

P2

P1

1. `SNAP:OFF`.
2. Choose **CREATE-POINT-POSITN-INTRSC** and carefully choose each hexagon line (P1) and then the circle (P2). Put 6 points on the circle at each intersection of the hexagon and circle.

Create Arcs Through Endpoints and Points

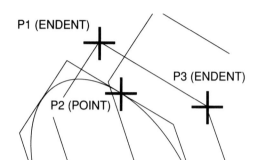

P1 (ENDENT)

P3 (ENDENT)

P2 (POINT)

1. Choose **CREATE-ARC-THREE-P-ENDENT** and select P1.
2. Choose **POINT** and select point P2.
3. Choose **ENDENT** and select P3.
4. Pan (**ALT-P**) get the other five locations. Rotate and zoom view as necessary. Note: you can create all six arcs without leaving the command—only changing location masks.
5. Save part file as **a:hexhead**.
6. Choose **DELETE—SELECT—SINGLE** and delete the front two hexagons.
7. **ESC** to the Main Menu.

Create Hex Planes

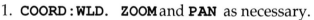

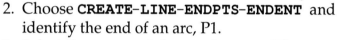

P2 (ENDENT)

P1 (ENDENT)

1. **COORD:WLD. ZOOM** and **PAN** as necessary.
2. Choose **CREATE-LINE-ENDPTS-ENDENT** and identify the end of an arc, P1.
3. Select the corner of the rear hexagon P2.
4. Connect the other curve ends with their respective rear hex corners.
5. **ESC** to the Main Menu.

Delete Points

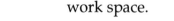

1. Choose **DELETE-SELECT-ALL DSP** in the front view **BY TYPE-GEOM-POINT-DONE**
2. CADKEY deletes only point entities from the work space.

Save as a Pattern

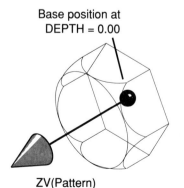

Base position at
DEPTH = 0.00

ZV(Pattern)

1. **DEPTH=0.00; SNAP:ON.**
2. Choose **FILES-PATTERN-CREATE-ALL DSP** in the front viewport, **ALL. CURSOR** snap to center of the hexagonal base.
3. Name the pattern **A:HEXHEAD.**
4. **ESC** to Main Menu.

The hexhead pattern is saved with the base point on the underside of the hexhead and with ZV(pattern) aligned with the fastener's axis.

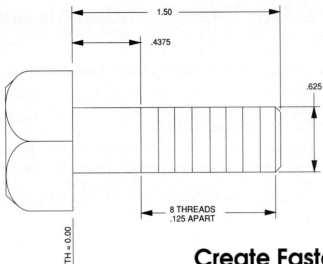

DEPTH = 0.00

Create Fastener Shank

1. **DEPTH=0.00; CONST:3D; SNAP:ON**.
2. Choose **CREATE—CIRCLE—CTR+DIA** and keyboard enter .625 as the diameter value.
3. Cursor snap to the grid point in the middle of the hex head. Click once.
4. **DEPTH=-.4375**; click again at the same location.
5. Use the **OFFSET** option to change depth -.125 eight times to produce 1 inch of threaded shank.
6. Change the diameter to .500 and offset to -.0625 and produce the chamfered end.
7. **ESC** to the Main Menu.
8. Save pattern again in the front view as **A:HEXHEAD** with the base at 0, 0, 0.

Load a:BLANK

1. CADKEY asks if you want to save the file. Respond **NO** because you have just saved the geometry.
2. Set the single viewport to **VIEW=1**.

Load Pattern File a:BASE

1. Choose **FILES—PATTERN—RETRIEV** and keyboard enter **a:base** <Enter>.
2. Choose **KEY-IN** and keyboard enter X=**0**, Y=**0**, Z=**0**, <Enter>. Press **ALT—A**.
3. **ESC** to the Main Menu.

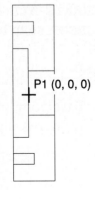

P1 (0, 0, 0)

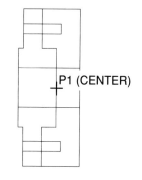

P1 (CENTER)

Load Pattern File a:CAP

1. Choose **FILES—PATTERN—RETRIEV** and keyboard enter **a:cap** <Enter>.
2. Choose **KEY-IN** and keyboard enter X=**0**, Y=**0**, Z=**0**, or choose **CENTER** and select the center of the cavity, P1.
3. **ESC** to the Main Menu.

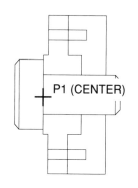

P1 (CENTER)

Load Pattern File a:PIN

1. Choose **FILES—PATTERN—RETRIEV** and keyboard enter **a:pin** <Enter>.
2. Choose **CENTER** and select the center of the Cap's boss, P1.
3. **ESC** to the Main Menu.

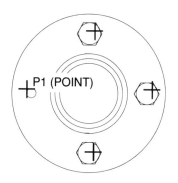

P1 (POINT)

Place Hex Heads on Cap

1. Choose **DISPLAY—VIEW—NEW—KEY-IN—RGT IN** and keyboard 90 <Enter> **—DONE. ALT—A** to auto zoom. This produces a left side view.
2. Choose **FILES-PATTERN-LIST/RTV** and keyboard enter **a:** <Enter>.
3. Cursor select **HEXHEAD**
4. Retrieve pattern and using the **POINT** mask for placing the pattern, place Hex Cap Screws on holes in the face of the Cap (P1). Respond **YES** to all of the defaults.
5. **SAVE** as **A:LAB10** <Enter>.

Note: You must be familiar with your plotting procedures. Make sure that you have identified the correct plotter in the **CONFIG** program, that your plotter is connected correctly to your computer, and that paper and pens are loaded correctly.

Plot Isometric of Your Assembly

1. Choose a one-viewport display. Make this view your view # 11(isometric view).
2. Choose **DISPLAY-ZOOM-AUTO.**
3. Choose **CONTROL-PLOT-AUTO-NO-PEN#-ALL DISP-ALL.**
4. Turn plotter on and assure that paper and pens are loaded correctly.
5. Press <Enter>. CADKEY plots the geometry displayed in the viewport.

End Lab 10

Engineering Drawings from 3D Models

▼ IN THIS CHAPTER

Planning Ahead
3D Models in Position
Editing 3D Models
Detail Drafting Entities
Border and Title Block
Lab 11

Tutor Topics

Complete **LINEAR** and **LAYOUT** in TUTOR. You will create pattern files that form the basis of an engineering drawing.

▼ INTRODUCTION

The subject of the chapters up to now has been modeling. However, anyone who has worked in industry knows and understands the importance of drawings for communicating design information between engineering and manufacturing, between production and marketing, and between clients and vendors. Traditionally, engineering drawings were produced very early in the design process because it was from these drawings that models and prototypes were built and tested. The drawings were used for scheduling, purchasing, and contracting.

CADD has changed some of this. Because CADD produces a numerical description of the design, this data base can be used for all of the activities previously mentioned as being the domain of engineering drawings. Where drawings had to be interpreted, the data base can be *postprocessed* in any number of ways to provide useful information. In fact, making traditional engineering drawings may not be necessary at all and, if it is, the drawings may be produced as an after-the-fact documentation procedure.

Still, there are times when traditional engineering drawings are useful and CADKEY Light provides several methods for producing them. First, 2D engineering drawings can be created from scratch using 2D construction techniques. This would be appropriate if the subject of the design were 2D, as with shims and gaskets which essentially have no depth, or when designing charts, diagrams, or schematics. This would also be appropriate if CADKEY Light were used as an automated drafting system and the data base not intended for postprocessing.

But there's a good chance that you have a 3D model of the design and it is the model that you will use as the basis of your engineering drawing.

The model will provide an accurate framework for the drawing. Still, many pieces of information will have to be added and some geometric data in the model will either be extraneous or redundant and will have to be removed.

CADKEY Light does not provide an automatic "smash" function where 3D model data can be translated into 2D drafting data. Still, with a minimum of effort, an engineering drawing can be created from 3D model data.

This chapter assumes that you understand how engineering drawings function and are knowledgeable about shape, size, and manufacturability. The laboratory exercise in this chapter makes use of the model geometry you used in the previous lab. For further assignments, refer to the engineering drawing texts listed in the bibliography.

▼ PLANNING AHEAD

If you recall from the previous chapter, the various parts of an assembly were created as patterns. Because the patterns were 3D, *any and all views* are available. To make the job of separating individual components of an assembly easier, it is helpful to have created them as individual patterns.

When making a model, you probably were not terribly concerned with line weights. You did, however, assign colors based not on some engineering drawing standard, but rather on the basis of how colors helped you understand and create the geometry. Standard engineering drawings make use of line weight change and generally omit color as a means of conveying information because engineering drawings are generally printed by monochromatic processes.

Model geometry may also lack limiting elements defining the outside of holes, cylinders, etc. These will have to be added. CADKEY Light does not differentiate between a .PRT file that is a 2D drawing and a .PRT file that is a 3D model. You may want to adopt a conventional designation system. For example, you may have the following files:

`BASE.PRT`	the part file of the 3D Base model
`BASE.PTN`	the pattern file of the 3D Base model
`BASEDWG.PRT`	the engineering drawing of the Base

▼ 3D MODELS IN POSITION

The main technique for turning a model into an engineering drawing is to position multiple instances of the model as patterns in a single viewport in such positions as to conform to standard view-projection. Because a single view is all that is necessary, engineering drawings are produced in a single viewport.

In order to achieve different views of the model, the pattern must be saved in different orientations. For example, the Base was originally saved in the position that might generally be deemed appropriate for the profile view (Fig. 15-1). But for a front view, ZV(pattern) needs to be aligned with the axis of the cylindrical geometry as shown in Fig. 15-2. When these two patterns are placed in the same viewport, ZV(pattern) is aligned with ZV(part) as shown in Fig. 15-3. The remaining task is to assure that the views are aligned. Figure 15-4 shows the two patterns as they would appear in the single viewport.

CADD Topics

▼ File Names.
The choice of names for your files is very important. You may have hundreds—even thousands—of files, so time saved identifying the desired file means increased productivity.

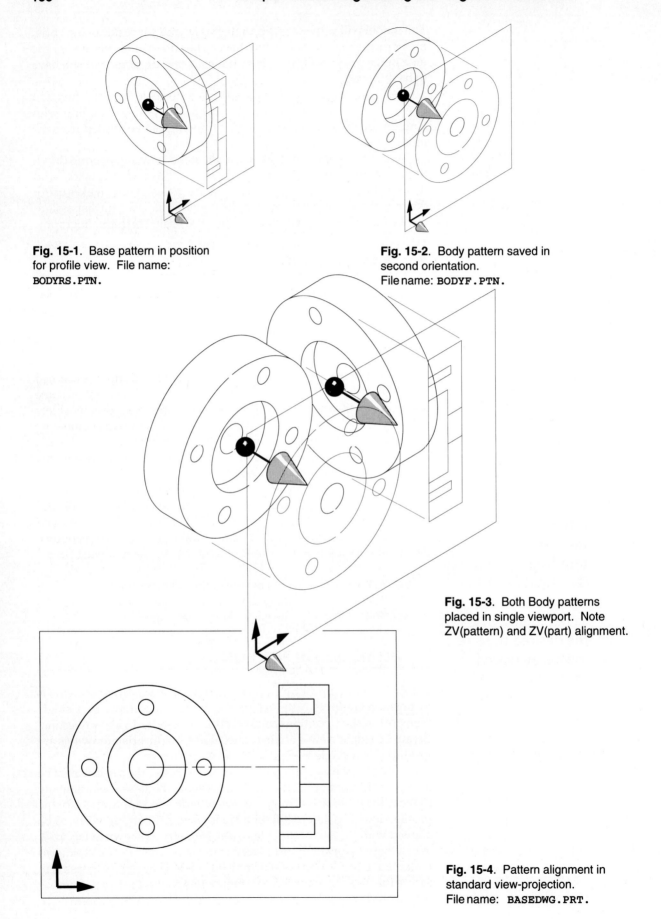

Fig. 15-1. Base pattern in position for profile view. File name: `BODYRS.PTN.`

Fig. 15-2. Body pattern saved in second orientation. File name: `BODYF.PTN.`

Fig. 15-3. Both Body patterns placed in single viewport. Note ZV(pattern) and ZV(part) alignment.

Fig. 15-4. Pattern alignment in standard view-projection. File name: `BASEDWG.PRT.`

▼ EDITING 3D MODELS INTO ENGINEERING DRAWINGS

Here the real work of making an engineering drawing begins. You will want to make use of location masks to assure accuracy. However, because the data in 3D, some apparent constructions cannot be accomplished. The most common operation is turning cylindrical models into a drawing.

Figure 15-5 displays the cylindrical model in position for two views. The limiting elements that would define the sides of the cylinder are missing from the wireframe model. But because these two positions on circles have no direct location mask position, point entities must be placed on the circles at 0 and 180 degrees and the points used to mask linework. The circle can then be deleted and the result is a flat projection of the model geometry. The circular view of the cylinder is more directly used without editing

Figure 15-6 shows a finished engineering drawing made from the model in Fig. 15-4.

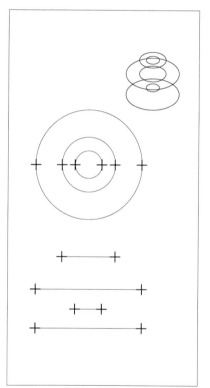

Fig. 15-5. Pictorial and wire frame top and front views of a cylindrical feature.

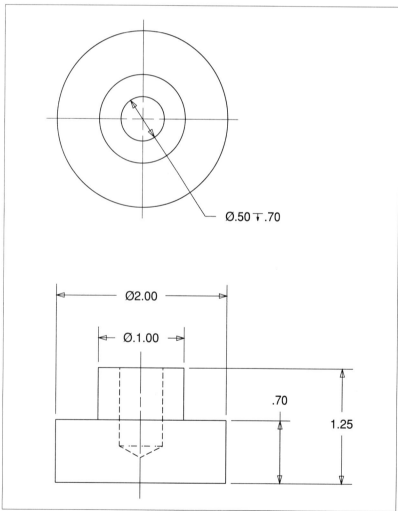

Fig. 15-6. Edited 3D model patterns with detail drafting entities added. The result is an engineering detail drawing.

▼ DETAIL DRAFTING ENTITIES

Detail drafting entities are treated much like geometric entities with the exception that they are not part of the numerical data base describing the geometry of a part. In postprocessing, drafting entities are either ignored or stripped from the file all together. Detail drafting entities appear only in the viewport in which they were created. It is convenient to create detail drafting entities on a layer separate from geometry so they can be manipulated independently of the geometry.

There are many detail drafting attributes that can be modified to produce the desired results on a drawing. Refer to Chapter 22 for a complete description of the Detail Menu.

Notes

A *note* is a passage of text placed on the drawing to convey information. Text in a note assumes the attributes currently established in **DETAIL–SET–TEXT**. Notes can be keyboard entered (**KEY-IN**), entered from **DISK** in ASCII format, or read from a text **FILE**. A note from keyboard or disk is saved with the part file. A note from file is not saved with the file but is linked to the part. When printed, plotted, or displayed, CADKEY Light must be able to locate and read the note. Use this option for notes exceeding 1024 characters. Figure 15-7 shows an example of a note on an engineering drawing.

1. SURFACES MARKED "X" ON RIGHT
   HAND & LEFT HAND SIDE OF HEAD
   MUST BE IN SAME PLANE.

Fig. 15-7. A detail drafting entity note. An <Enter> places copy on next line during text entry.

Labels

A label is a passage of text with a leader and an arrow and can be entered only from the keyboard. The text attributes of a label, like those of a note, assume those currently set in **DETAIL–SET–TEXT**. Use a label when a note pertains to a particular feature on the drawing and you want to point to it. Figure 15-8 shows an example of a label.

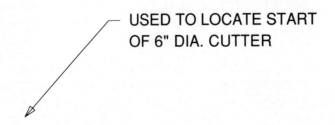

USED TO LOCATE START
OF 6" DIA. CUTTER

Fig. 15-8. A detail drafting entity label. The leader can extend from the right or left of the passage.

Dimensions

CADKEY Light produces dimensions parallel to the current viewport. For that reason, dimensions pertain only to distances normal in that viewport and not to dimensions in 3D space. For example, a vertical dimension in the top viewport would describe depth information from front to back.

If the object you are detailing is larger than the plotter paper size, you will need to **X-FORM—SCALE** the drawing. If this is done *before* dimensioning, the actual size of the object will be reduced, making dimension values not reflect the true size. If geometry and dimensions are scaled together, and the **AUTO UP** option is off, the values remain full-sized even though the drawing is scaled.

Hatching

When it is necessary to show an object in section, completely closed areas can be filled with a pattern of grouped lines. CADKEY Light provides seven patterns for cross-hatching (Fig. 15-9).

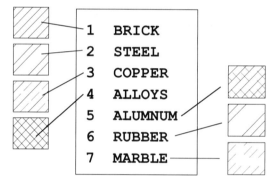

Fig. 15-9. Available cross-hatching patterns.

CADKEY in Industry

Making engineering drawings is serious business in engineering and technology. Most engineering projects require approval and funding appropriations long before the project is to begin. In addition, many who have to make decisions about the project do not have access to the design equipment that engineers use. These include managers, financial people, boards of directors, vendors, and regulatory agencies. Engineering drawings provide a transportable, reproducible, and effective means of distributing design information.

For engineering drawings to function they must adhere to exacting standards. Parts may be manufactured around the world by engineers and technicians speaking different languages. Engineering drawings must speak the same international language.

Many decisions previously made by engineers and draftsmen are programmed into CADD systems. Examples of these are line types and widths, standard dimensioning and tolerance symbology, hatch patterns, borders, and lettering. CADD operators must have a thorough understanding of these topics as well as shape and size description.

Though the emphasis of this book is on extracting drafting data from models, much engineering design is done in 2D. Some projects lend themselves to making engineering drawings during the design activity.

▼ BORDER AND TITLE BLOCK

Several **ANSI*** standard drawing sheet title blocks are available as CADKEY pattern files. Some of these have been included on your exercise disk and can be used to produce finished engineering drawings. Use the following steps as a general procedure for completing an engineering drawing:

1. Save model geometry in view position as separate patterns.

2. Place these patterns in alignment in a single viewport.

3. Edit model geometry into a standard engineering drawing and add detail drafting entities.

4. Save engineering drawing as a pattern.

5. Start a blank drawing.

6. Retrieve and place the desired border and title block at full scale.

7. Retrieve and place the engineering drawing inside the border. You may have to delete the drawing and replace it at a changed scale. Make sure that **AUTO UP** is set to **OFF** so that dimension values reflect their true sizes.

8. Add text to the title block as necessary.

9. Save drawing as a part with DWG included in its file name.

***ANSI** stands for the American National Standards Institute, an organization that establishes standards for engineering drawing sheet size and how most standard design components are shown and dimensioned.

▼ SUMMARY

For CADD to be used to its best advantage, model data are shared between the design process and engineering drawings. Since an unlimited number of views are possible with a 3D model, making engineering drawings from a model means less layout and drawing and a better assurance that the drawing reflects the shape and size of the design.

The technique most useful in CADKEY Light is one of capturing the model in various ZV orientations and saving these as separate patterns. The 3D patterns can then be arranged in a single viewport in traditional view-projection. It is from this multiple-model part file that an engineering drawing is constructed.

The models themselves provide the framework for the engineering drawing. Some model geometry may be deleted while additional lines are added to complete a description that adheres to drawing conventions. The model may be removed after enough drafting geometry has been found to make the drawing, or the model may remain, forming part of the drawing itself.

Detail drafting entities complete an engineering drawing. These entities include notes, labels, dimensions, and cross-hatching. The drawing can be saved as a pattern and scaled when being placed inside a border and title block. This final file is the result of nesting patterns within patterns within a part. When printed or plotted, you have a CADD engineering drawing.

▼ QUESTIONS

1. Explain the changing role for engineering drawings in light of CADD.

2. Describe what is meant by *postprocessing* the model's data base.

3. What is meant by "smashing" the data? Can CADKEY Light accomplish this?

4. What is the difference between geometric and drafting entities?

5. Can dimensions placed in the front viewport be made visible in the isometric viewport?

6. How many patterns of a model would be used to create a three-view drawing?

7. Describe a technique for distinguishing between a part file containing model geometry and a part file containing an engineering drawing of the model.

8. What is the difference between a **FILE** note and a **DISK** or **KEY-IN** note?

9. Describe the difference between a note and a label.

10. Must an area be completely closed in order to perform a cross-hatching operation?

11. What will happen to dimension values if geometry is scaled and **AUTO UP** is turned *on*?

12. How might layers be used to aid in producing engineering drawings?

13. Is it important to know what size paper on which an engineering drawing will be plotted? What two entity parameters might you have to adjust if this size changes?

CADKEY Light
Engineering Drawings

This exercise makes use of the pattern BASE.PTN that you used in Lab 10. It can be retrieved from your exercise disk.

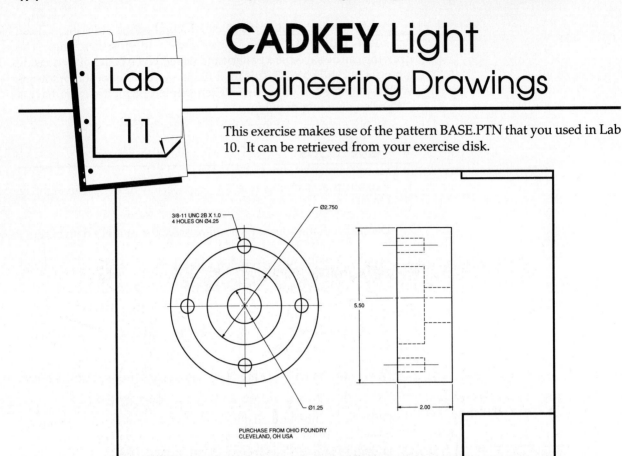

Start CADKEY Light with BLANK

1. **GRID:ON—ALL DSP; SNAP:ON;COORD:VW.**
2. Work in the default front viewport, View 1.
3. **ESC** to Main Menu.

Create Pattern of Right Side View

1. Insert exercise disk.
2. Choose **FILES—PATTERN—RETRIEV** and keyboard enter **a:base** <Enter>.
3. Accept all pattern defaults.
4. Allow the cursor to snap to a grid intersection and click once to place the pattern.
5. Insert your data disk.
6. Choose **FILES—PATTERN—CREATE—ALL DSP—ALL.**
7. **SNAP:OFF.** Choose **CENTER** from the Location Menu and select P1.
8. Keyboard enter **a:basers** <Enter>.
9. **ESC** to Main Menu.

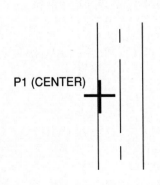

P1 (CENTER)

Create Pattern of Front View

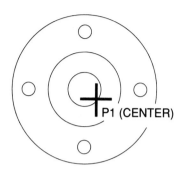

1. Choose **DISPLAY–VIEW–NEW–KEY-IN–RGT IN** and keyboard enter **90** <Enter>–**DONE**.
2. **ESC** to Main Menu.
3. Choose **FILES–PATTERN–CREATE–ALL DSP– ALL**.
4. Choose **CENTER** from the Location Menu and select P1.
5. Keyboard enter **a:basef** <Enter>.
6. **ESC** to the Main Menu.

Reload BLANK

1. **GRID:ON; SNAP:ON;COORD:VW**.

Place Right Side Pattern

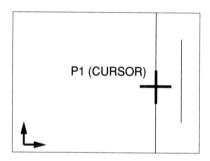

1. Choose **FILES–PATTERN-RETRIEV** and keyboard enter **a:basers** <Enter>.
2. Accept all pattern defaults.
3. Allow the cursor to snap to a grid point in the right middle of the viewport and click once (P1).
4. Press **ALT–H**.
5. **ESC** to Main Menu.

Place Front View Pattern

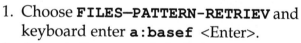

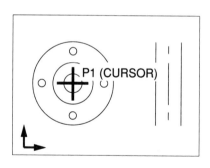

1. Choose **FILES–PATTERN-RETRIEV** and keyboard enter **a:basef** <Enter>.
2. Accept all pattern defaults.
3. Allow the cursor to snap to a grid point in the left middle of the viewport so that its center is in alignment with the placing point of the right side. Click once (P1). If views overlap or are separated by too much space, move pattern with **X-FORM–TRANS-A–MOVE**.
4. Press **ALT–A** <Enter>.
5. **ESC** to Main Menu.

Save Drawing

1. Insert your data disk.
2. Choose **FILES–PART–SAVE** and keyboard enter **a:basedwg** <Enter>.

Edit into Conventional Drawing

In order to complete drawing linework, point entities are placed at the top and bottom of the circles. Lines are created connecting the points.

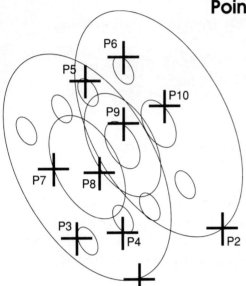

Points on Cylinders

1. Choose **DISPLAY—VIEW—NEW—KEY-IN—RGT IN** and keyboard enter **45** <Enter> **TOP OUT** and keyboard enter **35.267 —DONE** <Enter>.
2. Press **ALT—W** and draw a window around the model representing the right side.
3. Press **ALT—X** and select the color green.
4. Choose **CREATE—POINT—ON ARC** and select the circle P1. Keyboard enter **0** <Enter>.
5. Keyboard enter **180** <Enter>. Press **F10** backup.
6. **SNAP:OFF.** Select circle P2 and repeat for 0 and 180 degrees.
7. Select circles P3-P10 and place points at 0 and 180 degrees. **ESC** to Main Menu.
8. Press **ALT—X** and select the color white.

Cylinder Limits

1. Choose **CREATE—LINE—ENTPTS—POINT** and connect the points describing the outside of the body with solid lines.
2. Press **ALT—T** and select the dashed line.
3. Choose **CREATE—LINE—ENTPTS—POINT** and connect the points describing the tops, bottoms and depth of cylindrical cavities,
4. Press **ALT—T** and select the solid line.
5. **ESC** to Main menu.
6. Choose **DISPLAY—VIEW** and keyboard enter **1**<Enter>. The front view is displayed.

Delete Points

1. Choose **DELETE—SELECT—ALL DISP—BY TYPE—POINT—DONE**. Only the points are deleted. **ESC** to the Main menu.

Delete Pattern

1. Choose **DELETE—SELECT—GROUP—SELECT** and click once on the right side view (P1). The

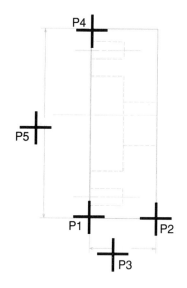

pattern is deleted, leaving the drawing lines. Press **CTRL–R** to redisplay the viewport.

Dimension Views
Right Side

1. **ESC** to the Main Menu. Press **ALT–A** to auto zoom viewport.
2. Choose **DETAIL–DIMENSN–HORIZTL–ENDENT** and select P1, P2, and P3. Accept if correct.
3. Press **F10** backup. Choose **VERTICL** and reselect P1, the select P4, and P5.

Front

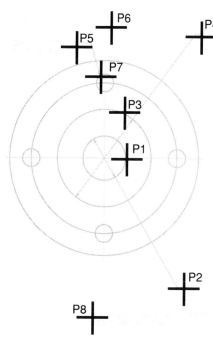

1. Press **F10** backup. Choose **DIAMETER**.
2. Select circle P1, text origin P2; Leader left.
3. Select circle P3, text origin P4; Leader left.
4. Press **F10** backup twice. Choose **LABEL**.
5. Keyboard enter **3/8-11 UNC 2Bx.35 DEEP** <Enter> **4 holes on 5.75 DIA**. Choose **SAVE TX–YES**. Select label position P5, leader side P6, and arrow position P7.
6. Press **F10, F10**. Choose **NOTE–KEYIN**.
7. Keyboard enter **PURCHASE FROM OHIO FOUNDRY** <Enter> **CLEVELAND, OHIO, USA** Choose **SAVE TX–YES**.
8. Select point P8 and click once.
9. **ESC** to Main menu. Press **ALT–A**.

Save as Pattern

1. Save all geometry in the viewport as **a:basedwg**.
2. Choose **CENTER** from the Locate Menu and select the Ø 5.5 circle as the pattern base.
3. **ESC** to the Main Menu.

Reload BLANK

Place Border

1. Choose **FILES–PATTERN–RETRIEV** and keyboard enter **a:bordb** <Enter>.
2. Accept all pattern defaults.
3. Click anywhere and press **ALT–A**.
4. **ESC** to Main Menu.

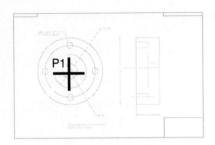

Place Drawing in Border

1. Choose **FILES—PATTERN—RETRIEV** and keyboard enter **a:basedwg** <Enter>.
2. Accept all pattern defaults.
3. Click at the position P1.
4. **ESC** to Main Menu.

Move Group if Necessary

1. Choose **X-FORM—TRANS-A—MOVE-GROUP—BY NAME** and keyboard enter the group name **basedwg.**
2. Click anywhere on the **basedwg** group.
3. Click on a new position for this reference point. Continue doing this until the drawing views are in the desired location.
4. **ESC** to Main Menu.

Add Text to Title Block

1. Press **ALT—W** and draw a window around the title block.
2. Choose **DETAIL—NOTE—KEYIN** and keyboard enter text appropriate for the different areas of the title block. Choose **SAVE TX** after each note.
3. Press **ALT—A** to auto zoom the drawing.

Save Engineering Drawing

1. Choose **FILES—PART—SAVE** and keyboard enter **a:basedwg** <Enter>.
2. **ESC** to Main Menu.

Plot Engineering Drawing

1. Press **ALT—A** to fill the viewport with the drawing.
2. Choose **CONTROL—PLOT—AUTO—NO—PEN#—ALL DSP—ALL**.
3. Turn plotter on and assure that paper and pens are loaded correctly.
4. Press <Enter>. CADKEY Plots the drawing contained in the viewport.

Experiment

You may notice that the depth of the Ø2.75 cavity is not shown. Turn the right side view into a full section and add this dimension.

End Lab 11

Technical Illustrations

▼ INTRODUCTION

A specialized use of CADD data is the preparation of technical publications—especially the preparation of pictorial illustrations showing the assembly of mechanisms. These illustrations are particularly useful in parts identification, training, maintenance, assembly, and marketing. Before CADD, engineering drawings were interpreted and the information contained in them translated by measuring or projection into pictorial views. These views were then rendered to give a realistic appearance with techniques such as line weight change to airbrushing.

CADD has changed this to some degree. If a part is described as a wireframe in 3D, as is the case with CADKEY Light models, much of the work in technical illustration has already been done—namely, the translation of principal (top, front, side) views into a pictorial orientation. It is the illustrator's job to take a viewing direction appropriate for the parts displayed and to place those parts in space so that they are shown to their best advantage.

CADKEY Light is capable of producing pictorial underlays over which traditional technical illustrations can be completed. In doing so, a 30%-60% time savings can be realized. Automatic hidden line removal is not a feature of CADKEY Light so the production of final engineering pictorial drawings is somewhat laborious, yet if the geometry exists in 3D data, the savings in layout time might well be worth the effort in manually editing the pictorial.

To be a technical illustration, a drawing has to be more than a simple single line weight pictorial. Note in Fig. 16-1 the subtle use of line transition, breaks, and line choice that gives the drawing a life like appearance even though it is just a line rendering. CADKEY Light can be used to selectively vary line weights according to the same rules that govern manual illustration, thus producing an approximation of a technical illustration.

179

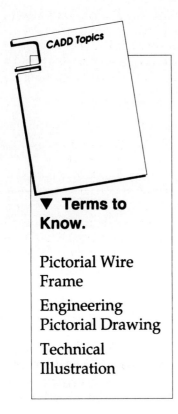

▼ Terms to Know.

Pictorial Wire Frame

Engineering Pictorial Drawing

Technical Illustration

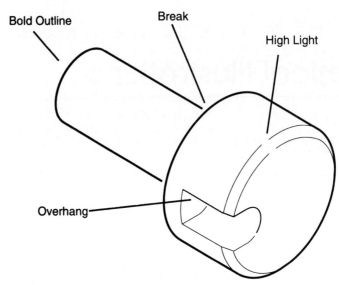

Bold Outline   Break   High Light

Overhang

Fig. 16-1. A technical illustration showing line weight rendering technique and cues to spatial depth.

▼ AXONOMETRIC VIEWS

CADKEY Light uses a parallel projection system that produces principal and axonometric views. Principal views are those in which two of the world axes appear normally and the third appears as a point. Axonometric views are those in which the world axes appear at angles. In CADKEY Light, you can view the world from any vantage, yielding an unlimited number of axonometric views.

The most common axonometric view is an *isometric view* where the three world axes appear equally angled—and thereby equally foreshortened (Fig. 16-2). Up to 90% of technical illustrations produced in industry are isometric for two reasons. First, in manual construction isometric does not require the use of special scales; second, because the axes are equally foreshortened, relative sizes in height, width, and depth can easily be compared. There are a limited number of isometric views. The isometric view in your template part **BLANK** is view 11. This was achieved by taking a new viewing direction from the front view:

RIGHT OUT 45   (this equally inclines the Z and X axes)
TOP OUT 35.266   (this equally inclines the Z, X, and Y axes)

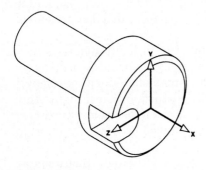

Fig. 16-2. An example of world axes in isometric position. Each axis is equally inclined to the viewport.

Were the first rotation kept at 45° but the second allowed to be some angle other than 35.266, the result would be a *dimetric view* where two of the axes are equally scaled but the third is different (Fig. 16-3). There are an infinite number of dimetric views. Measurements along the Z and X axes could be compared. However, distances along the Y axis could not be compared to those along the X and Z axes.

```
RIGHT OUT 45        (this equally inclines the Z and X axes)
TOP OUT ?           (the Y axis is inclined differently)
```

The third type of axonometric view is called a *trimetric view*. This describes the condition where the three axes are inclined unequally (Fig. 16-4). Distances along the three axes cannot be compared because each axis uses a different scale. Although trimetric axonometric views produce more realistic pictorials than do the other two, the difficulty in later combining portions of different pictorials makes trimetric appropriate for only specialized applications.

```
RIGHT OUT ?   (this unequally inclines the Z and X axes)
TOP OUT ?     (this unequally inclines the Z, X, and Y axes)
```

It is wise to consider an isometric orientation first. Because of its advantages, the vast majority of your illustrations needs can be met with an isometric. If certain geometric features are inappropriately hidden in the isometric, you may want to rotate or "tweak" the view slightly to get a better presentation.

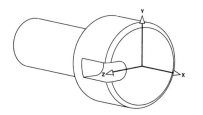

Fig. 16-3. A dimetric view where two axes (in this case Z and X) are equally inclined to the viewport.

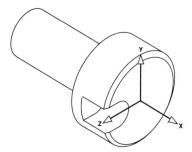

Fig. 16-4. An example of world axes in trimetric position. Each axis is unequally inclined to the viewport.

▼   USE AS AN UNDERLAY

If the part geometry is described in 3D, a print or plot in pictorial orientation will provide an accurate *underlay* over which a traditional manual illustration can be executed. Because in this case the wire frame simply provides the structure for the illustration, it does not have to be edited for visibility— the illustrator decides this while working on the finished overlay.

If the subject is a single part, it is unimportant where it is placed in space. However, if you are illustrating an assembly, the position of the parts one to another is critical in order to understand how the parts are assembled. You will probably want to begin with a main or central part into which the other components are assembled. Figure 16-5 shows an assembly with the central part identified.

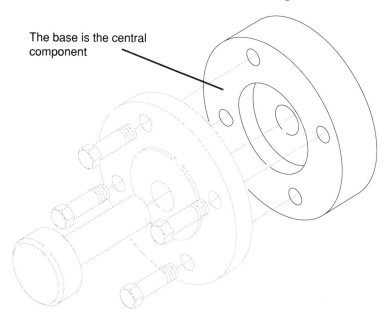

The base is the central component

Fig. 16-5. The central component in an assembly should be placed first.

To achieve optimum results, individual components of an assembly must be placed in space and the adjusted for desired spacing or overlap. To do this, consider these steps:

1. Save the components of the assembly as individual patterns with base positions on each axis of assembly.

2. Work in world coordinates.

3. Group each pattern when placing.

4. Place the patterns in a principal view without regard to depth position (Fig. 16-6) but in their correct position.

5. Switch to a single viewport and adjust axes for the desired view.

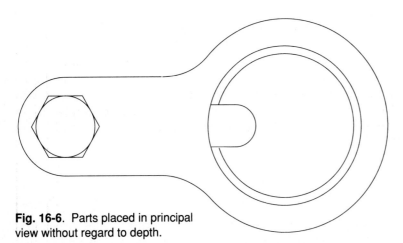

Fig. 16-6. Parts placed in principal view without regard to depth.

Begin with isometric (View=11).

6. Use **X-FORM** to move the patterns forward and back in world space until the desired view is achieved. Because you are using world coordinates, the parts are moved along world axes and not relative to the pictorial viewport (Fig. 16-7).

7. If necessary, use **DISPLAY—VIEW—NEW—ROT AXES** to "tweak" the pictorial view so that no important feature is hidden.

8. Use **DISPLAY—VIEW—SAVE** to save this new pictorial view. It becomes view 12.

9. Press **ALT—A** to auto zoom the pictorial.

Once the desired pictorial orientation has been achieved, the wire frame can be printed or plotted and used as an underlay for a traditionally rendered ink or polymer on mylar illustration. By carefully zooming the illustration, ellipses can be printed that closely match standard ellipse guide sizes.

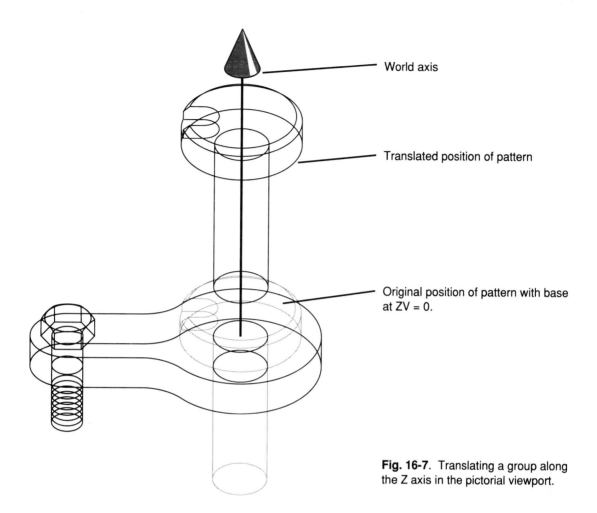

World axis

Translated position of pattern

Original position of pattern with base at ZV = 0.

Fig. 16-7. Translating a group along the Z axis in the pictorial viewport.

▼   EDITING FOR VISIBILITY

It may be practicable to use an engineering pictorial drawing—a pictorial that doesn't have variable line weights—as a finished illustration. To do this, the pictorial wire frame must be edited for visibility. This can be a laborious process but one that can produce credible results.

It should be noted here that once the editing process has begun, the visibility is correct *for that pictorial view only*. If the 3D data is subsequently rotated, visibility will be wrong (Fig. 16-7). For this reason, always keep an unedited version of the file so that the full wire frame can be reloaded and rotated into a new position if necessary.

The first step in editing is to **DEGROUP** all of the grouped components. This allows individual lines to be edited without answering questions each time about the group. Lines can be trimmed or extended or broken and the unwanted pieces deleted. Either method will produce the desired results. Save before a major editing sequence because CADKEY Light's **RECALL** command applies to deleted entities, not those that have been edited.

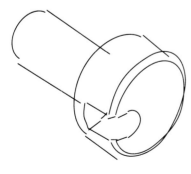

Fig. 16-8. The result of rotating an edited pictorial wire frame.

For example, consider the wire frame in Fig. 16-9. Limiting elements should be added as lines tangent to the appropriate ellipses. The ellipses can then be either trimmed and divided among the elements or broken with the unwanted portion deleted completely. The final visibility is shown in Fig. 16-10.

This editing process can be confusing at times when trying to decide what is in front and what is behind. You will want to work from near to far, starting with objects closest to you. Window up on individual intersections and zoom back to the complete component as necessary. Save the illustration *before* a major editing procedure.

The finished engineering pictorial can be used in lieu of a technical illustration. Because all lines are the same weight, less information is conveyed by the pictorial since many of the spatial cues present in a technical illustration are missing.

Limiting elements are 2D lines parallel to the pictorial viewport.

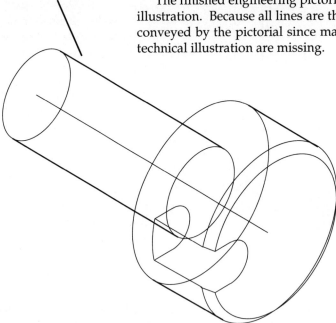

Fig. 16-9. Adding limiting elements to the pictorial wire frame.

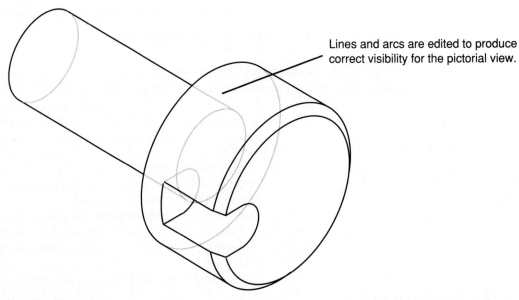

Lines and arcs are edited to produce correct visibility for the pictorial view.

Fig. 16-10. Trimming, breaking, and deleting elements to produce the correct visibility.

The finished engineering pictorial can be used in lieu of a technical illustration. Because all lines are the same weight, less information is conveyed by the pictorial since many of the spatial cues present in a technical illustration are missing.

▼   SIMPLE LINE RENDERING

You may want to apply rudimentary line weight shading techniques to CADKEY Light's pictorial engineering drawing. First, select all lines

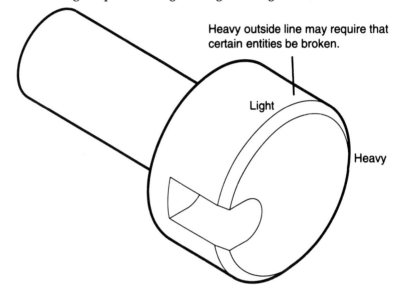

Heavy outside line may require that certain entities be broken.

Light

Heavy

Fig. 16-11. Outside lines changed to the third heaviest line.

and make sure they are the thinnest line.

Outside Lines

Change all outside lines to the third heaviest line (Fig. 16-11). This

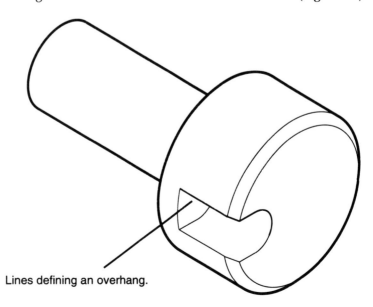

Lines defining an overhang.

Fig. 16-12. Portions overhanging are assigned the second heaviest line.

Highlights

Punch holes in lines that describe the top edges of cylinders (Fig. 16-13). This provides a certain "snap" to these lines. *Under no circumstance punch holes in outside or overhanging lines.*

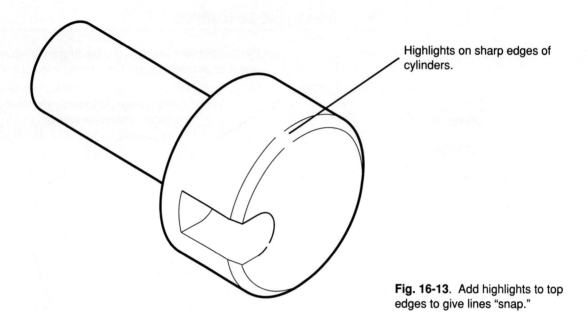

Highlights on sharp edges of cylinders.

Fig. 16-13. Add highlights to top edges to give lines "snap."

Breaks to Spatial Depth

Where one outside object line disappears behind another, the lines should not touch. Shorten the line to the rear so that a gap exists between the line to the front and the line to the rear (Fig. 16-14).

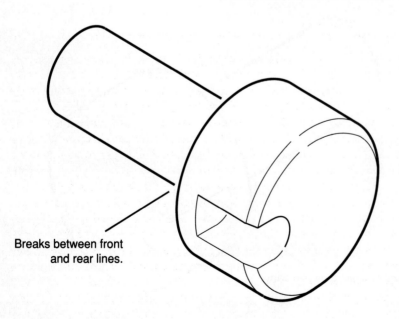

Breaks between front and rear lines.

Fig. 16-14. Shorten lines to the rear so that they don't actually touch the lines in front.

▼ CALL-OUTS

It is common that individual components of an assembly be identified either by name or by a reference number that refers to a listing in a bill of materials. CADKEY Light's **LABEL** detail drafting entity makes easy work of this. Call-outs can be aligned or freely placed (Fig. 16-15).

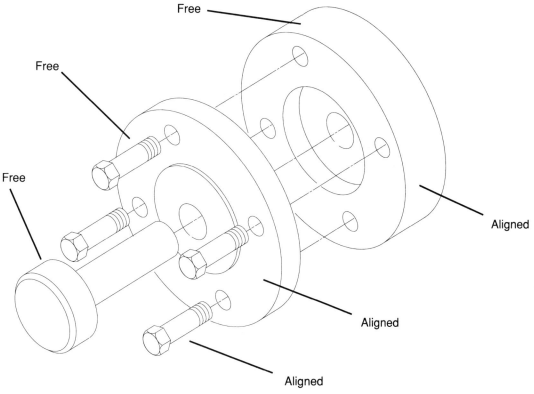

Fig. 16-15. Aligned and nonaligned call-outs.

▼ SUMMARY

Is CADKEY Light an illustration engine? Not in the sense that finished technical illustrations can be produced directly from the program. Accurate wire frame underlays can be produced that save considerable time over manual construction methods *if* the part has already been defined in 3D. This wire frame can be edited into an *engineering pictorial drawing* with uniform line weights. Or the attributes of this edited wire frame can be adjusted to approach the visual and spatial cues that are characteristic of a technical illustration.

The parallel projection system used by CADKEY Light produces orthographic views—both principal and axonometric. Axonometric views are those where the world axis system in inclined to the viewer, producing a *pictorial* view. Axonometric views can be *isometric, dimetric,* or *trimetric* depending on the number of axes that are equally inclined. Because X, Y, and Z measurements are equal and comparable in isometric, this pictorial view is preferred.

When used as an underlay, the CADKEY Light pictorial wire frame does not require editing. It may be scaled or zoomed before plotting so that ellipses will match standard ellipse guide sizes.

When the pictorial wire frame is edited for visibility, it becomes an engineering pictorial drawing and can be used as "quick and dirty" technical illustration. The editing process requires that groups be degrouped so that individual entities can be trimmed, extended, or broken more easily.

When line weight differences are applied to the engineering pictorial drawing, an even closer approximation of a technical illustration is achieved. By adding the visual cues of heavy outside and overhanging lines, highlights, and depth breaks, a better impression of the geometric characteristics is projected.

To identify individual components of an assembly, *call-outs* are used with part names, letters, or numbers. CADKEY Light uses the **LABEL** function to create a call-out with leader and arrow.

▼   QUESTIONS

1.   Describe the difference between an engineering pictorial drawing and a technical illustration.

2.   Why is it important to create a 3D part description for an eventual pictorial drawing?

3.   What is the difference between principal and axonometric views?

4.   Why should you first consider an isometric view for your pictorial orientation?

5.   Describe the difference, in terms of the inclination of the world axes to the viewport, of isometric, dimetric, and trimetric views.

6.   What does it mean to "tweak" a view? When is this done?

7.   Describe what results when a pictorial view that has been edited for visibility is rotated into a new position.

8.   Discuss the function of the four cues to spatial depth used when making a CADKEY Light technical illustration.

9.   What is a call-out? Which two methods of alignment can be used with them?

10. What is meant when it is said that the 3D data are used as an underlay?

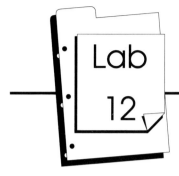

CADKEY Light
Technical Illustrations

This technical illustration exercise makes use of **HEXHEAD.PTN**, a pattern you created in Lab 10. On your exercise disk you will find **LINK.PTN** and **PIN.PTN**. These three patterns will comprise the components of an assembly you will edit into a technical illustration. You will be making an engineering pictorial drawing. Make sure that your exercise disk is in drive a: after you have turned on your computer and before starting CADKEY Light.

Start CADKEY Light with BLANK

1. Choose **DISPLAY—VIEW** and keyboard enter **1** as the number of the viewport <Enter>.

Retrieve Link

1. Choose **FILES—PATTERN—RETRIEV** and keyboard enter **a:LINK** <Enter>.
2. Group the pattern; accept all defaults.
3. Place the pattern anywhere in the viewport. Press **ALT—A** to auto zoom.
4. Press **F10** backup.

Retrieve Pin

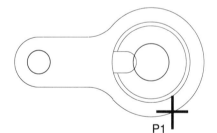

1. Retrieve **a:PIN**.
2. Group the pattern; accept all defaults.
3. Choose **CENTER** from the Location Menu and select P1 as the placing point.
4. Press **F10** backup.

Retrieve Hexhead

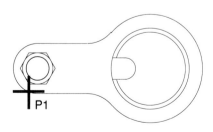

1. Assure that the disk containing your hexhead is in drive a:
2. Keyboard enter **HEXHEAD** <Enter>.
3. Group the pattern; use scale factor of **2**; accept all other defaults.
4. Choose **CENTER** from the Location Menu and select P1.
5. **ESC** to the Main Menu.

Change to Pictorial Viewport

1. Choose **DISPLAY—VIEW—NEW—KEY-IN—RGT IN**
2. Keyboard enter **45** <Enter>.
3. Choose **TOP OUT.** Keyboard enter **35.267**.
4. Choose **DONE. ESC** to the Main Menu.
5. Choose **DISPLAY—ZOOM—HALF**.
6. **ESC** to the Main Menu.

Reposition Hexhead

1. **COORD:WLD; CONSTR:3D.**
2. Choose **X-FORM—TRANS-R—MOVE—GROUP—BY NAME** and keyboard enter **HEXHEAD** <Enter>.
3. Keyboard enter + or - Z values until the pin is moved to slightly overlap the link. There is no change in X or Y values.
4. **F10** backup. **CTRL—R** to redraw display.

Reposition Pin

1. Choose **GROUP—BY NAME** and keyboard enter **PIN** <Enter>.

2. Keyboard enter + or - Z values until the pin is moved to slightly overlap the link. There is no change in X or Y values.
3. Press **ALT—A.**
4. **ESC** to the Main Menu.

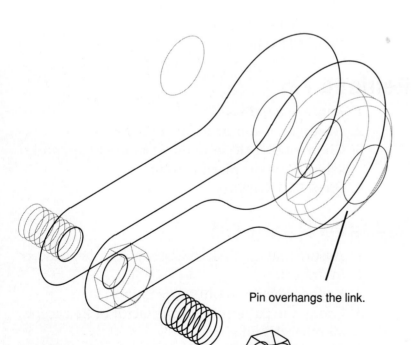

Pin overhangs the link.

The group HEXHEAD moved out along the Z axis.

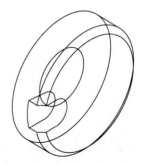

The group Pin moved out along the Z axis.

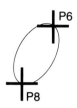

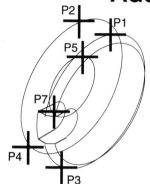

Save LAB12 on Your Data Disk

Add Limiting Elements

1. `COORD:VW; CONSTR:2D`
2. Press **ALT—W** and drag a window around the Pin.
3. Choose **CREATE—LINE—TAN/PRT—TAN TAN** and select the outer ellipse of the pin's head P1 and the rear of the head P2. Repeat for the bottom of the pin's head P3 and P4.
4. Select the beginning of the pin's shaft P5 and its end P6. Repeat this for the bottom limiting element P7 and P8.
5. Using the same procedure, add limiting elements to the top and bottom of the hex cap screw.

Add Flow Lines

1. `COORD:WLD; CONSTR:3D`
2. Choose **CREATE—LINE—ENDPTS—CENTER** and select the end of the pin P1.
3. Choose **DELTA** and rechoose **CENTER**. Reselect P1 as the delta reference point.
4. Keyboard enter Z=**-20**. There is no change in X or Y.
5. Repeat steps 1-3 for the hexhead's flow line.
6. **ESC** to the Main Menu.

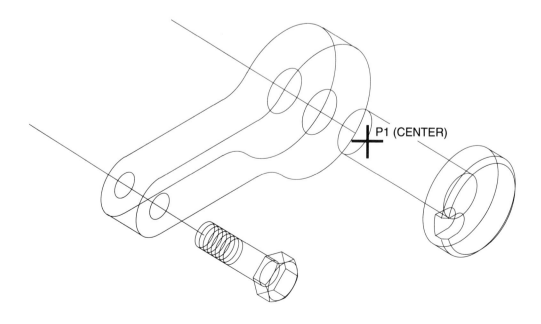

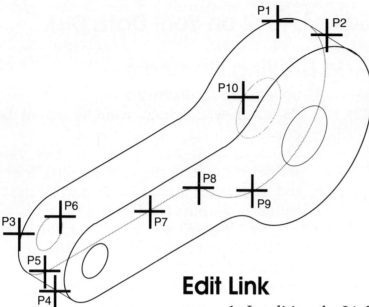

Edit Link

1. In editing the Link you will be performing one of the two basic operations used to turn the wire frame into a technical illustration: **breaking an ellipse**. You will want to come back to these steps when editing other objects.
2. Choose **EDIT—BREAK—FIRST** and select ellipse P1 and breaking entity P2; ellipse P3 and breaking entity P4. (You may want to use **ALT—W** to zoom up on the corner.)
3. **ESC** to the Main Menu.
4. Choose **DELETE—SELECT—SINGLE** and select entities P5- P10. Choose **ENTITY** each time you are queried.
5. Press **CTRL—F** to save. **ESC** to the Main Menu.

Edit Link Edge

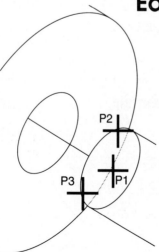

1. Choose **EDIT—BREAK—DOUBLE** and select the outer edge of the link, P1 and breaking entities P2 and P3.
2. **ESC** to the Main Menu.
3. Choose **DELETE—SELECT—SINGLE** and reselect P1 <Enter>. Choose **ENTITY** when queried.
4. **ESC** to Main Menu.

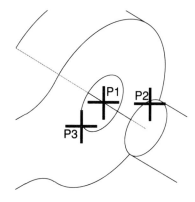

Edit Flow Lines

1. Zoom up on the Pin with **ALT—W**.
2. Choose **EDIT—TRM/EXT—FIRST** and select the flow line P1, trimming entity P2; flow line P1 again, trimming entity P3.

Edit Pin

Use the ellipse breaking and line-trimming procedures previously discussed to edit the Pin. Use **ALT-W** and **ALT-A** to display selected portions of the component.

1. Delete all full entities that are hidden.
2. Break ellipse at end of pin. Delete hidden portion.
3. Break ellipse at back of head. Delete hidden portion.
4. Break ellipse at rear of slot. Delete hidden portion.

Break Ellipse & Delete

Break Ellipse & Delete

Delete Ellipse

Trim Line

Break Ellipse & Delete

Delete Line

Break Ellipse & Delete

Edit Hexhead

Use the ellipse breaking and line-trimming procedures previously discussed to edit the Hexhead. Use **ALT-W** and **ALT-A** to display selected portions of the component.

1. Delete all full entities that are hidden.
2. Break chamfer curves on head. Delete hidden portions.
3. Trim limiting elements of fastener shank.
4. Break ellipses defining threads. Delete hidden portions.

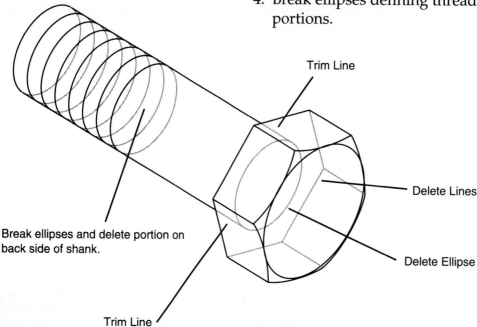

Trim Line

Delete Lines

Delete Ellipse

Break ellipses and delete portion on back side of shank.

Trim Line

Save Lab 12

End Lab 12

Experiment

Using the spatial cues of line weight, overhang, high lights, and breaks, continue to edit this engineering pictorial drawing into a technical illustration.

CADKEY Light **as a Design Tool**

▼   INTRODUCTION

This chapter presents methods and procedures for solving spatial and geometric problems. In traditional engineering drawing courses this has been the domain of *descriptive geometry* and has included true lengths, angles, and sizes; intersections and developments.

CADKEY Light provides two methods for determining this design data. First, viewing directions can be manipulated so that views are achieved that reveal the desired information. This is similar to view-projection in descriptive geometry. The other technique is to use CADKEY's ability to analyze the data base and display information about the geometry. This is done through the **CONTROL—VERIFY** command.

This chapter is by no means exhaustive of the methods available to aid in the design of mechanical or manufactured parts. It does, however, cover those topics of greatest interest and those which together can be used to solve more involved problems.

Being able to determine the normal or *true shape of a plane* is an important technique during design. Only when a plane appears normally can you do things like drill holes through it or cut it to a specific shape. Making flat pattern developments can be thought of as a process of assembling all of the normal planes of an object so that they can be folded in the correct manner.

If you can determine the *true angle* between planes or line elements, you can design connections, bracing, or gussets. This is a common procedure in structural design.

For piping and facilities design, it is often necessary to determine *shortest distances*. This might be between pipes for clearances, between flues or delivery tubes for connections, or between moving elements in an assembly to make sure that components don't interfere with each other.

By changing viewing direction, the intersection of geometric shapes can be determined. These intersections are important when determining clearances and when planning for openings in those shapes. By knowing the intersection, the amount of material needed to join the two—such as welding rod or adhesive—can be determined.

This chapter first presents an overview of fundamental design operations. This is intended to show you how geometric design problems can be solved. Then one of the techniques—finding the shortest connector between two lines—is explained in detail. In the laboratory exercise you will have the opportunity to implement these procedures.

▼   AN OVERVIEW OF DESIGN METHODS

Verify Coordinates

The **CONTROL—VERIFY—COORD** command provides information about entities and geometric conditions in the data base. For example, consider the lines in Fig. 17-1 to represent the axes of pipes. The coordinate location of the ends of the lines can be displayed on the prompt line using the **COORD** option. For example, you may wish to know how much higher one pipe end is than the other.

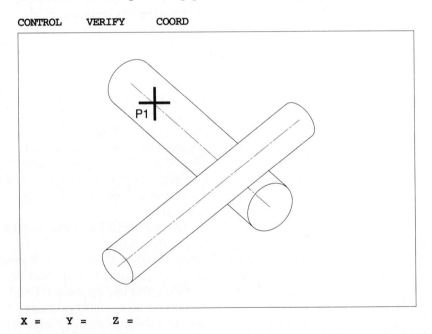

Fig. 17-1. Use verify coordinates to compare spatial locations.

Verify Angle

Using the **ANGLE** option, you can determine the true angle between any two intersecting lines—both the projected angle and the true angle (Fig. 17-2). This is a quick way to determine if you are looking normally at the plane containing the lines. If you are, the projected and actual angles will be the same.

`CONTROL    VERIFY    ANGLE`

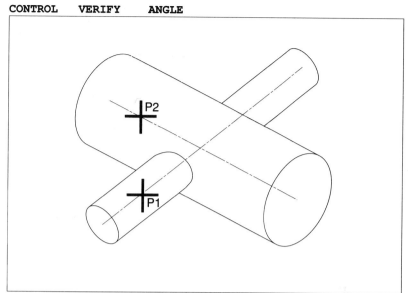

Fig. 17-2. Use **VERIFY ANGLE** to determine angle between intersecting lines.

`Angle in the plane of the lines =`

Shortest Distance

To arrive at the shortest distance between the two axes, system verification can be used to calculate this number. To determine the shortest distance between the two, ask CADKEY Light to determine the length of this connector by choosing **CONTROL–VERIFY–DIST** and choosing the two lines (Fig. 17-3). The shortest distance is displayed in the prompt line.

However, determining the location of this connector requires that you combine system verification and geometry rotation. This is explained in detail later and is the subject of the laboratory exercise at the end of this chapter.

`CONTROL    VERIFY    DIST`

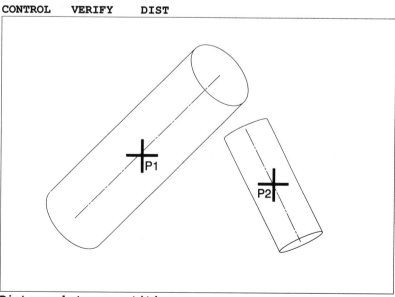

Fig. 17-3. Use **VERIFY DISTANCE** to have CADKEY Light calculate the true (shortest) distance between entities.

`Distance between entities =`

Normal Plane

Several methods are available to determine the normal view of a plane. The method used to determine the true shape of the planes connecting the axes in Fig. 17-4 (a) uses the **DISPLAY—VIEW—NEW—3 PTS** command. If the ends of the axes are used as the points using the **ENDENT** position mask, a new view is created normal (perpendicular) to the plane formed by the three points. This is shown in Fig. 17-4(b). Because the one axis formed by the three points is in that plane, it is also seen in true length.

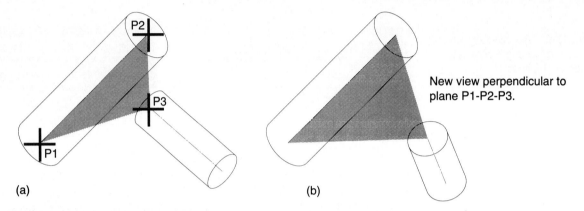

New view perpendicular to plane P1-P2-P3.

(a)   (b)

Fig. 17-4. Three points define a plane and a view normal to to that surface.

Intersections

Because CADKEY Light has the ability to trim, extend, and break entities, intersections can be found if one of the geometric forms has a sufficient number of elements to intersect and the other form can be viewed edgewise.

For example, two cylinders are shown in Fig. 17-5. One cylinder is defined by a number of elements and the other by the cylindrical surface edge (end planes). A view looking down the end of this second cylinder reveals where it crosses each and every element of the other cylinder (Fig. 17-6). When broken and removed, the intersection is found [Fig. 17-7(a&b)].

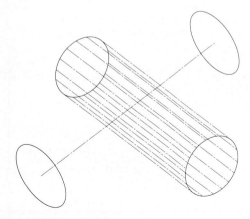

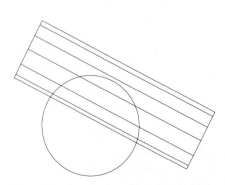

Fig. 17-5. Cylinders in space.   **Fig. 17-6**. End view crosses elements

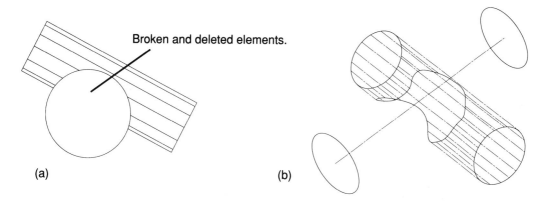

(a)

(b)

Fig. 17-7. Elements are broken and deleted, revealing intersection.

Developments

A development is the flat pattern which when folded up defines a 3D form. Some examples, such as double-curved (spheres, ellipsoids, tori) or warped surfaces, can only be approximated by flat pattern development. Prisms, pyramids, cylinders, and cones can be directly developed.

Figure 17-8(a) shows the front and top views of a prismatic shape. In the one of the two given views all four planes appear intrue shape. To construct a development, create patterns of the geometry defining each of the four planes. Begin a new part and place the patterns one to another, forming the development. Finally, change entity attributes so that folds are represented by dashed lines and the outside by solid lines [Fig. 17-8(b)].

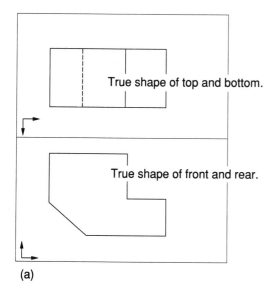

(a)

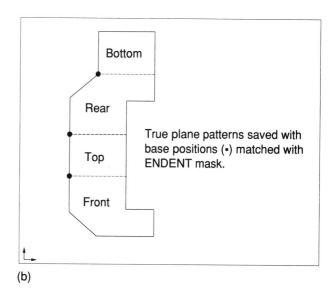

(b)

Fig. 17-8. Normal plane geometry saved as individual patterns and retrieved and placed on a development at construction depth.

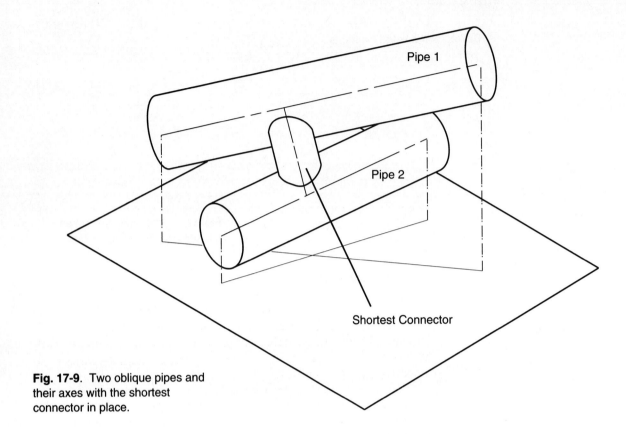

Fig. 17-9. Two oblique pipes and their axes with the shortest connector in place.

▼ A TYPICAL DESIGN PROBLEM

Figure 17-9 displays the situation that will be used to show CADKEY Light's design prowess. Two cylindrical pipes are in oblique orientation to each other. Their axes are represented by center lines in the examples that follow. A short connecting tube must be designed so that the two pipes are connected for support. To minimize material cost, this connector should be the shortest possible between the two pipes. This results in the connector being perpendicular to the two pipes. Remember, CADKEY Light will calculate the length of the connector. You must locate it by construction. You may want to change the color attribute of one of the lines to make the two easy to identify. To locate this connector:

1. Create a horizontal reference in the front view. Verify the 2D angle to determine the inclination above the horizontal (Fig 17-10).

2. Rotate all geometry the same number of degrees so the line is horizontal (true length in the top view). See Fig. 17-11.

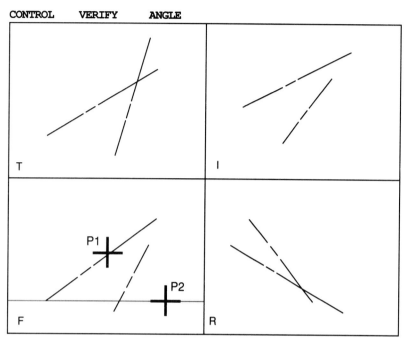

CONTROL   VERIFY   ANGLE

Angle in display plane =

Fig. 17-10. Verify angle to horizontal. Write this number down for future reference.

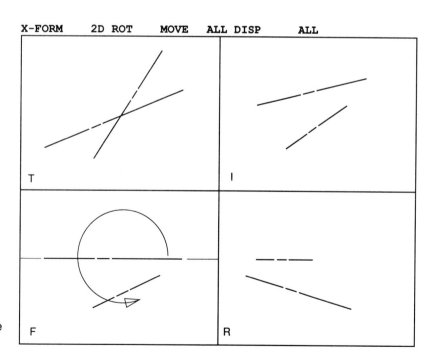

X-FORM   2D ROT   MOVE   ALL DISP   ALL

Fig. 17-11. Rotate geometry in the front view until line is horizontal. This makes the line true length in the top view.

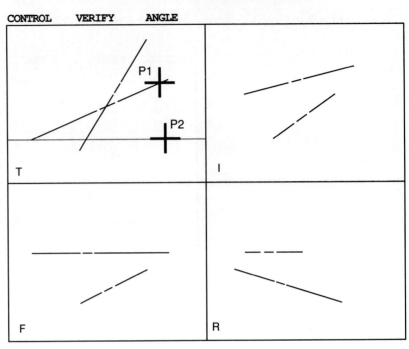

Fig. 17-12. Verify angle to frontal reference.

3. Create a horizontal reference in the top view through the end of the same line. Verify the 2D angle between the line and the frontal reference (Fig. 17-12).

4. Rotate all geometry the same number of degrees in the top view to get the line visually horizontal (Fig. 17-13). This line is true length in the front and top views and appears endwise in the side view.

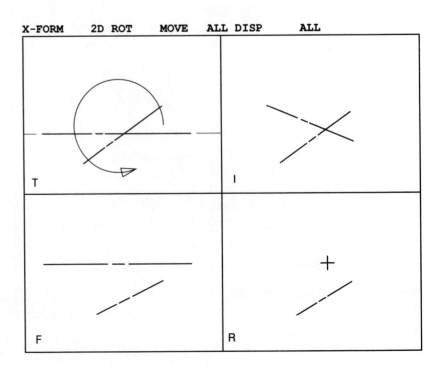

Fig. 17-13. Rotate geometry until line is frontal.

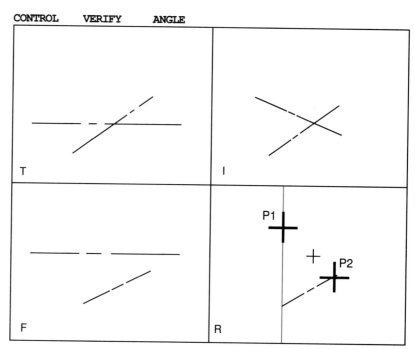

Fig. 17-14. Verify angle of second line to the vertical.

5. Create a vertical reference in the side view through the end of the other line. Verify the 2D angle to determine the inclination from the vertical (Fig. 17-14).

6. Rotate all geometry the same number of degrees so the line is vertical (Fig. 17-15).

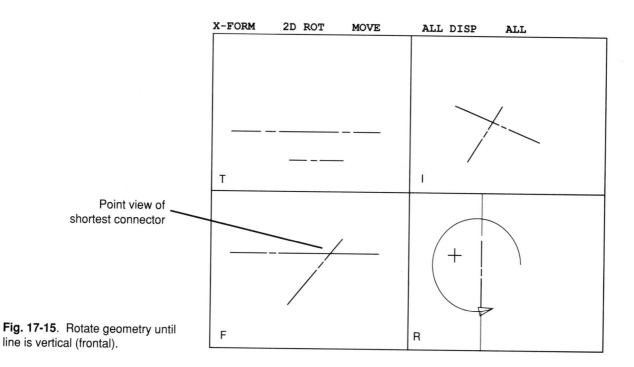

Point view of shortest connector

Fig. 17-15. Rotate geometry until line is vertical (frontal).

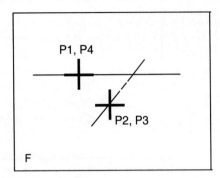 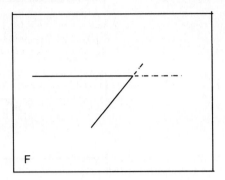

Fig. 17-16. Break axes at intersection.

7.   Both lines now appear true length in the front view. Their intersection represents the point view of the shortest connector (Fig. 17-15).

To construct this connector requires that you "trick" CADKEY Light. A line perpendicular to both axes cannot be directly constructed, but the lines *can* be broken at their apparent intersection and these breaks connected.

1.   Break both axes at the intersection of the other (Fig. 17-16).

2.   Create a line in either the isometric or top view using **ENDENT** location mask to connect the ends of the broken line (Fig. 17-17). This line is the axis of the shortest connector.

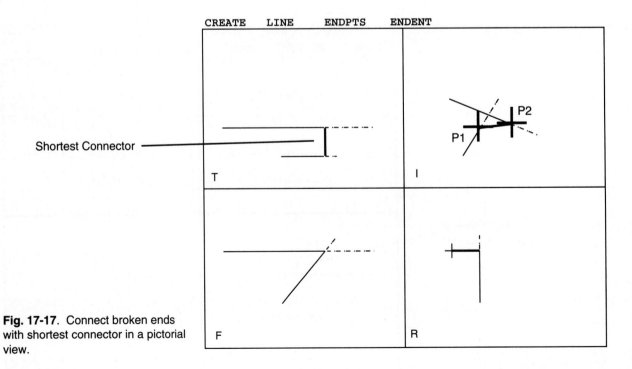

Fig. 17-17. Connect broken ends with shortest connector in a pictorial view.

▼ SUMMARY

CADKEY Light provides three methods for arriving at geometric design data: system verification, view change, and geometry manipulation. Through its **VERIFY** command, information such as coordinate data, angles, and distances can be automatically calculated and displayed. By changing view direction, spatial relationships can be examined and required geometry constructed. By keeping view direction constant and rotating the geometry, additional relationships can be determined. Any and all operations normally attributed to *descriptive geometry* can be performed by CADKEY Light.

Determining the *normal view* of a surface often requires the construction of two additional views using manual methods. CADKEY Light allows you to define a new view perpendicular to a plane defined by three points. Once this surface is displayed normally, it can be saved as a pattern, later to be assembled with other true shape patterns in a *development*.

Because CADKEY Light uses both 2D and 3D projective relationships, intersections can be found where entities cross visually. If you are able to view one surface as an edge and the other contains a sufficient number of surface elements to solve the problem, the intersection between the two can be determined.

It is often helpful to modify entity parameters—either color or line type—in order to aid in the design process. For example, you may want to make a cutting plane red and the object it is cutting yellow—just to be able to easily see the difference.

▼ QUESTIONS

1. Consider the difference between *representational geometry* and *descriptive geometry*. How might the two be different and how might they be used differently?

2. What is the difference between the angle between two lines in the projected view and in the plane of the lines? When might these two values be the same?

3. What is the *normal view* of a surface?

4. How can you tell if a normal view is displayed in a viewport?

5. How can you display the normal view of a surface?

6. In order to determine the intersections, must the entities actually touch?

7. What is a *development*? How is a development made in CADKEY Light?

8. Describe the difference between rotating a view and rotating the geometry within a view.

9. Define the terms *frontal*, *horizontal*, and *profile*.

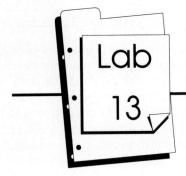

CADKEY Light
Design Exercise

This lab solves a basic design problem common in engineering and technology—locating the shortest connector between two skew lines. It also demonstrates the technique of isolating a problem with its fundamental geometry. Notice that only cylinder axes and ends are represented to solve this problem.

After the connector is found, it may be used to create a pipe which intersects the other two cylinders. Check the length of this line against the value CADKEY Light provides with **CONTROL–VERIFY–DIST**. Notice that CADKEY Light draws this line when it verifys the distance but that the line is only a marker and is not part of the geometric data base.

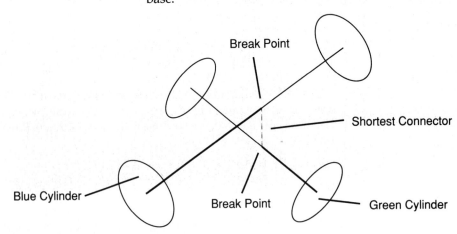

Start **CADKEY** Light **with a:LAB3**

1. **GRID:OFF; SNAP:OFF; COORD:WLD; CONSTR=3D.**
2. **ALEVEL=10; COLOR=2; LINE TYPE=2.**

Create Horizontal Reference

1. Choose **CREATE–LINE–HRZ/VRT–HORIZTL–ENDENT** and select the end of the blue line P1 in the front viewport.
2. **ESC** to the Main Menu.

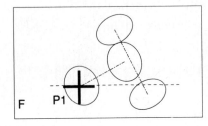

Verify Angle to Horizontal

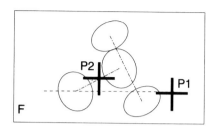

1. Choose `CONTROL—VERIFY—ANGLE`.
2. Select line P1, line P2.
3. Write down the value displayed in the prompt line as the angle in the display plane.
4. `ESC` to the Main Menu.

Rotate to Horizontal

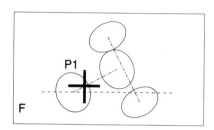

1. Choose `X-FORM—2D ROT—MOVE—ALL DSP` and click once in the front viewport, choose `ALL`.
2. Choose `CENTER` and select axis P1. Enter the value (-) you recorded above to rotate CW.
3. `ESC` to the Main Menu.
4. Delete the reference after rotating the axes.

Create Frontal Reference

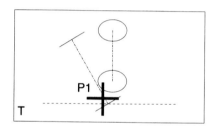

1. Choose `CREATE—LINE—HRZ/VRT—HORIZTL—ENDENT` and select the end of the blue line P1 in the top viewport.
2. `ESC` to the Main Menu.

Verify Angle to Front

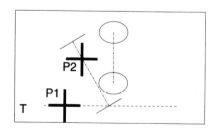

1. Choose `CONTROL—VERIFY—ANGLE`.
2. Select the red reference line P1, the blue cylinder axis P2.
3. Write down the value displayed in the prompt line as the angle in the display plane.
4. `ESC` to the Main Menu.

Rotate to Frontal

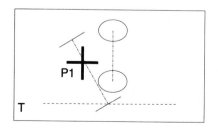

1. Choose `X-FORM—2D ROT—MOVE—ALL DISP` and click once in the top viewport, choose `ALL`.
2. Keyboard enter `1` as the number of desired copies.
3. Choose `CENTER` and select axis P1. Enter the value (+) you recorded above to rotate CCW.
3. `ESC` to the Main Menu.
4. Delete the reference after rotating the axes.

Create Frontal Reference

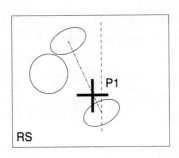

1. Choose **CREATE—LINE—HRZ/VRT—VERTICL—ENDENT** and select the end of the green line P1 in the right side viewport.
2. **ESC** to the Main Menu.

Verify Angle to Frontal

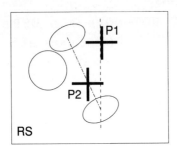

1. Choose **CONTROL—VERIFY—ANGLE**.
2. Select the red reference line P1, the green cylinder axis P2.
3. Write down the value displayed in the prompt line as the angle in the display plane.
4. **ESC** to the Main Menu.

Rotate to Vertical

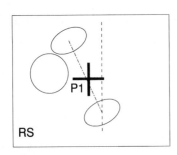

1. Choose **X-FORM—2D ROT—MOVE—ALL DSP**, click once in the right viewport, choose **ALL**.
2. Choose **CENTER** and select axis P1. Enter the value (-) you recorded above to rotate CW.
3. **ESC** to the Main Menu.
4. Delete the reference after rotating the axes.

Save LAB13 on Your Data Disk

Break Axes at Intersection

1. Work in the front viewport.
2. Press **ALT—X** and select the white color.
3. Press **ALT—T** and select the solid line.
4. Choose **EDIT—BREAK—BOTH** and select P1 and P2. **ESC** to the Main Menu.
5. CADKEY Light breaks the two axes at their projected intersection and assigns current entity parameters to the new sections of line.

Break Point (also the point view of the shortest connector)

Connect Broken Ends

1. Work in the isometric viewport. Press **ALT–W** and window up on the broken axes.
2. Press **ALT–X** and select the color red.
3. Press **ALT–T** and select the dashed line.
4. Choose **CREATE–LINE–ENDPTS–ENDENT** and select P1, P2.
5. **ESC** to the Main Menu.
6. Press **ALT–A** <Enter> to auto zoom all viewports.

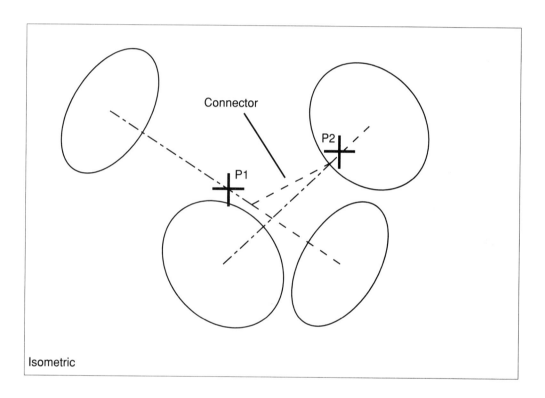

Connector

P2

P1

Isometric

7. Notice that this connector appears normally in the top and right side views. You may compare the length of this connector with the value returned by CADKEY Light when the **CONTROL–VERIFT–DIST** command is used.

Save LAB13 on Your Data Disk

End Lab 13

Experiment

Now that the shortest connector has been found, it can be used to define a cylinder. Assume that the connector's diameter is 50% of the diameter of the two pipes. Refer to the examples shown in Figs. 17-5 through 17-7 for the conceptual procedures necessary to solve this problem. Use the following steps as a guide.

1. Use **DISPLAY—VIEW—ENTITY** to achieve a normal view of the connector axis.

2. Repeat the sequence of reference creation, verification, and geometry rotation to get the connector into a position where a point view is seen.

3. Use **X-FORM—TRANS-A—COPY** and place a copy of the axis at the radial distance along the XV axis. This becomes an element on the surface of the cylinder and the one that will be copied around the axis to produce a cylinder.

4. Use **X-FORM—2D ROT—COPY** and place 12 copies at 30° using the shortest connector at the center and the **ENDENT** location mask.

5. View the blue cylinder from the end using **DISPLAY—VIEW—ENTITY** and trim the connector elements. See Fig. 17-7(a).

6. View the green cylinder from the end and trim the connector elements.

7. Return to views 1,9,10, & 11 and **ALT—A** <Enter> to fit the problem within the viewports.

PART THREE

CADKEY Light Menus

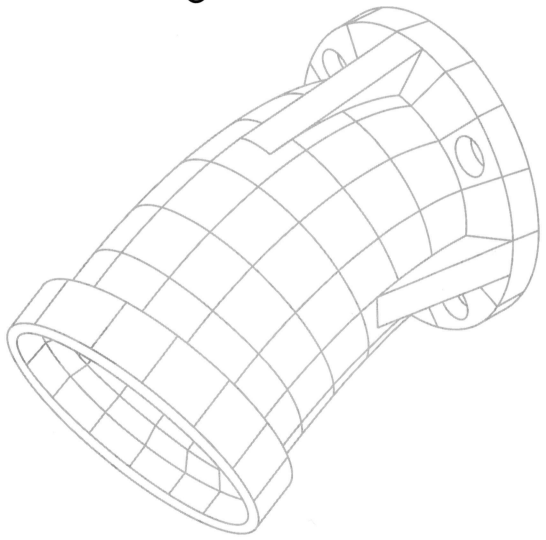

Position Menu

1	CURSOR
2	POINT
3	ENDENT
4	CENTER
5	INTRSC
6	ALONGL
7	POLAR
8	DELTA
9	KEY-IN

Required action / Method of indicating position

▼ HOW THE POSITION MENU FUNCTIONS

The Position Menu, also called the Location Menu in this book, offers options for indicating location in space and appears at appropriate times when creating geometry. The position menu cannot be selected directly but is displayed when an action in another menu requires location to be specified.

Each option displays instructions in the prompt line at the bottom of the screen. These instructions are divided into two parts separated by a slash (/). On the left of the slash is a description of the required action. To the right of the slash is the method used in locating the position. See the example of the prompt line above. Position menu options can be mixed and matched. For example, you can start a construction by locating the start point explicitly using the **KEY-IN** option and finish the action by using **ENDENT**. The most common mistake is to begin a construction using one position option and forget to change it for the second.

Not all position options may be available for the function you have chosen. When disabled, the option is replaced by a dash (-). When selected, an asterisk (*) is displayed beside the option. One position option can be used for the start of a construction and another selected for the end. If the cursor is not placed sufficiently close to a target end, center, point, or intersection, CADKEY Light will beep you and display an error message in the prompt line. Press <Enter> to reselect the point.

Locate by Cursor Position

1	CURSOR
2	POINT
3	ENDENT
4	CENTER
5	INTRSC
6	ALONGL
7	POLAR
8	DELTA
9	KEY-IN

Indicate start point / Cursor-indicate position

Indicate end point / Cursor-indicate position

▼   DESCRIPTION OF FUNCTION

A starting point is located by cursor position at the current working depth of the active view. If **SNAP** is on, cursor is attracted to snap interval. To use this function:

1. Select **CURSOR** from the Position Menu.

2. Move the cursor into the desired viewport.

3. Click once to indicate the start point.

4. Move the cursor to the desired endpoint.

5. Click once.

▼   OPTIONS

The start and end of the action do not have to be in the same viewport. Each position will, however, be at the construction depth of the view.

Locate to a Point Entity

1	CURSOR
2	POINT
3	ENDENT
4	CENTER
5	INTRSC
6	ALONGL
7	POLAR
8	DELTA
9	KEY-IN

Indicate start point / Select point

▼ DESCRIPTION OF FUNCTION

This function forces CADKEY Light to position the cursor at the location of a point entity. If 3D construction is selected, the cursor will be located at the X,Y,Z location of the point entity. In 2D construction, the cursor will be located at the projection of the point on the current construction plane. To use this option:

1. Select 2D or 3D construction from the Status Menu.

2. Select **POINT** from the position menu.

3. Move the cursor near the desired point entity.

4. Click once. If CADKEY Light cannot find the point or if a different point is located, you may want to either zoom in on the point or slightly rotate the view in order to get an unambiguous view of the point entity.

▼ OPTIONS

The construction can be changed from starting to endpoint by changing **CONST:** in the Status Menu. Note that CADKEY Light uses an "X "to mark positions. This is called a *point marker* can cannot itself be used for position.

Locate at End of Entity

1	CURSOR
2	POINT
3	**ENDENT**
4	CENTER
5	INTRSC
6	ALONGL
7	POLAR
8	DELTA
9	KEY-IN

Indicate start point / Select entity

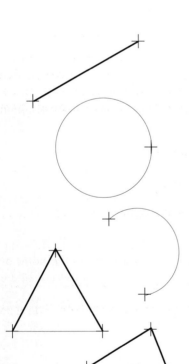

▼ DESCRIPTION OF FUNCTION

Lines, arcs, circles, polylines, and polygons have ends of entities. The end of a circle is the zero degree position on the circumference. The end of an arc is the nearest end point. The end of a polyline or polygon is the nearest vertex. To use this function:

1. Select **ENDENT** from the Position Menu.

2. Position the cursor near the desired end.

3. Click once. CADKEY Light moves the cursor to the end of the nearest entity.

▼ OPTIONS

In 3D construction, the position becomes the X,Y,Z location of the endpoint. In 2D construction the position is the projection of the point at the current construction depth.

Locate at Center of Entity

1	CURSOR
2	POINT
3	ENDENT
4	**CENTER**
5	INTRSC
6	ALONGL
7	POLAR
8	DELTA
9	KEY-IN

Indicate start point / Select entity

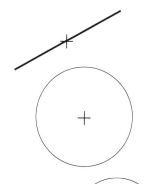

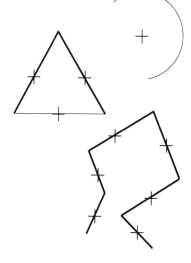

▼ DESCRIPTION OF FUNCTION

Lines, arcs, circles, polylines, and polygons haves centers of entities. The center of a circle is the actual radial center point. The center of an arc is the arc's center point. The center of a polyline is the midpoint of the nearest segment. The center of a polygon is the midpoint of the nearest side. To use this function:

1. Select **CENTER** from the Position Menu.

2. Position the cursor over the desired center.

3. Click once. CADKEY Light moves the cursor to the center point.

▼ OPTIONS

Not only can you change position option from start to end of action, each selection can be made in a different viewport.

Locate at Entity Intersection

1	CURSOR
2	POINT
3	ENDENT
4	CENTER
5	**INTRSC**
6	ALONGL
7	POLAR
8	DELTA
9	KEY-IN

Indicate start point / Select 1st entity

Indicate start point / Select 2nd entity

▼ DESCRIPTION OF FUNCTION

In 3D construction, the two intersecting entities must physically intersect or intersect by extension. In 2D construction the intersection is projected onto the construction plane at the current construction depth.

1. Select 2D or 3D construction option from the status menu.

2. Select **INTRSC** from the Position Menu.

3. Cursor select the first intersecting entity of the starting point (P1).

4. Cursor select the second intersecting entity (P2) of the starting point. CADKEY Light marks the intersection with a point marker. Note that this is not a point entity.

5. Change 2D or 3D construction if desired.

6. Repeat steps 3-4 for the end point of the construction.

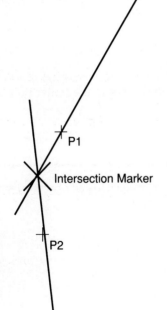

P1

Intersection Marker

P2

▼ OPTIONS

It is important to keep in mind the position option that has been selected. If, for example, the **INTRSC** option is still selected for the end point of the construction, CADKEY Light will look for an intersection. Change from 3D to 2D construction for entities that do not actually intersect.

Position Along Line

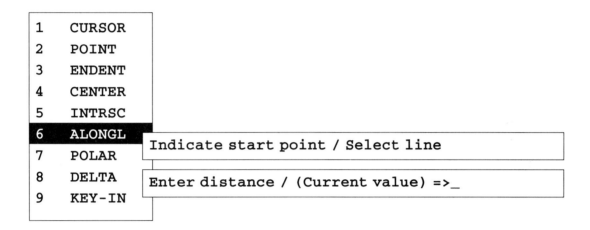

1	CURSOR
2	POINT
3	ENDENT
4	CENTER
5	INTRSC
6	ALONGL
7	POLAR
8	DELTA
9	KEY-IN

Indicate start point / Select line

Enter distance / (Current value) =>_

▼ DESCRIPTION OF FUNCTION

Allows position to be found a specified distance on a line from one of the line's ends. CADKEY Light marks the end from which the distance will be laid off with a point marker. The initial value displayed in the prompt line is the actual length of the line. In 3D construction, the position is on the line. In 2D construction, the position on the line is projected onto the construction plane at the construction depth.

1. Select **ALONGL** from the Position Menu.

2. Position the cursor near the end of the line from which you will be measuring and click once (P1).

3. CADKEY Light marks the reference end of the line with a point marker.

4. Keyboard enter the desired distance along the line from this reference.

5. Press <Enter>. CADKEY Light positions the cursor consistent with 3D or 2D construction.

Reference End
Point Marker

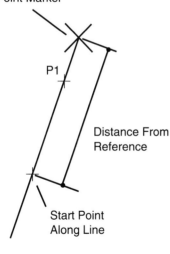

P1

Distance From
Reference

Start Point
Along Line

Polar Coordinate Position

1	**CURSOR**				
2	**POINT**	**1**	**CURSOR**		
3	**ENDENT**	**2**	**POINT**		
4	**CENTER**	**3**	**ENDENT**		
5	**INTRSC**	**4**	**CENTER**		
6	**ALONGL**	**5**	**INTRSCT**		
7	**POLAR**	**6**	**ALONGL**		
8	**DELTA**	**7**	**-**		
9	**KEY-IN**	**8**	**-**		
		9	**KEY-IN**		

```
Indicate polar origin / Cursor indicate position

                              Enter angle (0) =>_

                           Enter distance (0) =>_
```

▼   DESCRIPTION OF FUNCTION

Polar construction requires that a reference position, angle, and distance be specified. The reference or polar origin can be selected from a modified position menu as shown above. The angle is specified in positive degrees (CCW) or negative degrees (CW) from the polar circle's end. Distance is specified in current units.

In 3D construction, the depth value is the 3D position of the cursor. In 2D construction, depth is projected onto the current construction plane.

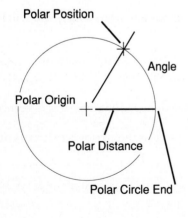

Polar Position

Angle

Polar Origin

Polar Distance

Polar Circle End

1. Select **POLAR** from the position menu.

2. Select the desired position option to locate the polar origin from the modified Position Menu.

3. Indicate the polar origin.

4. Enter the polar angle in degrees.

5. Enter the radial distance in current units.

6. CADKEY Light positions the cursor at the polar location and registers this as the start point before the construction.

Position From Reference

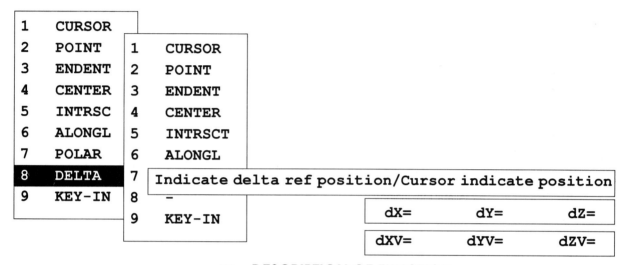

1	CURSOR
2	POINT
3	ENDENT
4	CENTER
5	INTRSC
6	ALONGL
7	POLAR
8	DELTA
9	KEY-IN

1	CURSOR
2	POINT
3	ENDENT
4	CENTER
5	INTRSCT
6	ALONGL
7	Indicate delta ref position/Cursor indicate position
8	-
9	KEY-IN

| dX= | dY= | dZ= |
| dXV= | dYV= | dZV= |

▼ DESCRIPTION OF FUNCTION

A **DELTA** position is located a specified distance from a reference position. The reference position can be any of the options in the position menu. In 3D, the reference position is at the X,Y,Z location indicated. In 2D, the reference is projected onto the construction plane at current construction depth. The offset from this reference is entered via the keyboard in current units.

1. Select **DELTA** from the Position Menu.

2. Select a position option from the modified Position Menu.

3. Locate the reference position.

4. Keyboard enter the X,Y,Z offset values. Press <Enter> after each value.

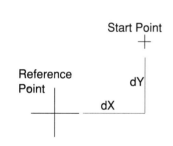

▼ OPTIONS

Either world or view coordinates can be in effect when using this position option. Offsets are labeled dX, dY, dZ in world coordinates and dXV, dYV, dZV in view coordinates.

Keyboard Enter Coordinates

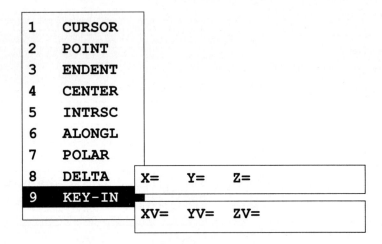

1	CURSOR
2	POINT
3	ENDENT
4	CENTER
5	INTRSC
6	ALONGL
7	POLAR
8	DELTA
9	KEY-IN

X=   Y=   Z=

XV=   YV=   ZV=

▼ DESCRIPTION OF FUNCTION

The precise location of start and end points can be entered via the keyboard by using the **KEY-IN** option. This option can be used in conjunction with any of the other position options.

1. Select **WLD** or **VW** coordinates from the Status Menu.

2. Select **KEY-IN** from the Position Menu.

3. Keyboard enter values for the Cartesian location.

4. Press <Enter> after each entry.

5. CADKEY Light positions the cursor at the exact Cartesian coordinates that were entered.

▼ OPTIONS

It is important to preselect world or view coordinates before beginning this command.

Masking Menu

▼ DESCRIPTION OF MASKING

To mask in CADKEY Light means to limit the system's search for certain entity types or attributes. In addition, masking can be done on levels. Masking can be performed on three types of data:

- Geometric entities (lines, arcs, etc.)
- Drafting entities (dimensions, notes, etc.)
- Attribute types (color, weight, type, etc.)

If entities conforming to the mask cannot be found, an error message is displayed in the prompt line. Press <Enter> and rechoose masking options. The view direction or display scale may need to be changed to include the target entity or entities in the viewport.

Masking as Part of the Command Sequence

The Masking Menu will appear any time a selection is made either *by type*, which sets inclusion, or *ex type*, which sets exclusion. If entities are included, they will be acted upon (deleted, moved, scaled, etc.). If entities are excluded, they will not be acted upon.

Masking as an Immediate Mode Command

Any command sequence can be interrupted by an *Immediate Command* (ALT-M) that invokes the Masking Menu. After masking toggles are set and control is returned to the function that was interrupted, the masks are active for that action.

The Difference Between DONE and <Enter>

Use <Enter> to move between Masking Menu options while turning toggles on. Use **DONE** or <Enter> to quit masking and return to the function that called the Masking Menu.

CALLING FUNCTION

MASKING MENU

GEOM	<Enter>
DETAIL	<Enter>
COLOR	<Enter>
L-TYPE	<Enter>
L-WIDTH	<Enter>
PEN #	<Enter>
DONE	

<Enter>

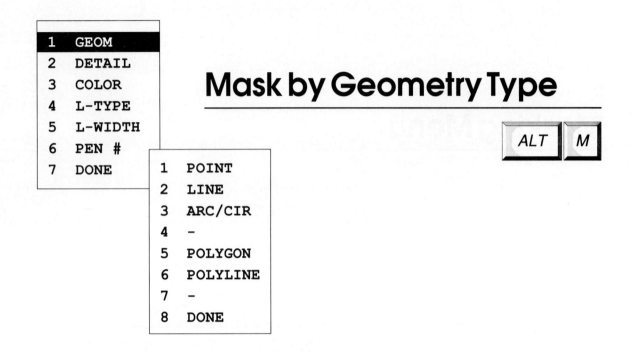

Mask by Geometry Type

ALT   M

▼ **DESCRIPTION OF FUNCTION**

Geometric entities may be masked by their type. Press <Enter> within each option to stay within the Masking Menu. Choose **DONE** to exit and execute the calling function.

▼ **OPTIONS**

POINT masks to point entities on all active layers. Point markers, because they are not geometric or drafting entities, cannot be masked.

LINE masks to line entities. Although an entity may appear as a line, it may in fact be a polyline or part of a polygon. Also, an arc of unusually large radius may appear to be a line.

ARC/CIR masks to either an arc or a circle.

POLYGON masks to polygon entities. What appears to be a polygon may actually be a pattern of line entities.

POLYLINE masks on polyline entities. If a polyline polygon (**N-GON**) has been created, it may be mistaken for a polygon.

DONE signals that you are finished choosing masking options in the current menu. Entities are selected, acted upon, and you are returned to the function that called the Masking Menu.

Multiple selections can, and should be made, one after the other before exiting the function. For example, if **POINT**, **LINE**, and **ARC/CIR** are chosen one after the other, the prompt line would read

```
Choose item(s) to mask on (current = 1-3)
```

An Example of Masking

To illustrate the process of masking, assume that four geometric entities are in the viewport:

- A solid black line 1 pixel wide (L1).

- A dashed black line 1 pixel wide (L2).

- A dashed red line 1 pixel wide (L3).

- A solid black arc 1 pixel wide (L4).

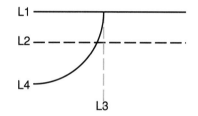

The dashed red line needs to be deleted. You wish to use the window option to delete the line.

1. Choose the delete option: **DELETE-SELECT-WINDOW**.

2. Invoke the Immediate Command **ALT—M**. The current command is interrupted and the Masking Menu is displayed.

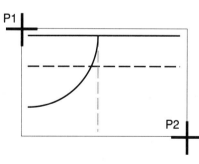

3. From the Masking Menu choose **GEOM—LINE** <Enter>. You stay in the Masking Menu.

4. From the Masking Menu choose **L—TYPE—DASHED** <Enter>. You stay in the Masking Menu.

5. From the Masking Menu choose **COLOR—RED** <Enter>. You stay in the Masking Menu.

5. From the Masking Menu choose **DONE**. You are returned to the **DELETE—SELECT—WINDOW** function ready to identify the selection window.

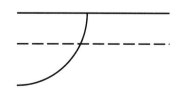

7. Click once to identify one corner of the window (P1).

8. Pull the window until all entities are included. Click the opposite corner of the selection window (P2).

9. The mask is in effect. Only red dashed lines are deleted.

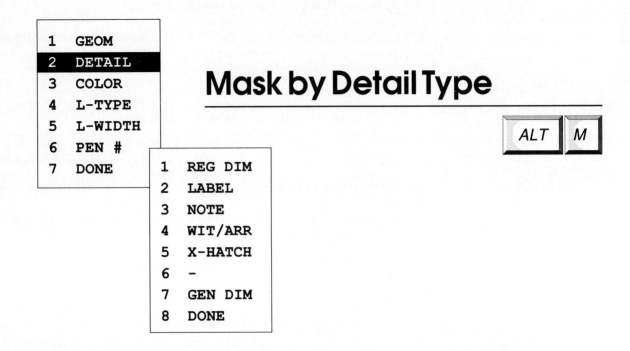

Mask by Detail Type

ALT   M

▼   **DESCRIPTION OF FUNCTION**

A *detail* is a non-geometric drafting entity. To mask on a detail removes the possibility of selecting model geometry by mistake.

▼   **OPTIONS**

REG DIM masks on angular, diameter, radial, and linear dimensions. A linear dimension can be horizontal, vertical, or parallel.

LABEL masks on label text.

NOTE masks on note text. Whether a block of text is a note or a label without a leader may not be readily apparent.

WIT/ARR masks on witness (extension lines in dimensioning) or on arrows.

X-HATCH masks on cross hatching.

GEN DIM masks on generic dimensions.

DONE signals that you are finished choosing masking options in the current menu. Entities are selected, acted upon, and you are returned to the function that called the Masking Menu.

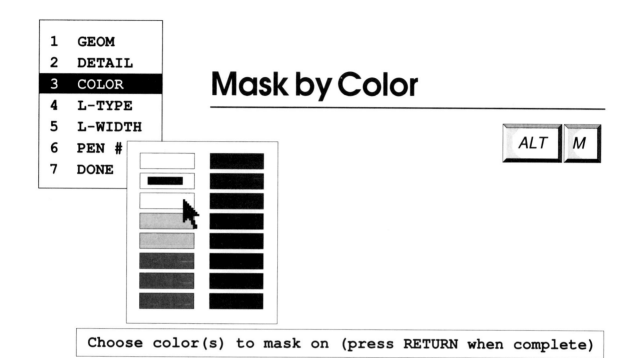

1	GEOM
2	DETAIL
3	COLOR
4	L-TYPE
5	L-WIDTH
6	PEN #
7	DONE

Mask by Color

ALT   M

```
Choose color(s) to mask on (press RETURN when complete)
```

▼ DESCRIPTION OF FUNCTION

This function allows masking of **GEOM** and **DETAIL** entities by color. When this option is chosen, a palette of colors is displayed. These colors are those available dependent on the graphics device installed and identified in the **CONFIG** program. All valid colors are displayed, although not all may be assigned to entities in the part file.

1. Move the cursor into the color palette. It changes to a pointer.

2. Choose the desired masking color by clicking once on that color. Deselect by clicking once again.

3. A dark panel appears on the color, signifying that it is an active mask.

4. Press <Enter> to accept the color mask.

5. Choose **DONE** to exit the Masking Menu. You are returned to the calling function and the function is executed.

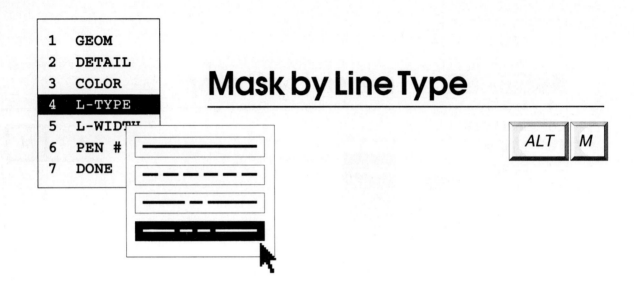

Mask by Line Type

| ALT | M |

▼ **DESCRIPTION OF FUNCTION**

Masking may be done by line type, sometimes called line style or line font. The four standard line types are solid, dashed, center, and phantom or cutting plane. When chosen, the line type appears in reverse video. Each line type may take on any of the eight widths as discussed on the next page.

1. Move the cursor into the type palette. It turns into a pointer.

2. Click once to select the type for masking. Click once on the style to deselect. When selected, the line appears in reverse video.

3. Press <Enter> to accept the chosen line mask.

4. Choose **DONE** to exit the Masking Menu. You are returned to the calling function and the function is executed.

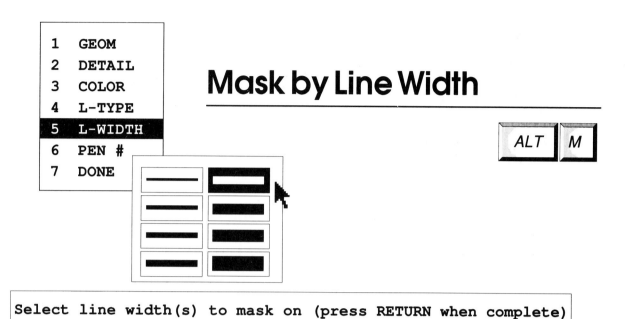

Mask by Line Width

```
1   GEOM
2   DETAIL
3   COLOR
4   L-TYPE
5   L-WIDTH
6   PEN #
7   DONE
```

$$\boxed{ALT} \quad \boxed{M}$$

```
Select line width(s) to mask on (press RETURN when complete)
```

▼   DESCRIPTION OF FUNCTION

Lines created in CADKEY Light can be 1, 3, 5, 7, 9, 11, 13, or 15 pixels in width. Line widths correspond to printer dot width or plotter pen stroke. For example, with the default pen width set to 1 (.3mm) in the **CONFIG** program, a line 3 pixels wide will print using 3 printer dots or 3 pen strokes. Line widths greater than 1 stroke produce corners that are not filled. Polylines produce connected ends and corners.

1. Move the cursor into the line palette. The cursor changes to a pointer.

2. Click once to choose a line width. Click again to toggle the selection off. When on, the line appears in reverse video.

3. Press <Enter> to accept the line width masks.

4. Choose **DONE** to exit the Masking Menu. You are returned to the calling function and the function is executed.

```
1   GEOM
2   DETAIL
3   COLOR
4   L-TYPE
5   L-WIDTH
6   PEN #
7   DONE
```

Mask by Pen Number

ALT M

```
Enter pen number(s) to mask on (current = ) =>_
```

▼   DESCRIPTION OF FUNCTION

When a CADKEY Light part file is sent to a plotter, entities in the data base can be assigned pen positions for execution on the plotting device. Plotters with 1-8 pens are supported by CADKEY Light. Note that there is an independent relationship between line width, as expressed in pixels, and pen # width, which is usually expressed in millimeters.

1.   Keyboard enter the number (1-8) for pen position on which to mask.

2.   Use hyphens (i.e., 1-4) to include a range of pens.

3.   <Enter> when done.

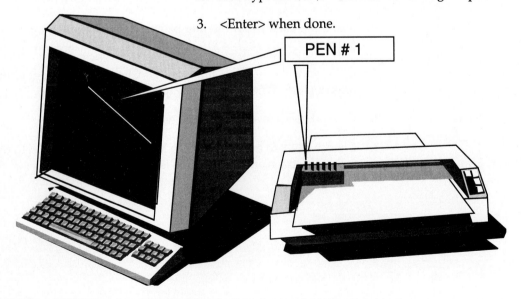

PEN # 1

1	GEOM
2	DETAIL
3	COLOR
4	L-TYPE
5	L-WIDTH
6	PEN #
7	DONE

Masking Completed

▼ DESCRIPTION OF FUNCTION

Choosing **DONE** signals CADKEY Light that all masking choices within the Masking Menu are complete. Control is returned to the function that either automatically invoked the Masking Menu, or the place in the command sequence that was interrupted to invoke the Masking Menu. Press **ESC** to exit the Masking Menu and return to the Main Menu without executing the calling function. Press **F10** backup to exit the Masking Menu and return to the current function.

Create Menu

▼ CREATING ENTITIES

This menu provides the tools to create model geometry. Many of the tools operate differently in 2D and 3D space so it is necessary to observe the status of the **CONST** switch in the Status Menu.

The Create Menu contains three levels:

> Level 1—Entities
> Level 2—Methods
> Level 3—Position

Entities are the geometric objects or primitives available in CADKEY Light. CADKEY Light considers all vectors making up entities to be curves, even though a particular curve may be called a line. This reference to curves may show up in the prompt.

Methods are the techniques available to construct the selected entity. As you might expect, the various entities have their own unique methods.

Position menu choices appear after a method has been chosen. Generally, this menu is identical for all entities unless a method for a particular entity precludes a location option. See pages 213-222 for a description of position options.

Line by Endpoints

1	CREATE
2	
3	
4	
5	
6	
7	
8	

1	LINE
2	ARC
3	CIRCL
4	POINT
5	POLYI
6	FILLE
7	-
8	POLYG

1	ENDPTS
2	STRING
3	PARALEI
4	TAN/PRE
5	HRZ/VRI
6	ANGLE
7	RECTANG
8	N-GON

1	CURSOR
2	POINT
3	ENDENT
4	CENTER
5	INTRSC
6	ALONGL
7	POLAR
8	DELTA
9	KEY-IN

▼ DESCRIPTION OF FUNCTION

ENDPTS allows the creation of lines by identifying each line's endpoints. A line can be 2D, in which case the line is constructed in the current view at construction depth. In 3D, endpoints assume the coordinates of the cursor in X,Y,Z space.

ENDPTS is used to create individual line entities. Any option from the Position Menu can be used to locate the endpoints. This command stays active, allowing the creation of additional lines. Use **ESC** to exit to the Main Menu.

Lines in 3D models represent the intersection of surfaces or solids or may be *elements* of the surfaces themselves. Lines in 2D drawings may represent intersections, as in 3D models, or may be used to show planes as they appear as *edges* or surfaces where a change of direction defines a *limit*.

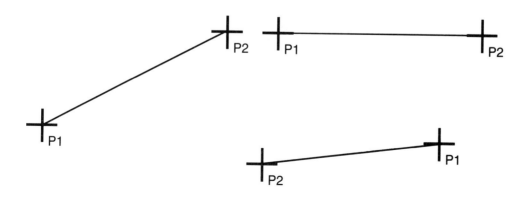

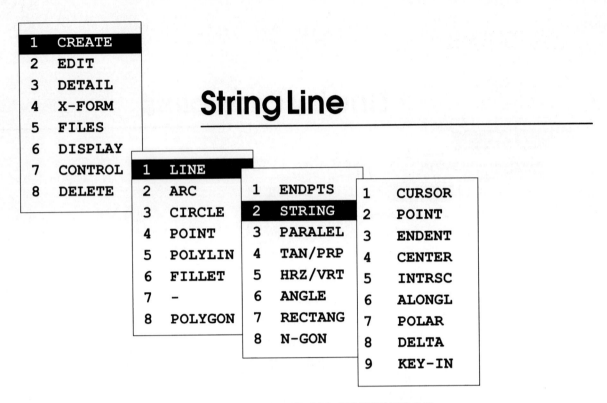

String Line

▼ **DESCRIPTION OF FUNCTION**

A string line assumes that the end of the last line created will be used as the beginning position of the next line. A string line is composed of individual line entities although they are physically connected. In 2D construction, the string line is created at construction depth in the current view. In 3D, the string line endpoints assume the 3D coordinates of the cursor.

This function remains active until **ESC** is pressed. All position options from the Position Menu are available to locate string endpoints.

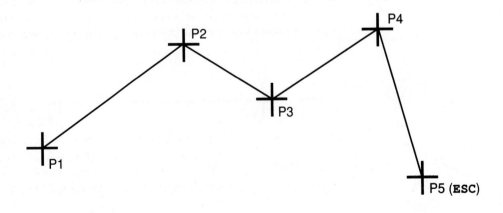

1	CREATE
2	EDIT
3	DETAIL
4	X-FORM
5	FILES
6	DISPLAY
7	CONTROL
8	DELETE

1	LINE
2	ARC
3	CIRCLE
4	POINT
5	POLYLIN
6	FILLET
7	-
8	POLYGON

1	ENDPTS
2	STRING
3	PARALEL
4	TAN/PRP
5	HRZ/VRT
6	ANGLE
7	RECTANG
8	N-GON

1	THRU PT
2	AT DIST

Parallel Line

▼ DESCRIPTION OF FUNCTION

A line can be constructed parallel to an existing line using one of two methods. In each case, the created line will be the same length as the original line. Control remains in this command, allowing a series of parallel lines to be constructed. Use **ESC** to return to the Main Menu.

▼ OPTIONS

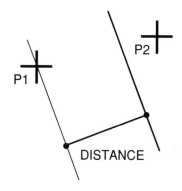

THRU PT creates a line parallel to an existing line through a point not on the line. This point can be any option from the Position Menu. In 2D, the line is projected to the current view (the view in which you define the point through which the parallel line must pass) at construction depth. In 3D, the line will lie in a plane formed by the referenced line and the point.

AT DIST creates a line parallel to an existing line at a specified distance. This action produces a parallel line of the same length as the referenced line in the current view at construction depth in either 2D or 3D construction. Note that P2 only identifies the side of the line on which the distance is measured.

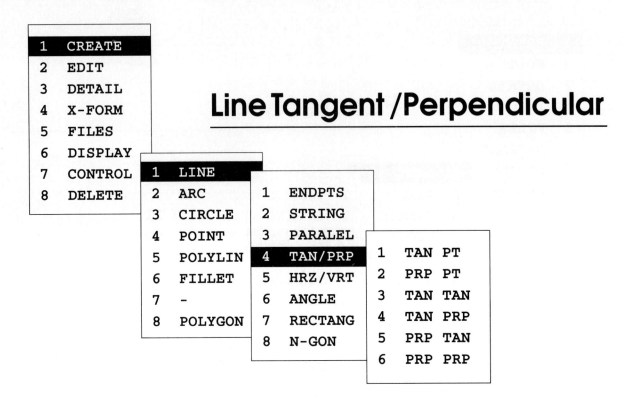

Line Tangent /Perpendicular

▼ **DESCRIPTION OF FUNCTION**

A line can be created tangent to an arc (which may be a circle) through a point, or to two arcs. In 2D construction, the tangent line is created in the current view at construction depth. In 3D, the entities must lie in the same plane.

Perpendicular lines must connect coplanar entities. In 3D, the perpendicular is created in the plane of the entities. An error message will alert you that the selected entities are not coplanar.

▼ **OPTIONS**

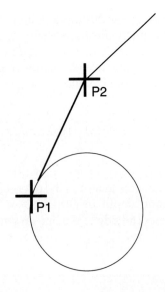

TAN PT creates a line tangent to an arc (circle) through a point and can use any point identified by the Position Menu. Select the arc near the anticipated point of tangency because more than one tangent condition may exist. The two entities must be coplanar or an error message will be displayed at the prompt line.

In the example to the left, P1 identifies the circle near the anticipated point of tangency. P2 uses the **ENDENT** position option to identify the end of a line entity. The tangent line is created between the circle and the end of the line.

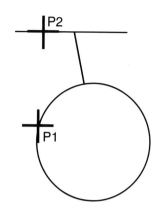

PRP PT creates a line perpendicular to an arc or line through a point not on the line. Any option from the Position Menu can be used to identify the point. A line perpendicular to an arc will pass, if extended, through the center of the arc. In the example to the left, a line has been created perpendicular to the circle using the **CENTER** option from the Position Menu.

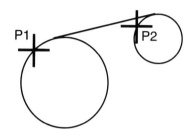

TAN TAN creates a line tangent to two arcs or an arc and a point. Identify the entities near the anticipated point of tangency. The entities must be coplanar for this function to work. When considering two arcs, carefully identify points P1 and P2 because four different tangent conditions exist.

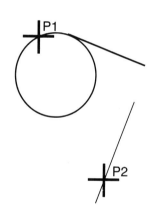

TAN PRP causes a line to be created tangent to the first entity selected and perpendicular to the second. The entities must be coplanar. Note that the created line need not actually touch the line or arc but would, were the line or arc completed.

PRP TAN causes a line to be created perpendicular to the first entity and tangent to the second. The entities must be coplanar, and the line is created in the plane of the two entities.

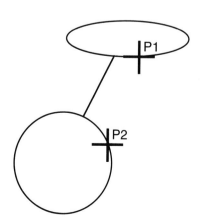

PRP PRP Creates a line perpendicular to both entities selected. In the case of lines, the perpendicular need not physically touch the two parallel lines. In the case of two arcs, the perpendicular line will extend from circumference to circumference (or their extensions) and be aligned with the arcs' centers.

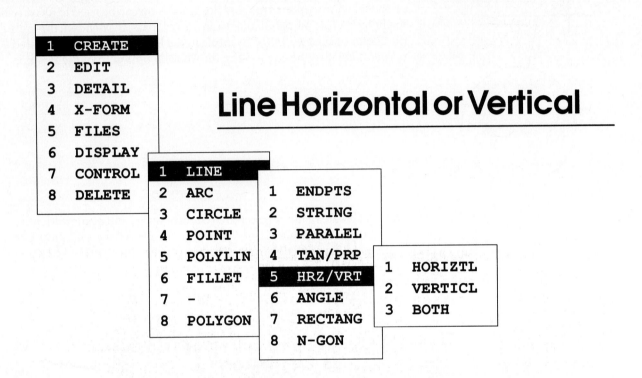

1	CREATE
2	EDIT
3	DETAIL
4	X-FORM
5	FILES
6	DISPLAY
7	CONTROL
8	DELETE

1	LINE
2	ARC
3	CIRCLE
4	POINT
5	POLYLIN
6	FILLET
7	-
8	POLYGON

1	ENDPTS
2	STRING
3	PARALEL
4	TAN/PRP
5	HRZ/VRT
6	ANGLE
7	RECTANG
8	N-GON

1	HORIZTL
2	VERTICL
3	BOTH

Line Horizontal or Vertical

▼ DESCRIPTION OF FUNCTION

This function provides an easy method of constructing lines parallel to the horizontal and vertical view axes. These lines extend to the limits of the viewport in which they are constructed.

In 2D construction, the lines are placed at the current depth in the current view. In 3D, the lines are created parallel to the XV and YV axes through the position indicated in 3D space. The option **BOTH** produces horizontal *and* vertical lines intersecting at the indicated position and extending to the limits of the viewport. Control is maintained until **ESC** is pressed.

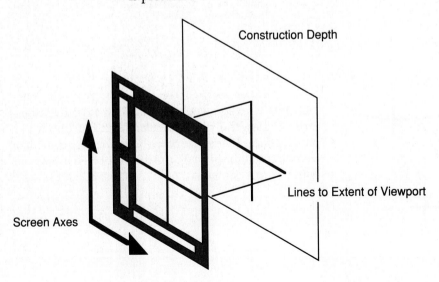

Construction Depth

Lines to Extent of Viewport

Screen Axes

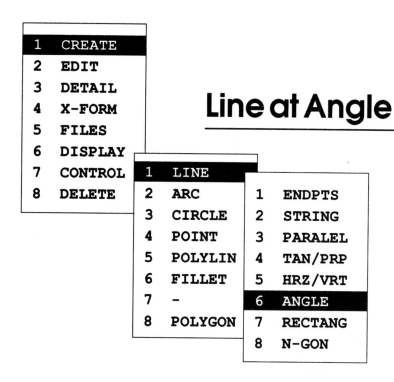

1	CREATE
2	EDIT
3	DETAIL
4	X-FORM
5	FILES
6	DISPLAY
7	CONTROL
8	DELETE

1	LINE
2	ARC
3	CIRCLE
4	POINT
5	POLYLIN
6	FILLET
7	–
8	POLYGON

1	ENDPTS
2	STRING
3	PARALEL
4	TAN/PRP
5	HRZ/VRT
6	ANGLE
7	RECTANG
8	N-GON

Line at Angle

▼ DESCRIPTION OF FUNCTION

Creating a line at an angle to an existing line is a common construction technique. The angled line is constructed from the end of a line using standard CW and CCW conventions. The angled line will extend from the end of the reference line and be the same length.

To produce a line of a specific length from a point other than the end of a line, use the **POLAR** position option in the Position Menu.

In 2D construction the line is projected onto the active construction plane in the current view. In 3D, the line is projected onto a plane parallel to the viewport through the end of the reference line.

▼ OPTIONS

The angle is determined based on which end of the reference line is selected. Note in the example below that two different results are achieved when different ends of the line are selected although the same angular specification is maintained.

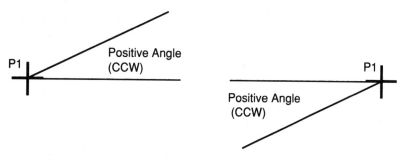

P1
Positive Angle
(CCW)

P1
Positive Angle
(CCW)

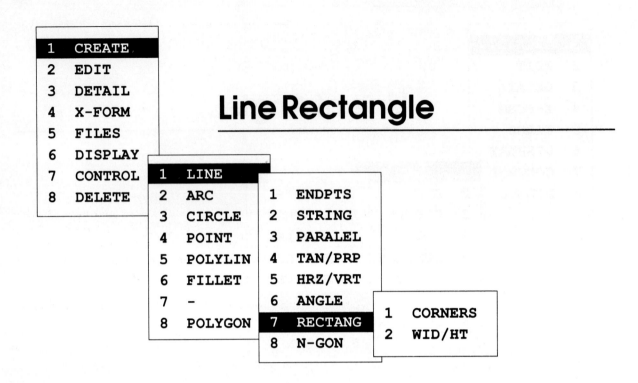

Line Rectangle

▼ DESCRIPTION OF FUNCTION

A line rectangle consists of four separate line entities. Regardless of 2D or 3D construction, a line rectangle is created at construction depth in the current view (the view in which you enter P2). Any option from the Position Menu can be used to locate the corners or starting point for the rectangle. Control is maintained until **ESC** is pressed.

▼ OPTIONS

CORNERS provides an interactive method of "rubber banding" the rectangle.

1. Set construction depth to the desired location in the intended view.

2. Click once to identify one corner of the rectangle (P1).

3. Move the cursor to the position of the opposite corner.

4. Click once (P2).

5. CADKEY Light creates a line rectangle at the current construction depth.

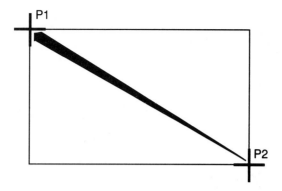

WID/HT allows exact numerical values to be used to define the line rectangle. Width is always parallel to XV; height is always parallel to YV. The same size line rectangle can continue to be placed. Use the **F10** backup break function command to change the dimensions of the rectangle. Press **ESC** to return to the Main Menu.

1. Set construction depth to the desired position in the intended view.

2. Keyboard enter the width and <Enter>.

3. Keyboard enter the height and <Enter>.

4. Indicate the lower left corner of the rectangle (P1).

5. CADKEY Light creates a line rectangle of the specified size at the current construction depth.

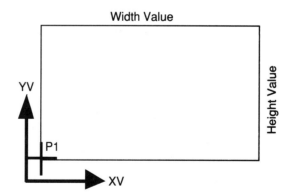

Line Polygon

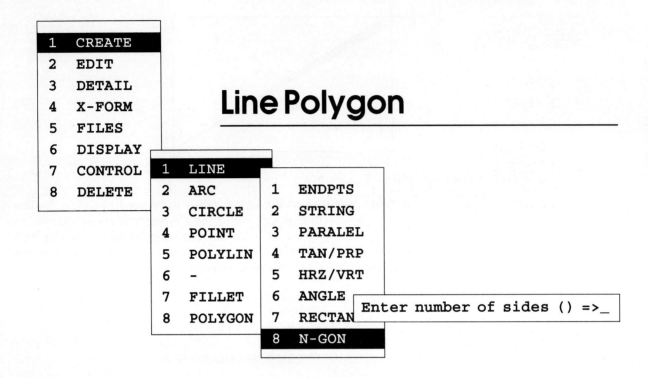

1	CREATE				
2	EDIT				
3	DETAIL				
4	X-FORM		1	LINE	1	ENDPTS
5	FILES		2	ARC	2	STRING
6	DISPLAY		3	CIRCLE	3	PARALEL
7	CONTROL		4	POINT	4	TAN/PRP
8	DELETE		5	POLYLIN	5	HRZ/VRT
			6	-	6	ANGLE
			7	FILLET	7	RECTAN
			8	POLYGON	8	N-GON

`Enter number of sides () =>_`

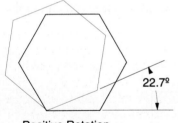

Positive Rotation

22.7º

▼ DESCRIPTION OF FUNCTION

A polygon consisting of individual line entities can be created with this function. You have the option of grouping the lines into a named group.

▼ OPTIONS

1. Enter the number of sides (3-100) and press <Enter>.

2. The line polygon is assumed to rest on a horizontal base at zero degrees of rotation. Rotation follows the positive (CCW) and negative (CW) convention.

3. Decide on the method of specifying size—either radius to corner or radius to flat.

4. Indicate the center of the polygon by choosing an option from the Position Menu.

5. Respond to the query for grouping.

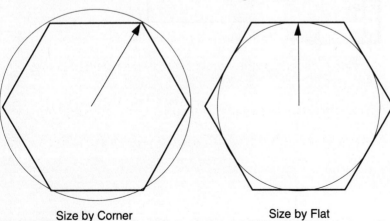

Size by Corner   Size by Flat

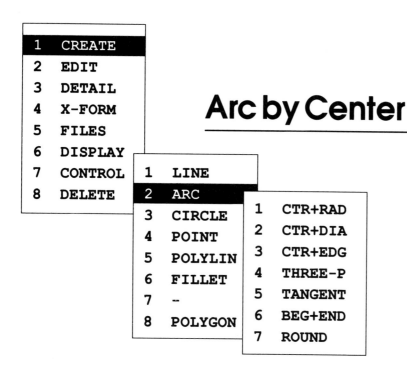

Arc by Center

▼ **DESCRIPTION OF FUNCTION**

An arc may be created using its center and one of three methods. These are appropriate when the center of the arc is known and the radius is either known or determinable. Positive (CCW) notation is used regardless of whether the start angle is positive or negative. In 2D, the center point is projected onto the construction plane in the current view. In 3D, the arc is constructed in a plane parallel to the current viewport but passing through the X, Y, Z coordinates of the center point.

▼ **OPTIONS**

CTR+RAD

1. Keyboard enter the radius in current units.

2. Keyboard enter a positive or negative start angle (SA) in degrees, <Enter>.

3. Enter a positive or negative end angle (EA) in degrees, <Enter>.

4. Indicate the center of the arc from any option in the Position Menu (P1).

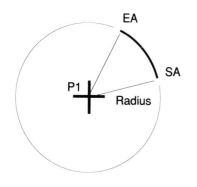

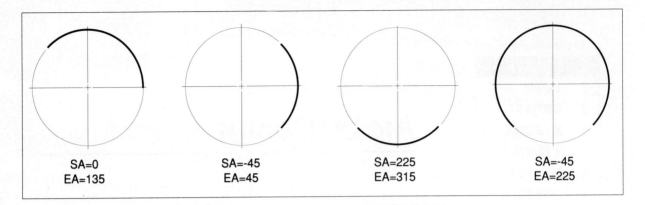

| SA=0 | SA=-45 | SA=225 | SA=-45 |
| EA=135 | EA=45 | EA=315 | EA=225 |

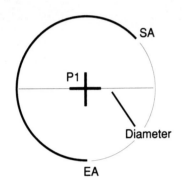

CTR+DIA

This option functions identically to the **CTR+RAD** option with the obvious difference in the way the arc's size is specified.

CTR+EDGE

This option may be thought of as creating an arc with a known center but of unknown radius either through a point or tangent to an entity.

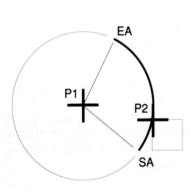

1. Keyboard enter a positive or negative start angle (SA) in degrees, <Enter>.

2. Enter a positive or negative end angle (EA) in degrees, <Enter>.

3. Indicate the center of the arc from any option in the Position Menu (P1).

4. Indicate an edge point using any of the options in the Position Menu (P2).

5. CADKEY Light creates an arc whose radius is the distance P1-P2 beginning at SA, ending at EA, and passing through P2.

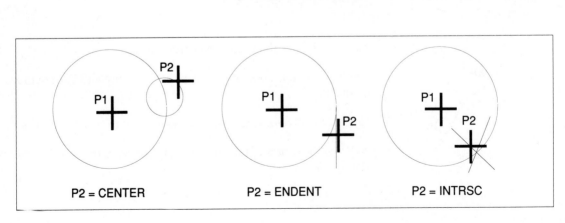

P2 = CENTER   P2 = ENDENT   P2 = INTRSC

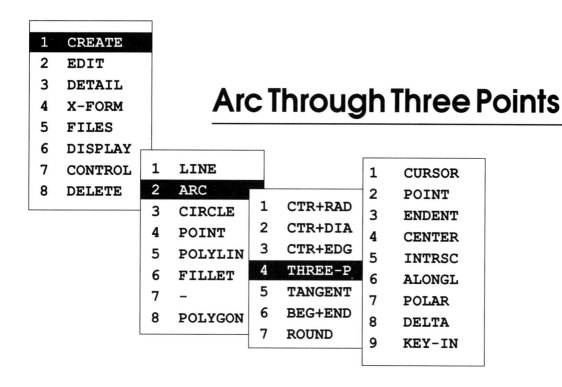

Arc Through Three Points

▼ DESCRIPTION OF FUNCTION

Three points not on the same line define a plane. An arc passing through those three points lies in that plane. In 2D construction, the arc is created at construction depth in the current view. In 3D, the arc is created in the plane defined by the three points. In 3D, then, the points can be identified in any combination of views with the same result.

The first point (P1) defines the beginning of the arc. Point P2 determines the direction of the arc and a second point on the circumference. Point P3 defines the end of the arc. Any option from the Position Menu can be used to indicate the three points.

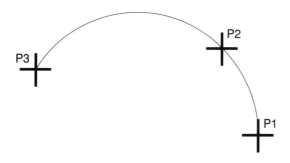

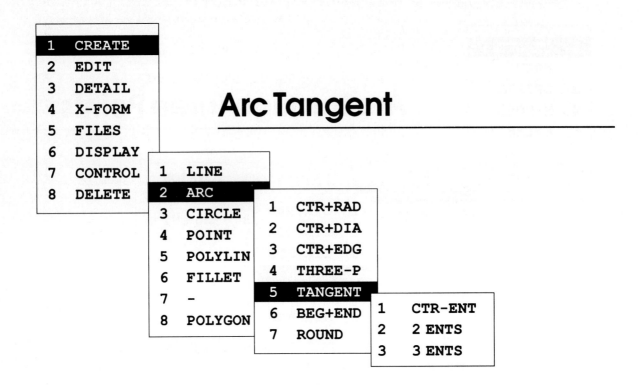

Arc Tangent

▼ DESCRIPTION OF FUNCTION

An arc can be created tangent to one entity with its center at a position indicated by any option from the Position Menu. Or an arc can be created tangent to two entities with a specified radius. Finally, an arc can be created tangent to three entities. Entities must be coplanar for these functions to work in 3D. Polylines and polygons cannot be used in 3D because they are not considered planar entities. In 2D, the arc is created at construction depth in the view the last point (center or entity) is indicated. Tangent arc requires that a start angle (SA) and an end angle (EA) be specified. The arc may be trimmed later if needed.

▼ OPTIONS

CTR-ENT allows an arc to be constructed tangent to an entity from a center indicated by an option from the Position Menu.

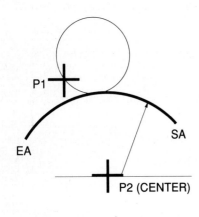

1. Keyboard enter the start angle (SA), <Enter>.

2. Keyboard enter the end angle (EA), <Enter>.

3. Cursor select the tangent entity near the anticipated point of tangency (P1).

4. Indicate the arc's center by using an option from the Position Menu (P2).

2 ENTS creates an arc tangent to two entities. If a tangent arc cannot be created, an error message is displayed. Press <Enter> to reselect entities.

1. Keyboard enter the start angle (SA), <Enter>.

2. Keyboard enter the end angle (EA), <Enter>.

3. Keyboard enter the desired radius, <Enter>.

4. Cursor select the first tangent entity near the anticipated point of tangency (P1).

5. Cursor select the second tangent entity near the anticipated point of tangency (P2).

6. CADKEY Light creates an arc tangent to the two entities beginning at SA and ending at EA.

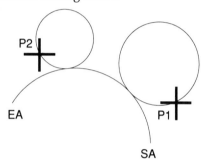

3 ENTS creates an arc tangent to three entities. The arc, as is the case in each of the three options, does not have to touch the tangent entities but would, were the arc completed into a circle. Use **F10** backup to cancel a selection and reselect an entity.

In 2D, the arc is created in the view in which P3 is indicated and at construction depth. In 3D, the arc is created in the plane of the selected entities.

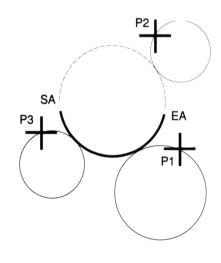

1. Keyboard enter the start angle (SA), <Enter>.

2. Keyboard enter the end angle (EA), <Enter>.

3. Cursor select the first tangent entity near the anticipated point of tangency (P1).

4. Cursor select the second tangent entity near the anticipated point of tangency (P2).

5. Cursor select the third tangent entity near the anticipated point of tangency (P3).

6. CADKEY Light creates an arc tangent to the three entities beginning at SA and ending at EA.

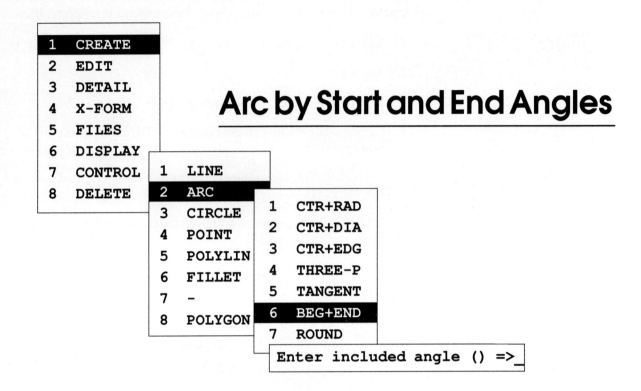

1	CREATE
2	EDIT
3	DETAIL
4	X-FORM
5	FILES
6	DISPLAY
7	CONTROL
8	DELETE

1	LINE
2	ARC
3	CIRCLE
4	POINT
5	POLYLIN
6	FILLET
7	-
8	POLYGON

1	CTR+RAD
2	CTR+DIA
3	CTR+EDG
4	THREE-P
5	TANGENT
6	BEG+END
7	ROUND

Enter included angle () =>_

Arc by Start and End Angles

▼ DESCRIPTION OF FUNCTION

An arc of a specified included angle may be created with start and end points (P1 and P2) indicated by any option from the Position Menu. The included angle (IA) is the angular portion of the arc specified in degrees that lies between P1 and P2. CADKEY Light determines the radius of the arc to fit the data you give it. The arc is created at construction depth in the current view.

1. Keyboard enter the included angle (IA) in degrees.

2. Indicate the start and end of the arc using an option from the Position Menu.

3. CADKEY Light determines the radius necessary to complete the desired arc.

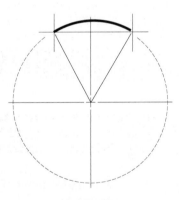

IA = 60º (INTRSC)

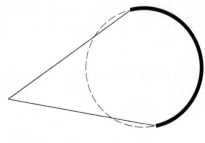

IA = 180º (ENDENT)

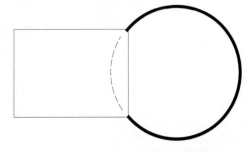

IA = 280º (ENDENT)

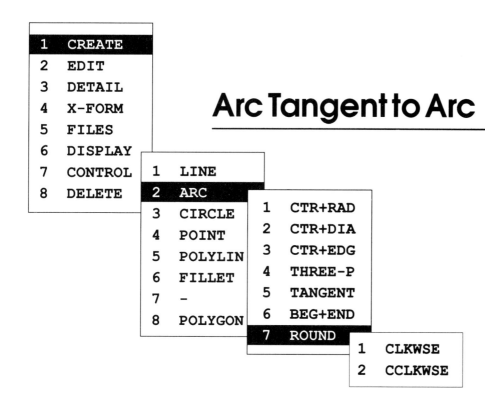

Arc Tangent to Arc

▼ **DESCRIPTION OF FUNCTION**

This function provides a way to construct *ogee* or reverse curves easily and quickly. Study the examples to become familiar with the difference in clockwise and counterclockwise directions. Ogee curves can be used to smoothly connect lines (straight curves in CADKEY Light) with curves as in highway or piping design. The curve is created in the current view at construction depth.

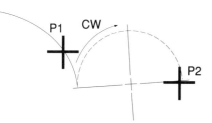

1. Select the curve that you wish an arc to be made tangent to near the desired end (P1). The curve must not appear as an edge. CADKEY Light marks the end with a small "X." Use **F10** backup to cancel a selection and reselect.

2. Indicate an end point for the arc (P2).

3. Assign a direction for the arc, either **CLKWSE** or **CCLKWSE**.

4. The arc is created using distance curve end-P2 as the diameter and the end of the curve and P2 as ends of the arc.

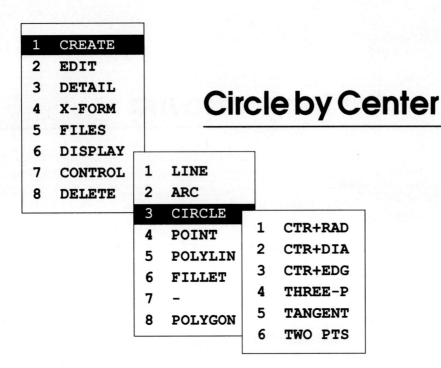

Circle by Center

▼ DESCRIPTION OF FUNCTION

This discussion covers the first two options in the **CIRCLE** function where the size and location of the circle's center are both known. Circles in 2D are created at construction depth in the view containing the last indicated point. In 3D, a circle is created in the current view on a plane parallel to the viewport containing the circle's center.

▼ OPTIONS

CTR+RAD provides a method of constructing a circle when the center point and radius are known.

1. Keyboard enter the radius, <Enter>.

2. Indicate the circle's center by an option from the Position Menu.

CTR+DIA functions identically to **CTR+RAD** with the exception that the circle is described by its diameter.

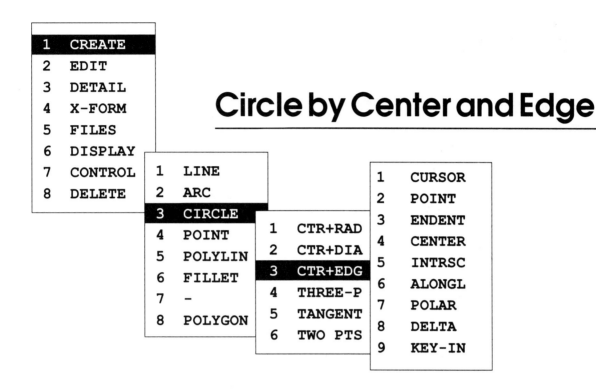

Circle by Center and Edge

1	CREATE
2	EDIT
3	DETAIL
4	X-FORM
5	FILES
6	DISPLAY
7	CONTROL
8	DELETE

1	LINE
2	ARC
3	CIRCLE
4	POINT
5	POLYLIN
6	FILLET
7	-
8	POLYGON

1	CTR+RAD
2	CTR+DIA
3	CTR+EDG
4	THREE-P
5	TANGENT
6	TWO PTS

1	CURSOR
2	POINT
3	ENDENT
4	CENTER
5	INTRSC
6	ALONGL
7	POLAR
8	DELTA
9	KEY-IN

▼ DESCRIPTION OF FUNCTION

This function allows a circle to be created when the center and a point on the circumference are known. In 2D, the center and edge are projected to construction depth in the current view. In 3D, CADKEY Light creates a circle on a plane containing the circle's center. This plane is parallel to the current viewport.

CTR+EDGE

1. Indicate the center of the circle using an option from the Position Menu (P1).

2. Indicate the edge point using an option from the Position Menu (P2).

3. CADKEY Light creates a circle using P1 as the center and the distance P1-P2 as the radius. Point P2 is on the circumference of the circle.

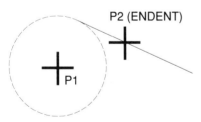

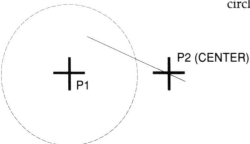

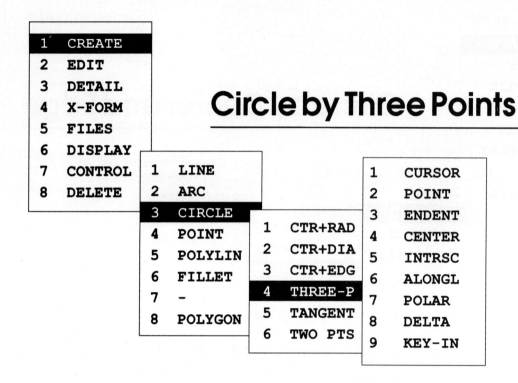

Circle by Three Points

▼ **DESCRIPTION OF FUNCTION**

A circle may be created through three points. These points can be in any location selected with an option from the Position Menu. In 2D, the circle is constructed at construction depth in the view in which P3 is indicated. In 3D, the circle is created in a plane defined by the three points. The order of selection does not change the circle as defined by three points.

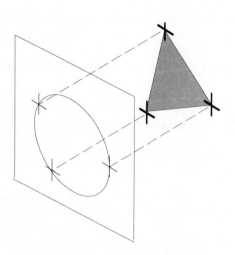

Circle by 3 Points in 2D Construction.

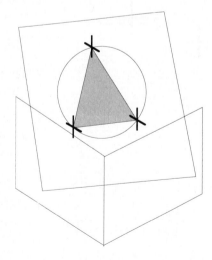

Circle by 3 Points in 3D Construction.

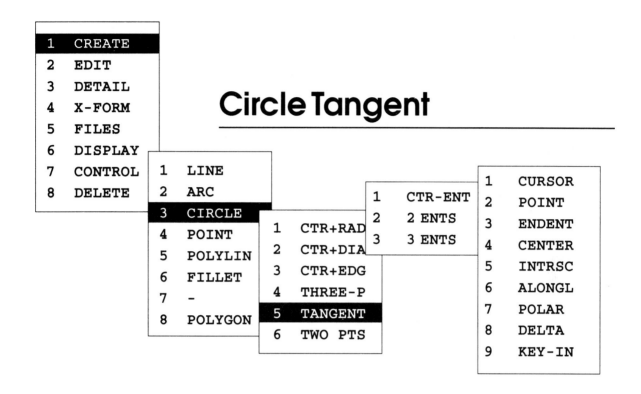

1	CREATE
2	EDIT
3	DETAIL
4	X-FORM
5	FILES
6	DISPLAY
7	CONTROL
8	DELETE

1	LINE
2	ARC
3	CIRCLE
4	POINT
5	POLYLIN
6	FILLET
7	-
8	POLYGON

1	CTR+RAD
2	CTR+DIA
3	CTR+EDG
4	THREE-P
5	TANGENT
6	TWO PTS

1	CTR-ENT
2	2 ENTS
3	3 ENTS

1	CURSOR
2	POINT
3	ENDENT
4	CENTER
5	INTRSC
6	ALONGL
7	POLAR
8	DELTA
9	KEY-IN

Circle Tangent

▼ DESCRIPTION OF FUNCTION

A circle can be created tangent to one, two, or three entities. If a tangent entity is a curve, arc, or circle, the entity must be selected in a view where it is seen as a curve. Any option from the Position Menu can be used to indicate position. Select tangent entities near the anticipated point of tangency. All entities are valid in 2D construction, and the circle is constructed at construction depth in the current view. All entities except polylines and polygons are valid in 3D. In 3D, entities must be coplanar and the circle is created in that plane.

▼ OPTIONS

CTR-ENT creates a circle tangent to one entity.

1. Cursor select the tangent entity (P1).

2. Indicate the center of the circle with an option from the Position Menu (P2).

3. CADKEY Light creates a circle centered at P2 tangent to the entity selected by P1. Note that CADKEY Light determines the correct radius.

2 ENTS creates a circle of specified radius tangent to two entities.

1. Keyboard enter the radius in current units, <Enter>.

2. Cursor select the first tangent entity (P1). Use **F10** backup to cancel a selection and reselect an entity.

3. Cursor select the second tangent entity (P2).

4. CADKEY Light creates a circle of specified radius at tangent to the two entities.

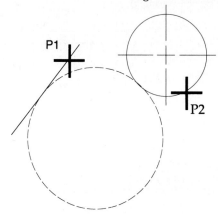

3 ENTS creates a circle tangent to three entities.

1. Cursor select the first tangent entity (P1). Use **F10** backup to cancel a selection and reselect an entity.

2. Cursor select the second tangent entity (P2).

3. Cursor select the third tangent entity (P3).

4. CADKEY Light determines the diameter of the circle that will be tangent to the three entities. See the note at the beginning of this function for 2D and 3D considerations.

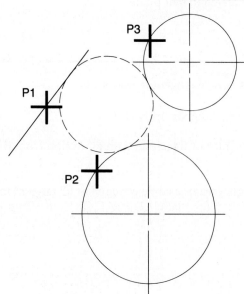

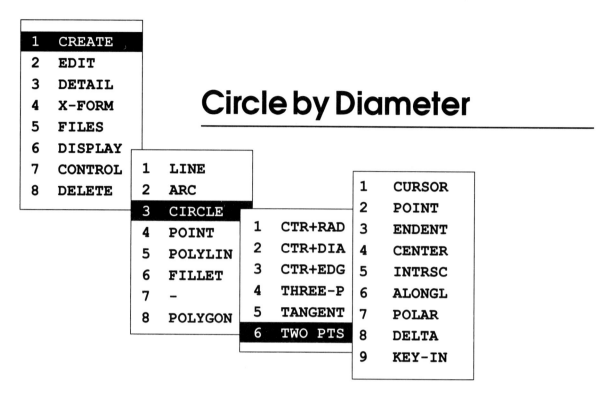

Circle by Diameter

▼ **DESCRIPTION OF FUNCTION**

This function is used to create a circle at the current construction depth and in the current view. This is true whether 2D or 3D construction is active. Options from the Position Menu are used to indicate the two points that define the circle's diameter.

1. Indicate the first end of the circle's diameter (P1).

2. Indicate the opposite side of the circle's diameter (P2).

3. The circle is constructed using distance P1-P2 as the diameter.

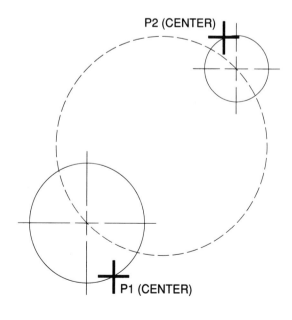

Point Entity

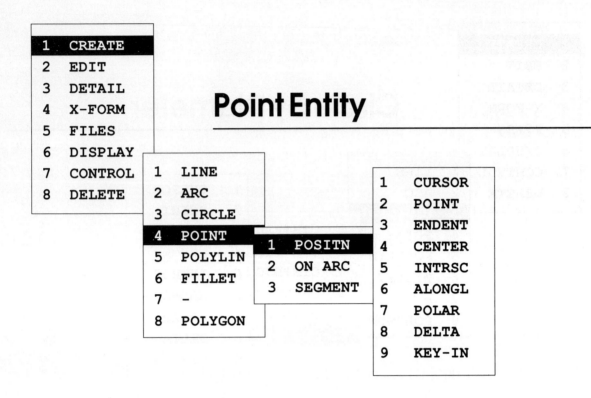

1	CREATE
2	EDIT
3	DETAIL
4	X-FORM
5	FILES
6	DISPLAY
7	CONTROL
8	DELETE

1	LINE
2	ARC
3	CIRCLE
4	POINT
5	POLYLIN
6	FILLET
7	-
8	POLYGON

1	POSITN
2	ON ARC
3	SEGMENT

1	CURSOR
2	POINT
3	ENDENT
4	CENTER
5	INTRSC
6	ALONGL
7	POLAR
8	DELTA
9	KEY-IN

▼ DESCRIPTION OF FUNCTION

A point entity (a "+") is a geometric entity that can be selected, used for positioning, and printed. It differs from a point marker (an "X") in that it is part of the geometric data base.

▼ OPTIONS

POSITN allows the creation of a point entity at any location in space using an option from the Position Menu. In 2D, the point is created at construction depth in the current view. In 3D, the point is constructed at the X,Y,Z coordinates of the indicated position. Control is maintained in this command, allowing repeated points to be constructed without leaving the function. **ESC** to the Main Menu to quit.

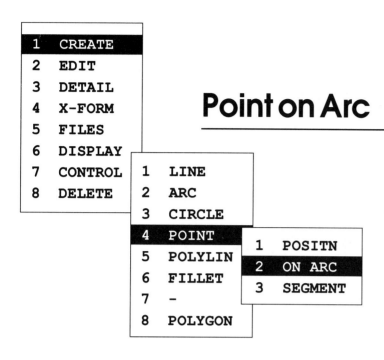

Point on Arc

▼ **DESCRIPTION OF FUNCTION**

A point on an arc or circle lies on the circumference or its extension. The point is physically put *on* the arc no matter the orientation of the curve in the current view. The point does not have to lie between the start and end of the arc, nor does it have to be within the limits of the viewport.

1. Select the desired arc or circle (P1).

2. Enter the angle in degrees. The angle is measured in the conventional positive (CCW) and negative (CW) manner.

3. The point is placed on the arc at the specified angle.

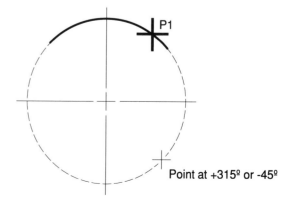

Point at +315º or -45º

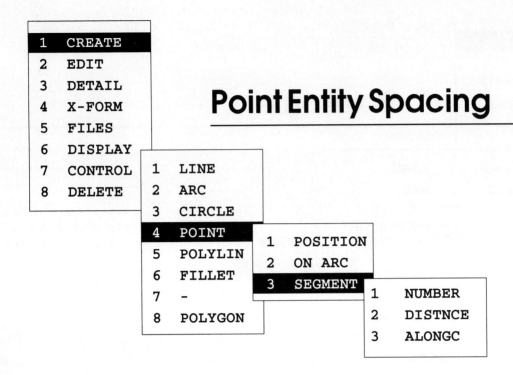

Point Entity Spacing

▼ DESCRIPTION OF FUNCTION

This function allows the placing of points on curves or lines at regular intervals. Up to 1,000 points can be created. **SEGMENT** is not affected by the 2D-3D switch setting. Points will always be placed on a curve or line in three-dimensional space.

▼ OPTIONS

NUMBER divides the entity into an equal number of spaces, each marked with a point entity. Points are placed at the beginning and end of a line or curve, and the distance between these limits is divided into the entered number. There will always be one more point created than the number of divisions specified.

1. Enter the desired number of segments, <Enter>.

2. Respond to the query about grouping the points, <Enter>.

3. Select the desired curve (P1).

4. The entity is divided into the specified number of segments.

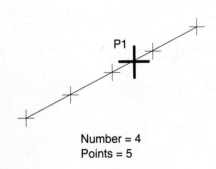

Number = 4
Points = 5

DISTANCE allows the specification of the interval between points. CADKEY Light places as many points at this interval as will be distributed along the line or curve. If the length is not an even multiple of the distance, a point will *not* be placed at the end of the line and there will be a remainder.

1. Keyboard enter the desired distance interval. It cannot be greater than the curve (line) length or less than .00005.

2. Respond to the query as to grouping of the points.

3. Select the line or curve at one end (P1). This end will be used for the beginning of the distribution of points.

4. The points are created beginning at the end closest to P1 at the interval specified. As many points as possible are created until either the remainder is less than the interval or until the remainder is zero.

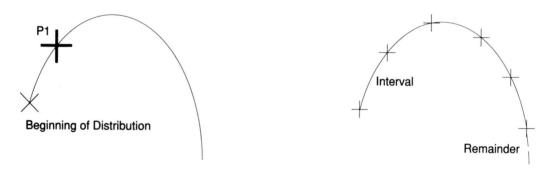

P1 — Beginning of Distribution — Interval — Remainder

ALONGC allows a point to be created a specified distance from one end of a line or curve.

1. Keyboard enter the desired distance. It must be less than the length of the line or curve and greater than .00005.

2. Select the line or curve near the reference endpoint (P1).

3. A point is placed on the entity the specified distance from the referenced endpoint.

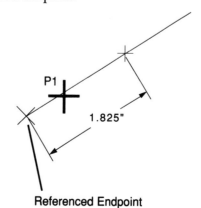

P1 — 1.825" — Referenced Endpoint

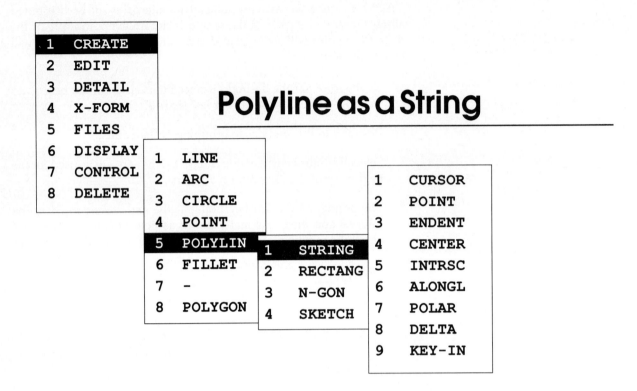

Polyline as a String

▼   **DESCRIPTION OF FUNCTION**

A polyline entity is a single continuous entity although it is usually an irregular line. As a single entity it can be manipulated as a unit without explicit grouping. The **STRING** option provides a method of specifying a polyline from vertex to vertex. In 2D, the polyline is created at construction depth in the current view. In 3D, the polyline vertices are located at the indicated X,Y,Z coordinates.

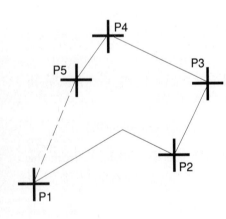

1.   Indicate the starting point (P1) for the polyline with any option from the Position Menu.

2.   Indicate subsequent vertices (P2-P5).

3.   End the polyline by **F10-F10** or <Enter>.

4.   Determine if the polyline should be closed to its starting point. Respond **YES** to close to P1. Respond **NO** to end the polyline at P5.

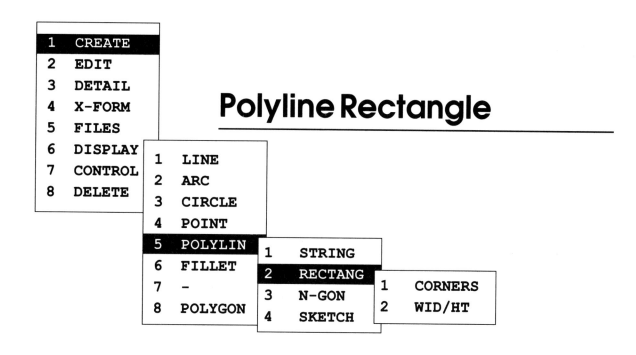

Polyline Rectangle

▼ **DESCRIPTION OF FUNCTION**

A rectangular polyline (single entity) can be manipulated as a whole. Although a rectangular polyline can be carefully created with the **STRING** option, the **RECTANG** option automates this process. Control is maintained in this function allowing multiple polyline rectangles to be constructed without reentering the commands. Use **F10** backup to change options. **ESC** to the Main Menu.

▼ **OPTIONS**

CORNERS allows the opposite corners to be cursor-indicated using any option from the Position Menu.

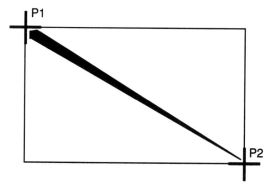

1. Cursor indicate P1.

2. Cursor indicate P2.

3. The polyline rectangle is created at construction depth in the current view.

WID/HT allows the creation of a polyline rectangle by the specification of its numerical size. In 2D, the polyline rectangle is created at construction depth in the view where the origin (lower left corner) is indicated. In 3D, the polyline rectangle is created in a plane parallel to the current viewport at the depth of the rectangle's lower left corner.

1.　Keyboard enter a value for the width, <Enter>.

2.　Keyboard enter a value for the height, <Enter>.

3.　Cursor indicate a position for the lower left corner using any option from the Position Menu.

Note that rectangle width corresponds to XV dimension and rectangle height to YV dimension.

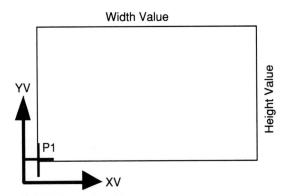

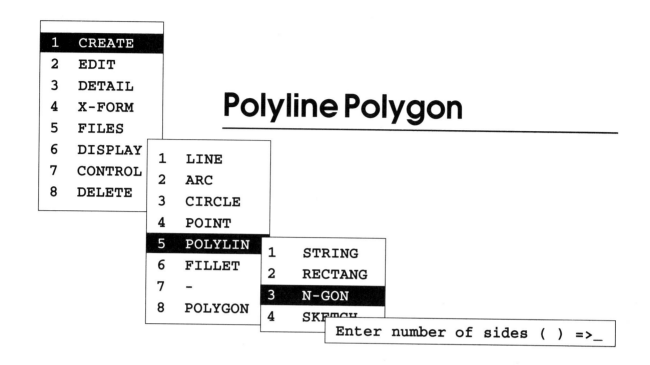

Polyline Polygon

1	CREATE
2	EDIT
3	DETAIL
4	X-FORM
5	FILES
6	DISPLAY
7	CONTROL
8	DELETE

1	LINE
2	ARC
3	CIRCLE
4	POINT
5	POLYLIN
6	FILLET
7	-
8	POLYGON

1	STRING
2	RECTANG
3	N-GON
4	SKETCH

Enter number of sides ( ) =>_

▼ DESCRIPTION OF FUNCTION

A polyline polygon is a single-entity regular polygon. In 2D, the polygon is created at construction depth in the current view. In 3D, the polygon is created on a plane parallel to the current viewport and containing the polygon's center.

1. Keyboard enter the number of sides (3-8), <Enter>.

2. Keyboard enter the rotation angle in degrees, <Enter>. The polyline polygon is rotated about its center.

3. Keyboard enter a radius value in current units, <Enter>.

4. Choose **CORNER** or **FLAT** as the construction method.

5. Indicate the center position using any option from the Position Menu.

22.8º

Positive Rotation

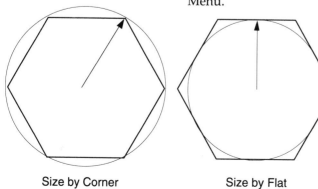

Size by Corner   Size by Flat

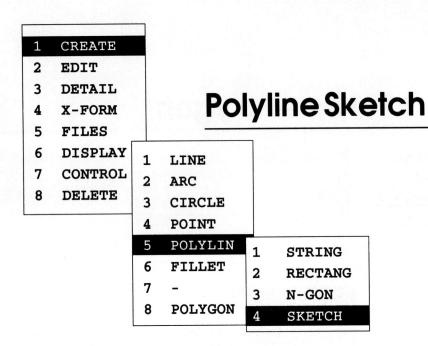

Polyline Sketch

▼ DESCRIPTION OF FUNCTION

This function provides a method of directly sketching a polyline in a freehand or continuous manner. With the cursor button held down, CADKEY Light samples the sketch and assigns polyline vertices to the path. Individual vertices can be specified by manually releasing and pressing the cursor button again. In 2D, the polyline sketch is created at construction depth in the current view. In 3D, each vertex of the sketch assumes the X,Y,Z coordinates of the cursor at that location. Use **F10** to back up and **ESC** to exit this command. You will be prompted to save the sketch. Press <Enter> to automatically store and end the sketch.

1. Cursor-indicate the starting point of the polyline sketch using any option from the Position Menu.

2. Continue the sketch by holding down the cursor button while sketching.

3. Press <Enter> when the sketch is complete.

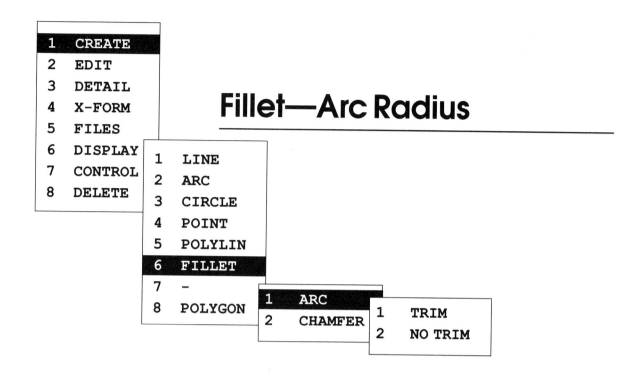

Fillet—Arc Radius

▼ **DESCRIPTION OF FUNCTION**

This function creates an arc tangent to two lines, an arc and a line, or two arcs. In 2D, this fillet is created in the current view at the construction depth active at the time the second entity is selected. In 3D, the filleted entities must be coplanar; the fillet is created in the plane of the two entities.

If the radius of the fillet is less than one-half the distance between the selected entities, a fillet cannot be constructed and an error message is displayed. Press <Enter> and enter a larger radius value.

▼ **OPTIONS**

NO TRIM creates the fillet tangent to the two entities without either being trimmed to the point of tangency.

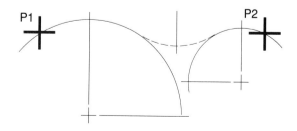

No Trim Option

TRIM removes the unwanted portion of the entities to the point of tangency of the fillet. Circles cannot be trimmed. Carefully select each entity on the portion that will be kept after trimming.

1. Choose the desired trim option.

2. Enter a value for the fillet radius, <Enter>.

3. Select the first entity near the anticipated point of tangency and on the portion to be kept if trim has been chosen.

4. Select the second entity near the anticipated point of tangency and on the portion to be kept if trim has been chosen.

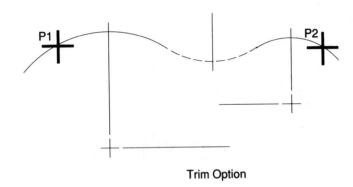

Trim Option

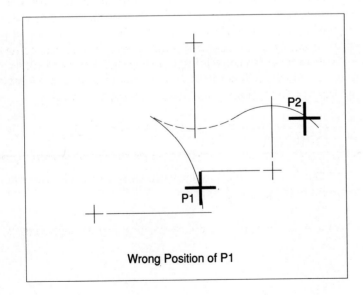

Wrong Position of P1

Note that CADKEY Light *keeps* the portion of the arc that has been identified. Compare the result of this example and the one above for the result of selecting each end of the arc.

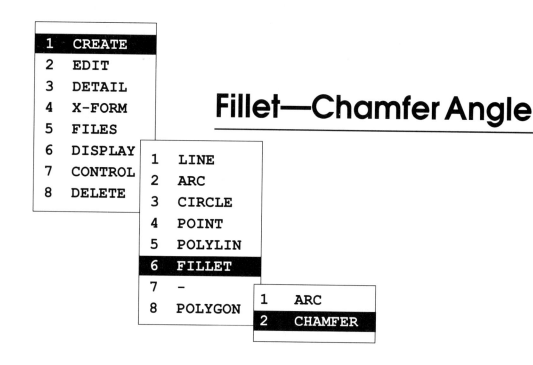

Fillet—Chamfer Angle

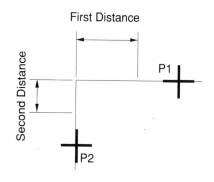

First Distance

Second Distance

P1

P2

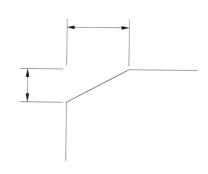

▼ DESCRIPTION OF FUNCTION

A chamfer angles two lines that either intersect or would intersect were they to be extended. The lines are automatically trimmed to the chamfer. The endpoints of the chamfer line are on the selected lines; the chamfer is then *in* the plane of the two lines.

The chamfer is specified by the distance each chamfer end lies along the entities from the intersection (or projected intersection).

1. Keyboard enter the first distance, <Enter>.

2. Keyboard enter the second distance, <Enter>.

3. Select the first line (P1). Note that the *first distance* lies along the *first line.*

4. Select the second line (P2).

5. CADKEY Light creates the chamfer and trims the two lines.

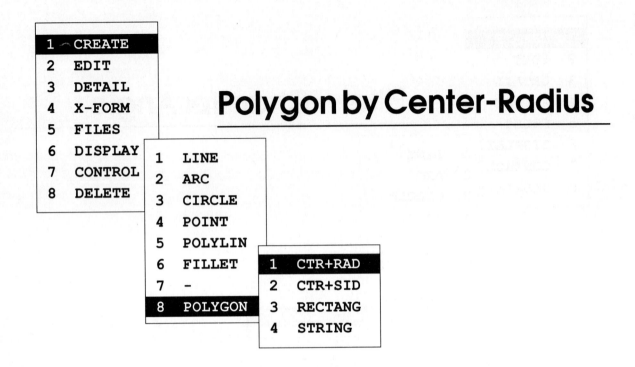

Polygon by Center-Radius

▼ DESCRIPTION OF FUNCTION

A polygon is a single entity and as such can be manipulated as a unit. Polygons can have 3-8 sides and can be created either in outline in the current color or filled with a user-specified color.

1. Keyboard enter the desired number of sides, <Enter>.

2. Keyboard enter the rotation angle in degrees, <Enter>.

3. Keyboard enter a value for the radius, <Enter>.

4. Choose either **FLAT** or **CORNER** as the construction method.

5. Choose either **OUTLINE** or **FILLED**.

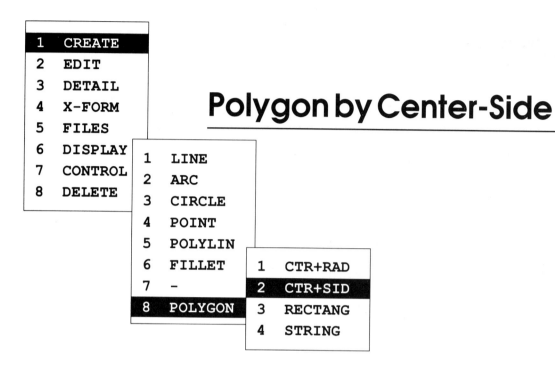

Polygon by Center-Side

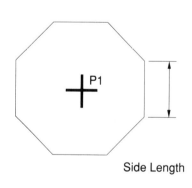

Side Length

▼ DESCRIPTION OF FUNCTION

CTR+SID provides a method of creating regular polygons when the side length is known. The polygon is a single entity and can have 3-8 sides. In 2D, the polygon is created at current construction depth in the current view. In 3D, the polygon is created in a plane parallel to the current viewport at the construction depth of the polygon's center point.

1. Keyboard enter the desired number of sides, <Enter>.

2. Keyboard enter a rotation angle, <Enter>.

3. Keyboard enter the length, <Enter>.

4. Choose either **OUTLINE** or **FILLED**.

5. Indicate the center position of the polygon using an option from the Position Menu (P1).

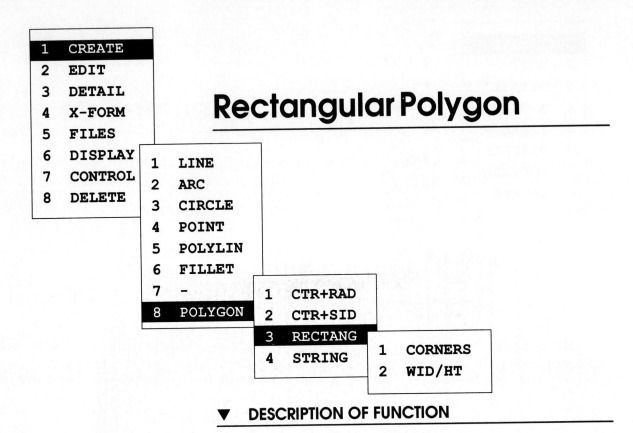

1	CREATE
2	EDIT
3	DETAIL
4	X-FORM
5	FILES
6	DISPLAY
7	CONTROL
8	DELETE

1	LINE
2	ARC
3	CIRCLE
4	POINT
5	POLYLIN
6	FILLET
7	-
8	POLYGON

1	CTR+RAD
2	CTR+SID
3	RECTANG
4	STRING

1	CORNERS
2	WID/HT

Rectangular Polygon

▼ DESCRIPTION OF FUNCTION

A rectangular polygon can be created in either outline of filled form. The rectangle is a single entity and can be manipulated as a unit.

▼ OPTIONS

CORNERS allows the opposite corners to be cursor indicated using any option from the Position Menu.

1. Choose either **OUTLINE** or **FILLED**.

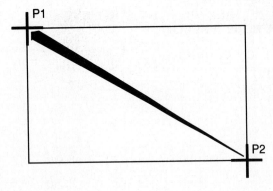

2. Cursor indicate P1 using any option from the Position Menu.

3. Cursor indicate P2 using any option from the Position Menu.

4. The polygon rectangle is created at construction depth in the current view.

WID/HT allows the creation of a polygon rectangle by the specification of its numerical size. In 2D, the polyline rectangle is created at construction depth in the view where the origin (lower left corner) is indicated. In 3D, the polyline rectangle is created in a plane parallel to the current viewport at the depth of the rectangle's lower left corner.

1. Choose either **OUTLINE** or **FILLED**.

2. Keyboard enter a value for the width, <Enter>.

3. Keyboard enter a value for the height, <Enter>.

4. Cursor indicate a position for the lower left corner using any option from the Position Menu.

Note that rectangle width corresponds to XV dimension and rectangle height to YV dimension. In 2D, the corner points are projected onto the current construction plane and the rectangle is created in the current view. In 3D, the polygon rectangle is constructed on a plane parallel to the current viewport containing the second corner of the rectangle.

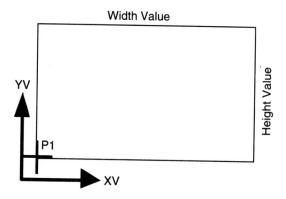

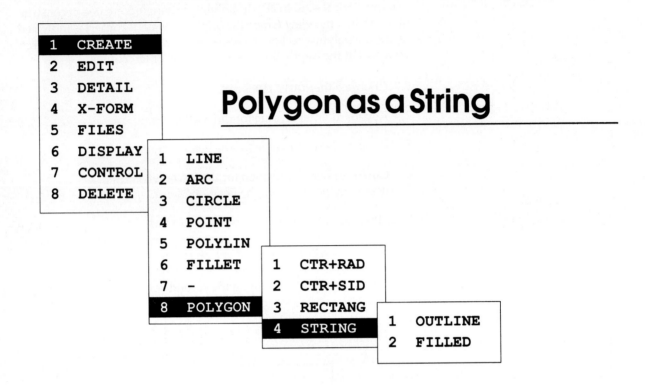

Polygon as a String

1	CREATE
2	EDIT
3	DETAIL
4	X-FORM
5	FILES
6	DISPLAY
7	CONTROL
8	DELETE

1	LINE
2	ARC
3	CIRCLE
4	POINT
5	POLYLIN
6	FILLET
7	-
8	POLYGON

1	CTR+RAD
2	CTR+SID
3	RECTANG
4	STRING

1	OUTLINE
2	FILLED

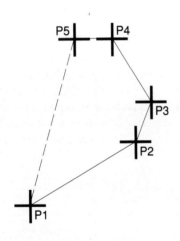

▼ DESCRIPTION OF FUNCTION

A string polygon is the function to use when an irregular polygon is desired. In 2D, the vertices of the polygon are projected onto the current construction plane in the current view. In 3D, the vertices of the polygon are located at the X,Y,Z coordinates of the indicated points. Note that a 3D string polygon may not be a planar figure.

1. Choose **OUTLINE** or **FILLED**.

2. Indicate the starting position (P1) using an option from the Position Menu.

3. Indicate subsequent vertices up to a total of eight.

4. The polygon is closed when <Enter> is pressed or automatically—from P8-P1 when the ninth vertex is indicated. Notice that vertex P9 is ignored when the polygon is closed.

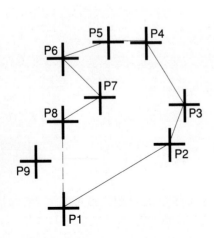

Edit Menu

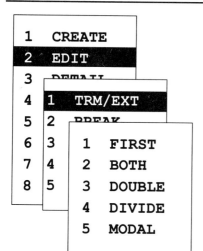

Trim or Extend Entity

▼ DESCRIPTION OF FUNCTION

Trimming and extending a line or arc in CADKEY Light is essentially the same operation: The line is extended or shortened along its locus or an arc is extended or shortened along its circumference. The entity that limits this trimming action is appropriately called the *trimming entity*. The operation takes place in 2D space. That is, the entities must either actually intersect or *appear* to intersect in the view in which the trimming is being done.

▼ OPTIONS

FIRST is used to trim or extend one end of a line or arc (P1) to the intersection or projected intersection of another entity (P2). The entity being trimmed is selected on that portion that is to remain (P1). Note the different results when P1 is moved to the other end of the entity.

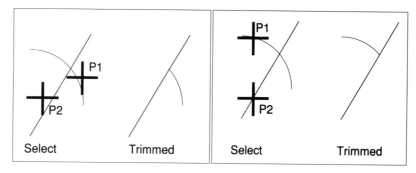

1	FIRST
2	**BOTH**
3	DOUBLE
4	DIVIDE
5	MODAL

BOTH allows two entities to be trimmed or extended to their intersection. Select each entity on the portion that is to remain. Only arcs and lines can be used with this option.

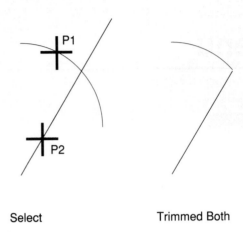

Select   Trimmed Both

1	FIRST
2	BOTH
3	**DOUBLE**
4	DIVIDE
5	MODAL

DOUBLE allows a line, arc, or circle to be trimmed or extended to the intersection of two entities. Select the part of the entity that is to remain (P1). Select the two trimming entities (P2 and P3).

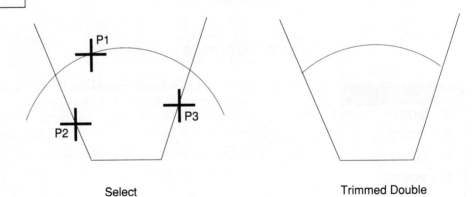

Select   Trimmed Double

1	FIRST
2	BOTH
3	DOUBLE
4	**DIVIDE**
5	MODAL

DIVIDE allows an entity (line or arc) to be divided and the portion in the middle to be removed. Notice that this is the opposite of other trimming options where the entity is selected on the portion that is to remain. Select the entity on the portion that is to be removed (P1). Select the two trimming entities (P2 and P3).

Select   Trimmed Divide

1	FIRST
2	BOTH
3	DOUBLE
4	DIVIDE
5	**MODAL**

MODAL trims multiple entities to a single entity. This removes the need to reselect entity and trimming entity as in the **FIRST** option. Select the entity to which all others will be trimmed (P1). Continue to select entities on the portions that are to remain until all are trimmed. **ESC** to the Main Menu or **F10** backup to change the edit function.

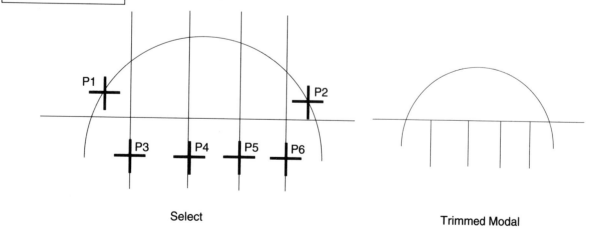

Select   Trimmed Modal

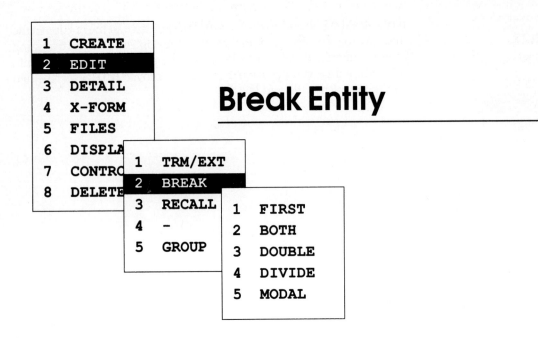

Break Entity

▼   **DESCRIPTION OF FUNCTION**

Breaking a line or arc divides the entity into several individual entities. New divisions assume what ever attributes are current. The selected portion of the original entity retains its original attributes.

Entities must extend past the expected intersection for that location to be used for a break point. For the following examples, assume that the original line type was a solid line and that the current line type is a dashed line.

▼   **OPTIONS**

FIRST allows a line or arc to be divided into two or three separate entities. Select the portion of the entity that will retain the original attribute (P1). Select the entity that will break the original (P2). Entity P1 now consists of two entities: the original portion and the new portion that took on the dashed line type.

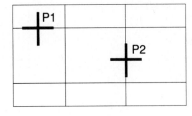

Select

Break First

BOTH allows you to break two entities into multiple segments. The portions selected will retain original attributes. The new divisions will assume the attributes in effect at the time the entity is broken.

1	FIRST
2	BOTH
3	DOUBLE
4	DIVIDE
5	MODAL

Select

Break Both

1	FIRST
2	BOTH
3	DOUBLE
4	DIVIDE
5	MODAL

DOUBLE allows an entity to be broken into three separate entities as determined by its intersection with two other entities. Select the portion that will keep the original properties (P1). Select the two breaking entities (P2 and P3).

Select

Break Double

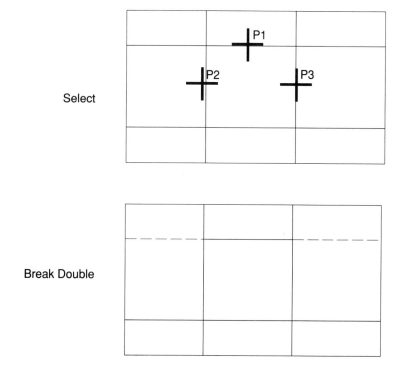

DIVIDE operates much like DOUBLE with the opposite effect. The interior portion takes on current properties and the outside segments retain the original properties.

1	FIRST
2	BOTH
3	DOUBLE
4	**DIVIDE**
5	MODAL

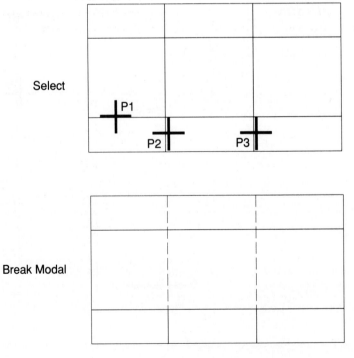

Select

Break Divide

MODAL allows multiple lines and arcs to be broken, each into two separate entities. The portion of each entity that is selected retains its properties and the new segment is assigned current properties.

1	FIRST
2	BOTH
3	DOUBLE
4	DIVIDE
5	**MODAL**

Select

Break Modal

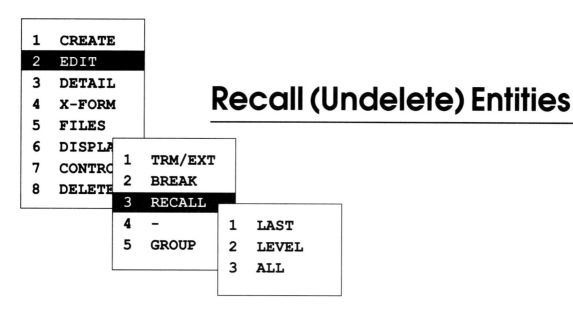

1	CREATE
2	EDIT
3	DETAIL
4	X-FORM
5	FILES
6	DISPLA
7	CONTRO
8	DELETE

1	TRM/EXT
2	BREAK
3	RECALL
4	–
5	GROUP

1	LAST
2	LEVEL
3	ALL

Recall (Undelete) Entities

▼ DESCRIPTION OF FUNCTION

Entities that have been deleted can be recalled back into the part file. Deleted entities can be recalled before or after a part file has been saved but not after a part has been cleared from the work space and reloaded. Entities cannot be recalled as a group. **ESC** to exit this function and return to the Main Menu.

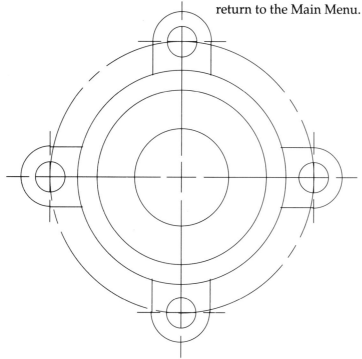

▼   OPTIONS

The **LAST** entity deleted can be recalled once for each delete action. If a window is used to select multiple entities, the entity that was created last will be considered last for the purposes of recalling.

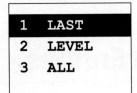

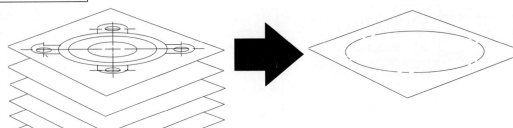

Recall of last delete if last was the bolt circle. Recall of **LEVEL** if the bolt circle was on the last deleted level. Recall of **ALL—BY TYPE** if there was only one circular center line.

LEVEL allows all entities on a deleted level to be returned to the part file. A level may be recalled once for each level deletion action. Keyboard enter a level number (1-256) and press <Enter>.

ALL recalls every entity that has been deleted since the part file was loaded. The **ALL** option returns all entities on all levels. Groups are brought in as ungrouped entities. **BY TYPE** allows the masking for inclusion to recall. **EX TYPE** recalls all entities *other than those masked.*

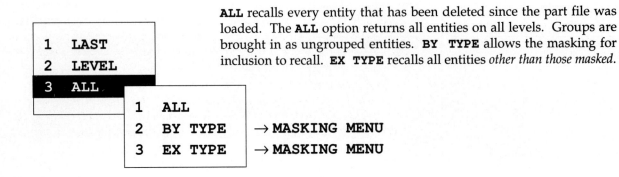

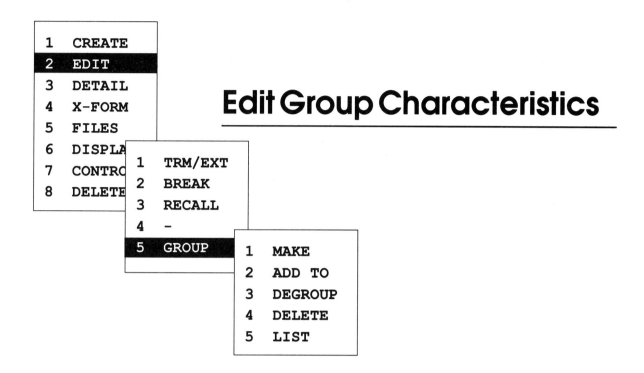

Edit Group Characteristics

▼ **DESCRIPTION OF FUNCTION**

A group can be any number of geometric entities that are treated as a unit. Grouping entities provides an easy way to change attributes or position. Groups can be selected by their name (up to eight alphanumeric characters) or by cursor selection. Groups can be created in two ways in CADKEY Light, each with different results.

Groups Within the Part File

A number of entities can be associated right on the part file. When this group is named and repeated on the part file by the **X-FORM..COPY** command, all copies belong to the group and no subgroups are created.

Groups Formed From Pattern Files

When a pattern file is placed in a part and grouped, each incidence of the pattern creates a subgroup. Groups and subgroups have a parent-child relationship. That is, attributes of the parent (group) can be changed and that change applied to all children (subgroups).

When a subgroup is selected, it may be acted upon in any of three ways: as a **GROUP,** which includes all subgroups,; as a **SUBGROUP,** which included only those entities in the selected subgroup; and as an **ENTITY,** which will change only the entity of the subgroup selected.

An Example of Group and Subgroup

Consider that a group **BOLTHEAD** has been named and repeated in nine locations. When the first group was created it was assigned the subgroup designation one (S1). Each additional grouping using **BOLTHEAD** as the name was assigned the next available subgroup number (S2-S9). The final subgroup was scaled larger. Assume that S4 has been selected for deletion by clicking on one of its entities (P1). You would have the following three options.

1. Delete the **GROUP** (S1-S9).

2. Delete the **SUBGROUP** (S4).

3. Delete the selected entity within S4.

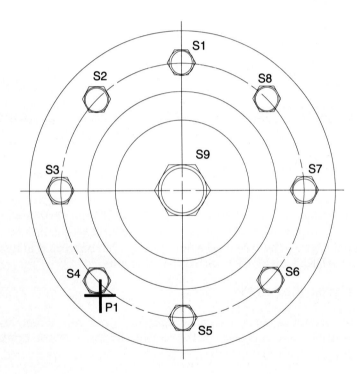

1	MAKE
2	ADD TO
3	DEGROUP
4	DELETE
5	LIST

▼ OPTIONS

MAKE allows selected entities to be treated as a unit. If additional groups are given the same group name, they are treated as subgroups.

1	MAKE
2	**ADD TO**
3	DEGROUP
4	DELETE
5	LIST

ADD TO allows additional entities to be added to a group after its original creation. Enter the group name when prompted. If subgroups exist, you must specify to which subgroup the additional entities will be added. Use the **LIST** option to check the validity and spelling of current groups.

1	MAKE
2	ADD TO
3	**DEGROUP**
4	DELETE
5	LIST

DEGROUP ungroups either the entity, the subgroup, or the entire group without removing its reference from the group table.

1	MAKE
2	ADD TO
3	DEGROUP
4	**DELETE**
5	LIST

DELETE removes the group name from the group table and degroups all subgroups. All entities continue to exist as separate entities.

1	MAKE
2	ADD TO
3	DEGROUP
4	DELETE
5	**LIST**

LIST provides a visual record of groups in the current part.

```
                              GROUP TABLE

        NAME   SUBGROUP    NAME  SUBGROUP      NAME    SUBGROUP

Seven Subgroups ———  BOLT   7
  One Subgroup ———    SCREW  1
     Degrouped ———    PIN    0
```

Detail Menu

```
┌─────────────────┐
│ 1   CREATE      │──┐
│ 2   EDIT        │1 │ DIMENSION │
│ 3   DETAIL      │2 │ NOTE      │
│ 4   X-FORM      │3 │ LABEL │ 1 │ HORIZTL  │
│ 5   FILES       │4 │ ARR/W │ 2 │ VERTICL  │
│ 6   DISPLAY     │5 │ X-HAT │ 3 │ PARALEL  │
│ 7   CONTROL     │6 │  -    │ 4 │ RADIUS   │
│ 8   DELETE      │7 │ CHANG │ 5 │ ANGULAR  │
└─────────────────┘8 │ UPDAT │ 6 │ DIAMETER │
                   9 │ SET   │
```

1	CREATE
2	EDIT
3	DETAIL
4	X-FORM
5	FILES
6	DISPLAY
7	CONTROL
8	DELETE

1	DIMENSION
2	NOTE
3	LABEL
4	ARR/W
5	X-HAT
6	-
7	CHANG
8	UPDAT
9	SET

1	HORIZTL
2	VERTICL
3	PARALEL
4	RADIUS
5	ANGULAR
6	DIAMETER

▼ DESCRIPTION OF FUNCTION

Dimensions for detail drafting can be created in any view. It may be most helpful to create dimensions on a separate level. This allows for selective display and editing. Several considerations need to be kept in mind.

- Dimensions are created using attributes changed in the **SET** option of this menu.

- Only those dimensions normal to a view (parallel to the view's viewport) will be displayed. Other dimensions will be suppressed.

- Linear distances can be dimensioned in *any* view regardless of the position of entities in that view. The linear dimensions will always be normal to the view in which they were created.

- For any arc or circle to be dimensioned it must lie in a plane parallel to the current viewport.

- Each dimension must be accepted by an explicit menu response.

- If the **DIM MOD** switch is set to **AUTOMAT**, the dimension value is automatically calculated and placed in the dimension. If the switch is set to **MANUAL**, the dimension text is keyboard entered at the prompt line.

- Dimensions are grouped entities that can be degrouped for editing.

Components of a Dimension

Study the following examples for the components of linear, radial, diametral, and angular dimensions.

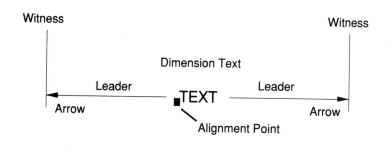

Horizontal,
Vertical, or Parallel
Dimensions

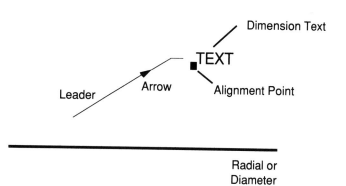

Radial or
Diameter
Dimensions

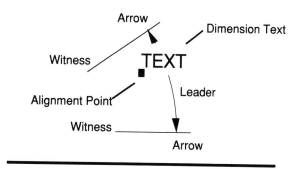

Angular
Dimensions

▼ OPTIONS

HORIZTL creates a dimension parallel to the XV axis.

1. Choose a position from the Position Menu.

2. Indicate the beginning of the dimension (P1).

3. Change the position option if necessary.

4. Indicate the end of the dimension (P2).

5. Indicate the position of the dimension text (P3).

6. Accept or reject the dimension.

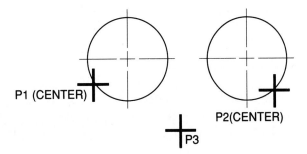

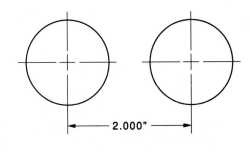

VERTICL creates a dimension parallel to the YV axis.

1. Choose a position from the Position Menu.

2. Indicate the beginning of the dimension (P1).

3. Change the position option if necessary.

4. Indicate the end of the dimension (P2).

5. Indicate the position of the dimension text (P3).

6. Accept or reject the dimension.

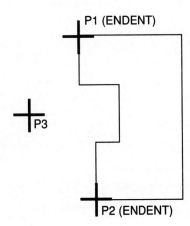

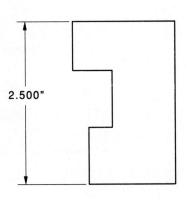

1	**HORIZTL**
2	**VERTICL**
3	**PARALEL**
4	**RADIUS**
5	**ANGULAR**
6	**DIAMETER**

PARALEL creates a dimension parallel to the line formed by P1-P2. This means that a parallel dimension *could* be parallel to either XV or YV or at any angle.

1. Choose a position from the Position Menu.

2. Indicate the beginning of the dimension (P1).

3. Change the position option if necessary.

4. Indicate the end of the dimension (P2).

5. Indicate the position of the dimension text (P3).

6. Accept or reject the dimension.

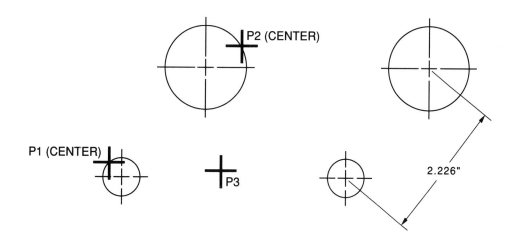

RADIUS creates a dimension of the radius of an arc or circle. In general practice, only an arc is dimensioned by its radius.

1	**HORIZTL**
2	**VERTICL**
3	**PARALEL**
4	**RADIUS**
5	**ANGULAR**
6	**DIAMETER**

1. Indicate the arc to be dimensioned (P1).

2. Indicate the dimension text position (P2).

3. Choose **LEFT** or **RIGHT** for leader position. In general, place the leader to the left of a right-hand dimension and to the right of a left-hand dimension.

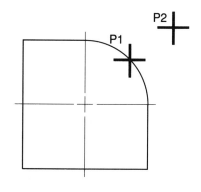

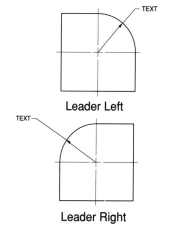

Leader Left

Leader Right

1	HORIZTL
2	VERTICL
3	PARALEL
4	RADIUS
5	**ANGULAR**
6	DIAMETER

ANGULAR allows you to dimension the angle in degrees between two nonparallel lines. These lines do not have to be coplanar. The *apparent angle* is dimensioned, not necessarily the true angle. Because there exist four possible angles between two lines, CADKEY Light superimposes dashed lines to the edge of the viewport over the angle. You are then prompted to cursor-indicate the desired angle.

1. Select the first line of the angle (P1).

2. Select the second line of the angle (P2).

3. Of the four angles displayed, cursor indicate the desired angle by clicking once in the angle's region.

4. Indicate the dimension's text position (P3).

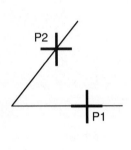
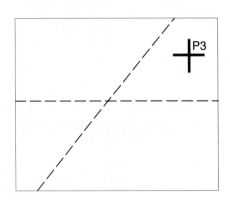
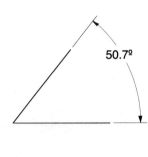

1	HORIZTL
2	VERTICL
3	PARALEL
4	RADIUS
5	ANGULAR
6	**DIAMETER**

A **DIAMETER** dimension is used for complete circles, holes, cylinders, or spheres.

1. Indicate the circle to be dimensioned (P1).

2. Indicate the dimension text position (P2).

3. Choose **LEFT** or **RIGHT** for leader position. In general, place the leader to the left of a right-hand dimension and to the right of a left hand dimension.

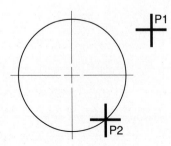
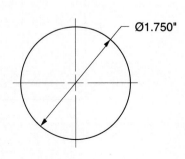

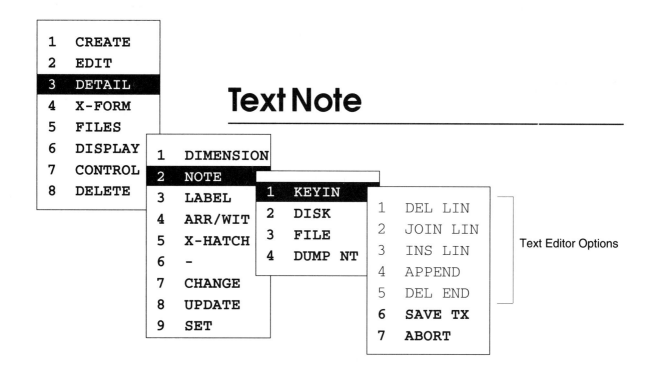

Text Note

▼ DESCRIPTION OF FUNCTION

A text note is a passage of text placed normally to the view of creation. It is visible only in that view. Text notes require several special considerations:

- Notes may use any of the following characters

!@#$%^&*()_+{}[]~'":;?/<.>,| \ 0-9, A-Z, a-z, $\pm$,°,Ø, space, <Enter>

- Notes cannot exceed 1,024 characters including spaces unless the text is read in from a text **FILE**. In that case there is no character limit.

- Line length cannot exceed 128 characters.

- Notes assume attributes set in **DETAIL–SET–TEXT**.

- Notes entered from the on-line text editor must first be saved with **SAVE TX** before placing.

- The origin of the text note (for placing and selecting) is determined by **NOT PLC**. You may want to use the window option for selection if you are unfamiliar with the location of a note's origin.

- Disk-based notes can be edited using the text editor options. See pages 302-303 for a discussion of text editing.

- File-based notes *cannot* be edited using the text editor.

▼   OPTIONS

KEYIN allows text notes to be created by keyboard input.

1. Keyboard enter the text note. Use <Enter> to place text on successive lines.

2. Choose **SAVE TX** to signal CADKEY Light that you are done entering text. Or,

3. Choose **ABORT** to return to the previous menu without placing the text.

4. Cursor indicate the text position in the desired viewport.

5. The text is placed each time the cursor position is indicated. Use **F10** backup to enter different text. Use **ESC** to return to the Main Menu.

DISK allows ASCII text that was created in a text editor or word processor to be used as a CADKEY Light text note. Replace tabs with spaces and use only the valid character set. A text note brought in from disk is saved as part of the data base of the part file.

1. Enter a complete path and file name including file extension. The extension is necessary because the text note is not a CADKEY Light file.

2. Indicate the position of the note origin.

3. The note is placed each time the cursor position is indicated. Use **F10** backup to respecify path and file name. Use **ESC** to return to the Main Menu.

FILE is much like the **DISK** option in that it provides a method of using text created in an editor or word processor in a CADKEY Light part drawing. However, a note read in using **FILE** is *not* saved with the part file. To print, plot, or view the note, CADKEY Light must be able to locate and read the text file. For this reason, use **FILE** only if the note exceeds the 1,024 character limit.

1. Enter a complete path and file name including file extension.

2. Indicate the position of the note origin.

3. The note is placed each time the cursor position is indicated. Use **F10** backup to respecify path and file name. Use **ESC** to return to the Main Menu.

DUMP NT provides a method of exporting a note on a CADKEY Light drawing to a text file. Use this option when you realize that a note will be used many times on different drawings.

1. Select the desired note using an option from the Selection Menu.

2. Keyboard enter the complete path and file name. If no path is specified, the **\NOT** subdirectory is used. If no extension is specified, the **.not** extension is used.

3. If the file exists at the specified location, respond **YES** or **NO** to replacing the original.

4. Use **F10** backup to return to the Note Menu. Use **ESC** to return to the Main Menu.

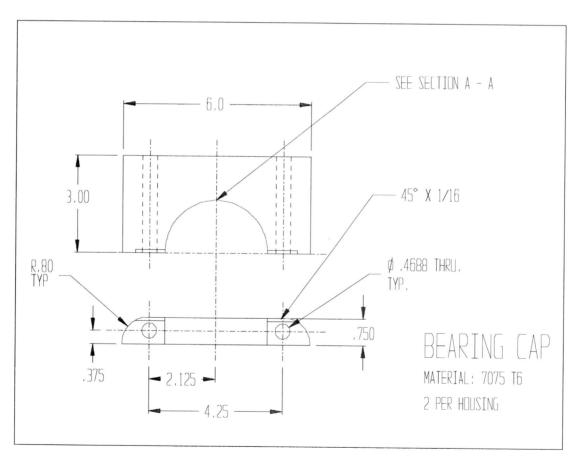

A CADKEY Light engineering detail drawing with notes and labels. Notice that a note provides general information applicable to the entire design. Labels (with leaders) provide information at specific locations on the design. Drawing by Vector Aeromotive.

```
1   CREATE
2   EDIT
3   DETAIL
4   X-FORM
5   FILES
6   DISPLAY
7   CONTROL
8   DELETE
```

```
1   DIMENSION
2   NOTE
3   LABEL
4   ARR/WIT
5   X-HATCH
6   -
7   CHANGE
8   UPDATE
9   SET
```

Text Label

▼ DESCRIPTION OF FUNCTION

A text label is a block of text with a leader and an arrow. Labels use the following guidelines:

- Up to 1,024 characters total, including spaces.

- Up to 128 characters per line.

- Use the label character set.

!@#$%^&*()_+{}[]~'":;?/<.>,| \ 0-9, A-Z, a-z, $\pm$,º ,Ø, space, <Enter>

- Labels assume the current text attributes.

- A label is created normal to and in the current view and is displayed in that view only.

- The leader can be drawn from either the right or left of the label.

- A text label can only be entered from the keyboard.

1. Enter the label's text from the keyboard using the label guidelines.

2. Choose **SAVE TX** when done.

3. Cursor indicate the label's origin or alignment point (P1). This origin assumes the position set in **SET—TEXT—NOT PLC**. In the example, the alignment point is at the right-bottom.

4. Cursor indicate the side for the label's leader (P2).

5. A rubberband line appears from the side of the label. Use **F10** backup to change the leader's side.

6. Choose any option from the Position Menu for the tip of the leader's arrow. Locate the arrow (P3).

7. Continue to cursor indicate the arrow's position until satisfied with the location. Press <Enter>.

8. Use **F10** backup to return to the Detail Menu. Press **ESC** to return to the Main Menu.

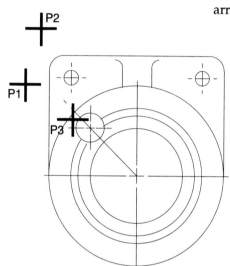

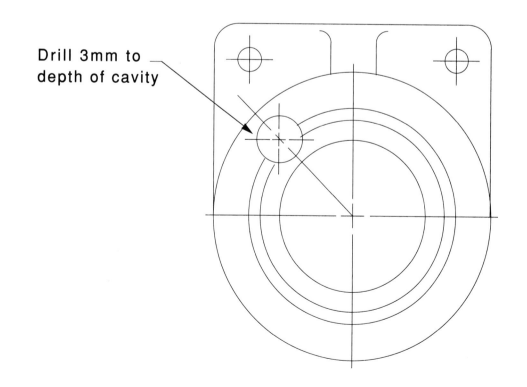

Drill 3mm to depth of cavity

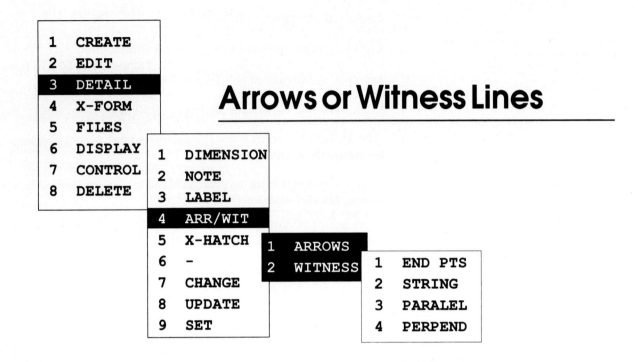

Arrows or Witness Lines

▼ **DESCRIPTION OF FUNCTION**

This option allows arrows and witness lines to be created that are independent detail drafting entities and not associated with dimensions, notes, or labels. The size of the arrow is controlled by the current dimension text height assigned in **SET—TEXT—DIM HT**. Each arrow includes an attached arrow shaft. A witness line is automatically spaced from the indicated starting position. Arrows and witness lines are created normal to the current view and visible only in that view.

▼ **OPTIONS**

END PTS creates arrows or witness lines by start and endpoints.

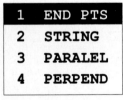

1. Cursor indicate a starting position for the entity using any option from the Position Menu (P1).

2. Cursor indicate the position of the tip of the arrow or end of the witness using any option from the Position Menu (P2).

3. Continue creating entities. **F10** backup to change to other entity type. **ESC** to the Main Menu.

STRING allows arrows or witness lines to be created end to end.

1	END PTS
2	STRING
3	PARALEL
4	PERPEND

1. Cursor-indicate a starting position for the entity using any option from the Position Menu (P1).

2. Cursor-indicate the position of the tip of the arrow or witness using any option from the Position Menu (P2). This point becomes the start point for the next entity.

3. Continue creating entities. **F10** backup to change to other entity type. **ESC** to the Main Menu.

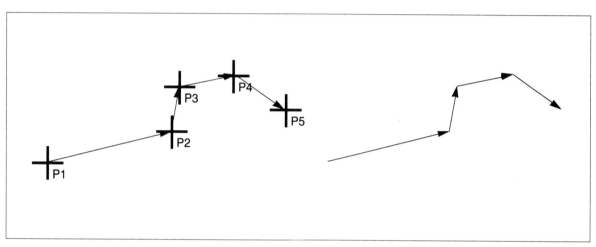

String line created with the end on one line being the start of the next.

1	END PTS
2	STRING
3	PARALEL
4	PERPEND

PARALEL allows arrows or witness lines to be created parallel to an existing line through some point. The line is created the same length, parallel to, and in the same direction (start to end) as the reference line.

1. Select the reference line (P1). See top of next page.

2. Indicate a reference point (P2) through which the entity will be created. Point P2 becomes the beginning of the line.

3. The entity will be created from P2 in the same direction as was the reference. Note how this may change the results.

4. **F10** backup to change options or **ESC** to the Main Menu.

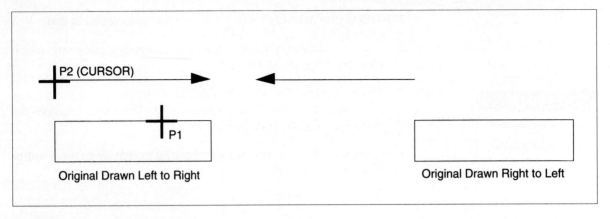

Line is parallel and same length in the direction the original

1	END PTS
2	STRING
3	PARALEL
4	**PERPEND**

PERPEND creates an arrow or witness perpendicular to an existing line through some point.

1. Select the reference line to which the new entity will be perpendicular (P1).

2. Choose a point using an option from the Position Menu through which the perpendicular will pass (P2). The perpendicular will be created either to the line or to the extension of the line.

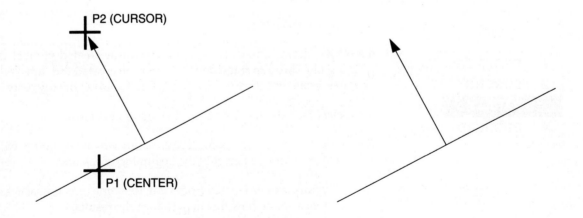

Line created perpendicular from the center to a free cursor location.

1	CREATE
2	EDIT
3	**DETAIL**
4	X-FORM
5	FILES
6	DISPLAY
7	CONTROL
8	DELETE

1	DIMENSION
2	NOTE
3	LABEL
4	ARR/WIT
5	**X-HATCH**
6	-
7	CHANGE
8	UPDATE
9	SET

Cross Hatching

▼ DESCRIPTION OF FUNCTION

Cross-hatching produces a pattern of grouped lines that fill a completely closed area. Only areas bounded by lines or arcs or circles can be cross-hatched. The hatch pattern itself can be selected and manipulated by functions that act on grouped entities. Entity attributes can also be changed.

▼ OPTIONS

Seven hatch patterns are available in CADKEY Light. Because you can vary spacing and angle, an almost unlimited number of hatching patterns can be created.

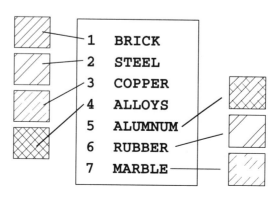

1	BRICK
2	STEEL
3	COPPER
4	ALLOYS
5	ALUMNUM
6	RUBBER
7	MARBLE

Valid Hatch Areas

The following are examples of valid hatch areas. Notice that the areas are bound, continuous, and unambiguous. That is, all lines begin and end on the perimeter of the area to be hatched.

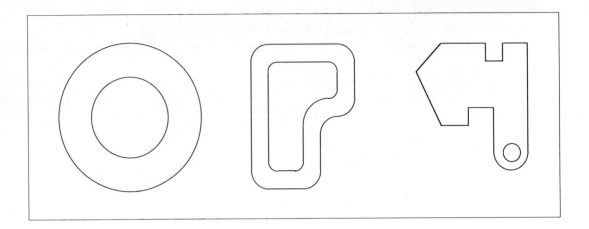

Breaking an Entity to Form a Valid Area

Because the arc does not start and end on the perimeter of the hatch area, it cannot be correctly filled. CADKEY Light may go ahead and try to fill the area with unpredictable results. If the arc is broken at P1 and P2, the middle portion of the arc becomes part of the perimeter of the valid area.

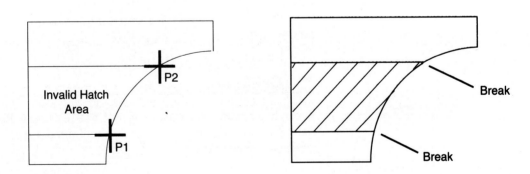

Nested Areas

It is often necessary to leave parts clear inside cross-hatch areas. CADKEY Light is able to do this by identifying in order the boundaries of each area. The first perimeter (A1) turns on the hatching. Perimeter A2 turns the hatching off. This may be done as may times as there are nested perimeters to identify. See the figure at the top of the next page.

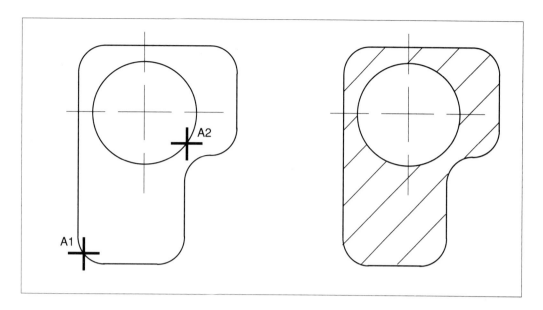

1   Choose the desired hatch pattern from the menu area.

2.   Keyboard enter the angle for the hatch lines or <Enter> to accept the default value.

3.   Keyboard enter the distance between hatch lines or <Enter> to accept the default value.

4.   Choose an option from the Selection Menu. You may want to invoke the immediate mode Masking Menu with **ALT—M**.

5.   Select the closed area(s). (First A1 and then A2, etc.)

6.   Choose **YES** to signal CADKEY Light that you have completed the selection of the area to hatch.

7.   Use **F10** backup to stay in the Hatching Menu but change options. Press **ESC** to return to the Main Menu.

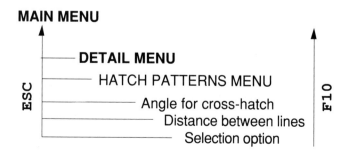

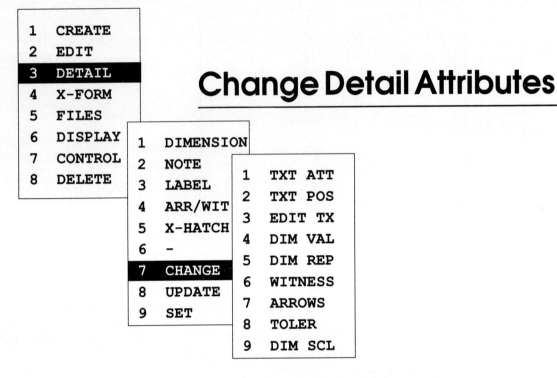

Change Detail Attributes

▼ **DESCRIPTION OF FUNCTION**

The **CHANGE** functions allows detail attributes for selected entities to be changed. Default attributes are not changed; attributes of unselected detail drafting entities are not changed.

Changing some attributes may cause the detail entity to be repositioned. This may require the entity to be moved or returned to its original attribute specification.

▼ **OPTIONS**

Text Attributes

FONT changes the font or text style of selected text. CADKEY Light offers two styles with slant and bold parameters. Six different type styles can then be displayed. Choose **DONE** to return to the Change Menu.

CADKEY
Box (no slant, no fill)

CADKEY
Bold (no slant, filled)

CADKEY
Box (slant, no fill)

CADKEY
Bold (slant, no fill)

CADKEY
Bold (no slant, no fill)

CADKEY
Bold (slant, filled)

HEIGHT allows you to change the height of text characters. The width of each character is adjusted by the current setting of **ASPECT**. Choose **DONE** to return to the Change Menu.

NOT ANG allows the base line of notes to be changed. Angles are measured counterclockwise from the positive X axis. Enter base line angle in degrees. Choose **DONE** to return to the Change Menu.

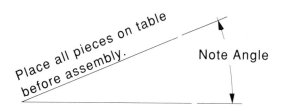

ASPECT changes the percentage of width to height for all text selected. For example, an aspect number of .5 established that the width of the text will be 50% of its height. The range of acceptable values is .01-100. Choose **DONE** to return to the Change Menu.

MIRROR revolves a selected text note 180° about the YV axis. The selection point of the text block remains at the same physical location relative to the block. Choose **DONE** to return to the Change Menu.

SLANT keeps the base line of selected text in the current position and inclines the characters either positive (to the left) or negative (to the right).

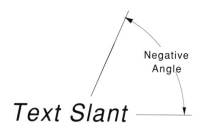

FILL Allows outline characters to be filled (made bold), and bold characters to be returned to outline form. Answer **YES** or **NO** for fill action: Yes means filled, no means not filled.

DONE signals CADKEY Light that you are finished changing text attributes. The Selection Menu is displayed and you select the text to be changed using one of the options. The text is redisplayed in changed form. If the text is too small to be read at the current display size, it is represented by a rectangular box. Press **ESC** to return to the Main Menu.

1	TXT ATT
2	TXT POS
3	EDIT TX
4	DIM VAL
5	DIM REP
6	WITNESS
7	ARROWS
8	TOLER
9	DIM SCL

Text position refers to where, within the block that defines the boundaries of the text, the selection point or origin will be found. This is not the same as *text justification* in that the orientation of the text to the block does not change. It is convenient to alter **TXT POS** if text placement relative to geometric or detail drafting entities is critical.

1. Select the detail entity. The default text position locates the selection point at the lower left of the first line of text. However, **TEX POS** may be at any of the nine locations.

2. When selected, a frame appears around the text block with the cursor attached at the current origin.

3. Move the cursor to any of the nine selection points and click once.

4. The text is adjusted to conform to this new position, and leaders, arrows, or witness lines are repositioned as necessary.

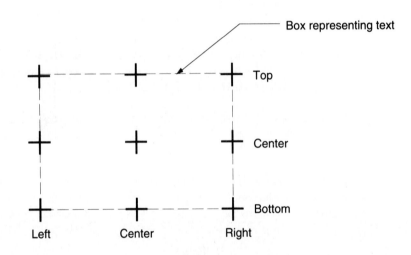

Box representing text

Top

Center

Bottom

Left   Center   Right

The On-Line Text Editor

CADKEY Light provides a means for editing text in previously created detail entities. The following guidelines should be used for text editing:

1	TXT ATT
2	TXT POS
3	EDIT TX
4	DIM VAL
5	DIM REP
6	WITNESS
7	ARROWS
8	TOLER
9	DIM SCL

Editable

- Dimensions with manually entered text.

- Notes with text entered from the keyboard .

- Labels.

Not Editable

- Notes that have been read in using the **FILE** option.

- Text editing is restricted to 128 characters per line and 1,024 characters per text block.

Text is edited using both menu options and special-function keystrokes. The special keystrokes allow the editing point to be moved within the text block while the menu options perform vital editing operations. New text is entered from the keyboard. Only the current line of text is displayed for editing in the editor while the entire text block is displayed in the viewport for reference. To save the text, press **F6**. To exit the text editor without saving changes and return to the Change Menu, press **F10**. To exit the text editor without saving changes and return to the Main Menu, press **ESC**.

Positioning Keys

After the text has been selected, use the following keys to position the editing cursor within the text block.

Home	Moves cursor to beginning of current line.
↑	Moves cursor up one line.
↓	Moves cursor down one line.
→	Moves cursor one character to the right on same line.
←	Moves cursor one character to the left on the same line.
End	Moves cursor to the end of the current line
Back Space	Deletes character to the left of the current position.
Delete	Deletes the character to the right of the current position.
Insert	Toggles between insert and overwrite modes.
<Enter>	In insert mode, saves all text up to the current cursor position by creating a new line of text to the right of the cursor position. In overwrite mode, saves all text up to the current cursor position and advances the cursor to the end of the next line.

Menu Functions

DEL LIN deletes the current line of text and displays the preceding line.

JOIN LIN joins the current line with the following line. Line length exceeding characters 128 is truncated.

INS LIN inserts a blank line above the current line.

APPEND inserts a blank line below the current line.

DEL END deletes all characters from the current cursor position to the end of the line.

SAVE TXT saves the edited text. If you are editing existing text, the detail

1	DEL LIN
2	JOIN LIN
3	INS LIN
4	APPEND
5	DEL END
6	SAVE TX
7	ABORT

entity is redrawn with the changes. If you are creating a new dimension, label, or note, you are prompted to indicate the entity's position.

ABORT exits the text editor without saving changes made to the text.

1	TXT ATT
2	TXT POS
3	EDIT TX
4	**DIM VAL**
5	DIM REP
6	WITNESS
7	ARROWS
8	TOLER
9	DIM SCL

DIM VAL provides a method of changing the dimension value currently associated with a dimension. The true size of the dimension is shown in parentheses as the default value. If the dimension value has already been changed, the text on the entity will not match the default text. Press <Enter> to accept the true dimension value or keyboard enter a new value. The <Enter> after this has been typed accepts the new value. Tolerances remain unchanged by this action.

DIM REP allows dimensions represented in one set of units to be changed to another. For example, decimal dimensions can be changed to feet and inches or fractional units. This option in **CHANGE** is used for existing dimensions. The same option in **SET** is used to change the default (modal) setting for all subsequent dimensions.

1	TXT ATT
2	TXT POS
3	EDIT TX
4	DIM VAL
5	**DIM REP**
6	WITNESS
7	ARROWS
8	TOLER
9	DIM SCL

1	DECIMAL
2	FRACTIN
3	FT / IN

If **DECIMAL** is chosen, fractional or **FT/IN** dimensions are displayed to the level of precision chosen from the menu. If **FRACTIN** is chosen, the current dimension is changed to a fractional value. Dimensions will be rounded to the nearest fractional unit and half units will be rounded down. Dimensions changed to **FT/IN** will be rounded to the nearest fraction chosen from the menu. Half units will be rounded down.

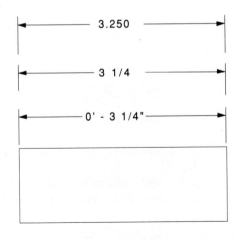

1	TXT ATT
2	TXT POS
3	EDIT TX
4	DIM VAL
5	DIM REP
6	WITNESS
7	ARROWS
8	TOLER
9	DIM SCL

1	BOTH
2	FIRST
3	SECOND
4	NONE

WITNESS allows the witness lines of existing dimensions to be omitted. The witness lines are considered as they are stored in the data base and depend on how the dimension distance was identified. Consider that a dimension is to be placed from P1 to P2 in the example. For the purposes of editing witness lines, the first witness line is that next to P1 and the second witness line is that next to P2. To keep from applying two reference lines at the same location, the **FIRST** witness line is suppressed.

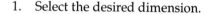

First witness supressed on
the 4.000 dimension.

ARROWS allows the orientation of dimension arrows to be changed. The position of dimension text and the length of witness lines is not changed. Two positions of arrows are supported—arrows inside witness lines and arrows outside witness lines. This option applies to horizontal, vertical, parallel, radial, diametrical, and angular dimensions. Use this option when the distance to be dimensioned is so small that text and arrows cannot fit inside witness lines.

1. Select the desired dimension.

2. Choose either **IN** or **OUT** as the position for dimension arrows.

3. Press <Enter>. Arrows are redrawn in the new position.

TOLER allows the tolerance value and type to be changed for selected dimensions. The **TYPE** option is used to assign a tolerance type to a dimension. The **VALUE** option is then used to change tolerance values.

1	TXT ATT
2	TXT POS
3	EDIT TX
4	DIM VAL
5	DIM REP
6	WITNESS
7	ARROWS
8	TOLER
9	DIM SCL

1	DIRECT

1	IN
2	OUT

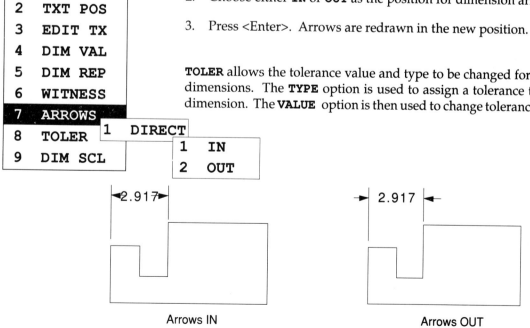

Arrows IN   Arrows OUT

A tolerance is the accepted deviation in a dimension. It does not change the dimension value itself. A positive tolerance establishes how much more than the dimension value will be accepted. A negative tolerance establishes how much less than the dimension value will be accepted. This range can be expressed as a +/- value after the dimension itself or as a set of dimension limits that the + and - values calculate. In a limit dimension the largest value is displayed over the smallest value.

Use **POS TOL** to keyboard enter a change in the positive limit. Use **NEG TOL** to change the negative or lower limit. **BOTH** is used to change both positive and negative values at the same time.

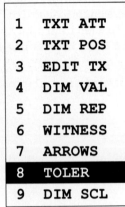

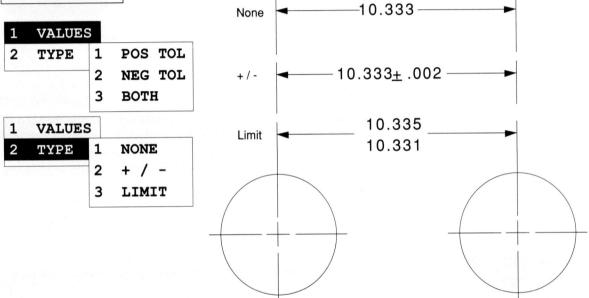

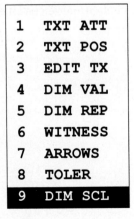

DIM SCL allows a dimension to be changed by applying a scale factor. This does not change the actual value of the detail drafting entity, only the value displayed in the dimension itself. The new scale factor is applied to the true entity value. Tolerance remain unaffected by the scaling. Angular dimensions and manually-entered dimensions are not scalable.

1	CREATE
2	EDIT
3	**DETAIL**
4	X-FORM
5	FILES
6	DISPLAY
7	CONTROL
8	DELETE

1	DIMENSION
2	NOTE
3	LABEL
4	ARR/WIT
5	X-HATCH
6	–
7	CHANGE
8	**UPDATE**
9	SET

Update Attribute Changes

▼ DESCRIPTION OF FUNCTION

This function changes selected detail entities to reflect attributes changed in **DETAIL–SET**. The following attributes can be updated.

- Note and label height, font, slant, and fill.

- Dimension height, font, value representation, dimension scale, trailing and leading zeros.

- Tolerance type and values.

It should be noted that the changing of certain attributes may result in entity text size that is inappropriate. The original or true dimension value is stored as part of the entity and will be presented as the default dimension value.

1. Select the entity or entities that you wish to update to reflect changes in **DETAIL–SET**.

2. Selected entities are updated and the screen is redrawn.

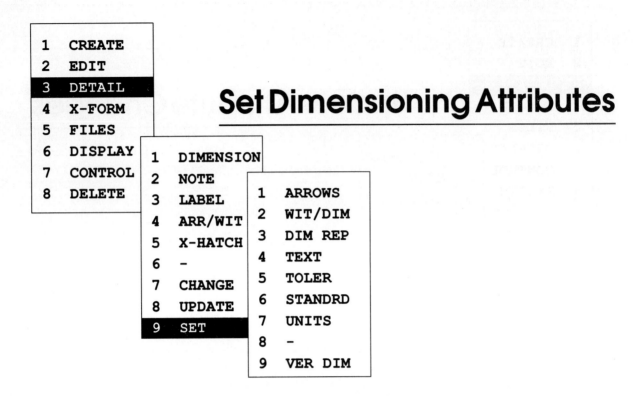

Set Dimensioning Attributes

▼ DESCRIPTION OF FUNCTION

The **SET** function changes the default or modal settings of CADKEY Light. These modal settings are those that will be used unless you change them. Many of the options are identical to those found in **DETAIL–CHANGE** discussed on pages 300-306. In this section, only those options unique to **DETAIL–SET** will be presented.

▼ OPTIONS

WIT/LDR allows witness lines and leaders to be changed. The witness part of this option is identical to that presented on page 305. The leader part is unique to this menu.

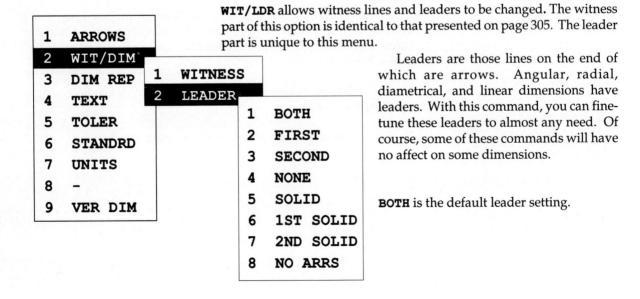

Leaders are those lines on the end of which are arrows. Angular, radial, diametrical, and linear dimensions have leaders. With this command, you can fine-tune these leaders to almost any need. Of course, some of these commands will have no affect on some dimensions.

BOTH is the default leader setting.

309

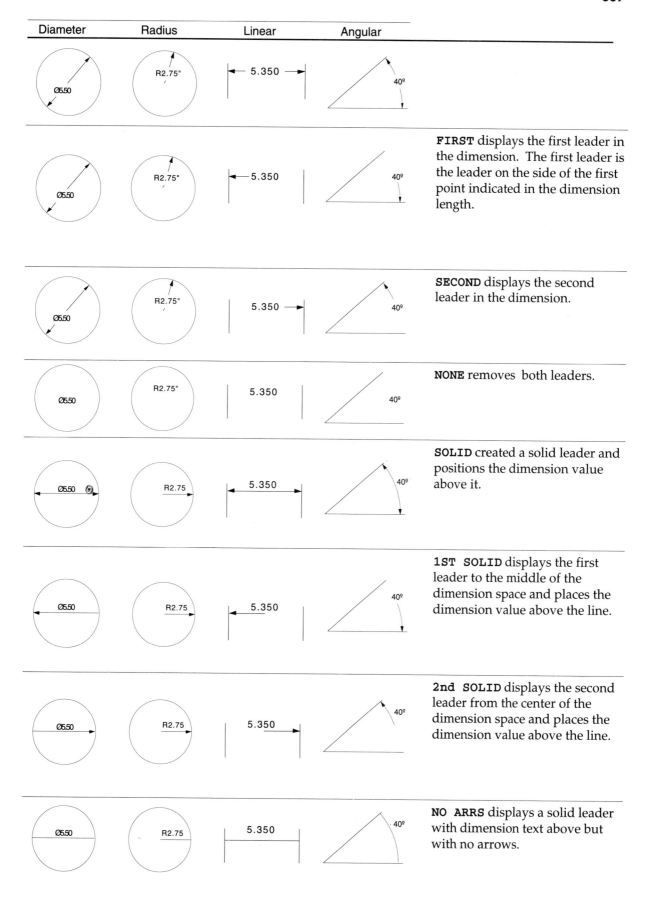

Diameter	Radius	Linear	Angular

FIRST displays the first leader in the dimension. The first leader is the leader on the side of the first point indicated in the dimension length.

SECOND displays the second leader in the dimension.

NONE removes both leaders.

SOLID created a solid leader and positions the dimension value above it.

1ST SOLID displays the first leader to the middle of the dimension space and places the dimension value above the line.

2nd SOLID displays the second leader from the center of the dimension space and places the dimension value above the line.

NO ARRS displays a solid leader with dimension text above but with no arrows.

TEXT allows the system default attributes associated with notes, labels, and dimensions to be changed. Once the settings are changed, any *new* detail drafting entities containing text will reflect these changes. For existing entities to reflect these settings, use **UPDATE**.

Each time CADKEY Light is started, text defaults are set. If you desire custom settings to start a work session, create a *template* or blank part file with the text settings established. The default text settings in CADKEY Light are as follows.

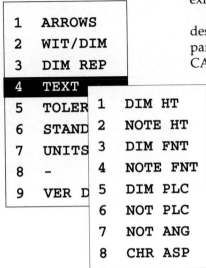

1	ARROWS
2	WIT/DIM
3	DIM REP
4	TEXT
5	TOLER
6	STAND
7	UNITS
8	-
9	VER D

1	DIM HT
2	NOTE HT
3	DIM FNT
4	NOTE FNT
5	DIM PLC
6	NOT PLC
7	NOT ANG
8	CHR ASP

CADKEY Light Text Defaults

	Dimension	Note or Label
HT	.3"/ 5mm	.3"/ 5mm
FNT	Box	Box
PLC	Center, Center	Left, Bottom
ASP	.5	.5
ANG	0.0	0.0

DIM HT allows the default height of text used for all dimensions to be set. This option may be set using the **DH** option in the Status Menu. Text height must be greater than .0005". Only dimensions created from this point on reflect the new setting.

NOTE HT allows the default height used for all notes and labels to be set. This option may be set using the **NH** option in the Status Menu. Only notes and labels created from this point on reflect the new setting.

DIM FNT allows the default font to be specified for all dimensions. The **DF** option in the Status Menu can be used for changing this setting. You have the option to slant the text or fill it for a bold affect. Box font displays faster than does bold font. Only dimensions created from this point on will reflect the font change.

NOT FNT allows the default font to be specified for all notes and labels. The **NF** option in the Status Menu can be used for changing this setting. You have the option to slant the text or fill it for a bold affect. Box font displays faster than does bold font. Only notes and labels created from this point on will reflect the font change.

```
1   HORIZTL
2   VERTICL
```

DIM PLC allows the placement point (called the *alignment point*) of dimensions to be changed. Alignment points are important in the placing of detail drafting entities in relation to other entities on a drawing.

There are nine possible alignment points based on *placement axis* and *placement point*. The alignment point is based on the greatest line width and the height of the first line of text. Only dimensions created after this setting is made will reflect the new alignment point.

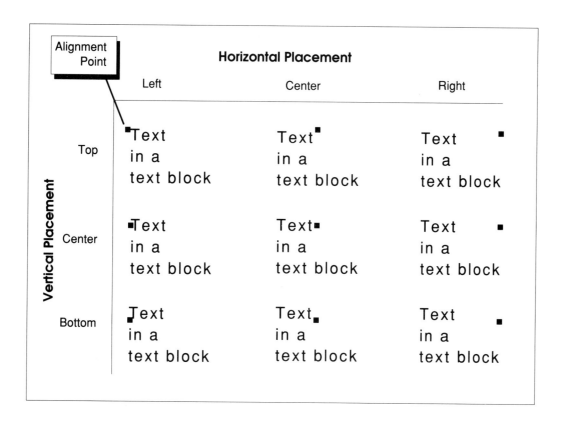

NOT PLC uses the same parameters for notes and labels as **DIM PLC** does for dimensions.

NOT ANG sets the angle of the base line of the note relative to the positive XV axis. The text is rotated about the current alignment point. Use the **RT** option in the Status Menu to set note angle. Only notes created after this point reflect the new angle setting.

CHR ASP allows the relationship of text width to height to be set for dimensions, notes, and labels. This attribute can be used to establish a hierarchical relation between notes, although text that varies by a great deal from the default (.5) is often difficult to read. Only detail drafting entities created from this point on will reflect the new aspect setting.

STANDRD allows several dimensioning standards to be set. These include enabling or disabling the display of leading or trailing zeros, the alignment of dimensioning text with either the dimension itself or the XV axis, and the toggling between automatic and manual dimensioning. Only detail drafting entities created after this option is set will be affected by the change.

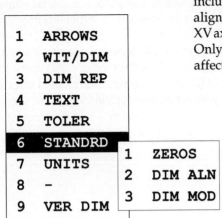

ZEROS turns on or off the display of leading or trailing zeros. Answer **YES** if you want leading or trailing zeros or answer **NO** if you want these zeros suppressed.

	Leading Zeros	Trailing Zeros
YES	0.375	.250
NO	.375	.25

DIM ALN sets the alignment of dimension text. Answer **YES** to align text with the dimension. Answer **NO** to align dimension text with the horizontal.

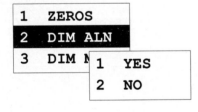

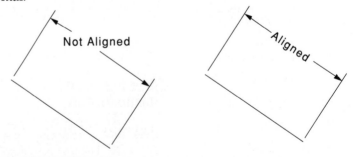

Not Aligned   Aligned

DIM MOD sets the mode of dimension creation—either automatic or manual. **AUTOMAT** places the system calculated dimension value at the indicated location. **MANUAL** allows the text to be entered from the keyboard with the limitations of 128 characters per line and 1,024 characters per string.

1	ARROWS
2	WIT/DIM
3	DIM REP
4	TEXT
5	TOLER
6	STANDRD
7	**UNITS**
8	–
9	VER DIM

1	INCH
2	MM
3	FEET
4	CM
5	YARD
6	METER
7	**USER**

UNITS provides a method of changing the active units used for dimensioning in CADKEY Light. The absolute magnitude of the dimension is not changed by a change in units. The absolute value is multiplied by a *scale factor*, which results in in the dimension being expressed in the selected units. User units can be any scale value that has appropriate meaning to the designer.

For example, a part 100" in length can be expressed in any of the units displayed. The value is rounded to the nearest scale division. Half units are rounded down. User units provides an option to scale geometry for custom applications.

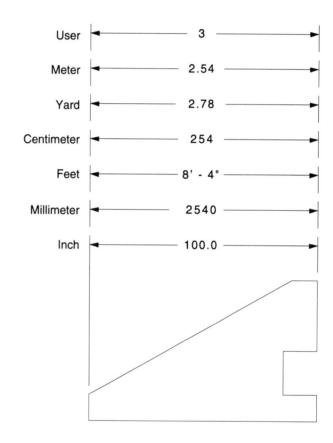

1	ARROWS
2	WIT/DIM
3	DIM REP
4	TEXT
5	TOLER
6	STANDRD
7	UNITS
8	–
9	**VER DIM**

1	YES
2	NO

VER DIM allows you to suppress or turn off the **NO/YES** Verification Menu that is displayed by default (no suppression). This menu requires an explicit acceptance of a dimension or label. Choose **NO** to *not* suppress this menu. Choose **YES** *to suppress* this menu.

X-Form Menu

1	CREATE
2	EDIT
3	DETAIL
4	**X-FORM**
5	~~FILES~~
6	1 TRANS-R
7	2 TRANS-A
8	3 2D ROT
	4 SCALE
	5 MIRROR

Transformation Methods

▼ DESCRIPTION OF FUNCTION

X-FORM provides a method of changing the spatial position of entities or groups of entities that already exist in the part file. Because CADKEY Light does not have an "Undo" command, it is important to save your part file before attempting a transformation function. All geometric entities and most detail drafting entities can be manipulated with this command.

Many of the transformations are similar in operation. It is important to have in mind positive and negative movement in relation to world and view axes. Totally different results will be obtained by changing directions or axis systems. To better understand transformations, the options in this menu are discussed before the actual commands are explained.

▼ OPTIONS

Translate Relative

A relative translation takes selected entities and moves them to another position in space by specifying a new location by *delta* coordinates. In this case, *delta* refers to change. For example, a change in world coordinates in the Y direction is referred to as *dY*. A change in view coordinates in the Y direction is referred to as *dYV*. All entities are moved by the translation amount and the relationship of the selected entities to each other is not changed by the translation.

Translated Position

dZ dX dY

Original Position

All entities moved by dX, dY, dZ.

Translate Absolute

An absolute translation takes selected entities and moves them to another position in space based on an original base point and a new base point. The relationship of the geometry to the base point is not changed by the translation, and the new geometry in the new position has the same orientation to the world axes as did the original (i.e., there has been no rotation).

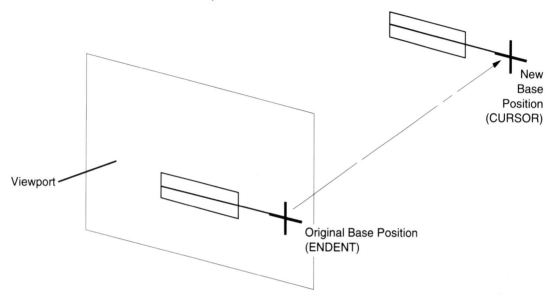

New
Base
Position
(CURSOR)

Viewport

Original Base Position
(ENDENT)

2D Rotation

This transformation rotates selected geometry about the ZV axis a specified number of degrees. In this transformation, geometry moves only in planes of rotation parallel to the viewport in which the rotation is being done. The geometry is rotated about a center point, and the relationship of the geometry to the center point is not changed by the translation.

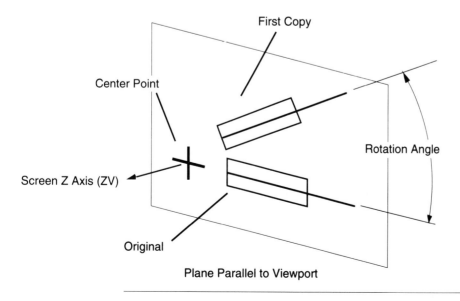

First Copy

Center Point

Rotation Angle

Screen Z Axis (ZV)

Original

Plane Parallel to Viewport

Scale

This transformation is fundamentally different from those mentioned above in that the data that describe the actual size of the selected entities are changed. A scaling center (P1) is identified around which the scaling is performed. A scale factor larger than 1 enlarges the selected entities. A scale factor of less than 1 makes the entities smaller. Note: *Scaling* changes the numerical size of the entities and associated automatic dimensions. *Zooming* reduces or enlarges the display of geometry in a viewport without altering actual entity specifications.

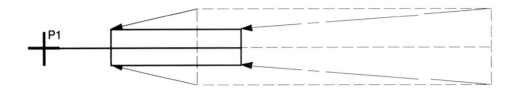

Scaled using ENDENT as the center of scaling.

Mirror

When selected geometry is transformed about an axis parallel to the viewport, it is said to be mirrored. Mirroring is performed such that XV and YV coordinates are changed while ZV coordinates remain the same.

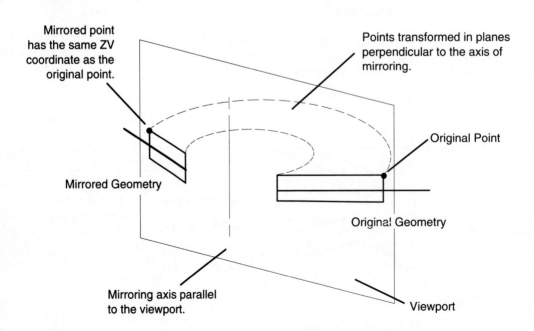

Mirrored point has the same ZV coordinate as the original point.

Points transformed in planes perpendicular to the axis of mirroring.

Mirrored Geometry

Original Point

Original Geometry

Mirroring axis parallel to the viewport.

Viewport

Transformation Methods

Three separate methods are available to each of the five transformation options. **MOVE** takes selected entities and relocates and/or scales them. **COPY** uses selected entities to produce copies. Each new copy is based on the previous copy. All copies are assigned to the same group and subgroup as the original. **JOIN** produces copies of selected geometric entities and automatically joins successive copies with appropriate entities.

Entities	Joined By	Color	Line Type	Line Width
Points	Lines	1	Solid	1
Lines	Lines	1	Solid	1
Polylines	Lines	1	Solid	1
Curve ends	Lines	Curve's	Curve's	Curve's
Polygons	Polygons	Polygon's	Polygon's	Polygon's

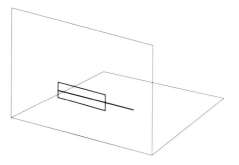 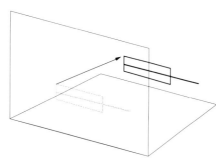

Original geometry is moved to a new location.

Move

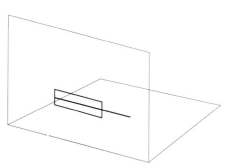 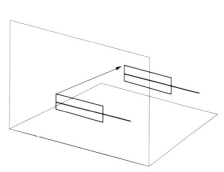

Original geometry is copied at a new location.

Copy

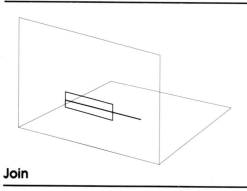 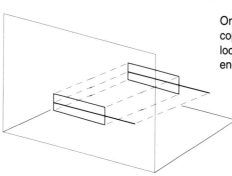

Original geometry is copied at a new location and entity ends are joined.

Join

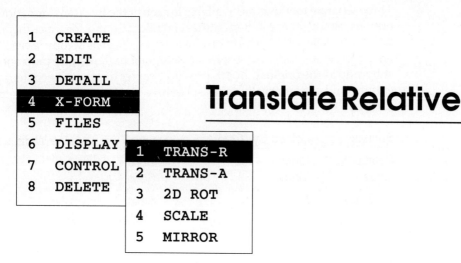

Translate Relative

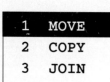

▼ DESCRIPTION OF FUNCTION

TRANS-R provides a way to relocate selected entities in relation to either view or world axes. If view coordinates are chosen, the ZV axis always runs in (-) and out (+) of the screen irrespective of the view and +XV and +YV are to the right and up, respectively. If world coordinates are chosen, make sure that the axis icon is turned on (**DISPLAY—AXES—DISP VW—ON**). This is the only way to determine positive (in the direction of the arrow) and negative (in the opposite direction) translation.

TRANS-R—MOVE takes the selected entities and moves them a specified distance from their current location based on a *delta* change in axis position.

1. Choose either World or View coordinates from the Status Menu.

2. Select the desired entities using an option from the Select Menu (see pages 338-341).

3. Indicate a new position for the selected entities by keyboard entering translation values in the three coordinate directions. You cannot change from View to World coordinates once this process has begun.

3. Press <Enter> to accept a zero value. Press **F10** to back up through the axes and correct mistakes.

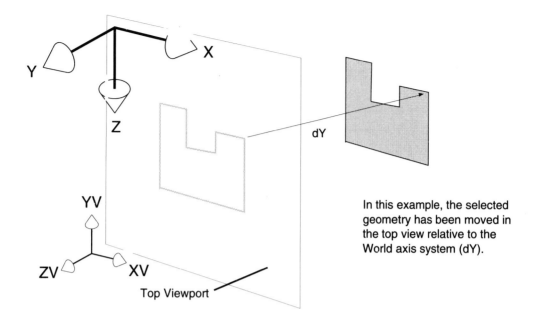

In this example, the selected geometry has been moved in the top view relative to the World axis system (dY).

1	MOVE
2	COPY
3	JOIN

TRANS–R–COPY leaves the selected entities at their original location and makes the number of copies specified at a *delta* change in position. The position of each copy is based on the coordinate location of the previous copy.

1. Choose either World or View coordinates from the Status Menu.

2. Select the desired entities using an option from the Select Menu.

3. Enter the desired number of copies from the keyboard.

4. Indicate the offset position for each copy by keyboard entering translation values in the three coordinate directions. You cannot change from View to World coordinates once this process has begun.

5. Press <Enter> to accept a zero value. Press **F10** to back up through the axes and correct mistakes.

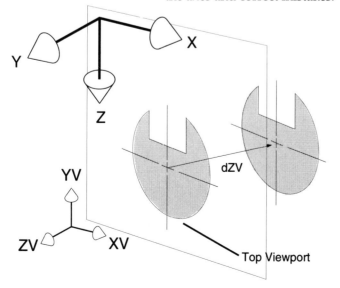

Selected geometry has been moved and copied relative to the view coordinate system (dZV).

1	MOVE
2	COPY
3	JOIN

TRANS—R—JOIN leaves the selected entities at their original location and makes the number of copies specified at a *delta* change in position. The position of each copy is based on the coordinate location of the previous copy and consecutive copies are joined at entity ends based on the chart found on page 317.

1. Choose either World or View coordinates from the Status Menu.

2. Select the desired entities using an option from the Select Menu.

3. Enter the desired number of copies from the keyboard.

4. Indicate the offset position for each copy by keyboard entering translation values in the three coordinate directions. You cannot change from View to World coordinates once this process has begun.

5. Press <Enter> to accept a zero value. Press **F10** to back up through the axes and correct mistakes.

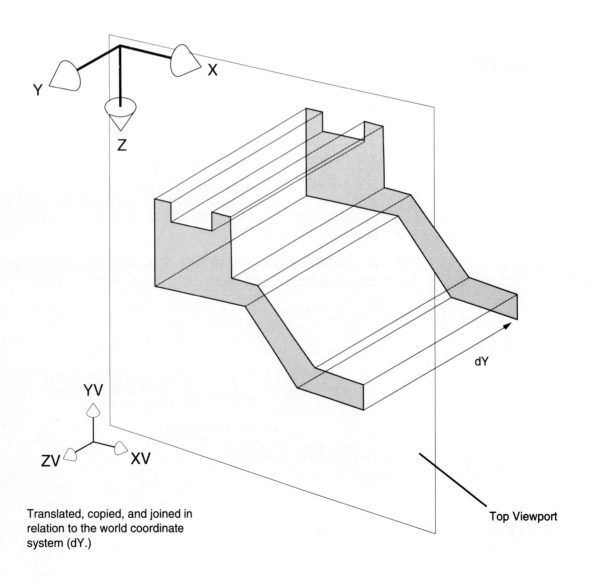

Translated, copied, and joined in
relation to the world coordinate
system (dY.)

1	CREATE
2	EDIT
3	DETAIL
4	**X-FORM**
5	FILES
6	DISPLAY
7	CONTROL
8	DELETE

1	TRANS-R
2	**TRANS-A**
3	2D ROT
4	SCALE
5	MIRROR

Translate Absolute

1	**MOVE**
2	COPY
3	JOIN

▼ DESCRIPTION OF FUNCTION

TRANS-A provides a way to translate selected entities in relation to an original base position and a new base position. The translation is accomplished parallel to the X,Y,Z axes and the geometry is *not* rotated. This option is appropriate if it is the relationship of the selected geometry to some position in the part file that is important. The actual translation distance need not, and usually is not, known.

TRANS-A—MOVE takes the selected entities and moves them to a new location by aligning an original base position with a new base position.

1. Select the desired entities using an option from the Select Menu.

2. Indicate a base position for the selected entities using any option from the Position Menu (P1).

3. Indicate a new base position for the selected entities using any option from the Position Menu (P2).

4. When the new position is indicated, the selected entities are translated in relation to the base point. Additional translations can continue to be made. Press **F10** backup to change the base position. **ESC** to the Main Menu.

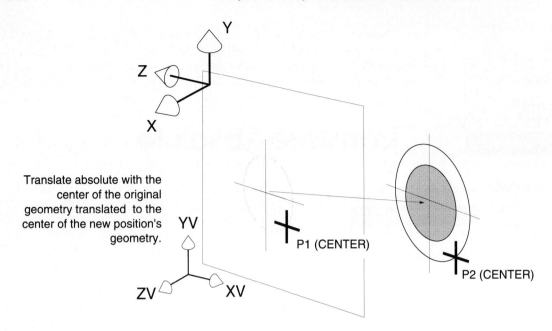

Translate absolute with the center of the original geometry translated to the center of the new position's geometry.

1	MOVE
2	COPY
3	JOIN

TRANS—A—COPY leaves the selected entities at their original location and makes the number of copies specified between the original and base points. The position of each copy is based on the number of copies and the distance between the original and base points.

1. Select the desired entities using an option from the Select Menu.

2. Keyboard enter the desired number of copies.

2. Indicate a base position for the selected entities using any option from the Position Menu (P1).

3. Indicate a new base position for the selected entities using any option from the Position Menu (P2).

4. When the new position is indicated, the selected entities are copied in relation to the base point. Additional translations can continue to be made. Press **F10** backup to change the base position. **ESC** to the Main Menu.

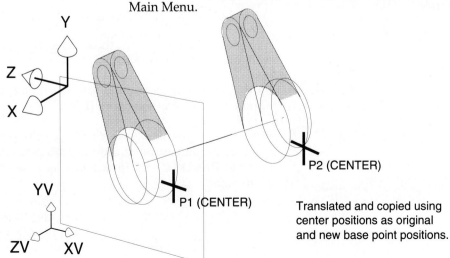

Translated and copied using center positions as original and new base point positions.

1	MOVE
2	COPY
3	**JOIN**

TRANS—A—JOIN leaves the selected entities at their original location and makes the number of copies specified between the original and base points. Corresponding endpoints of copies are joined with lines or polygons based on the chart found on page 317. The position of each copy is based on the number of copies and the distance between the original and base points.

1. Select the desired entities using an option from the Select Menu.

2. Keyboard enter the desired number of copies (in this case, 2).

3. Indicate a base position for the selected entities using any option from the Position Menu (P1).

4. Indicate a new base position for the selected entities using any option from the Position Menu (P2).

5. When the new position is indicated, the selected entities are copied in relation to the base point and the translations are joined. Additional translations can continue to be made. Press **F10** backup to change the base position. **ESC** to the Main Menu.

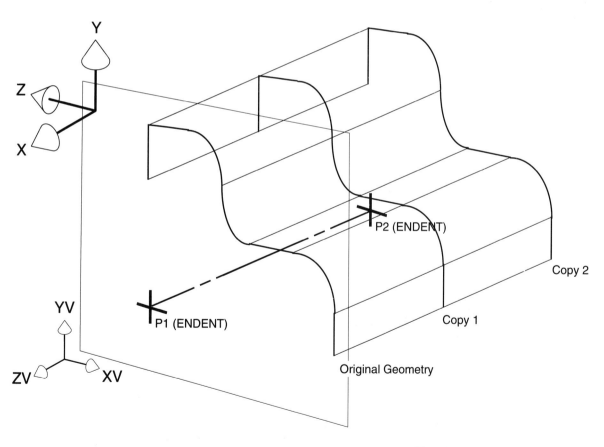

Translated by end of entity base positions with original and two copies joined.

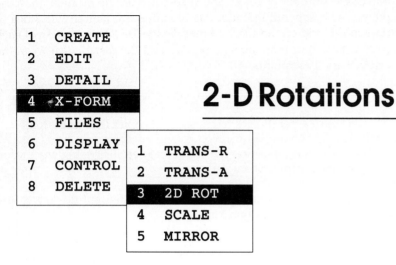

2-D Rotations

▼ **DESCRIPTION OF FUNCTION**

CADKEY Light provides a method of rotating selected geometry about an axis. This rotation, however, can be accomplished only in the plane of the viewport and only about the screen Z axis (ZV). When a world axis is aligned in a given viewport with ZV, the rotation is also about that world axis. Three-dimensional rotations *can* be done by rotating selected geometry in viewports where ZV corresponds to axes in world coordinates. Consider the following guidelines when performing rotations:

- Very small rotations (less than .25 degree) of arcs in a view other than one where the arc is normal may result in unpredictable results.

- Dimension text that is aligned with the dimension's leaders is automatically kept at a readable angle when rotated.

- Nonaligned dimension text is kept horizontal although the dimension itself may be rotated.

2D ROT–MOVE takes the selected entities and rotates them about a center point by either positive or negative degrees. All rotations cause a change in XV and YV coordinates but no change in ZV coordinates.

1. Select the desired entities using an option from the Select Menu.

2. Indicate a center point for the rotation using any option from the Position Menu (P1). Only XV and YV coordinates can be indicated.

3. Keyboard enter a rotation angle. Values can be positive (CCW) or negative (CW).

4. The selected entities are rotated about the designated XV,YV center point. Press **F10** backup to change center point or angle. **ESC** to the Main Menu.

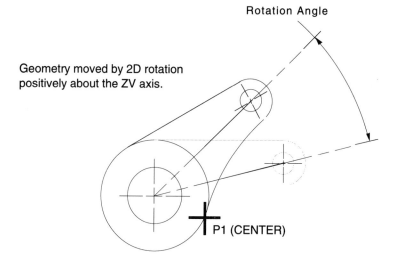

Geometry moved by 2D rotation positively about the ZV axis.

1	MOVE
2	COPY
3	JOIN

2D ROT—COPY takes the selected entities and rotates them about a center point by either positive or negative degrees, making a copy at the specified degree intervals. All rotations cause a change in XV and YV coordinates but no change in ZV coordinates.

1. Select the desired entities using an option from the Select Menu.

2. Keyboard enter the desired number of copies.

3. Indicate a center point for the rotation using any option from the Position Menu (P1). Only XV and YV coordinated can be indicated.

4. Keyboard enter a rotation angle. Values can be positive (CCW) or negative (CW).

5. The selected entities are rotated about the designated XV,YV center point and copied at each angle increment. Press **F10** backup to change center point or angle. **ESC** to the Main Menu.

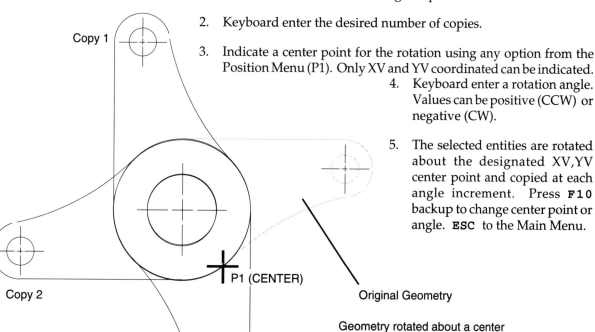

Geometry rotated about a center point with 3 copies made at 90º intervals.

1	MOVE
2	COPY
3	JOIN

2D ROT—JOIN takes the selected entities and rotates them about a center point by either positive or negative degrees, making a copy at the specified degree intervals. Corresponding endpoints of copies are joined with lines or polygons based on the chart found on page 317. All rotations cause a change in XV and YV coordinates but no change in ZV coordinates.

1. Select the desired entities using an option from the Select Menu.

2. Keyboard enter the desired number of copies.

2. Indicate a center point for the rotation using any option from the Position Menu (P1). Only XV and YV coordinates can be indicated.

3. Keyboard enter a rotation angle. Values can be positive (CCW) or negative (CW).

4. The selected entities are rotated about the designated XV,YV center point and copied at each angle increment. The lines or polygons that join each copy are created automatically. Press **F10** backup to change rotation angle, center point, or to choose again entities to rotate and join. **ESC** to the Main Menu.

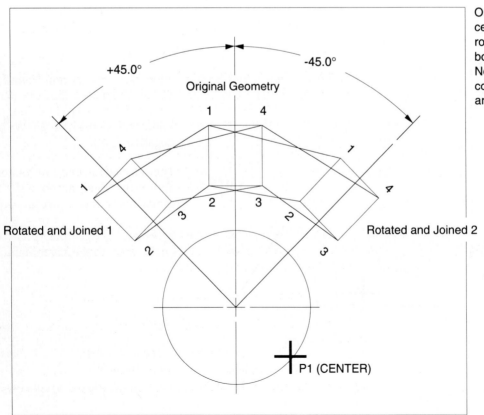

+45.0°   -45.0°

Original Geometry

1   4

2   3

Rotated and Joined 1   Rotated and Joined 2

P1 (CENTER)

Original geometry in center has been rotated and joined at both +45º and -45º. Note that corresponding corners are connected.

1	CREATE
2	EDIT
3	DETAIL
4	**X-FORM**
5	FILES
6	DISPLAY
7	CONTROL
8	DELETE

1	TRANS-R
2	TRANS-A
3	2D ROT
4	**SCALE**
5	MIRROR

Scale

▼ **DESCRIPTION OF FUNCTION**

This transformation is fundamentally different from those previously mentioned in that the dimensional size of the selected entities is scaled up or down. Consider the following guidelines when scaling geometric entities:

- If **AUTO UP** is selected **ON**, all text values in associated dimensions will be automatically updated to reflect the change in scale. Text in angular dimensions and manually entered text in dimensions will not be changed.

- 3D geometry can be scaled even though only XV and YV coordinates can be specified for the scaling origin. Change construction depth to locate scaled geometry along the ZV axis.

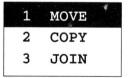

1	**MOVE**
2	COPY
3	JOIN

SCALE—MOVE allows selected entities to be translated and scaled at the same time. Entities are scaled around a center point. This point does not have to be at the center of the group of entities.

1. Select the desired entities using an option from the Select Menu.

2. Indicate with XV,YV the scaling origin using an option from the Position Menu.

3. Keyboard enter a scale factor and press <Enter>. This scale factor works on the current size of the entities if they have previously been scaled.

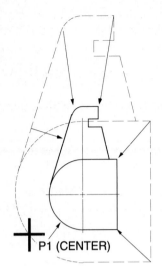

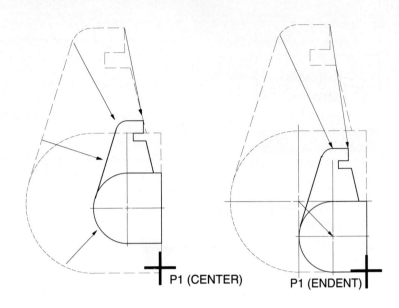

Geometry scaled about center, side, and corner.

4. The selected entities are scaled and moved into a new position relative to the indicated center point. Notice in the examples above how different center points change the final position but not actual size of the selected entities.

When the Scaling Origin Is Outside the Geometry

The examples at the top of this page are clear in how they depict geometry being scaled at the center, side, and corner of the figure. If the scaling origin is located outside the geometry that is to be scaled, it can be difficult to predict the location of the scaled geometry. Assume for this discussion the most simple case, one where construction depth has not been changed from that where the target geometry rests.

In the example below, the entire figure is to be moved at 25% scale based on the scaling origin, P1. Note the result in the second illustration. Every point on the original geometry is moved along a line from it to point P1 75% of the total distance. The result is a 25% figure at a position 25% of the distance from P1 to the original geometry.

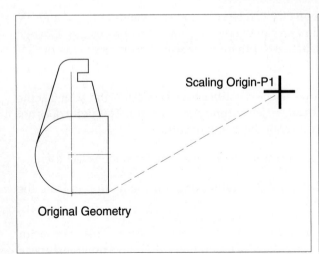

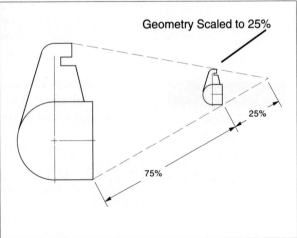

1	MOVE
2	COPY
3	JOIN

SCALE—COPY allows selected entities to be translated, scaled, and copied. Entities are scaled around a center point and each new set of copies is scaled based on the previous copy.

1. Select the desired entities using an option from the Select Menu.

2. Indicate with XV,YV the scaling origin using an option from the Position Menu (P1).

3. Keyboard enter a scale factor and press <Enter>. This scale factor works on the size of the previous copy or on the original's size in the case of a first copy.

4. The selected entities are scaled and copied relative to the indicated center point.

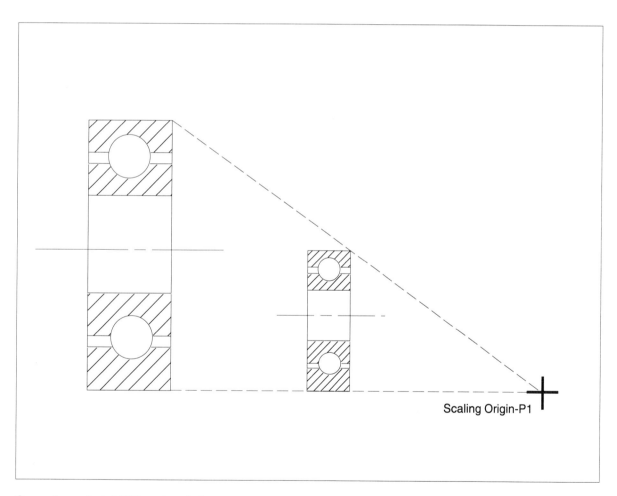

Geometry scaled at 50% and copied.

1	MOVE
2	COPY
3	JOIN

SCALE–JOIN allows selected entities to be translated, scaled, copied, and joined. Entities are scaled around a center point, and each new set of copies is scaled based on the previous copy. Corresponding end points of copies are joined with lines or polygons based on the chart found on page 317.

1. Select the desired entities using an option from the Select Menu.

2. Indicate with XV,YV the scaling origin using an option from the Position Menu. A change in construction depth at this time will result in a scaled and joined 3D model.

3. Keyboard enter a scale factor and press <Enter>. This scale factor works on the size of the previous copy or on the original's size in the case of a first copy.

4. The selected entities are scaled, copied, and joined relative to the indicated center point.

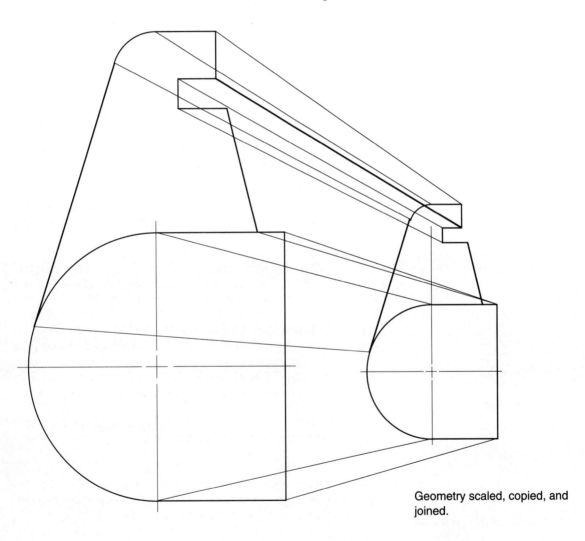

Geometry scaled, copied, and joined.

1	CREATE
2	EDIT
3	DETAIL
4	**X-FORM**
5	FILES
6	DISPLAY
7	CONTROL
8	DELETE

1	TRANS-R
2	TRANS-A
3	2D ROT
4	SCALE
5	**MIRROR**

Mirror

▼ **DESCRIPTION OF FUNCTION**

The **MIRROR** function provides a method to duplicate geometry 180° about an axis parallel to the current viewport. There is no change in ZV coordinates. Consider the following guidelines when mirroring geometric entities:

- Dimensions, notes, and labels cannot be mirrored using this function. Notes can be mirrored using **DETAIL—CHANGE—TEXT ATT—MIRROR** as described on page 301.

- The axis of mirroring can be indicated by any option in the Position Menu. Quite often one end of the axis is on the geometry to be mirrored and the other is either horizontal, vertical, or at some angle. Use *delta* coordinates or *polar coordinates* for the second point on the axis of mirroring.

- The status of the 2D-3D construction switch in the Status Menu does not affect this command.

1	**MOVE**
2	COPY
3	JOIN

MIRROR—MOVE allows selected entities to be mirrored or flipped across an axis. The selected geometry is moved from its original position until all points are the same distance from the axis but on the other side.

1. Select the entities for mirroring using any option from the Select Menu.

2. Choose a position option from the Position Menu.

3. Cursor indicate the position for one end of the mirror axis (P1).

4. Change position option if necessary.

5. Cursor indicate the position for the second end of the mirror axis (P2).

6. CADKEY Light mirrors the selected geometry about the axis.

7. Use **F10** backup to select additional entities to mirror or to change the mirror axis. **ESC** to the Main Menu.

Geometry mirrored about a
vertical axis using ENDENT
position masks.

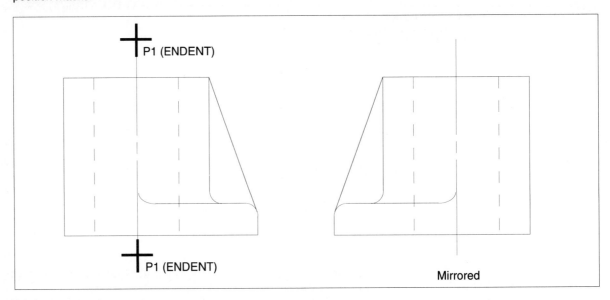

P1 (ENDENT)

P1 (ENDENT)

Mirrored

1	MOVE
2	COPY
3	JOIN

MIRROR—COPY allows selected entities to be mirrored with the selected geometry copied on the other side of a mirroring axis.

1. Select the entities for mirroring using any option from the Select Menu.

2. Choose a position option from the Position Menu.

3. Cursor indicate the position for one end of the mirror axis (P1).

4. Change position option if necessary.

5. Cursor indicate the position for the second end of the mirror axis (P2).

6. CADKEY Light mirrors and copies the selected geometry about the axis.

7. Use **F10** backup to select additional entities to mirror or to change the mirror axis. **ESC** to the Main Menu.

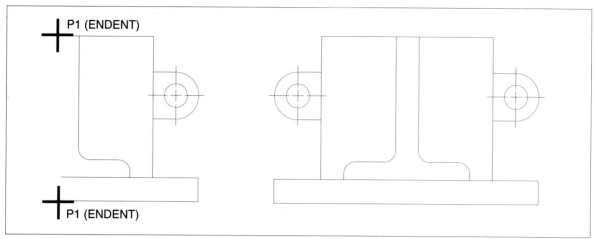

Mirror axis specified by entity position.

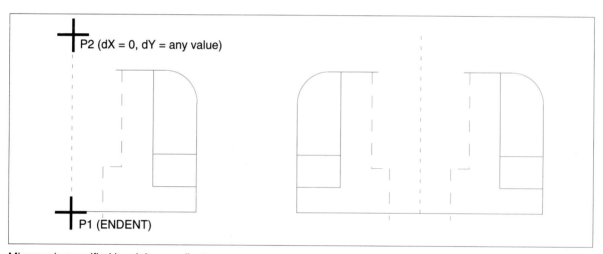

Mirror axis specified by *delta* coordinates.

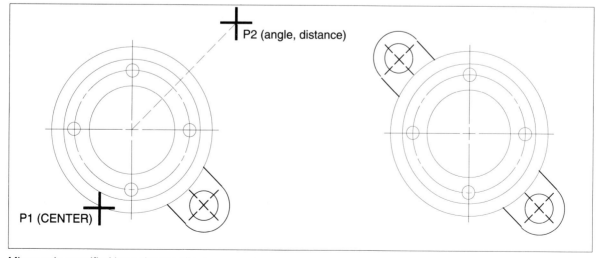

Mirror axis specified by *polar* coordinates.

1	MOVE
2	COPY
3	JOIN

MIRROR—JOIN allows selected entities to be mirrored and copied across an axis. The original geometry and the copy are connected. Corresponding endpoints of the original and the copy are joined with lines or polygons based on the chart found on page 317.

1. Select the entities for mirroring using any option from the Select Menu.

2. Choose a position option from the Position Menu.

3. Cursor indicate the position for one end of the mirror axis (P1).

4. Change position option if necessary.

5. Cursor indicate the position for the second end of the mirror axis (P2).

6. CADKEY Light mirrors the selected geometry about the axis.

7. Use **F10** backup to select additional entities to mirror or to change the mirror axis. **ESC** to the Main Menu.

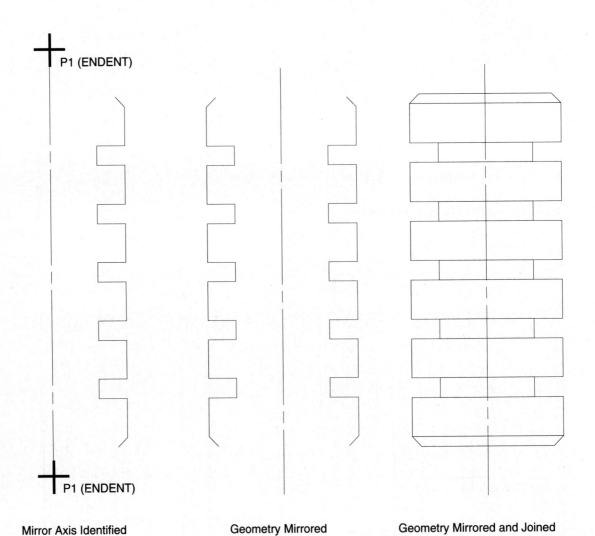

P1 (ENDENT)

P1 (ENDENT)

Mirror Axis Identified   Geometry Mirrored   Geometry Mirrored and Joined

Files Menu

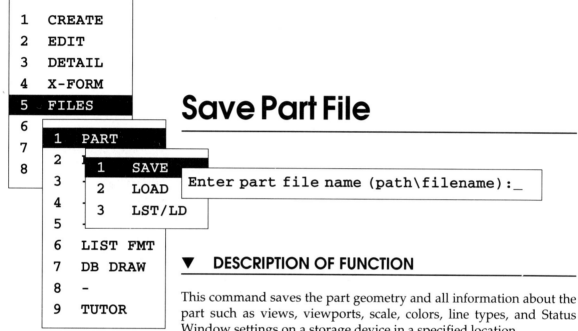

```
1  CREATE
2  EDIT
3  DETAIL
4  X-FORM
5  FILES
6
7       1  PART
8       2
        3        1  SAVE
        4        2  LOAD
        5        3  LST/LD
        6  LIST FMT
        7  DB DRAW
        8  -
        9  TUTOR
```

Save Part File

`Enter part file name (path\filename):_`

▼ DESCRIPTION OF FUNCTION

This command saves the part geometry and all information about the part such as views, viewports, scale, colors, line types, and Status Window settings on a storage device in a specified location.

CADKEY Light assumes that you want to save part files in **c:cadkey\prt**. This is set in the **CONFIG.DAT** file. To save a part elsewhere, specify the drive, path, and filename. File names must adhere to valid naming conventions specified by your operating system.

▼ OPTIONS

A new file begun by responding **ESC** at the initial CADKEY Light screen must be named during the first save. After that, the name and path become the default for all subsequent saves.

If the part file already exists when you save, you must respond explicitly **YES** or **NO** to overwrite the file. CADKEY Light does not return to the Main Menu after the save. Press **ESC** to return to the Main Menu.

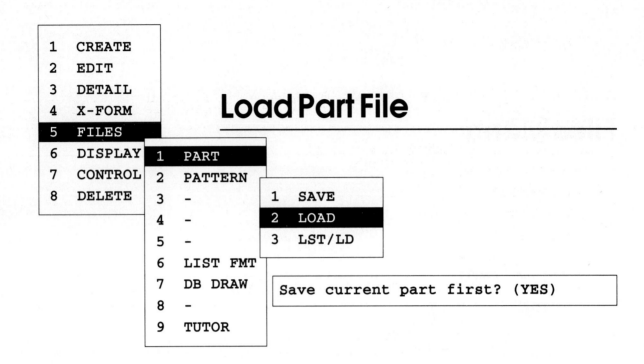

Load Part File

▼ DESCRIPTION OF FUNCTION

When a part file is loaded from the CADKEY Light program, a part must, by definition, be currently in the workspace. You are given the opportunity to first save the current part. The part is brought into CADKEY Light in a single viewport. To restore custom view assignments, see **DISPLAY—VIEW** on page 351.

    The path and the name of the part to be loaded must be entered exactly. If you are unsure of the name of a file, use the **LST/LD** option in this same menu.

▼ OPTIONS

If you respond **NO** to the save query, the current part is removed and any work since the last save is lost. If you respond **YES**, save the part in the manner described on page 335.

    CADKEY Light defaults to the part file path specified in the **CONFIG.DAT** file. Generally this will be the **/prt** subdirectory on your hard disk. If you simply type a file name CADKEY Light will look there for your part. If your part is on a diskette in drive **a:**, the filename *must* start with the drive specification.

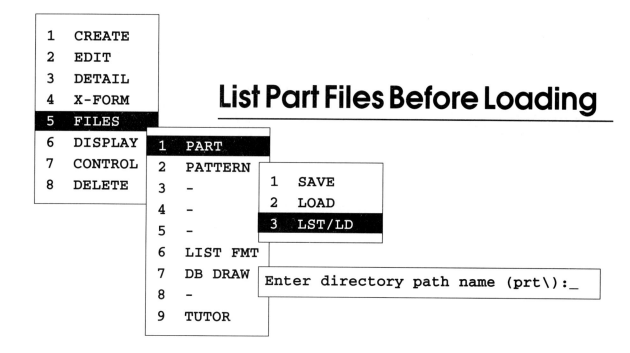

List Part Files Before Loading

▼ **DESCRIPTION OF FUNCTION**

When this option is used, a window listing the part files in the specified path is displayed. The screen information behind the window is written to a scratch file on your hard disk. For this reason, sufficient space must exist on your hard disk to use **LST/LD**.

prt/				page: 1
PARTA	.	.	.	.
PARTB	.	.	.	.
.	.	.	.	.
.	.	.	.	.
.	.	.	.	.
.	.	.	.	.
.	.	.	.	.
.	.	.	.	.

Forty files can be displayed on one page of the window and each page is numbered. To cycle through the stack of pages, highlight the page indicator and click the cursor button or press the space bar.

Cursor select the desired part file with a single click. CADKEY Light loads the selected part file and returns you to the **FILES-PART** menu.

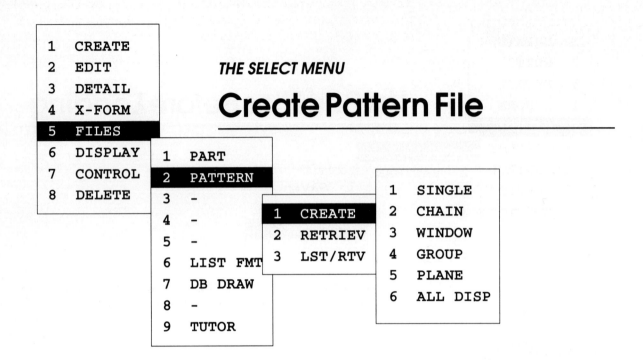

THE SELECT MENU

Create Pattern File

▼ **DESCRIPTION OF FUNCTION**

Pattern files can be merged with part files to build complex models and drawings. A pattern file need not be small. It can be of any size and complexity and can contain any combination of 2D or 3D elements. The **CREATE** option allows the selection of entities to be included in the pattern.

▼ **OPTIONS**

SINGLE allows the repetitive selection of individual entities. Use this option when items to be included are widely spaced or on different levels. Use **F10** to back up if an entity is mistakenly identified.

1	SINGLE
2	CHAIN
3	WINDOW
4	GROUP
5	PLANE
6	ALL DISP

Select entity 1 (Press RETURN when done)

```
1   SINGLE
2   CHAIN
3   WINDOW
4   GROUP
5   PLANE
6   ALL DISP
```

When entities physically are connected, as in a string line or polygon, they can be selected in **CHAIN**. The starting entity and direction of chaining must be specified. Only entities displayed fully in the viewport of selection are included in the chain.

```
Select start entity in chain
```

```
1   SINGLE
2   CHAIN
3   WINDOW
4   GROUP
5   PLANE
6   ALL DISP
```

Use **WINDOW** to select entities that are tightly grouped. Only entities contained totally in the final position of the flexible window are selected.

```
Indicate position for 1st selection window corner
```

```
1   SINGLE
2   CHAIN
3   WINDOW
4   GROUP
5   PLANE      1   SELECT
6   ALL DI     2   BY NAME
```

To include entities that have been grouped, decide whether you want to include all subgroups in the pattern. Choose **SELECT** to choose individual subgroups. Choose **BY NAME** to select all subgroups belonging to a parent group.

```
Choose group selection option
```

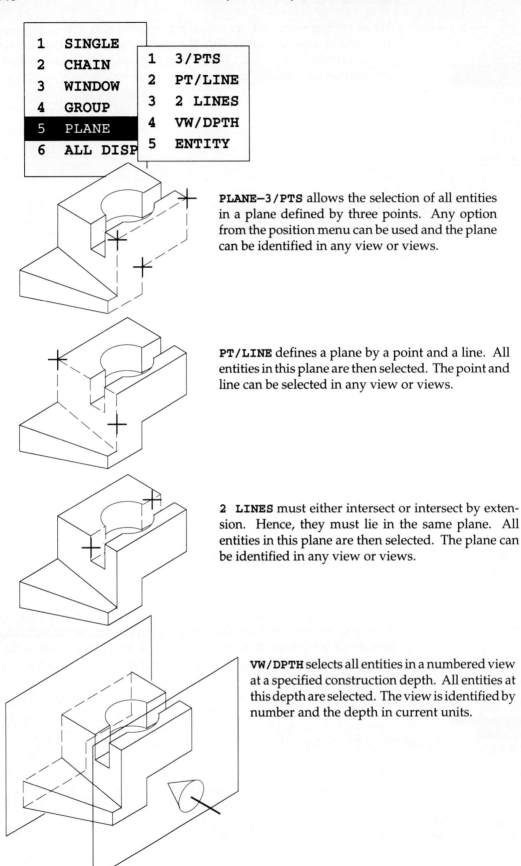

1	SINGLE
2	CHAIN
3	WINDOW
4	GROUP
5	**PLANE**
6	ALL DISP

1	3/PTS
2	PT/LINE
3	2 LINES
4	VW/DPTH
5	ENTITY

PLANE–3/PTS allows the selection of all entities in a plane defined by three points. Any option from the position menu can be used and the plane can be identified in any view or views.

PT/LINE defines a plane by a point and a line. All entities in this plane are then selected. The point and line can be selected in any view or views.

2 LINES must either intersect or intersect by extension. Hence, they must lie in the same plane. All entities in this plane are then selected. The plane can be identified in any view or views.

VW/DPTH selects all entities in a numbered view at a specified construction depth. All entities at this depth are selected. The view is identified by number and the depth in current units.

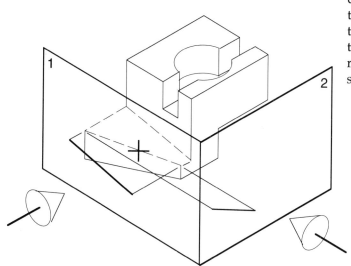

When a line is selected with **ENTITY**, a plane is defined containing the line that is perpendicular to the screen. Identify the line in a view in which the plane appears as an edge. Note in the example that identifying the same line in View 2 would result in a totally different set of entities being selected when compared with View 1.

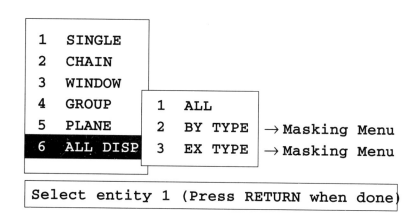

```
1   SINGLE
2   CHAIN
3   WINDOW
4   GROUP        1   ALL
5   PLANE        2   BY TYPE   → Masking Menu
6   ALL DISP     3   EX TYPE   → Masking Menu
```

```
Select entity 1 (Press RETURN when done)
```

ALL DISP—ALL allows the user to include or exclude entities by type or attribute. **ALL** provides a method for quickly identifying all entities that are within a specified viewport. Entities not totally within the viewport are not selected.

BY TYPE displays the Masking Menu and allows selection (by masking) of entities by attributes. Options within this menu can be changed without leaving the command to select dissimilar entities. Choose **DONE** when completed.

EX TYPE selects all entities totally displayed in the viewport *except* those identified by options in the Masking Menu. Choose **DONE** when completed.

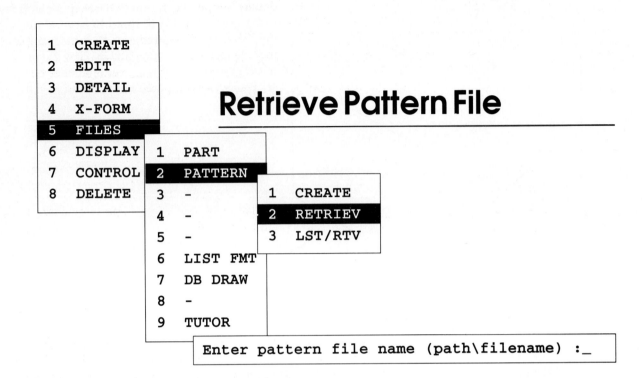

Retrieve Pattern File

1	CREATE
2	EDIT
3	DETAIL
4	X-FORM
5	FILES
6	DISPLAY
7	CONTROL
8	DELETE

1	PART
2	PATTERN
3	-
4	-
5	-
6	LIST FMT
7	DB DRAW
8	-
9	TUTOR

1	CREATE
2	RETRIEV
3	LST/RTV

```
Enter pattern file name (path\filename) :_
```

▼ DESCRIPTION OF FUNCTION

A pattern file is retrieved and placed into a part file. Patterns can be 2D or 3D and contain any CADKEY Light entity. When placed, the pattern's ZV axis is aligned with the ZV of the viewport into which you are placing the pattern. For example, a circle pattern created in the front view has a view Z axis perpendicular to the circle itself. Placing the pattern in TOP, RIGHT, and ISOMETRIC views aligns this pattern ZV axis with the ZV axis in each viewport. The cursor remains loaded with the pattern until you **ESC** the function. Use **F10** backup to change pattern parameters without leaving this function.

▼ OPTIONS

Grouping a pattern allows it to be easily moved, scaled, rotated, or deleted at a later time. Global changes to entity attributes can also be made easily although individual entities can be identified and modified. Multiple instances of a group are called subgroups. Subgroups can be used to keep track of how many times a group has been used (1-256 times) for bill of material data extraction and for making global changes to all instances of a group.

```
Group pattern entities? (YES)
```

```
Enter group name (pattern name):_
```

By default, the name of a grouped pattern is the pattern filename. The name can also be any valid filename you choose. You will probably want to use short, easy-to-remember group names.

```
1   CUR-LEV
2   ENT-LEV
3   KEY-IN
4   OFFSET
```

Pattern geometry can be placed on the current active level (**CUR-LEV**), on the levels on which they were originally created (**ENT-LEV**), on a keyboard-entered level (**KEY-IN**), or offset from their created levels by a positive or negative integer value. CADKEY Light will not let you assign a level outside the range 1-256.

```
Enter scale factor (1) =>_
```

Patterns are scaled about their origin or base. Enter a number greater than 1 to enlarge a pattern. Enter a number smaller than 1 to reduce a pattern. If the **AUTO UP** switch is set to **YES**, all dimension values, other than those manually entered, will reflect the change in scale.

```
Enter rotation angle (0) =>_
```

Rotation can be specified in positive degrees (CCW) or in negative degrees (CW). Multiple rotations (about X, Y, and Z axes) must be done after the pattern has been placed.

```
1   CURSOR
2   POINT
3   ENDENT
4   CENTER
5   INTRSC
6   ALONGL
7   POLAR
8   DELTA
9   KEY-IN
```

The pattern is placed with the pattern base aligned to the identified point using any of the options in the position menu. When using entity-related position options—**POINT, ENDENT, CENTER, INTRSC, ALONGL**—note that the construction depth setting is overridden and the pattern base is placed at the depth of the entity feature.

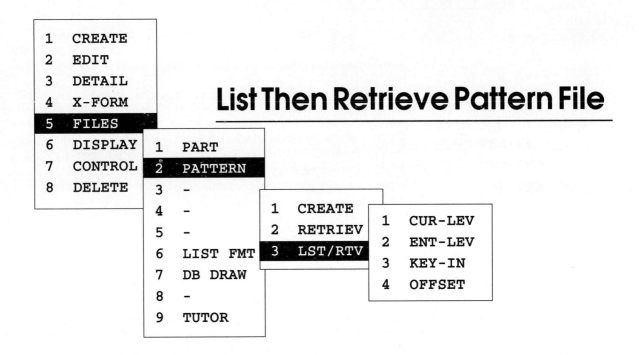

1	CREATE
2	EDIT
3	DETAIL
4	X-FORM
5	FILES
6	DISPLAY
7	CONTROL
8	DELETE

1	PART
2	PATTERN
3	-
4	-
5	-
6	LIST FMT
7	DB DRAW
8	-
9	TUTOR

1	CREATE
2	RETRIEV
3	LST/RTV

1	CUR-LEV
2	ENT-LEV
3	KEY-IN
4	OFFSET

List Then Retrieve Pattern File

▼ DESCRIPTION OF FUNCTION

Use this feature when the name, spelling, or location of a pattern is not known. If more than forty patterns are at the same path location, several pages of listings will be used. To turn the pages, highlight the page indicator and click the cursor.

Cursor select the desired pattern or press <Enter> to exit without choosing a pattern. Once selected, CADKEY Light displays the options for placing the pattern. Refer to pages 342-343 for a description of this procedure.

ptn/				page: 1
PATA	.	.	.	.
PATB	.	.	.	.
.	.	.	.	.
.	.	.	.	.
.	.	.	.	.
.	.	.	.	.
.	.	.	.	.
.	.	.	.	.

Cursor-select pattern to retrieve or press RETURN to exit

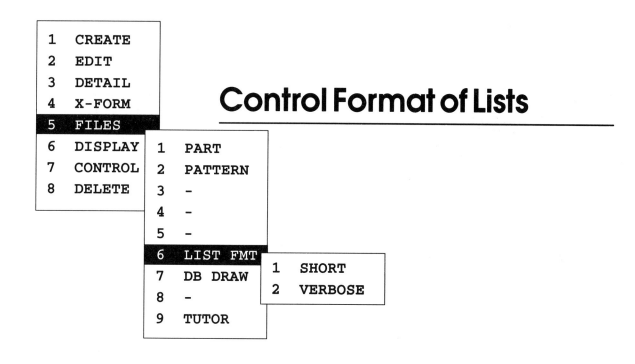

1	CREATE
2	EDIT
3	DETAIL
4	X-FORM
5	FILES
6	DISPLAY
7	CONTROL
8	DELETE

1	PART
2	PATTERN
3	-
4	-
5	-
6	LIST FMT
7	DB DRAW
8	-
9	TUTOR

| 1 | SHORT |
| 2 | VERBOSE |

Control Format of Lists

▼ **DESCRIPTION OF FUNCTION**

CADKEY Light defaults to a **SHORT** format for part and pattern lists. A short list contains only the name of the file. You will probably want to view lists this way most of the time. The list of patterns on the previous page is done in short format. A **VERBOSE** list contains the filename, size in bytes, creation date, and creation time. The longer format may be helpful to identify files when you know when they were created but not their names. Fewer files can be displayed on each page of the list, however. File size indicates model complexity and can be used to distinguish between similiar versions of a design.

| FILENAME | 273008 | 03-27-90 | 07:32a |

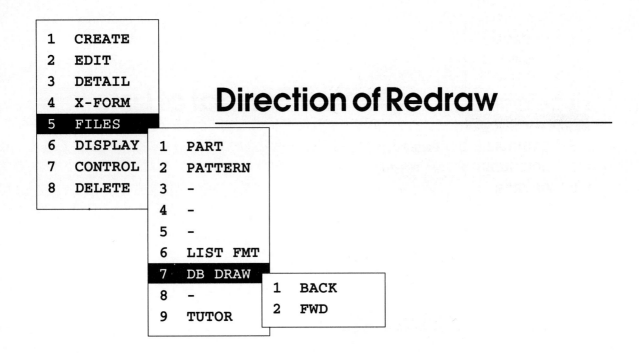

Direction of Redraw

▼ DESCRIPTION OF FUNCTION

This function controls the direction CADKEY Light uses to store or retrieve files. The default direction is forward—from the first entity created to the last. Choosing **BACK** reverses that direction. CADKEY Light will then read the last entity created first.

DB DRAW is helpful when identifying an entity that is at the beginning or end of the data base. Once that entity has been displayed, the further reading of the data base can be halted by pressing the **ESC** key.

1	CREATE
2	EDIT
3	DETAIL
4	X-FORM
5	**FILES**
6	DISPLAY
7	CONTROL
8	DELETE

1	PART
2	PATTERN
3	-
4	-
5	-
6	LIST FMT
7	DB DRAW
8	-
9	**TUTOR**

TUTOR

▼ DESCRIPTION OF FUNCTION

TUTOR appears in the Files Menu only if TUTOR has been installed. See pages 39-41 for the directions to install TUTOR. This function begins an instructional program that runs inside CADKEY Light. The general operation of TUTOR and the part and pattern files created use the same procedures as do the main program itself.

Display Menu

1	CREATE
2	EDIT
3	DETAIL
4	X-FORM
5	FILES
6	DISPLAY
7	CONTROL
8	

1	REDRAW
2	PAN
3	ZOOM
4	VIEW
5	VWPORTS
6	LEVELS
7	GRD/SNAP
8	AXES
9	CURSOR

Redraw Viewport

▼ DESCRIPTION OF FUNCTION

REDRAW erases and then redisplays the data base without changing the view or part geometry. All point and entity markers are removed, and entities that have been partially erased because of **EDIT** or **X-FORM** are cleaned up.

▼ OPTIONS

If you currently are using a single viewport, CADKEY Light automatically redraws that viewport. If a four-viewport display is being used, CADKEY Light prompts you for which viewport to redraw. To redraw all viewports press <Enter>.

```
Cursor-indicate viewport to REDRAW or press CR for all
```

To halt the redisplay of a viewport, press **ESC**. You may want to do this if the entity you need to work on has been redisplayed and you don't want to wait to see the entire part. See **DB DRAW** on page 346 to reverse the direction of display.

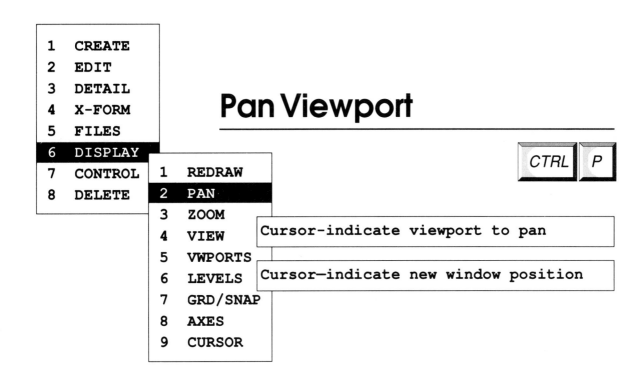

Pan Viewport

CTRL	P

Cursor-indicate viewport to pan

Cursor—indicate new window position

▼ **DESCRIPTION OF FUNCTION**

PAN allows the viewport to be moved relative to the part so that geometry currently outside the viewport can be seen. The function stays active, allowing successive pans, until a final position is accepted with <Enter>.

▼ **OPTIONS**

PAN can be accomplished using one of two methods. First, select **PAN** from the **DISPLAY** menu.

CURSOR METHOD
1. Click once in the viewport at the spot you want to use as a handle. If you want to move the viewport up, click near the bottom. If you want to move the viewport to the right, click near the left edge.

2. Move the viewport frame without depressing the cursor until it is in the desired position.

3. Click once to redisplay the part within the viewport's new position.

COORDINATE METHOD
1. Enter X and Y view coordinate values for the new center of the viewport. Press <Enter>.

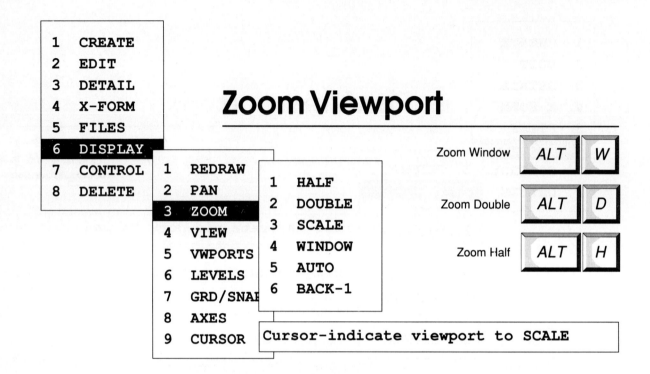

Zoom Viewport

1	CREATE
2	EDIT
3	DETAIL
4	X-FORM
5	FILES
6	DISPLAY
7	CONTROL
8	DELETE

1	REDRAW
2	PAN
3	ZOOM
4	VIEW
5	VWPORTS
6	LEVELS
7	GRD/SNAP
8	AXES
9	CURSOR

1	HALF
2	DOUBLE
3	SCALE
4	WINDOW
5	AUTO
6	BACK-1

Zoom Window   ALT   W

Zoom Double   ALT   D

Zoom Half   ALT   H

`Cursor-indicate viewport to SCALE`

▼ DESCRIPTION OF FUNCTION

The **ZOOM** command either increases or decreases the distance between the viewport and part geometry. This operation does *not* change the scale of the part geometry itself.

HALF reduces the display size 50% from the current size, keeping the geometry at the center of the viewport at the center when resized.

DOUBLE increases the display size 200% from the current size centered on the viewport.

SCALE allows the display to be increased or decreased by a numerical factor. The center point of the new display is cursor identified.

WINDOW allows a portion of the display to be "zoomed in." The window is defined by one cursor click at each corner of the flexible window. CADKEY Light automatically adjusts the display when the proportions of the window don't match the proportions of the viewport.

AUTO automatically sizes the part to fit in the viewport.

BACK-1 allows the previous zoom specification to be immediately recalled. CADKEY Light remembers the *current* zoom and the *previous* zoom. **BACK-1** can cycle from one zoom to the other.

▼ OPTIONS

All **ZOOM** commands can be invoked by immediate mode commands. This allows the display size to be adjusted during execution of a command.

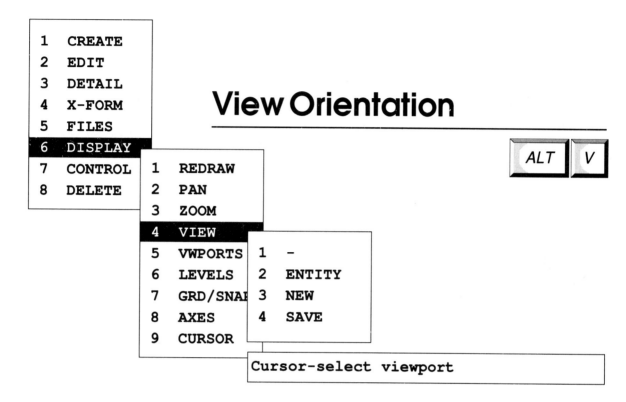

View Orientation

A view is the orientation of a viewport to the world axis system. CADKEY Light recognizes eight preset views that can be assigned to any viewport in any relationship by their view numbers

View Number	CADKEY Name	Axis Orientation
1	TOP	X, Y, positive Z
2	BOTTOM	X, Y, negative Z
3	FRONT	X, Z, negative Y
4	BACK	X, Z, positive Y
5	RIGHT	Z, Y, positive X
6	LEFT	Z, Y, negative X
7	ISOMETRIC	Pictorial
8	AXONOMETRIC	Pictorial

A view defined by **ENTITY** is taken normally or perpendicular to a planar entity (circle, arc, rectangle, polygon, etc.). This view is automatically assigned the next available view number and saved.

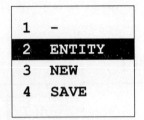

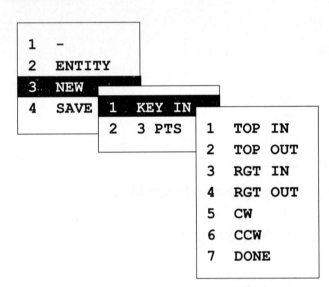

Creating **NEW** views of part geometry is fundamental to operating CADKEY Light. By using the **KEY IN** option, the view direction relative to the world axis system can be changed. This is done by visualizing the result of a change in viewing direction on the world axis system itself. This change is specified in degrees. It is important to understand that the object's position relative to the axes is *not* changed. Only the vantage from which the part is viewed is changed: stable geometry, moved viewing position.

TOP IN revolves the top of the axis into the screen.

TOP OUT revolves the top of the axis system out of the screen.

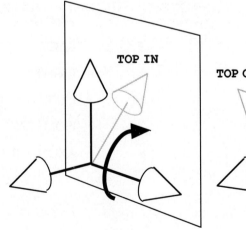

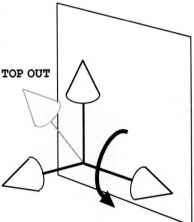

RGT IN revolves the right side of the axis system into the screen, thereby revolving the left side out of the screen.

RGT OUT revolves the right side of the axis system out of the screen, thereby revolving the left side into the screen.

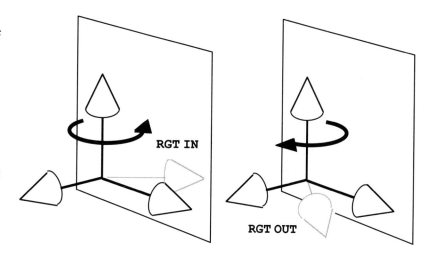

CW revolves the axis system clockwise and parallel to the screen.

CCW revolves the axis system counter-clockwise and parallel to the screen.

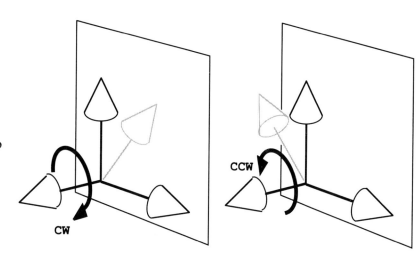

DONE signals CADKEY Light to perform the viewing transformations you have specified. A series of changes can be specified and the results seen in one redisplay. Any new view must be saved to be added to the view list and later recalled.

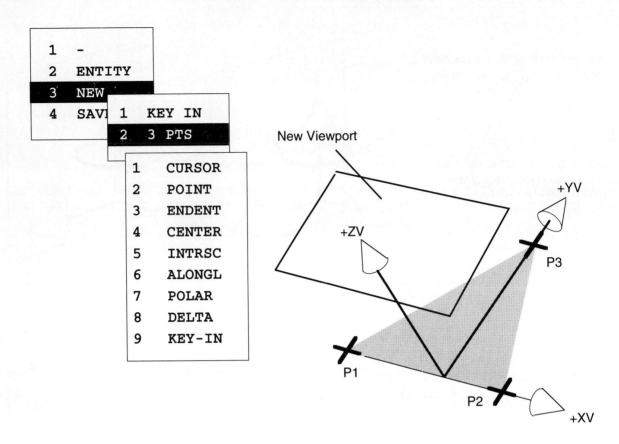

1	-
2	ENTITY
3	NEW
4	SAV

| 1 | KEY IN |
| 2 | 3 PTS |

1	CURSOR
2	POINT
3	ENDENT
4	CENTER
5	INTRSC
6	ALONGL
7	POLAR
8	DELTA
9	KEY-IN

New Viewport

+YV

+ZV

P3

P1

P2

+XV

A new view can be created normal to a plane defined by three points. Use this command when the direction is not defined by a planar entity but by points, lines, or ends or centers of entities.

Using the position menu, indicate the first two points, P1 and P2. This defines the positive X axis of the view coordinate system. The third point P3 defines the direction of the positive Y axis. The positive Z axis then defines the new view, normal to the plane defined by P1-P2-P3.

1	-
2	ENTITY
3	NEW
4	SAVE

Views created by **NEW** must use **SAVE** to be permanently added to the view list. New views begin with View 9. Check the view number assigned to the current viewport(s) by moving the cursor into a viewport. Its view number appears beside **VW:** in the Status Menu window. When CADKEY Light loads a part file, a single viewport is displayed by default. Choosing **AUTOSET** will display CADKEY's default four views, not the views you saved, however. You must assign your saved views to viewports explicitly.

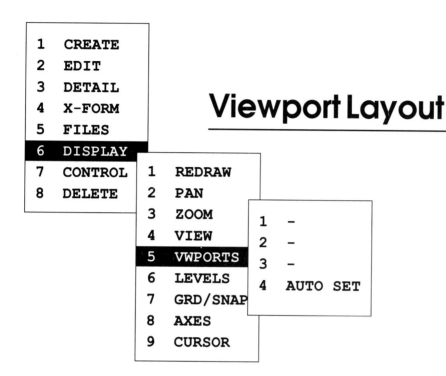

Viewport Layout

▼ **DESCRIPTION OF FUNCTION**

Two viewport arrangements are available in CADKEY Light: a single viewport and four equally sized viewports. When **AUTOSET** is chosen, the default CADKEY Light view assignments are made to the viewports. Views defined under **NEW** and saved can be assigned to the viewports by number.

Custom viewport assignments are not saved with part files. When a part is loaded, a single viewport with View 1 is used to display the geometry.

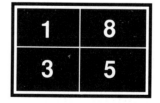

If the four viewport arrangement is chosen, CADKEY Light automatically assigns TOP-FRONT-RIGHT-ISOMETRIC views.

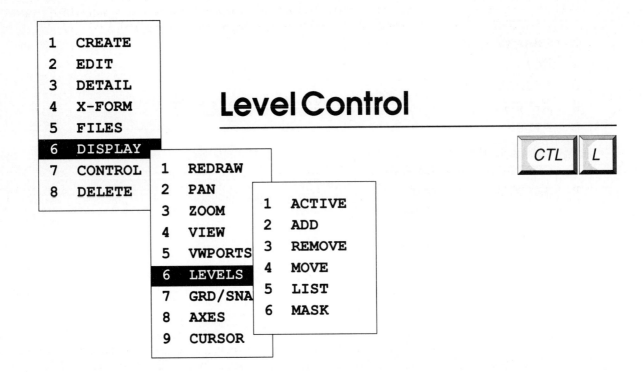

Level Control

CTL   L

1	CREATE
2	EDIT
3	DETAIL
4	X-FORM
5	FILES
6	DISPLAY
7	CONTROL
8	DELETE

1	REDRAW
2	PAN
3	ZOOM
4	VIEW
5	VWPORTS
6	LEVELS
7	GRD/SNA
8	AXES
9	CURSOR

1	ACTIVE
2	ADD
3	REMOVE
4	MOVE
5	LIST
6	MASK

▼ DESCRIPTION OF FUNCTION

The **LEVEL** function allows a part and its accompanying documentation (notes, dimensions) to be separated onto different layers for creating, editing, and display. Up to 256 levels are available, although level 256 is reserved for items that are not displayed but can be moved or copied to displayed levels. In understanding levels, keep the following definitions in mind:

ACTIVE LEVEL—level is visible; entities are selectable.

ADDED LEVEL—level is added to the display list and made visible.

TURN ON—level is made visible.

TURN OFF—level is made invisible.

MASKED—entities are not selectable.

If a level is **ACTIVE** it is displayed and all entities on that level can be selected. More than one level can be active at one time, although only one level can be the current level. To temporarily protect geometry on a level, use the **MASK** function.

1	ACTIVE
2	ADD
3	REMOVE
4	MOVE
5	LIST
6	MASK

```
Enter level number from 1-256 (current=1) =>_
```

The **ADD** function allows levels to be turned on. A level that has been added will be displayed after the next **REDRAW**. Use commas to separate levels (3,7,12) or hyphens to separate a range of levels (3-7, 12-15).

```
1   ACTIVE
2   ADD
3   REMOVE
4   MOVE
5   LIST
6   MASK
```

```
Enter level(s) to be added =>_
```

Removing a level from the display list causes it to not appear after the next **REDRAW**. A removed level that was active remains active, although it cannot be seen. This allows geometry to be placed on a level that is active but is not displayed.

```
1   ACTIVE
2   ADD
3   REMOVE
4   MOVE
5   LIST
6   MASK
```

```
Enter levels to be removed =>_
```

To **MOVE** entities from one level to another does not require that the target level be turned on and visible. Use **SELECT** to choose individual entities to move. Use **LEVEL** to move all entities on a certain level to another. Both of these options cause the display to be redrawn automatically.

```
1   ACTIVE
2   ADD
3   REMOVE
4   MOVE
5   LIST         1   SELECT
6   MASK         2   LEVEL
```

LIST changes the display status of levels. If a level is **ON** it is displayed and if a level is **OFF** it is not displayed. **TOGGLE** will reverse the status of either selected or nonselected levels. Click once to select a single layer. Click-drag across vertical columns or horizontal rows to select a range of levels. When finished, an \<Enter\> stroke redraws the screen with changes displayed.

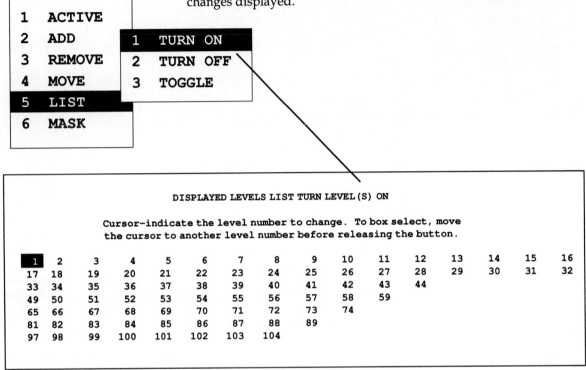

1	ACTIVE
2	ADD
3	REMOVE
4	MOVE
5	LIST
6	MASK

1	TURN ON
2	TURN OFF
3	TOGGLE

```
                    DISPLAYED LEVELS LIST TURN LEVEL(S) ON

           Cursor-indicate the level number to change.  To box select, move
              the cursor to another level number before releasing the button.

    1    2    3    4    5    6    7    8    9   10   11   12   13   14   15   16
   17   18   19   20   21   22   23   24   25   26   27   28   29   30   31   32
   33   34   35   36   37   38   39   40   41   42   43   44
   49   50   51   52   53   54   55   56   57   58   59
   65   66   67   68   69   70   71   72   73   74
   81   82   83   84   85   86   87   88   89
   97   98   99  100  101  102  103  104
```

Choose option from menu or Cursor-indicate level(s) to change

1	ACTIVE
2	ADD
3	REMOVE
4	MOVE
5	LIST
6	MASK

MASK allows active levels to be temporarily inactive. In other words, a level can be active but masked and will continue to be displayed. However, entities on masked levels cannot be selected. Use the same keyboard conventions for multiple masking as were described in **ADD**. Set **MASK** to zero to turn all masking off.

Enter level number or 0 for no mask (current=0) =\>_

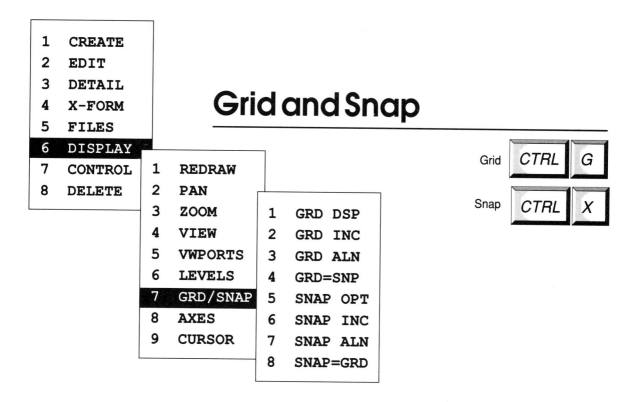

Grid and Snap

Grid	CTRL	G
Snap	CTRL	X

▼ **DESCRIPTION OF FUNCTION**

A **GRID** is a rectangular pattern of dots used as a guide in constructing rectilinear objects. Grid points cannot be printed or selected, although the cursor can be snapped to a grid point. If the level of **ZOOM** is such that individual grid points cannot be distinguished, the display of the grid will be temporarily disabled. The current grid increment is used to space the grid. CADKEY Light defaults to a .5 inch grid increment when inches are chosen in the **CONFIG** program.

▼ **OPTIONS**

GRD DSP toggles the display of grid points on and off. The primary display is the viewport identified as primary when the four-viewport setup was chosen. Otherwise, the grid is automatically displayed in a single viewport display. The display of the grid cannot be interrupted.

1	GRD DSP
2	GRD INC
3	GRD ALN
4	GRD=SNP
5	SNAP OPT
6	SNAP INC
7	SNAP ALN
8	SNAP=GRD

GRD INC allows the setting of grid point spacing along the X and Y axes. These increments can be set to different values. The grid does not have to be displayed for the increment to be changed.

1	GRD DSP	1	CURSOR
2	GRD INC	2	POINT
3	GRD ALN	3	ENDENT
4	GRD=SNP	4	CENTER
5	SNAP OPT	5	INTRSC
6	SNAP INC	6	ALONGL
7	SNAP ALN	7	POLAR
8	SNAP=GRD	8	DELTA
		9	KEY-IN

The grid can be aligned using any option from the position menu. If the grid is on, it is redrawn automatically.

1	GRD DSP
2	GRD INC
3	GRD ALN
4	GRD=SNP
5	SNAP OPT
6	SNAP INC
7	SNAP ALN
8	SNAP=GRD

When **GRD=SNAP**, the grid increment will be set equal to the snap increment. The grid is automatically redrawn if the grid is currently displayed.

SNAP is the attraction of the cursor to the snap increment. The snap increment and the grid increment can be set to different values and also aligned differently. Because the redisplay of a fine grid may be time-consuming, setting the grid to 4X the snap often allows easy construction and shortened redraw times. Snap can also be toggled on and off in the Status Window.

1	GRD DSP		
2	GRD INC		
3	GRD ALN		
4	GRD=SNP		
5	SNAP OPT	1	ON
6	SNAP INC	2	OFF
7	SNAP ALN		
8	SNAP=GRD		

1	GRD DSP
2	GRD INC
3	GRD ALN
4	GRD=SNP
5	SNAP OPT
6	SNAP INC
7	SNAP ALN
8	SNAP=GRD

SNAP INC adjusts the snap resolution. X and Y values can be set separately and are independent of grid increments. A keyboard shortcut for adjusting this increment is to use the PgUp and PgDn keys (with the NUM LOC off). Use PgUp to double the current X and Y snap increments. Use PgDn to halve the current X and Y increments.

1	GRD DSP	1	CURSOR
2	GRD INC	2	POINT
3	GRD ALN	3	ENDENT
4	GRD=SNP	4	CENTER
5	SNAP OPT	5	INTRSC
6	SNAP INC	6	ALONGL
7	SNAP ALN	7	POLAR
8	SNAP=GRD	8	DELTA
		9	KEY-IN

The snap increment can be aligned with any option from the Position Menu. To quickly align the snap to a grid, use the **SNAP=GRD** option.

1	GRD DSP
2	GRD INC
3	GRD ALN
4	GRD=SNP
5	SNAP OPT
6	SNAP INC
7	SNAP ALN
8	SNAP=GRD

This option adjusts the X-Y snap to be equal to and aligned with the grid X-Y increments.

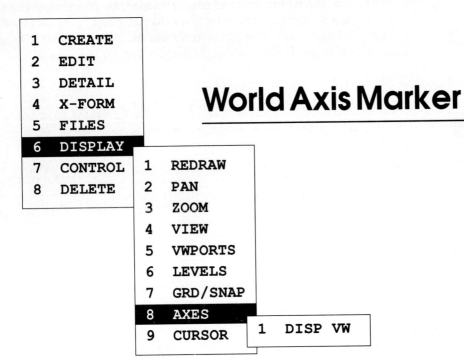

World Axis Marker

▼   **DESCRIPTION OF FUNCTION**

The display of the world axis marker provides a visual clue as to the orientation of the viewport to world space. This marker is always displayed in the lower left corner of the viewport and has no relation to the origin (0,0,0) of world space. These markers can be either turned on or off.

When creating a new view by the **KEY IN** method, it is most helpful to have the markers turned on so that the results of view changes can be observed. The marker is not part geometry and can't be plotted or selected. If one of the three axes points away from the screen, it is shown as a dashed line. Otherwise, the marker is shown with solid lines.

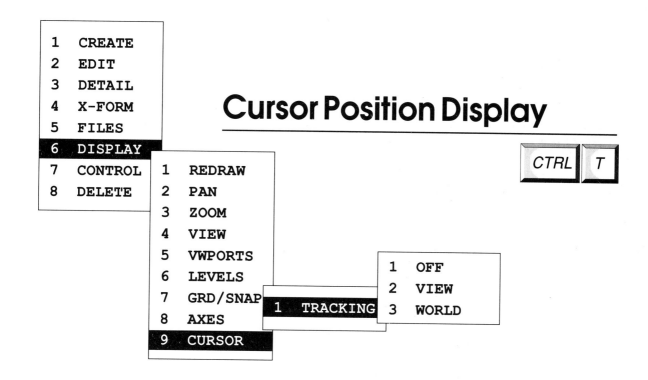

Cursor Position Display

CTRL   T

▼ **DESCRIPTION OF FUNCTION**

The Cursor Tracking Window records the position of the cursor in either view coordinates or world coordinates.

▼ **OPTIONS**

OFF   Does not record cursor position until the cursor is clicked in a viewport. This option works with the next two selections.

VIEW   Records the position of the cursor in terms of view or screen coordinates (XV,YV). The cursor can't record ZV coordinates because they are in and out of the screen. ZV position can be controlled by changing construction depth settings.

WORLD   Records the position of the cursor in terms of the world axis system (X,Y,Z). This option is helpful when determining the coordinate locations of points, centers, and ends.

Control Menu

```
1  VERIFY
2  ATT
3  CON         1  ATTRIB
4  COC         2  COORD
5  STA         3  DIST
6  PRI         4  ANGLE
7  PLOT
8  SYSCMD
```

```
1  CREATE
2  EDIT
3  DETAIL
4  X-FORM
5  FILES
6  DISPLAY
7  CONTROL
8  DELETE
```

Verify Entity

▼ DESCRIPTION OF FUNCTION

Entities currently in the data base can be checked for position and size by instructing CADKEY Light to **VERIFY** the selected entity. Only one entity can be checked at a time.

When **DIST** is chosen to verify the distance between positions and entities, two values are returned. The *projected distance* is the apparent distance parallel to the current viewport. The *actual distance* is the distance that would be seen if the measurement were viewed normally.

```
1  ATTRIB
2  COORD
3  DIST
4  ANGLE
```

▼ OPTIONS

ATTRIB allows entity attributes to be verified. The data concerning the selected entity are displayed in the prompt line. Press <Enter> to display successive lines of attribute information. The following attributes can be checked:

Prompt Line 1

      Type—a CADKEY Light generated reference number

      Form—a CADKEY Light generated reference number

      Level—the level to which the entity is assigned

      Def View—the view in which the entity was created

Prompt Line 2
___

> `Color`—a numerical value corresponding to the assigned color
>
> `Style`—a numerical value representing line type or text font
>
> `Width`—a numerical value representing line width
>
> `Pen`—the pen number assigned for plotting

Prompt Line 3
___

> `Grp Name`—the name of the group to which the entity is assigned
>
> `Grp #`—the group reference number
>
> `Subgrp #`—the subgroup reference number

Prompt Line 4 (if entity is a dimension)
___

> `TxT Ht`—text height size
>
> `Aspect`–the character aspect percentage
>
> `Arrow`—the arrow style number

To check the attributes of a geometric or detail drafting entity:

1. Select the entity using an option from the Position Menu.

2. Press <Enter> to display the next line of information at the prompt line.

1	ATTRIB
2	COORD
3	DIST
4	ANGLE

COORD allows the position of the selected entity in either world or view space to be verified. This option can be used to verify lines, arcs, circles, polygons, points, or dimensions. Coordinates reflect the status of the COORD toggle in the Status Menu. Information that you can expect to see on the prompt line by using this option depends on the entity selected. For arcs, degrees are displayed first with radians in parentheses. Here are the possibilities:

> **Center**—arcs, circles, lines, point
>
> **Sweep Angle**—arcs
>
> **Radius**—arcs, circles
>
> **St ang**—arcs, circle
>
> **End ang**—arcs, circle
>
> **Start point**—ine
>
> **End point**—line

To check the coordinates of a geometric or detail drafting entity:

1. Select the entity using an option from the Position Menu.

2. Press <Enter> to display the next line of information at the prompt line.

1	ATTRIB
2	COORD
3	**DIST**
4	ANGLE

DIST calculates the actual and projected distance between two positions in space, a position and an entity, or two entities. Because actual measurements may not occur in the current view, make sure that the 2D/3D construction switch in the Status Menu is set to 3D. Temporary lines are displayed to mark where the distance is measured—dashed for projected distance and solid for true distance. The numerical values are displayed on the prompt line in current units. These lines are erased when the screen is redrawn.

The distance between two positions (**2 POS**) in space can be calculated using any option from the Position Menu. For example, the true and projected distances between the center of the circle and the end of the line can be found using the **CENTER** and **ENDENT** position options. The distance between a position and an entity (**POS+ENT**) is marked using a temporary line. The position is selected using any option from the Position Menu. The entity is selected using any option from the Masking Menu. The shortest distance between two entities can be found using the **2 ENTS** option.

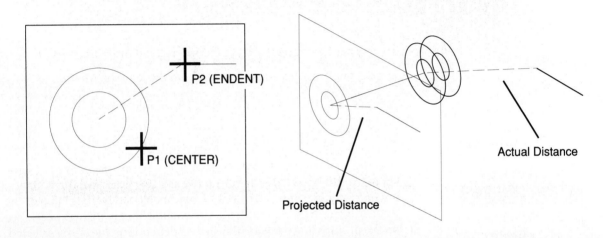

ANGLE verifies the angle formed by two intersecting lines. The projected angle is measured as the lines are projected onto the display plane. The true angle is measured in the plane formed by the two lines. The angle is reported in the prompt line in both degrees and radians.

1	ATTRIB
2	COORD
3	DIST
4	**ANGLE**

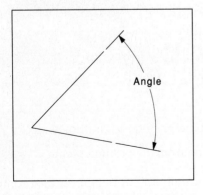

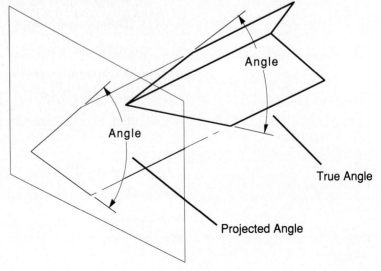

```
1  CREATE
2  EDIT
3  DETAIL
4  X-FORM
5  FILES
6  DISPLAY
7  CONTROL
8  DELETE        1  VERIFY
                 2  ATTRIB
                 3  CONSTR        1  COLOR
                 4  COORDS        2  L-TYPE
                 5  STATUS        3  L-WIDTH
                 6  PRINT         4  PEN #
                 7  PLOT          5  OUT/FIL
                 8  SYSCMD
```

Change Attributes

▼ DESCRIPTION OF FUNCTION

When attributes are controlled, they may be changed in either of two ways.

▼ OPTIONS

```
1  CURRENT
2  CHANGE
```

CURRENT allows you to make a change in the default attribute value. All entities created after this point using this attribute will reflect this change. This does not affect default values that are set in the **CONFIG** file and that are in place when CADKEY Light is started. Use this option when you know that a number of entities need to be created with this attribute.

CHANGE allows you to change the attribute of an existing entity in the data base. This does not change the default or *modal* attribute value. Each entity must be identified to be changed.

The attributes that can be controlled or changed are:

COLOR

L-TYPE

L-WIDTH

PEN #

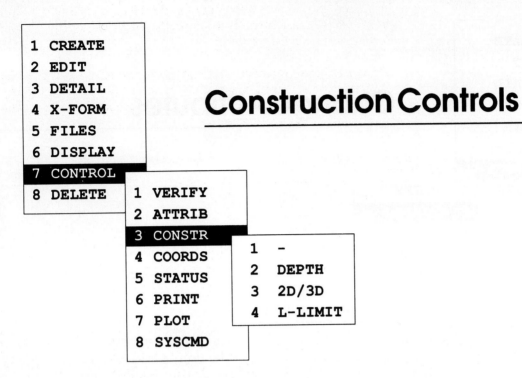

Construction Controls

▼ DESCRIPTION OF FUNCTION

This option allows the construction depth to be changed. The active construction depth of the viewport in which the cursor resides is displayed in the Status Menu. The default depth is 0.0 at start up. Negative construction depth is into the screen. Positive construction depth is out of the screen.

The current construction depth is referred to as the *working depth* and is specified along the ZV axis. For this reason, it is important to be in the view in which ZV depth has meaning when matched with world coordinates. For example, consider these settings:

View	ZV Depth
Front	Z Depth
Top	Y Height
Side	X Width
Isometric	Cube Diagonal

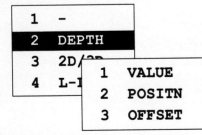

▼ OPTIONS

VALUE allows the changing of construction value by entering a numerical value from the keyboard. This might be thought of as *absolute construction depth*.

POSITN allows construction depth to be set using an option from the Position Menu. The **CURSOR** option is disabled because cursor input would be at the current construction depth. The ZV value of the position becomes the construction depth.

OFFSET may be thought of as *relative construction depth*. In this option, a change to the current construction depth is entered from the keyboard—a positive value brings the depth out, wheras a negative value moves the depth into the screen.

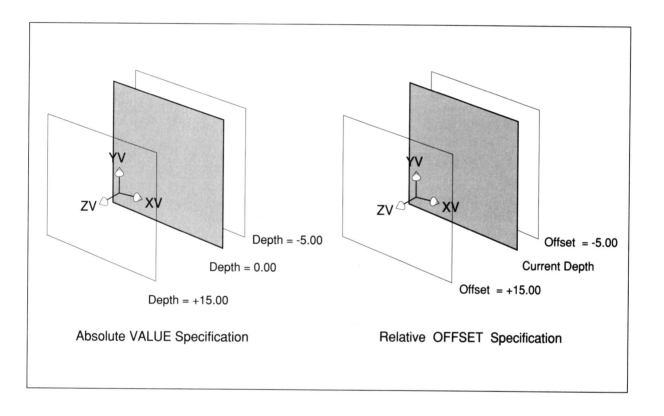

	Depth = -5.00
	Depth = 0.00
	Depth = +15.00

Absolute VALUE Specification

	Offset = -5.00
	Current Depth
	Offset = +15.00

Relative OFFSET Specification

1	–
2	**DEPTH**
3	**2D/3D**
4	**L-LIMIT**

2D/3D is a switch that allows suppression of Z axis coordinates. Set this switch before selecting other functions. Use this option when completing extensive 2D constructions.

1	–
2	**DEPTH**
3	**2D/3D**
4	**L-LIMIT**

L-LIMIT allows lines to be created according to the methods specified in the Create Menu. This is the default in CADKEY Light.

```
1  CREATE
2  EDIT
3  DETAIL
4  X-FORM
5  FILES
6  DISPLAY
7  CONTROL
8  DELETE        1  VERIFY
                 2  ATTRIB
                 3  CONSTR
                 4  COORDS
                 5  STATUS
                 6  PRINT
                 7  PLOT
                 8  SYSCMD
```

Construction Coordinates

| CTRL | W |

▼ DESCRIPTION OF FUNCTION

This switch toggles between view coordinates (XV, YV, ZV) and world coordinates (X, Y, Z). In view coordinates, the positive depth (ZV) axis is always out of the screen. Positive XV is to the right and positive YV is up. To work in 3D space, the 2D/3D switch must be set to 3D. In world coordinates, positive values are in the directions of the axis arrows of the axis icon.

View coordinates are appropriate when a view is defined that has no relation to the world axis system, as is the case with oblique construction planes. Here, only view coordinates are meaningful in the defined view. In principal views, it may be more meaningful to work in world coordinates.

It is important to be aware of the status of the coordinate switch before beginning a construction. Unless you are in the front view where world and view axes are the same, the same input in the two coordinate systems will yield different results.

▼ OPTIONS

VIEW coordinates require input in terms of the view or device axis system. When selected, all position values are returned in XV, YV, ZV format.

WORLD coordinates require input in terms of the world axis system. You will want to have the world axis icon displayed for reference when using world coordinates. When selected, all position values are returned in X, Y, Z format.

```
1 CREATE
2 EDIT
3 DETAIL
4 X-FORM
5 FILES
6 DISPLAY
7 CONTROL
8 DELETE      1 VERIFY
             2 ATTRIB
             3 CONSTR
             4 COORDS
             5 STATUS
             6 PRINT
             7 PLOT
             8 SYSCMD
```

Memory Status

▼ **DESCRIPTION OF FUNCTION**

This function provides a way to quickly check the amount of memory remaining for running the CADKEY Light program and the amount of hard disk space available for storing data (part files, pattern files, notes, scratch files, etc.).

When selected, this option displays the amount of memory and disk space available. Pressing <Enter> (RETURN) displays the second line of information. Press <Enter> again to return to the Control Menu.

```
Available memory = 72688 bytes      (press RETURN)
```

```
Free disk storage = 1036288 bytes   (press RETURN)
```

```
1  CREATE
2  EDIT
3  DETAIL
4  X-FORM
5  FILES
6  DISPLAY
7  CONTROL
8  DELETE      1  VERIFY
               2  ATTRIB
               3  CONSTR
               4  COORDS
               5  STATUS
               6  PRINT
               7  PLOT
               8  SYSCMD
```

Print Screen

▼ **DESCRIPTION OF FUNCTION**

This option is appropriate only if a dot matrix printer is connected to your computer. CADKEY Light sends the contents of the graphics screen to the printer at screen resolution. This can be used for check prints or for a quick record of a succession of steps.

Only entities actually displayed on the screen are displayed. You must have correctly specified your printer in the **CONFIG** program. The displayed geometry is automatically scaled to fit the limits of your selected printer.

1. Align the top of the paper with the printer head when prompted. Press <Enter>.

2. Printing can be halted by pressing **ESCAPE**. Respond to the **ABORT/RETRY** menu. Choose **ABORT** to cancel printing. Choose **RETRY** to begin the screen dump once again.

Note: Another method of taking a snapshot of the screen is to capture the entire screen as a *raster dump* or bit map. By pressing the **ALT** and **F** keys simultaneously, a file is sent to the **\prt** subdirectory beginning with **S1.SLD**, **S2.SLD**, **S3.SLD**... These slides are numbered by session and will be overwritten during subsequent sessions, so rename them with meaningful filenames. These bit-mapped graphic files can be edited in painting programs such as *DRHALO* by changing the file extension to that used by the painting program.

```
1  CREATE
2  EDIT
3  DETAIL
4  X-FORM
5  FILES
6  DISPLAY
7  CONTROL
8  DELETE      1  VERIFY
                2  ATTRIB
                3  CONSTR
                4  COORDS
                5  STATUS
                6  PRINT
                7  PLOT
                8  SYSCMD
```

Plot Active Viewport

Plotting Terms:

Scale—enlarging or reducing of the original geometry.

Rotation—angular displacement about the device Z axis.

Offset—XD and YD translation of the center of the geometry from the center of the paper.

▼   DESCRIPTION OF FUNCTION

This option sends those entities displayed in the active viewport to a plotter connected to your computer. CADKEY Light uses plotter parameters that were established when the **CONFIG** program was run.

An option from the Select Menu (see page 338) is used to identify those entities you wish to plot. An **AUTO** plot sends those entities in the active viewport to the plotter and uses automatic scaling factors and offsets to fit the geometry on the paper. **KEY IN** allows you to specify scale, Z device (ZD) rotation, and XD, YD offset or translation values. This option is helpful when plotting more than one file on a single piece of paper.

▼   OPTIONS

PEN # sends the plot to the plotter based on pen number attributes. CADKEY Light supports plotters with up to eight pens. The relationship of screen colors to pen numbers is totally independent and must be specified before plotting is begun. For example, it is possible to plot in color when using a monochrome (noncolor) display by using pen assignments.

COLOR sends the plot to the plotter based on the color assigned to each entity. Because there are 15 possible colors, it is possible to utilize a plotter with up to 15 pens. The **CONFIG** program allows colors to be assigned to pen numbers in any order or combination.

```
1 CREATE
2 EDIT
3 DETAIL
4 X-FORM
5 FILES
6 DISPLAY
7 CONTROL
8 DELETE      1 VERIFY
             2 ATTRIB
             3 CONSTR
             4 COORDS
             5 STATUS
             6 PRINT
             7 PLOT
             8 SYSCMD
```

Execute System Commands

▼ DESCRIPTION OF FUNCTION

The **SYSCMD** option allows DOS level operating system commands to be executed from within CADKEY Light. The operation of CADKEY Light is temporarily suspended. To do this the graphic screen is saved to disk so that when CADKEY Light is reentered, the screen image that was active when **SYSCMD** was chosen is displayed. Consider these guidelines when using this option:

- The amount of memory given up by CADKEY Light to run a system command or process is specified in the **CONFIG** program. CADKEY Light must have that memory back so *memory resident programs* cannot be run by **SYSCMD** commands. Memory resident programs should be installed before CADKEY Light is run.

- **SYSCMD** does *not* automatically save the current part file. Only the screen image is written to disk, so in the event of a system crash, part data will be lost unless an explicit save had been executed.

▼ OPTIONS

GRAPHIC uses the graphics display to execute a system command, temporarily suspending CADKEY Light. Press **ESCAPE** to restore the display and return to the CADKEY Light Main Menu.

NONE runs the system command without displaying the DOS prompt line or the action of the command. For this reason, this option should be used only when the system command is well known by the user—particularily if the operation doesn't require user action during operation. Press **ESCAPE** to restore the display and return to the CADKEY Light Main Menu.

SHELL allows you to enter the DOS operating system without exiting CADKEY Light. The graphic image is stored and the system shell is displayed on the screen specified in the **CONFIG** program. Press **ESCAPE** to restore the display and return to the CADKEY Light Main Menu. Type **EXIT** to restore the display and return to CADKEY Light.

Delete Menu

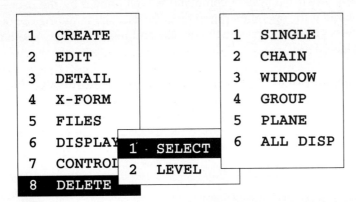

1	CREATE		1	SINGLE
2	EDIT		2	CHAIN
3	DETAIL		3	WINDOW
4	X-FORM		4	GROUP
5	FILES		5	PLANE
6	DISPLAY	1 SELECT	6	ALL DISP
7	CONTROL	2 LEVEL		
8	DELETE			

Delete Entity

▼ DESCRIPTION OF FUNCTION

Geometric and detail drafting entities can be removed from the data base with this command. Only entities that are visible in the viewport can be deleted. Any viewport in any combination can be used to select entities to delete. Use the **RECALL** (**CTRL—U**) option to bring back an entity that was deleted by mistake. It is highly advised that before major deleting, that the part file be first saved.

This command makes use of the Select Menu. You may wish to invoke the Masking Menu with the immediate mode (**ALT-M**) in conjunction with the Select Menu to further refine the selection process. When entities are selected an *entity marker* is placed on the screen. When entities are removed, blank spots may be formed on remaining geometry. To clean up the display, choose **DISPLAY—REDRAW**.

Dimensions are considered single entities. Individual dimension components such as witness lines, leaders, or text cannot be deleted. Entities that belong to a group can be deleted. At the time they are selected, you will be prompted as to whether you want the single entity or the group to which the entity belongs deleted. Once deleted, the entity loses its group assignment.

| CTRL | U | Recall Last Deleted Entity |

| CTRL | Q | Delete Single Entity |

```
1   SINGLE
2   CHAIN
3   WINDOW
4   GROUP
5   PLANE
6   ALL DISP
```

▼   OPTIONS

SINGLE (CTRL—Q) allows the repetitive selection of individual entities. Use this option when items to be included are widely spaced or on different levels. Use F10 to back up if an entity is mistakenly identified.

```
Select entity 1 (Press RETURN when done)
```

```
1   SINGLE
2   CHAIN
3   WINDOW
4   GROUP
5   PLANE
6   ALL DISP
```

When entities physically are connected, as in a string line or polygon, they can be selected in CHAIN. The starting entity and direction of chaining must be specified. Only entities displayed fully in the viewport of selection are included in the chain.

```
Select start entity in chain
```

```
1   SINGLE
2   CHAIN
3   WINDOW
4   GROUP
5   PLANE
6   ALL DISP
```

Use WINDOW to select entities that are tightly grouped. Only entities contained totally in the final position of the flexible window are selected.

```
Indicate position for 1st selection window corner
```

```
1   SINGLE
2   CHAIN
3   WINDOW
4   GROUP              1   SELECT
5   PLANE              2   BY NAME
6   ALL DI
```

To include entities that have been grouped, decide whether you want to delete all subgroups. Choose SELECT to choose individual subgroups. Choose BY NAME to select all subgroups belonging to a parent group.

```
Choose group selection option
```

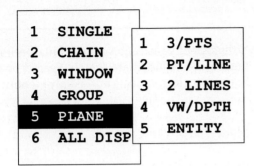

1	SINGLE	1	3/PTS	
2	CHAIN	2	PT/LINE	
3	WINDOW	3	2 LINES	
4	GROUP	4	VW/DPTH	
5	PLANE	5	ENTITY	
6	ALL DISP			

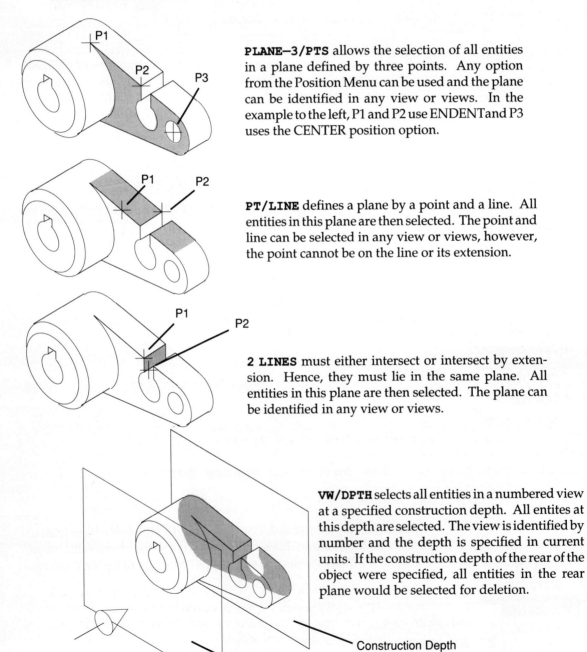

PLANE—3/PTS allows the selection of all entities in a plane defined by three points. Any option from the Position Menu can be used and the plane can be identified in any view or views. In the example to the left, P1 and P2 use ENDENT and P3 uses the CENTER position option.

PT/LINE defines a plane by a point and a line. All entities in this plane are then selected. The point and line can be selected in any view or views, however, the point cannot be on the line or its extension.

2 LINES must either intersect or intersect by extension. Hence, they must lie in the same plane. All entities in this plane are then selected. The plane can be identified in any view or views.

VW/DPTH selects all entities in a numbered view at a specified construction depth. All entites at this depth are selected. The view is identified by number and the depth is specified in current units. If the construction depth of the rear of the object were specified, all entities in the rear plane would be selected for deletion.

Construction Depth

Viewport

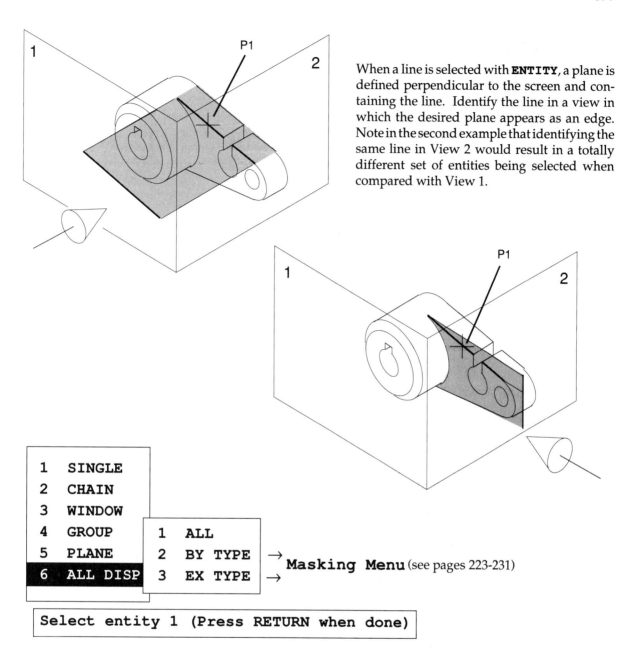

When a line is selected with **ENTITY**, a plane is defined perpendicular to the screen and containing the line. Identify the line in a view in which the desired plane appears as an edge. Note in the second example that identifying the same line in View 2 would result in a totally different set of entities being selected when compared with View 1.

1	SINGLE
2	CHAIN
3	WINDOW
4	GROUP
5	PLANE
6	**ALL DISP**

1	ALL	
2	BY TYPE	→
3	EX TYPE	→

→ **Masking Menu** (see pages 223-231)

Select entity 1 (Press RETURN when done)

ALL DISP—ALL allows the user to include or exclude entities by type or attribute. **ALL** provides a method for quickly identifying all entities that are within a specified viewport. Entities not totally within the viewport are not selected.

BY TYPE displays the Masking Menu and allows selection (by masking) of entities by attributes, Options within the Masking Menu can be changed without leaving the command to select dissimilar entities. Choose **DONE** when completed.

EX TYPE selects all entities totally displayed in the viewport *except* those identified by options in the Masking Menu. Choose **DONE** when completed.

```
1   CREATE
2   EDIT
3   DETAIL
4   X-FORM
5   FILES
6   DISPLAY
7   CONTROL
8   DELETE
```

Delete Entities by Level

```
1   SELECT
2   LEVEL
```

```
Enter Level to delete entities from =>_
```

▼ DESCRIPTION OF FUNCTION

This option allows all entities on a level to be deleted. The Masking Menu cannot be invoked to further refine the selection of entities. This command can be reversed by the **RECALL** option.

This does not alter assignments made in **DISPLAY–LEVELS**. To use this command wisely, preassign or move entities to levels by association. Then, if you wish to delete entities that have common characteristics, they will be on the same level.

1. Keyboard enter the number of the level containing the entities you wish to delete.

2. Press <Enter>. All entities assigned to this level are deleted. You are returned to the **DELETE** menu.

3. Choose **F10** to cancel a level delete before <Enter> has been pressed. Use **ESCAPE** to return to the Main Menu.

4. Choose **DISPLAY–REDRAW** to clean up the display.

Appendices

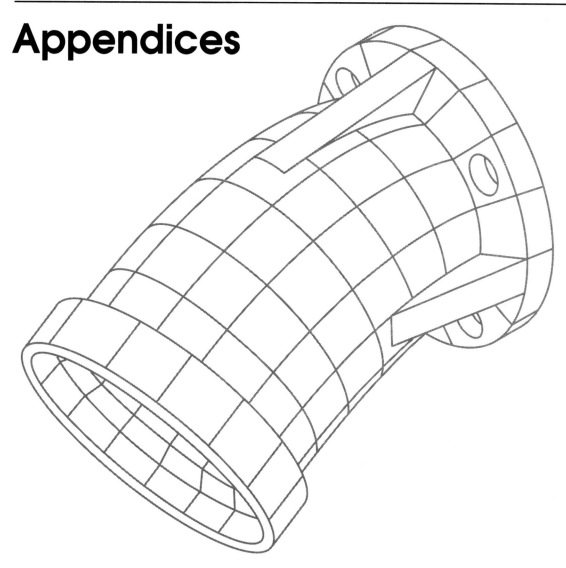

Glossary

GENERAL CADD TERMS

active area—block on a tablet which returns coordinate data.

ANSI—American National Standards Institute.

attribute—the line or color characteristics assigned to an entity or group of entities

axonometric view—a projection that appears inclined with three sides showing, and horizontal and vertical dimensions drawn to scale.

booting up—initializing or starting a system.

buffer—temporary storage unit.

cartesian coordinates—X, Y, Z absolute locations.

choose—to make a selection from a menu.

colinear points—points creating a straight line.

color palette—a selection of colors provided by the program.

configuration—the assigned hardware and computer system setup for a particular period of operation.

cursor—a symbol used to indicate a position in space or to select entities or their parts.

cursor button—a button assigned to the digitizer stylus or mouse which denotes a selection or position when pressed.

cursor control—part of an input device used for selection and position.

cursor indicate—define a position or location with the cursor.

cursor tracking—allows you to continuously display the cursor's coordinates.

data base management—defines the structure of data for accessing, entering, and deleting information.

default—a numerical value of menu option assigned by the program that may be accepted or changed by the user.

diagnostic—a program which identifies hardware configuration.

digitizer—a tablet or pad that converts graphic information into digital values.

digitizing area—block where the graphic cursor returns coordinate data or menu/status selections.

dimensioning—measurement of current parts and drawings that includes witness lines, leaders, and text.

drafting entity—type of entity used in dimensioning that appears in the view of creation (i.e., witness lines, arrows, labels, notes).

entity—basic, individual drawing component.

escape codes—a specific sequence of keystrokes to quickly access a function.

extension—used with a filename, identifies the type of file created (i.e., .PRT represents a part file).

file—collection of data, of any form, that are stored.

filename—a name assigned to a file that may be up to eight characters in length.

font—represents the style of text.

function keys—a set of 10 keys allowing direct access to menu options.

geometric entity—components of the drawing itself (i.e., lines, points, arcs).

gnomon—X, Y, Z world coordinate direction indicator icon.

hardware—the physical portion of a computer system (i.e., screen, disk drives, power unit, input device).

immediate mode—specific functions that may be invoked at any place in the menu structure.

initialize—to start up for the first time.

input device—a device that transfers data, or signals into a processor system (e.g., tablet or mouse).

ISO—International Standards Organization.

magnitude—in a vector, the length of the line segment.

masking—allows you to screen or designate certain entity or attribute types when making a selection.

numeric keys—the number keys 1-0 located across the top or at the right side of the keyboard.

n-gon—a polygon with three or more sides.

off-line program—a program that is initiated in a DOS environment versus from within another program.

on-line calculator—assigns variables and evaluates algebraic expressions according to given syntax rules.

origin—the intersecting point of coordinate axes.

orthogonal—intersecting or lying at right angles.

part—a complete file that contains all the information about a drawing's views, entity attributes, scale, etc.

pathname—the path taken to retrieve or store a file.

pattern—a component file that contains only entity information, independent of a part file.

pen velocity—the speed at which the plotter's pen moves.

peripherals—an input or output device connected to a computer.

placing point—the location in a part file where the base of a retrieved pattern is matched.

projected intersection—the intersection at which two lines meet if they were extended.

prompt—instructions or information displayed across the bottom of the screen.

radius—the distance from the center of an arc or circle to any point on the circumference.

reference point—a designated point to which a function is applied.

rubberband—an "elastic" line attached to the cursor that stretches as the cursor is moved.

rubberbox—an "elastic" box which may be increased or decreased in size to surround entities for selection purposes.

scale factor—a value by which you divide or multiply the displayed part for scaling purposes.

section—a profile of a part cut through by an intersecting plane

stylus—a pointing device used with a digitizer to specify position and location.

tangent vector—a directed line segment that can be translated into 3-D coordinates to intersect with exactly one point on a given line, arc, or circle.

toggle—turns a function on or off by the press of a key.

tolerancing—the total amount that a dimension is allowed to vary.

troubleshooting—changes the form, appearance, or placement of an entity.

vector—a directed line segment.

view coordinates—the x, y, z axis relative to the screen where x is horizontal, y is vertical, and z is pointing out from the screen

view dependent—the current part is not visible in any other view or from another perspective.

wire frame model—the description of a model in terms of vertices and connections.

work space—the electronic volume in which models are created.

world coordinates—the standard coordinate system where X and Y appear normally in the front view (view 1) and Z appears pointing directly out of the screen.

CADKEY LIGHT TERMS

ABORT (text editor)—exits the text editor without changing the text.

ACTIVE—chooses the level to which newly created entities are assigned.

ADD (LEVEL)—adds a level to the display list, allowing it to be seen.

ADD TO—adds entities to existing ordinate dimensions or groups.

ALL—selects all entities displayed.

ALL (RECALL)—recalls for display all entities deleted since the part was loaded.

ALL DSP—chooses all entities displayed on the screen.

ALONGC—creates a point on a curve at a specified distance from a designated end point.

ALONGL—creates a point on a line at a specified distance from a designated end point.

ANGLE (LINE)—creates a line entity at a given angle to a reference line.

ANGULAR (DETAIL)—dimensions the angle between two intersecting lines.

ANGULAR (TOLER)—assigns tolerancing values for angular dimensions.

APPEND (text editor)—joins the current line with the following line.

ARC—creates arc entities (portions of circles).

ARC (FILLET)—creates a tangent arc between two intersecting curve entities.

ARC/CIR—masks circle and arc entities.

ARR/WIT—creates arrows or witness lines as drafting entities.

ARROWS—changes or sets the direction of arrows relative to witness lines.

ASPECT—assigns the character width to height ratio of text.

AT DIST—creates a parallel line at a designated distance from a specified entity.

ATTRIB (CONTROL)—verifies or changes the attributes and form assigned to selected entities (i.e., color, line type, line width, pen #, outlined, filled).

ATTRIB (VERIFY)—displays attribute specifications of a selected entity.

AUTO—automatically scales the entire working part to fit in a viewport.

AUTOMAT—enables automatic calculation of dimension values.

AUTOSET—allows you to choose one of two viewport configurations.

AXES—defines and displays the gnomon (icon) that identifies the orientation of the world coordinate axes.

BACK—redraws from the last entity created to the first.

BACK-1—returns your drawing to the previous display.

BEG+END—creates an arc by specifying start and end points and the included angle.

BOTH (BREAK)—divides two intersecting curve entities into two (or three) separate entities at their common intersection.

BOTH (DETAIL)—displays both witness lines or leaders.

BOTH (TOLER)—assigns negative and positive values to tolerancing.

BOTH (TRM/EXT)—trims or extends intersecting entities to each other.

BREAK—divides curves into separate entities at their intersections.

BY NAME—allows selection of a group of entities by their group name.

BY TYPE—selects entities by type.

CENTER—locates the center of a selected entity as a specified position.

CHAIN—selects a series of entities by defining the start and end entities.

CHAMFER—creates an angled line that intersects two selected curve entities.

CHANGE (ATTRIB)—defines a new color, line type, line width, or pen number to existing entities.

CHANGE (DETAIL)—defines a new detail assignment to selected entities.

CHANGE (VIEW)—modifies the current display view.

CHR ASP—assigns the character width to height ratio of text.

CIRCLE—creates two-dimensional circles.

COLOR—assigns color to entities.

COLOR (masking)—allows you to mask by color attribute.

CONST (DEPTH)—allows you to assign the current working depth.

CONTROL—alters various modal parameters, displays detailed information about selected entities, allows you to print and plot and to access DOS from within the program.

COORD—displays coordinate data for a selected entity.

COORDS—sets view or world coordinate entry.

COPY—produces copies of selected entities without changing the original entities.

CORNERS—creates a rectangle by defining diagonal corners.

CP=DV—automatically sets the construction plane to the display view assignments.

CREATE—allows you to create geometric entities in the work space.

CREATE (FILES)—creates a pattern file, given the requested information.

CTR+DIA—creates arcs and circles by specifying a center position and a diameter.

CTR+EDG—creates arcs and circles by specifying start and end angles, center and edge points.

CTR-ENT—creates arcs and circles by specifying a center position tangent to a selected entity.

CTR+RAD—creates arcs, circles, and polygons by specifying a center position and a numerical radius.

CTR+SID—creates polygons by specifying a center position and number of sides

CUR LEV—assigns pattern file entities to the current active level during pattern file retrieval.

CUR TRK—displays the current coordinate positions of the screen cursor.

CURRENT—sets the existing modal attribute in effect.

CURSOR—locates a position using the cursor at current working depth.

DB DRAW—controls the order in which entities are drawn in the data base.

DBL UP—assigns both positive (+) and negative (-) symbols to the same line for tolerance values that are the same.

DECIMAL—changes or sets the type of decimal units used for dimensioning.

DEFINE (VIEW)—defines a new display view.

DEGROUP—ungroups selected entities.

DEL END (text editor)—deletes all characters from the current cursor position to the end of the line.

DELETE—removes levels, displayed entities, or groups from the data base.

DEL LIN (text editor)—deletes the current line and displays the preceding line.

DELTA—indicates a screen position by entering coordinates relative to a reference point.

DEPTH—changes the working depth.

DETAIL—creates drafting entities that add dimensions and text to a drawing.

DETAIL (masking)—allows you to select drafting entities for masking.

DIAMETR—dimensions the diameter of a circle in degrees or radians.

DIM ALN—aligns the dimension text using horizontal or vertical positioning.

DIM FNT—changes or defines the type of font used for displayed dimensions.

DIM HT—changes or defines the height of displayed dimensions.

DIM MOD—permits you to toggle between automatic calculation of dimension values and manual entry of dimension text.

DIM PLC—sets the placement position of text in dimensions.

DIM REP—changes the existing linear, radius, diameter, or ordinate dimension's representation to decimal feet, inches, or fractions.

DIM SCL—changes the value of a dimension by a designated scale factor.

DIM VAL—changes dimension values.

DIMENSN—calculates different radius, diameter, distance, and ordinate dimensions.

DIRECT—alters or sets the direction of the arrows relative to witness lines.

DISK—reads in an existing ASCII text file of no more than 1,024 characters.

DISP VW—turns the display view gnomon (world axis icon) on and off.

DISPLAY—affects how your drawing looks on the screen but does not physically alter or change coordinates of the geometry itself.

DISPLAY (AXES)—displays the desired axis icon.

DIVIDE (BREAK)—breaks a selected curve into three separate entities defined by two intersections with the inner portion assigned the current attributes.

DIVIDE (TRM/EXT)—separates a curve entity into two entities by selecting the portion of the entity to be trimmed or extended.

DOUBLE (BREAK)—breaks a selected curve into three separate entities defined by two intersections with outer portions taking on current attributes.

DOUBLE (DISPLAY)—scales the current display to twice its size.

DOUBLE (TRM/EXT)—trims or extends a curve to selected curve entities.

DUMP NT—outputs the text from an existing note to a disk-based ASCII text file.

EDIT—changes or revises a drawing.

EDIT TX—invokes the on-line text editor.

ENDENT—locates the endpoint of an entity as a position.

ENDPTS—creates a line entity, arrow, or witness line by specifying the start and end points.

ENTITY—defines a selection plane using a selected line, arc, or circle.

ENTITY (VIEW)—defines a view using a planar entity.

ENT-LEV—assigns retrieved pattern file entities to the levels that were in effect when the pattern was created.

EX TYPE—selects all entities except those specified.

EXIT—leaves CADKEY Light and returns you to DOS.

FILE (NOTE)—reads an existing ASCII text file with no size limitation.

FILES—creates, retrieves, or lists part and pattern files.

FILL—allows you to select a font and fill its character area.

FILLED—fills a polygon or polyline with a color from the color palette.

FILLET—connects two non parallel curve entities with an arc or an angled line.

FIRST (BREAK)—divides the first curve selected into two (or three) separate entities with current entities assigned to the broken portion of the line.

FIRST (DETAIL)—displays the first of two witness lines or leaders.

FIRST (TRM/EXT)—trims or extends the first entity selected.

1ST SOL—displays a leader line under a dimension extending to the first dimension point.

FONT—assigns type of text font displayed.

FORWARD—redraws from the first entity created to the last.

FRACTIN—changes or assigns the current dimension to a fractional value.

FT/IN—changes the current dimension value to feet and inches mode.

GEN DIM—masks generic dimensions.

GEOM—masks to selected geometric entity types.

GRAPHIC—executes system commands or programs without exiting the program.

GRID—displays a two-dimensional matrix of dots on the screen.

GRID ALN—aligns the grid to a selected point.

GRID DISP—turns grid on and off.

GRID INC—sets the X and Y interval of the grid.

GRID=SNAP—sets grid to current snap increment.

GROUP—links entities together so they can be selected individually or as a complete unit.

HALF—scales the display to one-half its size.

HEIGHT—changes text height.

HORIZTL (DIMENSN)—displays the horizontal dimension between two points.

HORIZTL (SET)—positions the horizontal alignment for text.

HRZ/VRT—draws horizontal and vertical line entities.

IN—redisplays dimension arrows pointing in.

INS LIN (text editor)—inserts a blank line above the current line.

INTRSC—locates a position at the intersection of two selected curve entities.

JOIN—copies selected entities and connects their endpoints.

JOIN LN (text editor)—joins the current line with the following line.

KEYIN—defines a direction by entering delta values from the keyboard.

KEY-IN—enters a Cartesian coordinate position from the keyboard.

KEY-IN (NOTE)—enters a note via the keyboard.

KEY-IN (RETRIEV, LST/RTV)—enters a level assignment for retrieved file entities via the keyboard.

L-LIMIT—enables certain line creation methods to produce lines to limits of the current viewport.

L-TYPE—defines the type of lines drawn: solid, center line, dashed, and phantom.

L-TYPE (masking)—allows you to mask selection by line type.

L-WIDTH—defines the width of a line according to the number of pixels assigned.

L-WIDTH (masking)—allows you to mask by line width.

LABEL—creates a label with leaders and arrows.

LAST—recalls the last entity deleted.

LEAD—assigns zeros before the decimal point of any dimension or tolerance less than 1.

LEADER—controls the display of leader lines in dimensions.

LEVELS—adds, changes, deletes, or recalls layers of a drawing.

LIMIT—displays the high limit of tolerancing above the low limit.

LINE—creates line (straight curve) entities.

LINEAR—assigns tolerance values to linear dimensions.

LIST (GROUP)—lists group name and contents.

LIST (LEVELS)—generates a list of levels to add or remove from the display list.

LOAD—retrieves a part file.

LST FMT—assigns short or long filename listing.

LST/LD—lists the contents of the current part file directory for cursor selection.

LST/RTV—lists the contents of the current pattern file directory for cursor selection.

MAKE—groups selected entities.

MANUAL—enables manual entry of dimension text.

MASK (LEVELS)—screens out desired levels in a part.

MIRROR (TXT ATT)—changes a selected note by rotating the entity about its mirroring axis within its current text position.

MIRROR (X-FORM)—duplicates selected entities about the mirroring axis in the plane of the screen.

MODAL (BREAK)—divides multiple curve entities based in intersections with a common entity into two separate entities assigning current attributes to the new portions.

MODAL (TRM/EXT)—continuously trims or extends selected curve entities to selected curve entities.

MOVE (LEVELS)—moves selected entities to specified levels.

MOVE (X-FORM)—operates on selected entities by changing the position and or scale.

N-GON—creates a polygon or polyline with equal length sides.

NEG TOL—assigns negative tolerancing values.

NEW—defines a new view using viewing rotation techniques.

NO ARRS—displays a solid dimension leader line without arrows.

NO TRIM—allows selected entities to remain in their original condition when arc fillets are added.

NONE (SYSCMD)—executes a system command or program without leaving the existing program while suppressing text output to the screen.

NONE (TOLER)—displays no tolerance with a dimension.

NONE (WITNESS/LEADER)—displays no leader or witness lines in a dimension.

NOT ANG—changes or sets the angle of text.

NOT FNT—changes or sets the type of font used for notes or labels.

NOT PLC—sets the placement position of text in notes and labels.

NOTE—adds general note text.

NOTE HT—changes or sets the height of text characters in notes or labels.

OFFSET (DEPTH)—allows you to change the working depth from the current depth.

OFFSET (FILES)—assigns retrieved pattern entities to levels of creation adjusted by an integer value.

ON ARC—creates point entities on a selected arc.

OUT—displays dimension arrows pointing outward.

OUT/FIL—changes the current status of polygons or closed polylines to outline or filled form.

OUTLINE—assigns the current color to a selected polygon or polyline.

PAN—moves the viewport parallel to XV and YV.

PARALEL (ARR/WIT)—creates witness lines or arrows parallel to a designated line.

PARALEL (DIMENSN)—dimensions the distance between two points.

PARALEL (LINE)—creates a line parallel and the same length to an existing line.

PART—contains the basic information about a drawing file in part form.

PATTERN—creates a part-independent file containing entities that can be added to a part file.

PEN #—assigns a pen number to selected entities for plotting purposes.

PEN # (masking)—allows you to mask by pen number.

PERPEND—creates an arrow or witness line perpendicular to a line.

PLANE—defines a plane using orientation and depth for selection.

PLOT (CONTROL)—initiates the plotting procedure.

POINT—indicates a point entity as the location for a position.

POINT (CREATE)—creates point entities.

POLAR—indicates a position based on a reference point, angle, and radius.

POLYGON—creates a polygon entity with equal length sides.

POLYLINE—creates a polyline entity.

POS TOL—assigns positive tolerancing values.

POSITN (DEPTH)—indicates a depth position in 3-D space.

POSITN (POINT)—creates a point entity at an indicated position.

PRINT—initiates a screen dump to printer.

PRP PRP—creates a line perpendicular to two selected entities.

PRP PT—creates a line perpendicular to a selected entity through a selected point.

PRP TAN—creates a line perpendicular to a line and tangent to a circle or arc.

PT/LINE—defines a projection plane using a point in space and two endpoints.

PT/LINE (PLANE)—defines a selection plane using a point in space (not necessarily a point entity) and two endpoints.

RADIUS—dimensions the radius of a circle or arc in degrees or radians.

RECALL—returns deleted entities to the screen.

RECTANG—creates a rectangle using four separate lines or one continuous polygon or polyline.

REDRAW—repaints the screen, removing entity markers.

REG DIM—masks angular, diameter, radius, or linear dimensions.

REMOVE (LEVEL)—removes designated levels from the display list.

RETRIEV—recalls a pattern file and adds it to the current part file.

ROUND—draws an arc tangent to the endpoint of an existing line or arc.

SAVE—saves a part file under a specified filename and path.

SAVE (VIEW)—stores a view with part file description so it can be recalled.

SAVE TX (text editor)—saves edited text.

SCALE—increases or decreases the geometric size of selected geometry.

SECOND—displays only the second of two witness or leader lines.

2ND SOL—displays the leader line under the dimension and extends the line to the second dimension point.

SELECT—moves selected entities.

SET—reassigns modal parameters used in dimensions and labels.

SET X,Y—sets the spacing between grid points or snap increments.

SHELL—enters the system environment without leaving the program.

SHORT—lists only the filenames.

SINGLE—selects single entities.

SKETCH—generates a continuous polyline.

SLANT—allows slanted text between -31º and +31º.

SNAP—sets a resolution for cursor attraction.

SNAP ALN—aligns the snap interval to the current grid position.

SNAP INC—allows you to enter the X and Y coordinates for cursor snap.

SNAP OPT—turns snapping on and off.

SNAP=GRD—sets the snap interval to the current grid spacing.

SOLID—displays one solid leader line.

STANDRD—assigns whether trailing or leading zeros are displayed with a dimension. Controls whether dimension text is aligned with leaders and toggles between automatic dimensioning and manual dimension entry.

STATUS—displays the amount of memory left for program use.

STRING—draws continuous lines, polygons, polylines, arrows, or witness lines from continuous endpoints.

SYSCMD—allows external or system processes to be run from within the program.

TANGENT (ARC, CIRCLE)—creates an arc or circle tangent to one, two, or three selected entities.

TAN/PRP—creates a line tangent or perpendicular to two selected entities or to an entity and a position.

TAN PRP—creates a line tangent to a selected entity and perpendicular to another.

TAN PT—creates a line tangent to a selected entity through a specified point.

TAN TAN—creates a line tangent to two selected entities.

TEXT—alters the size, font, or alignment of text.

TEXT (SYSCMD)—executes a system command or program without exiting the program environment by displaying a graphic screen.

3 ENTS—creates an arc or circle tangent to three selected entities.

THREE-P—creates an arc or circle by specifying the start, middle, and end points.

3 PTS (PLANE)—defines a plane using three positions in space.

3 PTS (VIEW)—defines a new display plane with three positions in space.

THRU PT—creates a parallel line through a designated position.

TOLER—specifies or changes the variability of lines or angles.

TRAIL—displays zeros after the decimal point in a dimension.

TRACKING—displays the location of the cursor's coordinates.

TRANS-A—translates entities from one location to another by referencing original and new base positions.

TRANS-R—translates entities by specifying an X, Y, Z shift relative to the world coordinate system.

TRIM (FILLET)—trims two entities as a fillet is created between them.

TRM/EXT (EDIT)—trims or extends curve entities to projected intersections with other curves.

2-D ROT—rotates selected entities about the ZV axis.

2-D/3-D—sets the construction mode to 2D or 3D.

2 ENTS—creates an arc or circle of specified radius tangent to two entities.

2 LINES (PLANE)—defines a selection plane using the endpoints of two lines and their 3D intersection.

TWO-PTS—creates a circle by specifying the diameter.

TXT ATT—changes font, height, angle, and aspect ratio of notes and labels. Mirrors selected notes.

TXT POS—changes text position.

TYPE—assigns the type of tolerance used.

USER—assigns a user-defined scale factor to the current part.

VALUE—assigns a numerical value to the current working depth.

VALUES—changes a dimension's tolerance value.

VERBOSE—lists filename, size, creation date, and directory date.

VERIFY—displays area, attributes, coordinate data, angles, perimeter, and distance information of selected entities.

VERTICL (DIMENSION)—displays the vertical dimension between two points.

VERTICL (SET)—aligns position of text.

VIEW (COORDS)—allows you to create a part in view coordinates.

VIEW (DISPLAY)—defines or changes the display view.

VW/DPTH—defines a selection plane using a specified view and depth.

WID/HT—constructs a rectangle using numerical values for width and height.

WINDOW—produces a "rubberbox," which can be shrunk or enlarged to fit around a specific entity or area for selecting, editing, or transforming.

WIT/ARR—masks witness lines and arrows.

WIT/LDR—specifies or changes the display of witness or leader lines.

WITNESS—creates two drafting entity lines that extend from the points being dimensioned.

WITNESS (CHANGE/SET)—specifies or changes the display of witness lines.

WORLD (COORDS)—displays the world axis icon at the lower left of a viewport.

X-FORM—performs coordinate transformations on selected entities.

X-HATCH—fills a specified closed area with the current hatch pattern.

0 REP—controls the display of zero tolerancing.

ZEROS—controls the display of zeros in a dimension.

ZOOM—Moves the viewport along the ZV axis.

A   P   P   E   N   D   I   X   B

Bibliography

Bertoline, G.R., *Fundamentals of CAD*, Albany, N.Y.: Delmar.

Besant, C.C., *Computer-aided Design and Manufacturing*, New York: Wiley.

Earl, J.H., *Engineering Design Graphics*, Reading, Mass.: Addison-Wesley.

Foster, R.J., Rogers, H.F., and Devon, R.F., *Graphic Communication Principles: A Prelude to CAD*, New York: McGraw-Hill.

Goetsch, D.L., *Introduction to Computer-Aided Drafting*, Englewood Cliffs, N.J.: Prentice Hall.

Lamit, G., and Paige, V., *Computer-Aided Design and Drafting*, Columbus, Ohio: Merrill.

Luzadder, W.J., and Duff, J.M., *Fundamentals of Engineering Drawing*, Englewood Cliffs, N.J.: Prentice Hall.

Index